The National States
Rights Party

ALSO BY MICHAEL NEWTON
AND FROM MCFARLAND

Unsolved Civil Rights Murder Cases, 1934–1970 (2016)

*The Ku Klux Klan:
History, Organization, Language, Influence and Activities
of America's Most Notorious Secret Society* (2007; softcover 2014)

*White Robes and Burning Crosses:
A History of the Ku Klux Klan from 1866* (2014)

*Hate Crime in America, 1968–2013:
A Chronology of Offenses, Legislation and Related Events* (2014)

*The Texarkana Moonlight Murders:
The Unsolved Case of the 1946 Phantom Killer* (2013)

The FBI Encyclopedia (2003; softcover 2012)

The Mafia at Apalachin, 1957 (2012)

Chronology of Organized Crime Worldwide, 6000 B.C.E. to 2010 (2011)

The Ku Klux Klan in Mississippi: A History (2010)

The FBI and the KKK: A Critical History (2005; softcover 2009)

Mr. Mob: The Life and Crimes of Moe Dalitz (2009)

The National States Rights Party
A History

MICHAEL NEWTON

McFarland & Company, Inc., Publishers
Jefferson, North Carolina

ISBN (print) 978-1-4766-6603-7
ISBN (ebook) 978-1-4766-2881-3

LIBRARY OF CONGRESS CATALOGUING DATA ARE AVAILABLE

British Library cataloguing data are available

© 2017 Michael Newton. All rights reserved

No part of this book may be reproduced or transmitted in any form or by any means, electronic or mechanical, including photocopying or recording, or by any information storage and retrieval system, without permission in writing from the publisher.

Front cover image of Arkansas Governor Orval Faubus (reading statement), nominated for president by the NSRP in 1960 (Library of Congress); *top* National States Rights Party flag

Printed in the United States of America

*McFarland & Company, Inc., Publishers
Box 611, Jefferson, North Carolina 28640
www.mcfarlandpub.com*

In memory of
Lawrence Daniel Duke, Sr.
(1913–1986),
for fighting the good fight

Acknowledgments

Most nonfiction books are written alone, but not without aid from those possessing special knowledge and resources. As so often in the past, I wish to thank old friend David Frasier, now retired as a librarian from Indiana University, for his skill in plucking ancient journal articles out of "the cloud," which I will never understand. I also owe grateful thanks to the ever-helpful staff at Indiana's Brown County Library; to Scott Butler, assistant metro and daily editor with the *Florida Times-Union*; to Amanda Hawk, with the University of Maryland's research team; to Waid Prather, editor-publisher of *The Carthaginian*; to Joseph McCain, publisher of the *Winston County Journal*; to Bill Riddle, senior librarian for California documents at the California State Library; to Amada DeWilde at the Sacramento Public Library; to the Albany (Georgia) Civil Rights Institute; to Alex La Pierre and Shay Meredith at the Thronateeska Heritage Center in Albany, Georgia; to Wayne McNeer, adult librarian at the Philadelphia–Neshoba County Public Library; to Lisa Calvert at the St. Johns County Public Library; to Laura Baas, librarian specialist at the State Library of Florida; to Kelly Enright and Blake Pridgen at Flagler College; to Maggie Thomas, genealogy assistant at the Switzer Library in Cobb County, Georgia; to Jill Anderson at Georgia State University's library; to Myra Evans and Bill Torpy at the *Atlanta Journal-Constitution*; to David Johnson, human resources director for Fairburn, Georgia; to William de Marigny Highland, St. Bernard Parish historian/manager, Los Islenos Museum Complex; to David M. Hardy, section chief of the FBI's Record/Information Dissemination Section; to Kevin Chatham, library assistant at the Meridian–Lauderdale County Public Library; to the Ivan Allen, Jr., Reference Department of the Atlanta–Fulton Public Library; to Mary Beth Newbill at Birmingham Public Library; to Julie Saylor, EPFL Maryland Department, Baltimore Public Library; to Rose Donoway, Princess Anne branch manager, Somerset County Library; and to Nancy Oliver, library technician at the St. Louis Public Library's central branch. Party founder Edward Fields was generous with insightful commentary and rare documents. Finally, as always, thanks to my wife, Heather, for her support while I pursued subjects as alien to her and to her loving personality as any distant galaxy. I wouldn't have made it without you, Sunshine.

Table of Contents

Acknowledgments	vi
Preface	1
Author's Note	2
Introduction: The American Reich	3
1. Dragon's Teeth	11
2. "All deliberate speed"	31
3. Birth of the Party	42
4. Shock Waves	52
5. Reading, Writing and Riots	65
6. Mayhem	86
7. "It happened like I told you"	100
8. A "segregated superbomb"	115
9. Dirty Wars	124
10. Ballots and Bullets	130
11. Un-American	141
12. Night Terrors	153
13. Dream Killers	163
14. Rumors of War	174
15. Under Fire	189
16. Last Gasp?	198
Appendix A. NSRP Constitution (1958)	209
Appendix B. "Why Vote States Rights" (1960)	233
Appendix C. NSRP Platform (1980)	236
Chapter Notes	239
Bibliography	254
Index	259

Preface

I first encountered the National States Rights Party (NSRP) in 1965, at age fourteen, as part of what became my lifelong research on the Ku Klux Klan. Over the next quarter-century I corresponded with the party and many other far-right groups of similar persuasions, using sundry pseudonyms and alternate addresses to remain at arm's length from the fringe. During the course of that research, I accumulated reams of racist literature, an even larger mass of mainstream books and media reports, personal letters, and government files released under the Freedom of Information Act. On several occasions, I attended public rallies of extremist groups to hear their rhetoric first-hand. From that pursuit, I learned it takes all kinds to build a radical movement. Some leaders join the hate game seeking cash and power over others. Many more, particularly in the lower ranks where violence breeds, are perfectly sincere in their beliefs concerning various minorities—and that's what makes them dangerous.

For three decades, the NSRP was America's most active, most dangerous Nazi organization. Its members and associates fomented or participated in race riots spanning at least six states and were responsible for multiple murders, bombings, and acts of arson. The doctrines it espoused remain the bulwark of our fascist fringe today—including 142 Nazi groups, 115 "white nationalist" organizations, and 119 racist skinhead gangs, operating at last count across 47 states and the District of Columbia. While technically defunct today, the NSRP survives after a fashion, its aged founder still publishing a variation of its original *Thunderbolt* newsletter, now retitled *The Truth at Last* and disseminated to a wider audience than ever, via the World Wide Web. The plague has not been purged. It spreads.

Author's Note

Except in direct quotations, the work in hand does not refer to "neo-Nazis," a phrase coined to suggest that modern fascists differ from those of World War II in some essential way besides chronology, geography, or personal identity. In truth, "new" Nazis pore over *Mein Kampf* and idolize its author, celebrate *Der Führer*'s birthday annually, and make no secret of their plans to launch a fresh "Final Solution" if they ever manage to seize power. While that goal remains a pipe dream, they still dress in variations of the Third Reich's uniforms and flaunt its symbols where the law permits, perpetuate its myths of "Aryan blood" and a "Master Race," arm themselves for battle come *der Tag,* and terrorize innocent victims given any opportunity. They hallucinate their own alleged "superiority," and many have adopted ancient Nordic cultism to emphasize imaginary links to Western Europe. They despise all Jews and nonwhites, gays and "leftists" (as viewed through the prism of fascist perspective), all labor unions and socially conscious progressives. In short, despite the change in scene and a new century's advent, they're really nothing new at all.

Introduction:
The American Reich

They should have seen it coming, all those "experts"—analysts, economists, investors, journalists and politicians—yet "Black Tuesday" managed to surprise them in October 1929. Within a year its shock waves had been felt around the globe, with tens of millions jobless, banks and industries collapsing almost overnight, and everybody looking for a scapegoat.

As it happened, one was ready-made, at least for some: the Jews.

Anti-Semitism was as old as history and stubbornly refused to die. From Martin Luther to Russia's pogroms, Jews were denounced as "Christ-killers," practitioners of human sacrifice, and covert masters of the world's economy. Nine years before the Wall Street crash, Detroit automobile tycoon Henry Ford took a respite from promotion of his Model Ts to vilify the Jews in print, serializing a Czarist forgery, *The Protocols of the Learned Elders of Zion* in his *Dearborn Independent* newspaper, then collecting those articles in a set of four bound volumes titled *The International Jew*. Ford wrote none of the articles personally, later blaming them on *Independent* editor William Cameron when Aaron Sapiro filed a libel action against him in December 1927. Incredibly disclaiming any knowledge of the eight-year series, Ford settled the case by penning an apology of sorts to the Anti-Defamation League (ADL) of B'nai B'rith, but he still cheerfully accepted the Grand Cross of the German Eagle—the Third Reich's highest medal for a foreigner—in July 1938.[1]

While Ford sought to appease Jews he'd offended, thus averting costly boycotts, Europe teemed with radical extremists of the Right and Left. Benito Mussolini's National Fascist Party seized control of Italy in 1922, suppressing Communism by brute force.[2] Stateside, *Il Duce*'s methods so impressed the American Legion—bastion of "100-percent Americanism"—that Commander Alvin Owsley cited Italian fascism as the new model for America's defense, telling reporters in 1923, "If ever needed, the American Legion stands ready to protect our country's institutions and ideals as the Fascisti dealt with the destructionists who menaced Italy! ... The American Legion is fighting every element that threatens our democratic government—Soviets, anarchists, IWW [Industrial Workers of the World], revolutionary socialists and every other red…. Do not forget that the Fascisti are to Italy what the American Legion is to the United States." Mussolini, though flattered, declined repeated invitations to address Legion conventions, the last in 1930.[3]

Fascism took longer to gain control in Germany, where the National Socialist German Workers' (Nazi) Party battled from 1919 to 1933 before installing Adolf Hitler first

Henry Ford (center) receives the Grand Cross of the German Eagle on July 30, 1938, from Fritz Hailer, German consul to Detroit (left), and Karl Krupp, consul to Cleveland (Library of Congress).

as chancellor, then as *Führer* (leader) of a single-party dictatorship.[4] Six months after Hitler's rise to power, in July 1933, retired Marine Corps General Smedley Butler—a two-time Congressional Medal of Honor winner and Philadelphia's director of public safety—exposed a conspiracy by wealthy businessmen and American Legionnaires to violently depose President Franklin Roosevelt. No one was prosecuted in that case, which the *New York Times* dismissed as a "gigantic hoax," though it appears that certain plotters did approach Butler before losing their nerve.[5]

Roosevelt's quasi-socialistic New Deal reforms, reviled to this day by conservative critics, eventually pulled America out of the Great Depression, but not without far-right resistance. Opponents included Paul Castorina's Fascist League of North America, premiering in summer 1923; George Edward Deatherage's American Nationalist Confederation, created in August 1927, succeeded by his Knights of the White Camellia in August 1935; Harry Jung's American Vigilant Intelligence Federation, incorporated in December 1927; Holt J. Gewinner's Atlanta-based Order of Black Shirts, aka the American Fascisti Association, launched in spring 1930; Kurt Ludecke's Swastika League of America, formed in 1932; William Dudley Pelley's Silver Shirt Legion of America, created in January 1933; the Khaki Shirts of America, aka U.S. Fascists, introduced by Arthur J. Smith in July 1933; Heinz Spanknoebel's Friends of the New Germany, founded in October 1933; the

Chattanooga-based Crusader White Shirts, organized by George W. Christians in December 1933; Gaetano Asone's United States of America Union of Fascists, founded in March 1934; the short-lived American White Guard, chaired by one "Colonel McCord" for a few months in 1935; Anton Haegele's American National-Socialist Party, announced in July 1935; Fritz Kuhn's German-American Bund, launched in March 1936; lifelong anti-Semite Gerald Lyman Kenneth Smith's Committee of One Million, created in April 1937; Dr. J. G. Lambert's Blue Shirts of Canada, spreading to claim 15,000 members in the American Midwest after May 1938, when it split from Montreal's *Parti National Social Chrétien*; the American Destiny Party, founded by Joseph Elsberry McWilliams in May 1940; the America First Committee, formed by Yale law students in September 1940, claiming aviator Charles Lindbergh as its primary spokesman; and Mrs. J. Henry Orme's Americanism Defense League of Hollywood, created seven months before Pearl Harbor. Separately or in concert, those and other groups rallied, marched, harassed ethnic minorities, and sometimes brawled in city streets with labor union members.[6]

American Legion Commander Alvin Owsley declared his group "the Fascisti of America" in 1923 (Library of Congress).

News from Europe, Africa, and the Far East blackened fascism's image for many Americans, years before the outbreak of World War II in 1939 and America's entry to the conflict two years later, but far-right passions died hard. In August 1940, some 800 members of the German-American Bund rallied with 200 Ku Klux Klansmen at the Bund's Camp Nordland in New Jersey, cheering as Deputy *Bundesführer* August Klapprott told his audience, "The principles of the Bund and the principles of the Klan are the same." Imperial Wizard James Colescott disagreed, expelling Grand Titan Arthur Bell and one of his subordinates for approving the rally, but the controversy highlighted a schism in the Klan, concerning its embrace of Nazism, that continues to the present day.[7]

Home front antipathy to fascism increased after Pearl Harbor, but members of the anti–Semitic fringe continued agitation through the war years, led by Gerald Smith, Elizabeth Dilling of the Patriotic Research Bureau and sundry others, virtually to the eve of V-E Day in 1945. Some, like William Pelley, espoused the strange tenets of British Israelism—later dubbed Christian Identity—claiming that Western Europeans are the true "Lost Tribes of Israel." A variation of that theme, christened the "dual-seedline" doctrine, asserts that after Eve bore Adam's son Abel, she copulated with Satan in serpentine form to produce Cain, the first murderer and patriarch of all Jews.[8]

The best known Identity spokesman in postwar America was Wesley Albert Swift, a onetime Methodist preacher born in 1913. Onetime instructor of a Klan rifle team,

Deputy *Bundesführer* August Klapprott (at microphone) leads a joint meeting of the Ku Klux Klan and German-American Bund at Camp Nordland, New Jersey, August 1940 (Library of Congress).

Swift shared the stage with Gerald Smith on a West Coast tour in 1949 and became the legal representative of Smith's Christian Nationalist Crusade in 1953. On his own, he founded diverse Identity-based groups including the California League Against Communism, the Anglo-Saxon Christian Congregation, the Christian Defense League, and the California Rangers. His Church of Jesus Christ—Christian, launched in 1946, grew into a chain of congregations spreading nationwide, subsequently morphing into the Aryan Nations.[9]

Federal prosecutors reacted slowly to the rise of fascist groups. In January 1940 FBI agents arrested 18 members of the Christian Front, founded by radio-ranting Father Charles Coughlin two years earlier, on charges of plotting to "overthrow, put down and destroy by force the Government of the United States," using stolen weapons supplied by infiltrators within New York's National Guard. Trial convened in June, but the results were anticlimactic: one defendant killed himself, while jurors acquitted 10 more and failed to reach verdicts on seven, whose charges were dropped.[10]

Perhaps discouraged, the Justice Department stalled its next move until July 21, 1942,

Opposite, top: Fritz Kuhn, *Bundesführer* of the German-American Bund. *Opposite, bottom:* Teamsters Union members battle William Pelley's Silver Shirts in Detroit, August 1938 (Library of Congress).

when it issued the first of three indictments filed under the June 1940 Alien Registration Act, better known as the Smith Act after its principal author, Virginia congressman Howard Smith. The indictment named 28 outspoken anti–Semites as defendants: Courtland "Court" Asher, a Ku Klux kleagle (recruiter) and publisher of the Klan newsletter *The X-Ray*; David John Baxter, founder of the Social Republic Society of America; political cartoonist Otto Brennemann; Howard V. Broenstrupp, a Silver Shirt associate of William Pelley; Oscar Brumback, author of *America, Awake!*; Prescott Freeze Dennett, head of the Columbia Press Service, considered a front for German propaganda; Constantine Leon de Aryan, editor of an anti–Semitic California newspaper, *The Broom*; Hudson de Priest, a columnist for Gerald Winrod's publication, *The Defender*; Hans Diebel, a member of the German-American Bund; Elizabeth Dilling; Robert E. Edmondson, a self-styled American Vigilante Patriot, described by 21st-century Nazis as "a prolific Jew-wise researcher and leading propagandist equal to Germany's Joseph Goebbels"; brothers Elmer J. and James F. Garner, Kansas publishers of the magazine *Publicity*; William Griffin, publisher of *The New York Evening Enquirer*; Charles Bartlett Hudson, publisher of the newsletter *America in Danger!*; Ellis Oliver Jones, a columnist for *Publicity* and founder of the isolationist National Copperheads in May 1941; William Ernest Kullgren, a magazine publisher and Silver Shirts member; William Robert Lyman, Jr., a member of Baxter's Social Republic Society of America; Dr. Donald McDaniel, distributor of Otto Brennemann's cartoons; Robert Noble, founder of an anti-war group, the Friends of Progress; William Pelley; Eugene Nelson Sanctuary, a regular contributor to Winrod's *Defender*; Herman Max Schwinn, western director of the German-American Bund; Edward James Smythe, publisher of *Our Common Cause* and national commander of the Protestant War Veterans Association; Ralph W. Townsend, alleged agent for Imperial Japan; James B. True Jr., cofounder of America First, Inc., and inventor of the patented "kike killer" truncheon in 1935 (available in men's and women's sizes); George Sylvester Viereck, a Third Reich propagandist; and Gerald Burton Winrod, a fundamentalist preacher, Jew-bashing publisher, and a failed U.S. Senate candidate in 1938. Despite its sweep and headline-grabbing drama, the mass indictment misfired, all charges subsequently dismissed.[11]

Justice tried again with a second round of indictments on January 4, 1943. Defendants named a second time included Asher, Baxter, Brennemann, Broenstrupp, Brumback, Dennett, de Aryan, de Priest, Diebel, Dilling, Edmondson, the Garners, Griffin, Hudson, Jones, Kullgren, Lyman, McDaniel, Noble, Pelley, Sanctuary, Schwinn, Smythe, Townsend, True, Viereck, and Winrod. New additions to the list included Frank W. Clark, chairman of the National Liberty Party; George Deatherage; Frank K. Fernenx, a California member of the German-American Bund; anti–Semitic author and lecturer Paquita de Shishmareff (aka "Leslie Fry"), who tried to buy the KKK for $75,000 in 1939; Lois de Lafayette Washburn, founder of the National Gentile League and national secretary of the American Gentile Protective Association; and *The New York Evening Enquirer*. Additionally, 13 other groups and 12 publications were named as unindicted coconspirators—but once again, the charges never went to trial.[12]

Prosecutors took their third and final swing one year later, on January 3, 1944. Repeat defendants included Baxter, Broenstrupp, Deatherage, Dennett, Diebel, Dilling, Edmondson, Fernenx, Elmer Garner (minus his brother), Hudson, Jones, Lyman, Noble, Pelley, Sanctuary, Schwinn, Smythe, True, Viereck, and Winrod. Third-round additions facing charges for the first time were Garland Leo Alderman, Sr., national secretary of the

Black Legion regalia and weapons seized by Michigan police in 1939 (National Archives).

National Workers' League and past chairman of the America First Committee in Pontiac, Michigan; Frank W. Clark, Washington state leader of the Silver Shirts and ex-national secretary of Pelley's Christian Party; Lonnie Lawrence Dennis, an Atlanta lawyer and onetime "Mulatto Boy Evangelist" turned collaborator with Third Reich propagandists; Ernest Frederick Elmhurst, head of the Pan-Aryan Alliance, organizer for the American National Socialists and the German-American Bund; Bundist August Klapprott; Gerhard Wilhelm Kunze, successor to Fritz Kuhn as Bund leader in December 1939; Joseph

McWilliams; Eugene John Parker Sage, founder of Michigan's Black Legion KKK spinoff in 1935, cofounder and treasurer of Detroit's National Workers' League three years later; Peter Hans von Stahrenberg, founder of America's first openly Nazi group, the American National-Socialist Party, in 1935; and Lois de Lafayette Washburn, a leader of the National Liberty Party, founder of the National Gentile League, and national secretary of the American Gentile Protective Association. Conspicuous omissions once again included "big fish" Father Coughlin and Gerald Smith, the latter investigated three times by the FBI but never charged.[13]

Trial convened in Washington, D.C., before Judge Edward Eicher, on April 17, 1944. Edward Smythe missed opening day, arrested on April 18 near New York's Canadian border, ostensibly while fishing on vacation. On May 4, Elmer Garner died at age 80, shipped home to his widow in a pine box, reportedly nude. Judge Eicher severed David Baxter and James True from the trial due to physical ailments, and Robert Noble for his unruly conduct. The proceedings dragged on for 119 days, minus a two-week summer recess, until Eicher suffered a fatal heart attack on November 29. His replacement, Judge Bolitha Laws, initially asked prosecutors if they wished to start a new trial, then privately reviewed the evidence, declaring a mistrial for all defendants on December 7. On June 30, 1947, the Circuit Court of Appeals for the District of Columbia affirmed dismissal of the indictments.[14]

Collapse of the government's case did not relieve all the defendants from jeopardy, however. Ellis Jones and Robert Noble faced prison for their August 1942 conviction under California's sedition statute, resulting in sentences of ten and five years, respectively. Franz Ferenz, convicted in the same case, remained in San Quentin Prison until an appellate court dismissed his charges in 1945. Gerhard Kunze received a 15-year sentence on his 1942 conviction for violating the 1917 Espionage Act. Germans Hans Diebel and Herman Schwinn were interred until war's end as enemy aliens. William Pelley had the bulk of a 15-year sentence to serve, imposed after his April 1942 Indiana conviction for sedition and high treason. Frederick Elmhurst resumed his Nazi activities in New York City, where police arrested him with cohorts Dr. Herman Homer Gustav Maerz and Kurt Mertig of the Citizens Protective League in October 1945, all charged with unlawful assembly and selling pamphlets on Jewish ritual murder. Elmhurst and Mertig drew six-month sentences, while Maerz was sentenced to one year. In 1947 ten of the original 30 sedition defendants filed a libel suit against Chicago's *Sentinel*, a weekly Jewish newspaper, for its coverage of their trial. Four prevailed in that case, collecting $24,100 in damages.[15]

Many Americans supposed that the Allies' triumph in World War II—defeating Nazi Germany in April 1945, crushing Imperial Japan four months later, exposing Hitler's concentration camps and placing various Axis leaders on trial for war crimes between October 1945 and April 1949—ended the fascist threat worldwide. Unfortunately, they were wrong, and on an epic scale. Barely a year after V-J Day, the nation's native Nazis were in action once again. In fact, as news reports revealed, they'd never left.

Chapter 1

Dragon's Teeth

The ashes of Berlin and Tokyo were barely cool before a wave of racist violence swept through Dixie. Lynching resumed after a wartime lull, and Atlanta obstetrician Dr. Samuel Green revived the KKK, officially dissolved by federal tax liens in 1944, renaming it the Association of Georgia Klans while he expanded into other states. The Klan dominated Atlanta's police force and its police union under Marion Hornsby, chief since 1937 and a proud member of Green's Klavern No. 1. Klan attorney Vester Marvin Ownby chartered a new racist group, We the People, in 1944, while fellow Klansman James Shipp launched the Commoner Party in 1946, soon changing its name to the American Gentile Army. Edward Smythe scouted Atlanta as headquarters for his latest venture, the Protestant War Veterans. That organizational fervor sprang in part from the return of African American veterans, eyes opened to a wider world, and a dramatic increase in black voter registration—fivefold in Atlanta alone since V-J Day.[1]

For Georgia's racist whites, hope lay with two-term former governor Eugene Talmadge, an admitted flogger, suspected Klansman, and silent partner in Vigilantes Inc., founded by Georgia Public Safety Commissioner John Goodwin in 1942, during Talmadge's second gubernatorial term. Seeking a third, Talmadge campaigned for white supremacy and suppression of black voting statewide. In March 1946 Talmadge met with Samuel Roper, his former chief of the Georgia Bureau of Investigation, lately an Atlanta detective and exalted cyclops of AGK Klavern No. 297. When Roper asked the best way to keep blacks from the polls, Talmadge grabbed a scrap of paper and wrote: "Pistols." He also promised the Klan a "free hand" if any riots erupted during his next administration. Six days before the Democratic primary Talmadge broadcast a statewide message, warning, "Wise Negroes will stay away from white folk's ballot boxes on July 17."[2]

Kluxers took their cue from Talmadge, whose newspaper, *The Statesman*, published a poem titled "White Georgia Thanks God for the Klan" on April 15. White officials collaborated with the AGK, challenging 20 percent of Putnam County's registered blacks "on grounds of incompetence due to lack of education, intelligence, or character"; purging 50 percent of Ellaville's black registrants, 25 percent in Gainesville, 400 in Baxley, 800 in Colquitt County, 180 in Spaulding, 100 in Lamar, 294 in Moultrie, 800 in Appling—more than 20,000 altogether statewide. In Atlanta's East Point district, 81 were challenged by attorney Ike Wingrow, who defended Klan floggers at a 1940 clemency hearing. In Fitzgerald, on July 16, Klansmen tacked signs to the doors of African American homes reading: "The first nigger who votes in Georgia will be a dead nigger." The net result was victory for Talmadge on July 17, guaranteeing his election in November.[3]

That atmosphere drew bigots to Atlanta from around the nation. Two who heard

Daniel Duke (right) confronts Governor Eugene Talmadge during a clemency hearing for convicted Klan floggers, 1941 (Library of Congress).

the siren song of race and destiny were Emory Carney Burke and Homer Leslie Loomis, Jr. Alabama born in 1915, Burke attended high school in Montgomery and joined the debating society, poring over the Klan-centric novels of Thomas Dixon, Jr. (1902–05), Madison Grant's *The Passing of the Great Race* (1916), and Klansman Lothrop Stoddard's *The Rising Tide of Color* (1920). Graduating in 1933, he studied architectural drafting then moved to New York in 1935, working with future sedition trial defendant Ernest Elmhurst to publish the *American Bulletin* and *The Storm*. Daniel Duke, Georgia's assistant attorney general, would later say Burke's name appeared on the masthead of "nearly every fascist organization in the country prior to World War II." After Pearl Harbor, Burke moved to Marietta, Georgia, working at the Bell Bomber Plant.[4]

Native Manhattanite Homer Loomis was born in 1914, son of a wealthy admiralty lawyer, and graduated from St. Paul's School in Concord, New Hampshire, an Episcopal Church preparatory boarding school. He enrolled at Princeton University in 1933 and left in February 1935, blaming his expulsion for drunkenness on Jews. Back in New York, he earned a playboy's reputation and appeared in gossip columns prior to marrying a woman whom he seemingly tried to drive crazy. In divorce court, she described Loomis forcing her to read aloud "A Mad Man's Manuscript" from *The Pickwick Papers*, about a man plotting uxoricide, while Loomis remarked that he'd given the matter much thought.

Soon remarried, Loomis moved to Virginia but failed as a would-be gentleman farmer and divorced again, telling neighbors, "Hitler has the right idea. He's not going to let the German race get mixed up with a lot of inferior races." Such views notwithstanding, he was drafted in 1944, serving with the army's 2nd Armored Division in Europe. Loomis later claimed he bribed army officers to let him roam freely, meeting Nazi leaders and using his father's financial connections to help them, rewarded with advice on starting a movement in America. Honorably discharged in February 1946, he met with Mississippi Senator and Klansman Theodore Bilbo in Washington, then traveled to Atlanta with dreams of founding his own fascist party, saying, "I'm going to be the Hitler of America."⁵

Homer Loomis, Jr. (left), in uniform with Columbians charter member Roy Whitman (National Archives).

***

In May, Loomis found work as a fry cook at The Varsity, a now-famous hamburger joint two blocks from the Georgia School of Technology, and fell into conversation about white supremacy with fellow employee James Akin, already acquainted with Emory Burke. The next day all three met at Burke's home. While polar opposites in background, Burke and Loomis clicked, became fast friends, and hammered out the framework of a group they called the Columbian Workers Movement, soon truncated to Columbians Incorporated—named in honor of explorer Christopher Columbus (ironically, a Jew who feigned Catholicism to avoid persecution). They agreed that Burke would serve as president and Loomis as secretary-organizer. Georgia Tech drafting student and ex–Eighth Army Air Force bombardier John Henry Zimmerlee joined as treasurer. The group's tone was set when recruits donned khaki uniforms with lightning-bolt shoulder patches reminiscent of Hitler's SS, admonished to greet their secretary-organizer with a brisk "Heil, Loomis!"⁶

Klan attorney Vester Ownby filed a state charger petition for the Columbians, billing it as a nonprofit "patriotic and political" group. Said charter was routinely granted, though reports of the event list dates ranging from August 8 to 18, 1946. Senator Bilbo's influence was evident in the group's first publication: a pamphlet titled *Separation or Amalgamation*, which anticipated the title of Bilbo's polemic, yet unpublished: *Take Your Choice: Separation or Mongrelization*. Headquarters was a rundown three-room suite on Bartow Street, where members slept on cots and mattresses, someone always present to field "emergency calls" of "generally troublesome Negroes" or black families pricing homes in white neighborhoods. Loomis told recruits and visitors, "The Negro would behave himself if it wasn't for the Jews. It's the Jews' fault that the Negroes are getting out of line." The office library of 50 books included *Mein Kampf* and histories of the Nazi movement.[7]

With charter in hand, the Columbians accelerated recruiting. In theory they welcomed "all members of the white man's community," but most members came, in Burke's words, from "those of our brothers and sisters that many of the politicians call 'poor white trash.'" Applications asked potential recruits three questions: "Number one: Do you hate niggers? Number two: Do you hate Jews? Number three: Have you got three dollars?"[8] For those who met those qualifications, a more detailed Columbians Creed required them to swear:

> I believe America today is a battlefield upon which two forces are contending for mastery; those two forces are the authentic American spirit and the anti–American, anti-western spirit of invasion and materialism.
>
> I believe the question which most clearly marks the line of battle between these two opposing, world shaking forces, is the subject of race.
>
> I believe the idea of Race Purity is born of the authentic American spirit, and those who champion this holy idea count among their fellow fighters the spirit of our great dead.
>
> I believe the idea of Racial Amalgamation is spawned by that anti–American, anti-western, alien spirit and that those who carry the banner of this idea are in mortal conflict with the whole depths of the American soul.
>
> I believe the time has come for every man to step forward and enlist to fight in the struggle either on the side of the American Spirit or on the side of the alien Asiatic spirit.
>
> I take my stand to fight in the ranks of those who believe in the holy American ideals of RACE, NATION and FAITH.[9]

***

Atlanta's reigning racist group, the AGK, was ambivalent toward the upstart Columbians. The Klan officially rejected collaboration, and Dr. Green fumed when *Atlanta Constitution* editor Ralph McGill accused the Columbians of running a "cut-rate hate racket," taking three dollars from recruits when the AGK demanded ten. White professionals, including lawyers, judges, and Atlanta's police chief still cherished the Klan, while Burke and Loomis courted blue-collar workers and students. Still, Columbians held their Thursday night meetings at the Whitehall Street home of the Plumbers and Steamfitters Local 272, where Atlanta Klavern No. 1 met on Mondays, and Loomis addressed the klavern on October 3, drawing applause when he said, "Nowadays we hear a lot of talk about 'let's give the nigger political equality, but not social equality.' But don't you know that, given political equality, one-third of the Georgia legislature would be black? We promise that all the niggers in America be shipped backed to Africa, with time-bombs on board the ships as an economy measure." Five days later, Georgia chartered the West End Cooperative Corporation, founded by Joseph M. Wallace, chairman of the AGK's "Housing Kommittee"—created to terrorize blacks who sought homes in "white" districts.[10]

Meanwhile, in August, Columbians published the first issue of their newspaper, *The Thunderbolt,* headlined: "Columbians Organize To Save White Supremacy." Only one more issue followed, but the paper and its title would be resurrected 12 years later.[11]

On August 26 the Columbians held their first public rally in East Point Auditorium. Flanked by lightning-bolt flags and posters, Burke addressed an audience of 300, denouncing the "horrors of Communism" and America's melting-pot ideal, attacking "Jew-Communists," and proclaiming himself the group's "sole authority on matters of policy." After saying, "We are not preaching hatred against the Negroes or any other races," he demanded a government drive to deport blacks and Jews "before race-war breaks out." So it went for 45 minutes, after which John Zimmerlee enlisted 40 recruits. Loomis congratulated Burke on his "magnificent address," then advised reporters, "Our approach will have to be toned down for the crowds, then we'll really have them pouring in to join." For the next three weeks, Columbians seemed to vanish. Even so, donations arrived from Gerald Smith and a new rising light of the fringe, Jesse Benjamin Stoner, Jr.[12]

***

Stoner—"J. B." to the world at large—already had a history of racist agitation at the tender age of 23. Born on April 13, 1924, to parents who ran a sightseeing company in Chattanooga, he survived polio at age two, with a permanent limp from his damaged left leg. Stoner lost his father in 1929, later attending the McCallie School on Missionary Ridge, founded in 1905 as "a first-class university school." Already an active admirer of Theodore Bilbo, Stoner suspected a conspiracy to encourage racial intermarriage. A lifelong bachelor who found "no woman smart enough" for him, he admitted no Jew or African American had ever personally harmed him, but from an early age he recognized their scheming to destroy the white race.[13]

In 1941, the year his mother died, Stoner organized Chattanooga's chapter of the America First Committee, then joined the Klan and was appointed kleagle by Imperial Wizard James Colescott one year later. At odds with many postwar Klansmen over Jews, he forged ahead with plans that marked him as "perhaps the most outspoken and obsessive anti–Semite in American history." In 1944 he petitioned Congress for passage of a resolution declaring that "Jews are the children of the Devil, and that, consequently, they constitute a great menace to the United States of America." Ignored on Capitol Hill, he launched the Stoner Anti-Jewish Party in 1945, committed to "make being a Jew a crime, punishable by death." Stoner told reporters, "I think Hitler was too moderate. He didn't have anywhere near the race problem we got." Given the chance, his party would kill Jews with gas chambers, electric chairs, firing squads, "or whatever seems most appropriate." In October 1946 author Earl Conrad called on federal authorities to ban Stoner's postcards from the mail, but they declined.[14]

Through it all, Stoner remained Chattanooga's top Klansman. On July 13, 1946, he addressed Atlanta's Klavern No. 1, declaring, "We ought to get all Jews out of our country, and I don't mean send them to some other country. I'll never be satisfied as long as there are any Jews here or anywhere. I think we ought to kill all Jews just to save their unborn generations from having to go to Hell." One observer in the audience, Klansman and police informer Stetson Kennedy, deemed Stoner "stark, raving crazy" and marked him for future study. Prior to that speech, Stoner told some reporters he was out of the Klan, "engaged in distributing anti–Jewish literature" and planning to "out–Hitler Hitler" with his new party, but in fact he remained a Klansman for at least two more years, perhaps as long as four, and would return to it spasmodically throughout his life.[15]

***

While Stoner, Gerald Smith and others sent cash and best wishes, others joined the Columbians for action. George Michael Bright was born in August 1923, either in New York or Tennessee (reports differ), and was an industrial engineer when he reached Atlanta in 1946, already nursing a hatred of Jews. Founding member Ira Jett, born in

1901, was an attorney and a member of the AGK. James Ralph Childers, 17, worked as a trucker in the war, visiting "Chicago and other states," then landed in Atlanta as a fry cook. William H. Couch Jr., was on terminal leave from the army's 349th Bomber Squadron when he signed up. Shot down over Sicily in August 1943, he spent time at Stalag Luft III POW camp in Silesia and survived the "Black March" from there, across Czechoslovakia to Germany, in which 2,200 Allied prisoners died. Despite his wartime trials, he told fellow Columbians in 1946, "We have the worst men in the world at the head of the American Army. Of course you know Eisenhower is a Jew." (In fact, Dwight Eisenhower—then that army's chief of staff—was Presbyterian.)[16]

Another battle veteran, 20-year-old Lanier Waller, was born in Georgia but raised in a Texas orphanage until he fled at age 14. He "worked tug boats in Houston," then falsified his age to join the Marine Corps after Pearl Harbor, fighting in the Pacific until he contracted malaria, whereupon doctors learned his true age and discharged him with a brief disability pension. By the time Waller was old enough to reenlist the war was over. Cherishing memories of the Corps and "killing Japs," he met James Childers in Atlanta and was introduced to Burke, concluding "I thought it was a pretty good thing, segregating and killing the niggers. I thought everything was pretty legal."[17]

An early Columbian more in the mold of Emory Burke was Holt Gewinner, Georgia born in 1915, a former boxing promoter and "investigator" for the KKK, cofounder at age 15 of the Order of Black Shirts. In the Great Depression members marched through Atlanta with placards reading "No Jobs for Niggers Until Every White Man Has a Job." Georgia soon revoked the Black Shirts' charter, prompting founders to try again in Orlando, Florida, but Gewinner was home again by 1946, serving as a member of the AGK's "Committee to Investigate Un-American Activities." On August 26 he shared a flatbed at the Exposition Cotton Mills, in West Midtown, with Burke, Loomis, and Vester Ownby. Gewinner asked listeners to organize by streets to "combat nigger bloc voting. There are just two ways to fight these things—with ballots and with bullets. We are going to try ballots first."[18]

The youngest Columbian was Edward Reed Fields, born in Chicago on September 30, 1932, resettled in Atlanta by 1946 as a student at the Marist School, a preparatory school founded in 1901 by the Catholic Society of Mary. A precocious Nazi, Fields remembered Hitler well enough to idolize *Der Führer*'s memory and tried in vain to organize a "pro–National Socialist" student group called the Black Front. At 13 Fields published his first anti–Semitic screed, *The Jew Comes to America*. Next, he formed a club supporting Eugene Talmadge, but it hardly mattered, since his classmates couldn't vote. At 14 a friend invited him to a Columbians meeting and Fields recalled, "We were enthused by what we saw." With three dollars in hand, Fields took his fledgling step toward a lifelong sojourn on the fascist fringe.[19]

As summer waned, Burke and Loomis claimed 2,000 dues-paying members, though critics placed the total between 200 and 500. Publicity followed, and while most of it was negative—highlighting comments like Loomis's remark: "Briefly, the mission of the Columbians is to separate the white man from the nigger, and the Jew from his money"—even bad press spurred the movement's growth. Soon, small chapters were reported from Philadelphia, New York City, Indianapolis, and Gary, Indiana. Raymond Vick led the Indianapolis unit, traveling to Atlanta for orders, but the effort collapsed when reporters exhumed his arrest record for assault and battery, disorderly conduct, drunkenness and vagrancy, with a one-year prison term for robbery.[20]

Soon after founding the Columbians, Burke visited kindred spirit Earnest Sevier Cox in Virginia. A lieutenant colonel in World War I and a committed white supremacist, Cox co-founded the Anglo-Saxon Clubs of America with composer John Powell in 1922, promoting Madison Grant's nordicist ideology. A year later he published *White America*, calling for "repatriation" of black Americans to Africa, subsequently mediating peace between southern racists and Marcus Garvey's "Back to Africa" movement. In 1924 Cox helped pass Virginia's Racial Integrity Act, banning miscegenation, and two years later promoted the Massenburg Bill, requiring segregation in public places. Harry Laughlin's *Eugenical News* predicted that "the removal of Negroes would make Cox a greater savior of his country than George Washington," and *White America* was incorporated into the University of Virginia's biology curriculum, but despite his admiration for Emory Burke, Cox never joined the Columbians.[21]

Back in Atlanta, letters poured into headquarters. Porter R. Mitchell Jr., of Bridgeport, Ohio, urged Columbians to organize the Buckeye State, recruiting former members of the Klan and its 1930s spin-off, the Black Legion. "Over 200" prospects were ready, he wrote, and "several former Klan leaders have agreed to assist in establishing the order." From Minneapolis, 23-year-old University of Minnesota student Maynard Orlando "Max" Nelsen wrote to the Columbians before police arrested him for plastering the campus with stickers reading "Kill Jews" and "Dead Niggers Make Good Fertilizer." A raid on his apartment disclosed a "formidable arsenal" and a map marking prospective American conquests in "World War III." Also jailed was Raymond J. Healey, self-styled "Irish Hitler" of Chicago. When fellow Nazis failed to spring him from the lockup he turned informer, spilling everything he knew on colleagues including Emory Burke. From Florida, longtime "kludd" (Klan chaplain) Allen C. Shuler urged Columbians to colonize Jacksonville. Informer Stetson Kennedy later claimed he "nipped it in the bud," but offered no details.[22]

Meanwhile, advice and donations arrived in Atlanta from a *Who's Who* of the radical right. Gerald Smith sent cash and on behalf of his new Christian Nationalist Crusade urged affiliated groups to do likewise. Sedition trial defendant Edward Smythe visited Atlanta to learn how the Columbians generated headlines. Fellow acquittee George Deatherage dispatched cash and best wishes from Baltimore, where he ran a contracting business and penned speeches for decorated army veteran George Van Horn Moseley, who retired as Commanding General of the Third United States Army in 1938. Settled in Atlanta, Moseley described Jews as a permanent "human outcast" race, "crude and unclean, animal-like things ... something loathsome, such as syphilis." In December 1941 Moseley wrote that European Jews were "receiving their just punishment for the crucifixion of Christ ...

Retired army general and Columbians supporter George Van Horn Moseley (Library of Congress).

whom they are still crucifying at every turn of the road." His answer was a "worldwide policy which will result in breeding all Jewish blood out of the human race."[23]

***

Unknown to the Columbians, their ranks were infiltrated almost from day one by hostile spies. One such was Stetson Kennedy, who joined the order and the AGK, purportedly the fifteenth Columbian recruit in August 1946. A Florida native, born in 1916, Kennedy was a Klansman's nephew who despised the KKK after his family's black maid was flogged and raped in 1924, for "sassing" a white streetcar conductor who short-changed her. Kennedy was present when the maid described her ordeal to his mother, later recalling, "I didn't understand everything that was being said, but I had seen enough to turn me against the Klan forever." In 1946 he used his uncle's Klan membership card to join the AGK and Columbians as "John Perkins." Over time, Kennedy rifled the Columbians' files and picked through their garbage for fan mail, reporting all he found to Assistant Attorney General Duke and the private Non-Sectarian Anti-Nazi League, including Homer Loomis's advice to new recruits: "We don't want anybody to join who's not ready to get out and kill niggers and Jews."[24]

Kennedy was not the only NSANL informer inside Columbians headquarters. Founded in 1933 as the American League for the Defense of Jewish Rights, the group was organized to lead a world boycott against the Third Reich. The early 1940s found agents investigating Gerald Smith, Joseph McWilliams, and Father Charles

Left: Stetson Kennedy, in Klan regalia with Columbians literature, infiltrated both groups and reported their activities to law enforcement in 1946 and 1947 (Library of Congress). *Right:* Betty Penland, Columbians secretary and paramour of Homer Loomis, Jr. (National Archives).

Coughlin's Christian Front. NSANL moles within the Columbians included "John Brown" (né William Bishop), who offered opening prayers at many meetings, and "Renee Forrest" (née Fruchtbaum), a petite New York blonde who served as office secretary. During her tenure at headquarters, three young men from the NSANL lurked outside, ready to charge in if Renee threw a drinking glass through the window to signal danger. Even after their traitorous roles were revealed, Bishop and Fruchtbaum obtained confessions to various acts of mayhem from members James Childers and Lanier Waller.[25]

Heedless of the enemy within, Columbians courted disaster. First, Loomis and secretary Betty Kite Penland were charged with cohabitation after police caught them in a hotel room at 2 a.m. Judge A. W. Callaway fined them each $50, and Penland's brother later attacked Loomis at headquarters, forcing him to leap out a window and flee. Loomis ignored the irony of his arrest on morals charges when he demanded that female headquarters employees shun alcohol and tobacco, going to bed by 10:30 p.m. Emory Burke, even more chauvinistic, vowed someday to lynch "women who drank, smoked, wore lipstick, and danced."[26]

More serious charges surrounded the group's racist schemes: armed patrols of "white" neighborhoods, plans to bomb a convention of African American Baptist ministers (foiled by a dearth of dynamite), and discussion of "hits" on Dan Duke, Ralph McGill, and Mayor William Hartsfield. In newly integrated districts, Columbians posted signs reading "Zoned as a White Community," while Vester Ownby played both sides, offering white home owners "protection" for $3 as Columbians, simultaneously prodding them to sell—through him—and escape the black "invasion." When officials reacted, John Zimmerlee became an early casualty, forced to resign as treasurer or be expelled from Georgia Tech.[27]

On October 15, 1946, Loomis signed up 47 new members at a rally commemorating recent violence. He invited all to join him in Monroe four days hence, celebrating a quadruple lynching at Moore's Ford on July 25. On that day, a probable Klan firing squad executed

Columbians poster widely distributed in Atlanta, warning African Americans against purchase of formerly "white" homes (author's collection).

two black couples—George and Mae Dorsey, Roger and Dorothy Malcom—on suspicion that George stabbed a white farmer. Loomis planned his demonstration to "beard the FBI in its den" and was cheered by a turnout of 500 racists, plus widespread media coverage. J. Edgar Hoover scrawled a memo reading, "Certainly spotlight should be put on The Columbians," then erroneously ended by asserting, "It is just a front for the KKK."[28]

Violence escalated. Black West End residents reported bricks and stones hurled through their windows, usually late on Thursday nights after Columbians meetings. On October 24 a stick of dynamite thrown from a car bounced off one victim's porch, shattering nearby trees and shrubs. James Childers, confessing later, said Loomis sent him and James Akin out repeatedly during October with "orders to beat up any Negroes who were passing through.... When we did this we were supposed to wear our shirts with the patch ... and if we had to kill one, to put a knife in his hands and tell the policeman he drew a knife on us." Childers estimated they had jumped "a dozen or so" men who never filed police reports.[29]

On October 28 officers answered a call from Formwalt Street. They arrived to find Childers, Akin, Clarence Kite, and a Columbian known only as "Red" holding 23-year-old Clifford Hines at gunpoint in the backseat of their car, bloodied from a blackjack beating. Police jailed both Childers and Hines, while sending the other three home. Loomis bailed Childers out on October 30 and presented him with a "Medal of Honor."[30]

On Halloween some 400 persons rallied at Columbian headquarters, including a squad of Jewish War Veterans who jeered and began shredding Nazi literature while Burke spoke from the dais. Scuffling ensued, with guns drawn, before police arrived to clear the hall. When Edward Fields told officers Jews started the brawl, one replied, "We have our orders." From then on, Fields recalls, "I learned that persecution was expected and only through sacrifice would America be saved." Later that night, drive-by bombers demolished the porch of a home newly purchased by Goldsmith and Minnie Sibley on Ashby Street. Other black victims reported gunfire and stoning. Dan Duke told Stetson Kennedy of seven racist bombings in the past two weeks.[31]

While authorities eyed the Columbians, Loomis opened November by announcing formation of a women's auxiliary led by girlfriend Betty Penland, divorced sister of Clarence Kite. Members would sew flags and patches, bake "snacks," perform secretarial duties, and clean up headquarters—all in line with Burke's demand that women hew to "hearths and kitchens." At the same meeting, November 1, Burke described Columbians as "the long-awaited movement which is destined to save first the South and then the nation." How? Loomis called elections the first step, saying, "If we want to bury all niggers in the sand, once we come to power we can pass laws enabling us to bury all niggers in the sand."[32]

November 2 marked the movement's high tide, when Loomis led a squad to block Frank Jones and his wife from their new West End home. Five hundred observers included 200 Jewish veterans, and a melee was brewing when police arrived to charge Loomis, Akin, Jack Price and R. I. Whitman with inciting a riot. On November 18 a grand jury indicted Loomis, Whitman, and Emory Burke on that charge, plus usurping police powers. Meanwhile, critics piled on. *Newsweek* magazine branded the Columbians "toy Hitlers," the *Atlanta Journal* linked Burke to Nazi leaders from the 1930s, and Ralph McGill editorialized: "The Nazi type mind is cracked and lends itself to all sorts of aberrations, including those of sex.... Without exception, all members of this group, who

Columbians provoke a near-riot in Atlanta's West End on November 2, 1946 (Library of Congress).

have come to the public eye, are failures who have never managed to hold a job, but who blame someone else for their own laziness and their own failures."[33]

***

The noose tightened. Chief Hornsby declared "total police war" on Columbians, viewed by some as a move to eradicate the AGK's competitors. Governor Ellis Arnall announced a four-point plan to rid Georgia of Nazis. Dan Duke alternately called Burke's troopers "juvenile delinquents of the Klan" and speculated that the AGK "set up the Columbian outfit as their dynamite detail." On November 15 persons unknown teargassed the order's headquarters. Eleven days later the House Committee on Un-American Activities announced a Columbians investigation as its "first order of business in 1947" (never pursued). In early December, James Childers, Lanier Waller, and member Jess Johnson—a "one-armed well digger"—signed confessions, all quickly leaked to the press. Fresh indictments on December 13 charged Burke, Loomis, and Ira Jett with illegal possession of dynamite. At their arraignment, Dan Duke punched Burke for impugning his honesty. The judge excused it, saying his "head was turned at the time."[34]

Dynamite seized from Columbians headquarters. Left to right: turncoat members Lanier Waller and James Childers; Solicitor General E. E. Andrews; James Sheldon, chairman of the Non-Sectarian Anti-Nazi League; NSANL undercover agent Mario Buzzi; Detective I. M. Eason; and Atlanta Chief of Police Marion Hornsby, a longtime Klansman (Library of Congress).

Setbacks continued when Eugene Talmadge died on December 21, three weeks before inauguration. Thus began the "Three Governors Controversy," with son Herman Talmadge claiming his father's seat, defying rivals Ellis Arnall and Melvin Thompson. The AGK backed Talmadge, who addressed Dr. Green's birthday party on November 18, saying, "I believe in the Ku Klux Klan and will fight for it and white supremacy with the last drop of my blood." Columbians were present in January, when Talmadge barricaded himself in the governor's office and Arnall retreated to a nearby information booth, soon tear-gassed by enemies. Georgia's Supreme Court settled the issue in March, naming lieutenant governor-elect Thompson the rightful winner, but a special election in September 1948 returned Talmadge to power, with substantial aid from AGK terrorists.[35]

With trials looming, the Columbians decided to "fix" Dan Duke in Fairburn, where Duke served as mayor. Stetson Kennedy was present when "several hundred countrymen" turned out, *sans* women and children, "prepared for action." Emory Burke spoke first, followed by P. M. Adams, "one of the Columbians' graybeard adherents, an ex–Shakespearean actor currently engaged in selling baby shoes from door to door." Duke followed Adams, denouncing the brownshirts for "craven, bald-faced falsehoods," branding them "unintelligent cowards." When Loomis brandished a copy of the *Pittsburgh Courier*, decrying

Duke's interview "in a nigger paper," Duke countered that the interviewer had been Irish Catholic. After Duke challenged Burke to fight, the troopers fled, Burke shouting, "We'll be back."[36]

Chief Hornsby died on January 31, and his replacement abolished the Klan-ridden police union two days later, a first step toward cleansing the department. In April, Fulton County Solicitor General Paul Webb declared "the back of the Columbians has been broken," though the group's charter remained in force until June 27. Ed Fields joined George Moseley on a Free Emory Burke Committee, with aid offered by Edward Smythe, but Homer Loomis later complained, "That bum Smythe is running all over the North collecting money for a 'Columbian defense fund,' and pocketing every cent of it himself." Betty Penland considered turning state's evidence after police charged her brother with auto theft and robbing a Chinese laundry. Quarreling over cash and trial strategy, Clarence Kite and James Akin fought outside Columbians headquarter, both booked by police for disorderly conduct.[37]

Burke and Loomis initially retained attorney James Reagan Venable—a Klansman since 1924, owner of Stone Mountain and ex-mayor of a nearby town with the same name—as their chief defense counsel. Venable's plans were disrupted, however, when Homer Loomis, Sr., abandoned his New York admiralty practice to defend his son personally. Unversed in criminal law, Henry Sr., alienated Venable with his arrogance, prompting Venable to focus on Burke's defense while passing Henry Jr.'s case to bumbling family law practitioner George Thomas. Thus hampered, Henry Jr., faced trial first, insisting on his right to make an unsworn statement immune to cross-examination, rambling on for two hours of "master race" dogma. Jurors convicted him on February 15, resulting in a March 27 sentence of 30 months in a "public labor camp"—the chain gang—and two years' probation. Leaving court, he vowed to write his own *Mein Kampf,* titled *Thunder in the South,* and said, "They can put me behind forty feet of granite and I'll still shout white supremacy!"[38]

Burke fared no better at trial in February, despite James Venable's best efforts. Like Loomis, he insisted on delivering a speech—this one four hours long, declaiming at length on the works of his favorite racist authors—but jurors remained unimpressed. They deliberated only 15 minutes before convicting Burke, whereupon he received a three-year sentence. Appeals, all denied, left both men free until 1950. Loomis spent much of that time working for Gerald Smith's Christian Nationalist Crusade, based in St. Louis. James Akin moved to Columbus, Georgia, joining longtime Klansman Evall Grady "Parson Jack" Johnston's newly formed Christian Crusaders League as a typesetter. Loomis returned briefly in June, announcing formation of an all-white People's Progressive Political Party, but no one joined and he soon returned to Missouri. In December 1947 the Columbians rated a spot on the U.S. Attorney General's list of subversive organizations, lumped with eight others that "adopted a policy of advocating or approving the commission of acts of force and violence to deny others their rights under the Constitution of the United States"—four Klans and four groups defunct since the 1930s.[39]

***

Politics eclipsed the Columbians in 1948. Herman Talmadge had Georgia's gubernatorial race sewn up, with help from nightriders, while a heated presidential race engrossed America.

No one in Washington expected "accidental" president Harry Truman to become a civil rights crusader. Prior to predecessor Franklin Roosevelt's death in April 1945—and long afterward—Truman filled his private speech, letters and diary with bitter slurs against "niggers," "Kikes," "Japs" and other "inferior" races, yet by 1947, at least in public, he voiced concern for the rights of African Americans. He promised the NAACP federal aid to eliminate lynching and segregation, while prodding Democrats to include a civil rights plank in their 1948 platform. Minneapolis Mayor Hubert Humphrey and Illinois Senator Paul Douglas prepared to push that plank at the party's Philadelphia convention in July.[40]

That trend appalled southerners who worshiped at the shrine of white supremacy. In Alabama, "big mule" Sidney Smyer and ex-governor Frank Dixon (nephew of novelist Thomas Dixon, Jr.) hatched the "Birmingham Plan" to redeem their party from liberalism. Their choice as spokesman at the convention: Theophilus Eugene Connor, named by his parents for a bank robber, nicknamed "Bull" for plays he fabricated as a radio sports announcer, serving since 1937 as Birmingham's commissioner of public safety. A crude racist who worked hand-in-hand with the Klan, in Philadelphia Connor railed against Truman's "civil strife" program and mocked it by donning a feathered headdress, whooping through the aisles while demanding "civil rights for Indians." When Truman's plank passed by a vote of 651½–582½, Alabama and Mississippi delegates stormed out. Connor came home smiling, even as he told reporters, "They crucified us."[41]

Overnight, southern racists formed the States' Rights Democratic Party, better known as "Dixiecrats." They convened at Birmingham's Municipal Auditorium on July 17, just three days after bolting from Philadelphia. Favored presidential nominee Frank Dixon declined to run, but northern reporters rebuked him for sounding as if he were

"Dixiecrats" rally in Birmingham to nominate Strom Thurmond as their presidential candidate, July 1948 (Library of Congress).

"addressing the Ku Klux Klan convocation." With Gerald Smith and Jesse Stoner in the audience, cadging favors and booing "liberal" Governor James Folsom's remarks, the comparison seemed apt. Another delegate, Klan attorney Horace Wilkinson, told reporters, "I'm against Truman for the same reason I was against Al Smith [in 1928]. He thinks too damn much of the nigger." Deprived of Dixon, the Dixiecrats nominated South Carolina Governor Strom Thurmond for president, with Mississippi Governor Fielding Wright as his running mate. President Truman retaliated on July 26 with Executive Order 9981, establishing the President's Committee on Equality of Treatment and Opportunity in the Armed Services to desegregate the U.S. military.[42]

Truman faced another problem in his race against Republican rival Thomas Dewey. The left wing of his party, some of them Communists, also bolted in July 1948, forming the Progressive Party, nominating ex–Vice President Henry Wallace and Idaho Senator Glen Taylor as its standard bearers. Bull Connor had met Taylor in May, arresting him when he used a "colored" door to enter a meeting of the Southern Negro Youth Congress, later convicting Taylor of disorderly conduct. Smirking for reporters, Connor remarked, "There's not enough room in town for Bull and the Commies." On November 2, Dixiecrats carried Alabama, Louisiana, Mississippi, and South Carolina with 1,169,021 votes, Progressives claimed 1,157,172 ballots, and Truman *still* amazed pundits, defeating Dewey by a margin of 2.18 million votes. Civil rights, however sluggishly, became a brooding fact of life across the South.[43]

Lost in the national furor, Gerald Smith also ran for president in 1948, backed by former America First Party candidate Harry A. Romer on the Christian Nationalist Party ticket, embarrassed with a mere 48 popular votes. Jesse Stoner had more modest goals in Tennessee, running as an independent in the state's 3rd Congressional District. He fared better than Smith, but still placed third among three candidates, with 934 votes out of 96,357 ballots cast.[44]

***

Native Nazis learned from the Columbians' example. First to grasp the fallen torch was German immigrant Kurt Mertig, whose Citizens Protective League the DOJ declared "subversive" in 1948. In January 1949 he launched the New York-based National Renaissance Party, borrowing the thunderbolt emblem without apology, naming his group from a comment in Adolf Hitler's political testament that after *Der Führer*'s death "the seed of radiant renaissance of the National Socialist Movement" would arise. Mertig soon abandoned his brainchild to found the German-American Republican League, branded "subversive" in 1949, while 22-year-old occult fascist James Hartung Madole took over the NRP, aided behind the scenes by German transplant Frederick Charles Weiss.[45]

The fledgling NRP drew recruits from ex-members of the Christian Front, Citizens Protective League, German-American Bund, and William Henry McFarland Jr.'s Nationalist Action League (designated "subversive" in April 1949). Madole, influenced by sedition trial defendant and sci-fi writer Charles Hudson, previously formed the Animist Party before joining McFarland's NAL in 1948. Decades later, Nazi insider Rick Cooper claimed that the NRP "consisted of a small number of sincere patriots, [but] was backed, at least in part, by Jewish money and infiltrated by a group of homosexuals." Two he named, who play important roles in our later story, were Eustace Clarence Mullins, Jr. (never chairman of the Fair Employment Practices Commission, as Cooper claims) and Matthias Koehl, Jr., who joined the NRP around age 17, in 1952.[46]

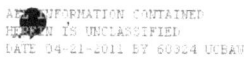

A publication of the National Renaissance Party, highlighting black crimes against whites (author's collection).

Six months after the NRP's creation, in July, white rioters attacked would-be African American neighbors in the Chicago suburbs of Englewood and Park Manor. On November 9, 63-year-old Joseph Beauharnais chartered the White Circle League of America, pledged to "keep white neighborhoods free from negroes [sic]." Charging recruits a mere dollar to join, Beauharnais published *The White Circle News* and aspired to public office, failing to become Chicago's mayor in 1951.[47] His group's first pamphlet read (uncorrected):

WANTED

ONE MILLION SELF RESPECTING WHITE PEOPLE IN CHICAGO TO UNITE UNDER THE BANNER OF THE WHITE CIRCLE LEAGUE OF AMERICA to oppose the National Campaign now on and supported by TRUMAN'S INFAMOUS CIVIL RIGHTS PROGRAM and many Pro Negro Organizations to amalgamate the black and white races with the object of mongrelizing the white race!

THE WHITE CIRCLE LEAGUE OF AMERICA is the only articulate white voice in America being raised in protest against negro aggressions and infiltrations into all white neighborhoods. The white people of Chicago MUST take advantage of this opportunity to become UNITED. If persuasion and the need to prevent the white race from becoming mongrelized by the negro will not unite us, then the aggressions ... rapes, robberies, knives, guns and marijuana of the negro, SURELY WILL.

The Negro has many national organizations working to push him into the midst of the white people on many fronts. The white race does not have a single organization to work on a NATIONAL SCALE to make its wishes articulate and to assert its natural rights to self-preservation. THE WHITE CIRCLE LEAGUE OF AMERICA proposes to do the job.

WE ARE NOT AGAINST THE NEGRO! WE ARE FOR THE WHITE PEOPLE!

We must awaken and protect our white families and neighborhoods before it is too late. Let us work unceasingly to conserve the white man's dignity and rights in America.[48]

***

Columbians alumni followed various paths when the organization collapsed. Homer Loomis, Jr., and Betty Penland stayed in St. Louis during 1948, where she toiled as a secretary in a brokerage house, moonlighting as a nightclub photographer. Following parole, Loomis left the Nazi fringe and went "straight" as CEO of the Rexair Rainbow Vacuum Cleaner Corporation.[49]

Emory Burke worked with Gerald Smith through 1949, shadowed by G-men to meetings with James Shipp, George Moseley, James Venable, Jesse Stoner, and others. Burke served his time in Georgia and emerged to publish a booklet, *Chain-Ganged by the Jewish Gestapo*, then spent the remainder of his life as an icon of various Nazi fringe groups.[50]

Ira Jett, already a Klansman, joined the AGK's Klavalier torture squad in 1948, and in April or May 1949 (accounts differ) founded Atlanta's American Bilbo Club, honoring the senator lost to cancer August 1947.[51]

Ex-Columbians treasurer John Zimmerlee served in the Korean War as a first lieutenant and B-26 bomber navigator. His plane was shot down over North Korea on March 22, 1952, lost with all hands aboard.[52]

Would-be Columbian Max Nelsen served a six-month workhouse sentence for plastering the campus with racist fliers, founded the Minneapolis-based Democratic Nationalist Party in 1947, then graduated from Minneapolis Business College, later working as comptroller for several small companies. He married German immigrant Thea Kappl in 1953, while pursuing his Nazi activities.[53]

Movement supporter Edward Smythe edited the *Protestant Statesman and Nation* from Washington, D.C., in the early 1950s, receiving a one-year sentence for mail fraud in April 1952. He also penned a nativist jingle to the tune of "God Bless America."[54] Its lyrics ran:

> God Bless America
> The Jews own it
> The Catholics run it
> The Negroes enjoy it
> The Protestants founded it, but
> The Communists will destroy it[55]

Jesse Stoner and Ed Fields pursued active far-right careers after leaving the Columbians. Stoner was expelled from the Klan for launching a campaign to purge Chattanooga's Jews, but sources disagree on timing: some claim Dr. Green banished him before the Dixiecrat revolt of 1948; others say Sam Roper did the honors when he succeeded Green and renamed his group the Associated Klans of America in 1950.[56] Either way, the exile didn't stick. Stoner led, joined, or fraternized with various Klans for the remainder of his life.

Ed Fields segued from the Columbians to Atlanta's short-lived American Anti-Communist Society, and during 1949–50 wrote several letters to *The Broom*, seeking members for a "Defense Committee" to "protect Americans from the terror of the Kike." When the first desegregation challenge targeted Atlanta's schools in 1950, he passed out pamphlets headlined: "Jewish Communists Behind Atlanta's School Segregation Suit." That same year, he tried military service but received a general discharge from the U.S. Naval Air Force for "unsuitability." When he sought to reenlist in 1951 Fields described himself as a self-employed "Anti-Jewish Crusader," whose duties included "Distribution of anti–Jewish literature and organize youths for anti–Jewish activities—Death to the Communist Traitors." He specified refusal to serve "in the U.N. police or any Jew-controlled international force."[57] The medic who examined him filed a report on December 15, 1952, concluding:

> Abnormal Psychiatric—Paranoid personality—is not qualified for induction.... He states that Jews caused him to be expelled from both college and the Navy. He appears calm, unperturbed, and somewhat arrogant during the interview.... He looks immature and he lacks the force of personality usually observed in paranoid individuals.... He is seriously sick and the chances of eventually becoming frankly insane are excellent.[58]

He went further, contacting FBI agents who filed a report that the doctor was "quite anxious that someone with authority to commit this man to an institution be notified. We told him that we knew of no such person at the moment."[59]

From military dreams Field turned to law school in Atlanta, and there, in 1952, met classmate Jesse Stoner. With comrade Emmett O'Neil Morris, they overhauled the Stoner Anti-Jewish Party, renaming it the Christian Anti-Jewish Party. Stoner appointed himself "Arch Leader," while Fields became Chief Secretary. One of their early pamphlets bore the headline: "Defend the White Race. The Great White Race Has a Right to Live." Another, announcing a party rally, appended the warning: "Only Whites Invited. Jews Stay Away."[60]

In 1953 Fields changed his mind again, quit law school, and decamped to study at

Opposite: **A flier distributed from Jesse Stoner's Christian Anti-Jewish Party (author's collection).**

JEWS BEHIND RACE MIXING

"JEWISH LIFE", official organ of the Jewish section of the Communist party, in its June, 1950 issue on page 8, states:

"Our job as Jewish Communists is to take the lead in educating the Jewish masses on the meaning of white supremacy and to enroll the Jewish community in an all-out fight against it. This is paramount in our work in the struggle for negro rights. This is vital to the struggle of the Jewish people for their own security and future."

It has surprised some people to find out that the president of the National Association for the Advancement of Colored People [NAACP] is NOT a Negro BUT the JEW ARTHUR SPINGARN. It is the Jews who are leading the fight to destroy segregation in Atlanta schools.

The NAACP is sponsoring suits all over the country and in the U. S. Supreme Court to break down Racial Segregation and open up our White schools, restaurants, busses and hotels to negroes. All important Jewish organizations are against Segregation and have petitioned Congress for an anti-White FEPC law.

A Jew, Julius Rosenwald, spent $30 million financing organizations and writers that promote mongrelization. A race once mongrelized is mongrelized forever.

America must awaken to the Jew attack against White People!

For more information on the Jew menace to the White Race write:

CHRISTIAN ANTI-JEWISH PARTY

P. O. BOX 48   ATLANTA GA.

the Palmer School of Chiropractic in Davenport, Iowa. Stoner stuck to his guns, both politically and academically, obtaining his law degree and passing Georgia's bar exam, briefly sharing offices with Klan "klonsel" James Venable. Like most of Stoner's business ties, that one failed, but the attorneys would remain friends and fellow fanatics throughout the tumultuous era ahead.[61]

CHAPTER 2

"All deliberate speed"

On May 17, 1954, the U.S. Supreme Court issued a unanimous ruling in the case *Brown v. Board of Education of Topeka*, reversing the court's 1896 "separate but equal facilities" ruling in *Plessy v. Ferguson*, finding that "separate educational facilities are inherently unequal." When various Jim Crow states dragged their feet, blustered in Congress, and debated abolition of their schools to defy the ruling, the Court reiterated its judgment on May 31, 1955, ordering state authorities to begin integration "with all deliberate speed."[1]

While some racists feigned surprise in 1954, despite three years of warning as the *Brown* case wound its way through lower courts, others anticipated the court's decision. In February 1954 Edward Fields joined another student from Palmer School of Chiropractic to rebel against National Brotherhood Week, plastering Davenport and two nearby towns with stickers reading: "This store owned by Jews" and "Anti-Jewish Week, Feb. 21–28." Police filed no charges but Fields was reportedly placed on academic probation. Nonetheless, he continued interspersing his studies with racist mass mailing and picketing, all the while corresponding with Jesse Stoner and building a network of like-minded fascists nationwide.[2]

Stoner, for his part, remained as active as ever. Convinced that African Americans lacked the intelligence to coordinate a mass protest movement, he blamed Jewish communists for pressing the *Brown* case, and for all subsequent demonstrations against segregation anywhere. As he wrote in a treatise titled "The Philosophy of 'White Racism'": "The negro [sic] is not the enemy. The Jew is THE enemy of our White Race and the Jew is using the negro in an effort to destroy the White Race that he so passionately hates." On August 16–17, 1954, Stoner and five other members of his Christian Anti-Jewish Party—Fields and Atlanta resident Robert Bowling among them—picketed the White House, protesting the *Brown* decision.[3]

***

Meanwhile, in the South, Virginia Senator Harry Byrd, Sr., organized the "Massive Resistance" movement in February 1956, declaring, "If we can organize the Southern States for massive resistance to this order I think that in time the rest of the country will realize that racial integration is not going to be accepted in the South." In mid–March, Byrd and 95 other racist members of Congress signed a "Southern Manifesto," branding the *Brown* ruling "a clear abuse of judicial power," encouraging all segregated states to resist the mandate. Various southern public schools were closed before Virginia's Supreme Court and a special panel of federal judges from the Eastern District of Virginia declared those actions unconstitutional in January 1959.[4]

Meanwhile, in July 1954, Mississippi plantation manager Robert "Tut" Patterson founded the first Citizens' Council, swiftly recruiting 15,000 politicians, professionals, and others from the "cream" of white-supremacist society to resist integration on every front, by all legal means. Suggestions included economic harassment of blacks who supported racial equality, establishment of private white "academies," resistance to black voter registration, and later, deportation of southern blacks to the "liberal" North on "reverse freedom rides." While proclaiming themselves "respectable," outwardly shunning "the nefarious Ku Klux Klans," Council members soon crossed the line into violence, including riots, bombings, and murder, earning a public reputation as an "uptown Klan," a "white collar Klan," a "button-down Klan," and a "country club Klan." In fact, despite professed screening of applicants, many Klansmen joined the Citizens' Councils soon after their inception, and some Council organizations—such as future NSRP member Asa Earl Carter's Northern Alabama Citizens' Council—were essentially front groups for covert Klan units. Others, like Frederick John Kasper's Seaboard White Citizens' Council, openly rallied with Klansmen while inciting criminal violence.[5]

The Councils' baptism by fire occurred in February 1956, when Autherine Lucy won a three-year court battle to become the University of Alabama's first African American student. University administrators had accepted her in 1952, before they learned her race,

Rioters protest the admission of African American coed Autherine Lucy to the University of Alabama in February 1956 (Library of Congress).

then reversed themselves, initiating bitter litigation. Finally compelled to honor the *Brown* decision, officials enrolled Lucy on February 1, while still denying her a campus dormitory room. Lucy attended her first classes on February 3, but that night and the weekend brought furious white demonstrations to campus, with many of the protesters visibly older than university students. Some were members of Asa Carter's Birmingham-based Citizens' Council, aka the Original Ku Klux Klan of the Confederacy. Of the four off-campus whites briefly detained but never tried, one was longtime Klansman and NACC member Robert Chambliss, dubbed "Dynamite Bob" for bombing numerous black homes and churches around Birmingham. After their release, the four filed million-dollar damage suits against Lucy and the NAACP.[6]

Asa Carter—"Ace" to friends and enemies alike—was an Alabama native, born in 1925, who joined the navy during World War II, then attended the University of Colorado. He returned to Birmingham in 1953, working as a radio announcer and mouthpiece for the racist American States Rights Association, but lost those jobs in February 1955 after a string of broadcasts bitterly reviling Jews. By November he had organized the NACC, appealing to a "redneck" clientele (Emory Burke among them), the worst siphoned off to join his secret Klan. The Lucy riots were the group's debut. Other incidents included an attack on singer Nat "King" Cole at Birmingham's Municipal Auditorium in April 1956, the turpentine-soaked castration of black victim Edward Aaron in September 1957 (sending four of Carter's men to prison), the attempted murder of civil rights activist Fred Shuttlesworth that same month, and finally Carter's shooting of two Klansmen who questioned his handling of their dues, which finally dissolved the group. Carter's allies were Birmingham Public Safety Commissioner Bull Connor and attorney Arthur Hanes, Sr., ex-FBI agent, CIA contract employee, alleged closet Klansman, and future mayor of Birmingham.[7]

Asa Carter harangues a segregationist audience on August 31, 1956 (National Archives).

***

Carter was not alone in rousing rabble during those frenetic years. A more unlikely candidate, given his background, was Frederick John Kasper—normally called "John," later preferring "Fred" when he retired from racist activism. New Jersey born in 1929, Kasper began life as a social liberal, attended South Dakota's Yankton College, then graduated from Columbia University before settling in Manhattan's Greenwich Village, where he dated at least one African American woman and ran a small bookshop described by a newspaper reporter as "a recognized center for the distribution of pro–Negro books and magazines ... patronized chiefly by Negroes and Negrophile whites."[8]

That changed with Kasper's descent into near-pathological adoration for Ezra Pound, a famed poet arrested in 1945 for broadcasting fascist propaganda—he called Adolf Hitler "a Jeanne d'Arc, a saint"—and committed to a psychiatric hospital in Washington, D.C., where he remained until April 1958. Kasper encountered Pound's work at Columbia and began corresponding with the poet, whom Kasper addressed as "Grandpaw" and "Master," extolling Pound as "god and the greatest of all men." Before it closed, Kasper's Greenwich bookshop began peddling *Mein Kampf* and *Protocols of the Learned Elders of Zion*, while he excoriated Jews in weekly group discussions. Kasper moved to Washington in 1956, the better to visit Pound and lobby for his release, while sharing rooms with fellow Pound devotee and future NSRP associate Eustace Mullins.[9]

That same year, Kasper focused his attention on the threat of integrated schools to "racial purity." In June 1956 he chartered the Seaboard White Citizens' Council in Virginia, with aid from Ace Carter. Within a month FBI agents named Kasper as their prime suspect in cross-burnings at the Washington homes of Chief Justice Earl Warren, Solicitor General Simon Sobeloff, and New York Senator Herbert Lehman.

Poet Ezra Pound offers a fascist salute upon his arrival in Italy, following release from a U.S. mental institution in April 1958 (Library of Congress).

After "brief scouting trips" through the Upper South, Kasper and Carter targeted Charlottesville, Virginia, in July and August, harassing civil rights activists, burning a cross at the home of white liberal Sarah Patton Boyle, and invading a meeting of the Virginia Council on Human Relations, where Kasper warned, "We of the Citizens' Council have declared war on you." Kasper logged his first arrest in Charlottesville, for distributing hate literature, but his efforts came to naught and local schools integrated without incident—as they also did in Louisville, Clay, and Sturgis, Kentucky, despite Kasper's best efforts. Still, that Bluegrass trip was not a total waste, as he forged an alliance with Citizens' Council leader Millard Dee Grubbs, another future NSRP ally. Aside from Council work, Grubbs—then 70 years old—headed the Continental League of Christian Freedom, regarded by some as a Klan front, and in 1955 founded the militant Christian Sentinels of Kentucky.[10]

After several false starts and reams of printed literature paraphrasing—if not plagiarizing—Ezra Pound, Kasper finally found fertile soil for his belated fascism in Tennessee. His first target was Clinton, seat of Anderson County, where impending high school integration had roused white racists to the boiling point. Kasper arrived on August 25, 1956, and began haranguing locals on the street, sleeping in his car by night. On August 26, after he ignored an order to leave town, police jailed Kasper overnight for vagrancy and inciting to riot. Fifty whites protested integration on August 27, and jurors acquitted Kasper at his trial the following day, for lack of evidence. He swiftly organized a picket line at Clinton High School, while enlisting white students for a Junior Citizens' Council. Those recruits began attacking black students on August 28, prompting some to leave school, while federal marshals interrupted Kasper's speech to 1,000 admirers, serving

Top: Rioters inspired by John Kasper and Asa Carter attack black motorists in Clinton, Tennessee, August 1956 (Library of Congress). *Bottom:* John Kasper (in suit) greets supporters after posting bail in Clinton, Tennessee, August 1956 (National Archives).

him with a temporary restraining order. On the 30th, while disorderly protests continued, a judge found Kasper guilty of contempt. Asked if he had anything to say, Kasper replied, "Stop the integration of Clinton High School" and received a one-year-sentence. En route to jail he told reporters, "Woe to those whose only right is their power. The wild grass will grow over their dead bodies."[11]

With Kasper temporarily incarcerated, spokesmen for the Tennessee Federation for Constitutional Government picked up his torch, augmented on August 31 by Ace Carter, who addressed a crowd of 2,000, lambasting the NAACP, the Supreme Court, and the "carpetbagging judge" who sentenced Kasper. The mob ran amok, shouting, "We want Kasper!" and marching on Mayor Buford Lewallen's home, threatening to dynamite that residence and the county courthouse. While city officials armed and deputized a 47-man "home guard," and Governor Frank Clement dispatched 633 National Guardsmen with 10 armored vehicles, Kasper posted bail and decamped for Birmingham, telling an audience of Carter's stalwarts, "I'm a rabble-rouser, a troublemaker. I'm not through up there. We want trouble. We want it now.... Some of us may die and I may die, too. It may mean going back to jail, but I'm going back to fight. We went as far as we could have gone legally. Now is the time to fight, even if it involves bloodshed." A grand jury indicted Kasper for sedition *in absentia*, but jurors acquitted him in November, while Ezra Pound hailed his protégé for using the trial to garner "a little publicity for the NAACP being run by kikes and not by coons."[12]

True to his word, Kasper was not "through up there" in Tennessee. Forsaking Clinton—where racists burned more crosses, beat a white Baptist minister who backed integration, shot up homes, detonated dynamite in an African American neighborhood, and finally bombed Clinton High in October 1958—Kasper embarked on a speaking tour of the South and published more screeds with titles such as *Virginians Awake!* and *Segregation or Death*. He logged a fresh arrest at Oak Ridge in September 1956 but failed to block the city's voluntary school desegregation. Next he turned to Nashville, variously posing as president of the Tennessee Citizens' Council and an officer of the Tennessee Federation for Constitutional Government. His message was the same as always and inspired the same response from bigots anxious "to protect and defend the purity of the white race." After speaking of "the shotgun, dynamite, and rope," Kasper became a prime suspect in the September 1957 bombing of newly integrated Hattie Cotton Elementary School, but police found no basis to charge him, despite a Klansman's confession that Kasper helped him hide a cache of dynamite one night before the blast. Kasper's name came up again in March 1958, when bombers struck a local Jewish Community Center, but again he escaped indictment. He *was* convicted of conspiracy in Clinton, but posted bail again pending appeal, calling for a new terrorist underground network to combat the federal government. Kasper ultimately served time in two federal prisons, released in August 1958, but by then many of his former friends had turned against him.[13]

Kasper's apparent downfall as a rabble rouser was induced, at least in part, by the American Jewish Committee leaking details of his Greenwich Village days to southern authorities. Word of his interracial dating soon reached Klansmen, resulting in a ban on Kasper speaking at their rallies. In March 1957 he visited Miami for the trial of Citizens' Council officer Fred B. Hockett, charged with cross-burning and stockpiling 100 boxes of dynamite to be deployed at Kasper's direction. Hockett escaped with a fine, and while Kasper ducked further charges, his plan to organize a local youth branch of the Council was derailed by a subpoena to Tallahassee, where a state legislative committee grilled

Police survey bomb damage at Nashville's Hattie Cotton Elementary School, September 1957 (National Archives).

Retired admiral and perennial fascist political candidate John Crommelin, before retirement from the navy (Library of Congress).

him on his background and alliance with the Klan. Before incarceration, he was last seen in Wetumpka, Alabama, where the Citizens' Council denied him its podium.[14]

Still, even *in extremis,* Kasper had friends on the far right. One of them was ex–Rear Admiral John Geraerdt Crommelin, Jr., an Alabama native born in 1902 and a decorated naval officer forced to retire in 1950 after a series of quarrels with Pentagon superiors, whom he branded "a Prussian General Staff system of the type employed by Hitler." Back in civilian life, convinced his ouster was plotted by Jews, he launched the first in a series of failed political races, seeking to unseat incumbent Alabama Senator Lister Hill. Crommelin tried and failed again in 1954, running third among four in his bid to depose Senate incumbent John Sparkman. By 1956, when he challenged Hill again, John Kasper was living in Crommelin's home and offering campaign advice that failed to help Crommelin win May's Democratic primary. Still, Crommelin admired Kasper enough to join him on subsequent trips to Clinton, Tennessee, telling one local audience, "You may not see it, and your children may not see it, but someday a statue will be erected on this courthouse lawn to John Kasper."[15]

***

While future NSRP activists Kasper, Carter, and Crommelin made their respective headlines across the South, Edward Fields remained in Iowa, graduating from the Palmer School of Chiropractic in 1956. That same year he served as acting Iowa chairman of the Constitution Party, backing ex–Commissioner of Internal Revenue T. Coleman Andrews for president; visited Chicago for a convention held by Northern Friends of the South, led by 1940s sedition defendant Joe McWilliams; and in September joined in a National States Rights Conference in Memphis.[16]

Fields surfaced next in Louisville, Kentucky, newly married, practicing chiropractic and battling integration with Citizens' Council leader Millard Grubbs, while using the title "Doctor" to impress his fellow fascists.[17]

***

Jesse Stoner had other matters on his mind in 1957, chief among them foundation of yet another racist group—the Christian Knights of the Ku Klux Klan—which he served Imperial Wizard, while remaining "Arch Leader of the Christian Party"—both operating from an Atlanta post office box. Some scholars date creation of Stoner's Klan from 1959, but its inauguration was heralded by Stoner's first letter to the Nation of Islam, aka Black Muslims, at the group's Chicago headquarters in February 1957. Twelve years later, NOI leader Elijah Muhammad published Stoner's missive for all posterity. It read, uncorrected:

Elijah Muhammad, leader of the Black Muslims and a personal *bête noir* of Jesse Stoner in the late 1950s (Library of Congress).

Infidels:
  Repent of Mohammedanism or burn in hell forever, throughout eternity.
  The Lord Jesus Christ is the only begotten Son of God and He is the only One Who can save your infidelic souls and lead you into Heaven. Read the Holy Bible. St. John 6:35—"And Jesus said unto them, I am the bread of life. He that cometh to me shall never hunger; and he that believeth on me shall never thirst." St. John 6:47—"Verily, verily, I say unto you. He that believeth on me hath everlasting life" St. John 8:12—"Then spake

2. "All deliberate speed"

Jesus again unto them, saying, I am the light of the world; he that followeth me shall not walk in darkness, but shall have the light of life." Acts 16:31—"And they said, Believe on the Lord Jesus Christ and thou shall be saved and thy house." Acts 4:12—"Neither is there salvation in any other: for there is none other name under heaven, whereby we must be saved." Therefore, Muhammad can do you no good.

It does not surprise me to hear that Islam is growing among the Africans of America. It is easy to understand because Islam is a nigger religion. It has only been successful among Africans and mix-breeds and never among the white people never. As you probably know, Christianity was well established throughout North Africa by white people before Mohammed was born. As time went on more and more people in North Africa became mongrelized with African blood. Therefore, they were no longer able or willing to stand up and fight for Christianity when persecution came upon them from Arabia. Their faith in Christ was shallow and weak. Then came the bloody Islamic conquerors from Arabia who slaughtered white Christian leaders but spared the black people and mix-breeds. The Africans quickly forgot Christ, the true religion, and became Mohammedans. Some scholars have wondered why, but not me. I know why. Islam is a product of the colored race. Islam is a dark religion for dark people. I don't know why Africans would support Islam for any other reason except of race. There are several reasons why niggers should oppose it. One reason is that the Qur-an forbids Muslims to drink intoxicating drinks, whereas most niggers like to get drunk. It says also that thieves should have their hands cut off. How many niggers would be left with hands?

Christianity, the one and only true religion, has only been successful in white nations among white people, as recognized in the literature of the Christian Party. Christianity prevails in every white nation, even when outlawed, but does not appear to have roots in any colored nation that could withstand tribulation. Therefore on a racial group basis, it would appear that only the superior white race is capable of appreciating Christianity and that the dark inferior races prefer a heathen religion like Islam. Therefore, it is obvious that we Christians should work hard to preserve the great white race. Not only will we benefit; missionary work and be instrumental in saving the individual souls of millions of colored people in spite of their racial weakness and racial inferiority. We white Christians love the souls of all men, with all due respect to the racial differences that God Himself created. If GOD had only wanted one race, He would have created one race.

To every place it has spread, Islam has been a blight and brought darkness. Islam's armies conquered much of Asia and Africa and even of Europe and caused darkness in every country that it entered and it decayed their civilizations that the great white race had built.

Muslims, in their efforts to conquer the world, occupied most of Spain and even invaded ancient France. Fortunately, there was a great white Christian leader, Charles Martel. He saved Civilization and the white race by defeating the Mohammedans at the Battle of Tours in the year of our Lord 732 thus stopping the Islamic invasion of Europe. Later the Islamic Turks invaded white Christian Europe from the East. The Turks, under Suleiman the Magnificent, got as far into the heart of Europe as the gates of Vienna before they were stopped in AD 1529. In AD 1683, during the reign of Mohammed IV, they besieged Vienna again, but were soundly defeated by the great King John Sobieski in Poland, the hero of white Christiandom and perserver of civilization.

One of the main purposes of Mohammedan invasion of white Europe was to capture white women. Only white women are beautiful. When ruling over white sections of Europe, part of the tribute required of the conquered people was the regular giving of beautiful white women to the Muslims as slaves. They didn't like their own dark women. The African race has never produced a beautiful woman so the Muslims were naturally not satisfied with their own black women. If the Africans were as good as whites, they would be happy with their own women instead of lusting for our white women. Your desire for white women is an admission of your own racial inferiority. One reason why we whites will never accept you into our white society is because a nigger's chief ambition in life is to sleep with a white woman thereby polluting her. Every time a demented white woman marries a nigger, your newspapers brag about the sin. The day will come when no nigger will be allowed to even look at a white woman or a white woman's picture. That will be a sad day for the men of your race who have no respect for their own women won't it? For your information, nigger is the Latin word for black, so why are you ashamed of it?

Yes, Africans in America are ashamed of their own race. They regret that they are what they are. As proof, look at the nigger newspaper that advertise skin whiteners, and so-called hair straighteners. If blacks are as good as whites why aren't they proud of their black skins and the kinky wool on top of their heads? If you aren't ashamed of your race, why don't you strive to keep it pure and preserve it and its characteristics.

You blacks have a lower opinion of your own race than we whites have. You hate, yes hate your own African race so much that you want to destroy it by mixing your blood with white blood. You want white blood pumped into your race because you think white blood is better and will improve you and make you less negroid, less African. You are trying to forget your heritage and your race by associating with your white superiors.

If you were as good as whites and equal to us, you would not be trying to force yourselves into white society. You would be happy with the company of your fellow Africans. Or, is the odor too much for you? Since you niggers don't respect your own race and don't love your race enough to preserve it, how can you expect white people to respect it? I have more respect for an African who believes in Black Supremacy and racial purity than I do for an African who hates his own race and tries vainly to disown it. I admire the African who says that no white man is good enough to shake hands with him.

I hope you will appreciate the fact that I am not a hypocrite like some Yankees who preach race-mixing and practice segregation. I actually express the sentiments and feelings that are in the hearts of most white people everywhere when I tell you that I believe in white supremacy and the inferiority of all dark races.

Why should we whites let Africans infiltrate our civilization when Africans have never been able to build or maintain a civilization of their own? You Africans are afraid to do it alone. You are afraid that you would get lost without the white man to guide you and help you. Yet with your mania for mongrelization, you are trying to destroy the white race that has given you civilization on a silver platter. You are striving to kill the white goose that laid the golden egg of civilization. If you succeed, you will not be able to get more golden eggs because the white goose will be dead.

A new independent African nation will be born in a few days on March 6th, 1957. Now known as the rich Gold Coast, it will become known as Ghana. Blacks will run it from top to bottom. Do you think they are capable of success or does their black blood doom them to their failure? The black Prime Minister graduated from Lincoln University here in America. Many of Ghana officials have studied in America. English is a common language in Ghana. If the Africans had self-respect and ability, they would go to Ghana in Africa and prove their racial ability by helping to build a great African nation. They won't go because they have no confidence in themselves.

They know that their race is a lower form of humanity and cannot stand on its own feet. The Africans of America are afraid to be without the white man, and thus, admit their own inferiority.

The British West Indies that lie off the coast of the United States will also become a new independent black nation soon. They speak English there. However, American's black people won't even go that short distance to help build a black nation because there won't be enough whites to control them and lead them around. The Africans of America are convinced that they would perish without the white race to help and protect them. Blacks even claim that white teachers are superior to black teachers. Inferiors always demand the right to associate with their superiors. When the black man cries against segregation, he is actually singing praises to the white race.

They never intended for America to fall into the possession of a dark race. Many of the founders of this nation owned blacks as slaves, such as Washington, Jefferson, and the great Patrick Henry who said: "Give me liberty or give me death."

America is a white Christian nation and no infedelic religion such as Islam, has a right to exist under the American sun. Your Islam, your Mohammedanism is not a white religion. Mohammedanism is a nigger religion. The white race will never accept it, so take it back to Africa with you. It is like the Holy Bible says about GOD'S plan for the nations of men in Acts 16:31—"And hath determined the times before appointed, and the bounds of their habitation." Therefore you have no place in America with your African race or your Islamic African religion.

The Christian Party becomes stronger every day. When we are elected to power we will legally drive you out. Remember AD 1492 when those two great white Christian monarchs, King Ferdinand and Queen Isabella, expelled the Muslims from Spain. The Christian Party will be even more ruthless. We will not tolerate your infidelic Christ-hating religion on American soil. We will drive Islam into the ocean. America isn't big enough for the Christian Party and Black Islam, so Islam must go.

You Muslims should be ashamed of yourselves for trying to lead the poor darkies of America into your Mohammedam hell. If they are smart, they will shun Mohammed and follow the Lord Jesus Christ, the Son of God, into Heaven and a happy and everlasting life.

Repent and confess the Lord Jesus Christ or you will burn in hell forever, you infidels. Your false religion is an insult to the true living GOD.

May God have mercy upon your heathen souls.

With many wishes for the failure of Islam in America, I am, Yours for Christ, Country and Race,
    J. B. Stoner[18]

Despite his facetious sign-off, Stoner's letter marked the start of an obsession with the Muslims that consumed him for at least the next two years.

Chapter 3

Birth of the Party

Few historical topics are more fraught with chaos, contradiction, and conundrums than the origins of fringe political movements. Participants' memories radically differ, while outsiders pile on supposition, rumors, and opprobrium. Such is the case with the National States Rights Party's creation.

In autumn 1957 Edward Fields produced a pamphlet, subsequently delivered to the FBI by informer "LS T-2."[1] Titled *America Salutes the Heroes of Nashville*, it read (uncorrected):

> White America looks with pride upon its brave and courageous sons who battle for racial purity in Nashville. You made a great show of strength and determination. We congratulate you Patriots who fought against the Communist Judges, crooked politicians, and lying newspapers. Your demonstrations have encouraged the people of Little Rock and other places to stand firm and rise up against the mongrelizers. Round one of this life and death struggle is over.
>
> Only by police brutality in Nashville, and Federal bayonets in Little Rock are the integrationists making any headway. Integration is slowly grinding to a dead stop.
>
> The time has come for all White organizations to unite and form a White Political Party, to put our people on the ballot and vote the traitors out of office. Such scum as Benny West, Clement, the Nashville School Board, and Nashville Police Chief, must be run out of office for their crimes against Whitemen.
>
> We must take over every town and state in the South, Legally and politically, then we can meet Eisenhower's troops with forces of our own. Then we can arrest Communist Federal judges for disturbing the peace, vagrancy, loitering, etc. With the State guard and police on our side we will tell Eisenhower to go to HELL!
>
> Eisenhower is starting a Civil War against all the White South. Federal bayonets in the backs of our sweet innocent little children is a crime against our people, which demands justice and vengeance. United, the Whiteman has the strength of steel, the cry of our Freedom Fighting Forefathers was "The Redcoats are coming," in the same spirit of '76, our cry will be "The Red Courts are coming." Let this warning awaken the workers and farmer, to crush the invaders as was done by George Washington and Robert E. Lee.
>
> We will soon be in Nashville to help you Whitefolks form a White Democratic Nationalist Party. To find out what part you can have in this movement, or extra copies of this leaflet—write to
>
> DR. EDWARD FIELDS
> 1617 Bardstown Road
> Louisville, Kentucky[2]

When the promised gathering occurred, however, it would not be at the heart of Nashville's battleground, but in Knoxville, 181 miles farther east.

***

3. Birth of the Party

On November 10, 1957, fascists from around the country gathered in Knoxville to form the party envisioned by Fields, but discarded his proffered name to call it instead the United White Party. Various accounts present different lists of those present, but all agree that the delegates included Fields; Jesse Stoner; Emory Burke; Wallace Hugh Allen, handicapped from age 16, in 1941, after a train struck his car; Neubert Newman "Ned" Dupes, a Knoxville car salesman and friend of John Kasper; Kasper himself, by some accounts, presumably free on appeal from his latest conviction; C. Daniel Kurtz (born A. Casimir Kudelski in 1891), ex-leader of the Christian Front's Minute Men in Queens, New York, lately affiliated with the National Renaissance Party and co-founder with Bryant Bowles in 1953 of a National Association for the Advancement of White People; and Matt Koehl, Jr., a friend of Ed Fields since 1953, born in Milwaukee to Hungarian immigrants of German descent, and a member of the NRP's Elite Guard.[3]

Also present, although overlooked in some reports, was U.S. Navy Commander George Lincoln Rockwell. Already familiar with Wallace Allen—a fellow commercial artist—Rockwell was tipped to the impending conclave by colleague DeWest Hooker (né Lendrum De West Murrelle, Jr.), a film and television producer, oil broker and president of the Independent Refining Cooperative Inc., and a committed fascist who advised Rockwell to espouse hard-core Nazism. Taking Hooker's advice, Rockwell arrived in Knoxville on November 9, briefing Emory Burke and others on his "Lincoln Plan" for repatriation of blacks to Africa by paying each emigrant family $10,000. Burke loved the idea but advised Rockwell to delete Nazi jargon from his final presentation, which Rockwell did when addressing the assembled delegates on Sunday. Afterward, Wallace Allen offered Rockwell a job selling advertising in Atlanta. Rockwell moved his family to Georgia but gave it up in February 1958, passing on to Virginia and eventual foundation of his American Nazi Party in 1959.[4]

Some southern newspapers approvingly noted the UWP's stated goal of opposing all "race mixing groups and individuals." Historians still debate whether the UWP was simply Stoner's Christian Anti-Jewish Party renamed, or whether it was a wholly new organization. In any case, Fields and Stoner were in charge. The sometime chiropractor's first contribution to the UWP was a 12-page pamphlet titled *Documented Proof: Jews Behind Race Mixing*.[5]

***

Three months later, on February 1, 1958, native fascists convened an "Ultimatum Conference of Loyal Americans" at the Henry Clay Hotel in downtown Louisville. Keynote speaker John Crommelin, described in FBI reports as being on "extended furlough" prior to final separation from the navy, had in fact he formally retired in May 1950. From the dais, Crommelin boasted of his friendship with John Kasper and urged attendees to support his upcoming gubernatorial race in Alabama.[6]

Others spotted at the meeting included Millard Grubbs and James William Cole. Still leading the Kentucky Citizens' Council, Grubbs had attended another Louisville meeting on August 3, 1957, where he introduced a resolution calling for impeachment and hanging of U.S. Supreme Court justices for their ruling in the *Brown* case. That resolution was later memorialized in a pamphlet titled *The American Eagle*.[7]

James Cole was even more intriguing. Born in 1924, a World War II veteran, he acquired the nickname "Catfish" while driving a taxi in hometown Kinston, North Carolina, then became a traveling tent evangelist, founder with wife Carolyn of Southern Bible

Louisville's Henry Clay Hotel, site of the "Ultimatum Conference of Loyal Americans," February 1958 (author's collection).

College in Marion, South Carolina, and voice of the nondenominational *Free Will Hour* radio program on Sunday mornings. Cole was finally ordained in 1958 by the Wayside Baptist Church in Summerfield, North Carolina, but his true allegiance lay with the North Carolina Knights of the Ku Klux Klan, which he founded in 1956 and led as Grand Dragon. After failing to drive the NAACP from his native state, thwarted by members of a paramilitary Black Armed Guard, Cole focused on Lumbee Indians in Robeson County—whom he dubbed a

North Carolina Klan leader James "Catfish" Cole attacked Lumbee Indians in January 1958 and suffered humiliating defeat, plus a prison term (Library of Congress).

"mongrel race"—and was humiliated when tribesmen mobbed a rally at Maxton on January 18, 1958, seizing Klan regalia, while Cole wound up convicted of inciting a riot. Early the following year he was convicted again, this time for impersonating a licensed private detective. Outside the Klan he was a laughingstock, but within the narrow confines of the fascist fringe, Cole still possessed a certain cachet for trying, even when he failed.[8]

Nothing more was heard about the "Ultimatum Conference," but John Crommelin proceeded as planned with the Alabama Democratic gubernatorial primary in May, aided by Emory Burke, his fliers declaring "the key to segregation of the races and survival of the Christian White Race is a thorough understanding by White Christian voters of the Communist-Jewish conspiracy." The field was crowded with 14 contenders, chief among them Attorney General John Malcolm Patterson and Circuit Judge George Corley Wallace, dubbed the "the fighting little judge" for his background as a boxer. Patterson, already famous for driving the NAACP from Alabama as an unregistered "foreign corporation" in 1956, appealed directly to the Klan, mass-mailing an appeal for votes on official stationery, citing the name of "mutual friend" Robert Shelton—lately expelled from the U.S. Klans to lead his own Alabama Knights. Wallace criticized Patterson's alliance with Klansmen, trailing Patterson by 34,424 primary votes, while Crommelin placed eleventh in the field with a mere 2,245 ballots. Patterson did even better in June's general election, eclipsing Wallace by 64,902 votes, leaving Wallace to complain, "The sonofabitch out-niggered me, but I'll never be out-niggered again."[9]

The most important part of Crommelin's campaign was the reintroduction of George Rockwell and Matt Koehl, casually friendly since the UWP's founding convention in November, both doing their best to elect the ex-admiral. They parted company before year's end, Koehl joining the NSRP, while Rockwell went on to found his ANP, but they would reunite in 1960, when Koehl switched allegiance to the Virginia-based party. Other future NSRP members active in Crommelin's failed campaign and those that followed were Oren Fenton Potito, an early minister for Wesley Swift's Church of Jesus Christ—Christian; Gordon Winrod, son of 1940s sedition defendant Gerald Winrod and an Identify minister; and Charles Conley Lynch, another Swift devotee, known to friends and enemies alike as "Connie."[10]

***

More needless confusion surrounds the actual birth of the NSRP, occurring in August 1958. FBI reports persist in claiming the party was founded at Knoxville in 1957, and some scholars follow that mistaken lead. Eldridge Duffee, Jr., in his massive doctoral dissertation on the party, stuck with Knoxville as the party's birthplace, while fudging the date to sometime in the summer of 1958. In fact, the founding convention met in Louisville, then home to Edward Fields, over the weekend of August 30–31. One normally reliable source places the event at "Liberty Hall, Louisville," but Kentucky's only Liberty Hall stands in Frankfort, 54 miles east of Louisville. Most likely, the author meant Freedom Hall, opened in 1956 as part of the Kentucky Fair and Exposition Center, five miles from downtown.[11]

Roughly 100 delegates from 18 states attended the party's birth. Among those present were Ed Fields and Jesse Stoner; John Crommelin; Millard Grubbs; Dan Kurtz; Florida Klan leader William Hendrix; Ned Dupes; Connie Lynch; George Rockwell; Matt Koehl; Emory Burke; Gordon Winrod; Wallace Allen; industrial engineer and ex–Columbian George Michael Bright; Pennsylvania native James Konrad Warner; John Wilson Hamilton, leader of the St. Louis–based National Citizens Protective Association and editor of its newsletter, *The White Sentinel,* a former associate of Gerald Smith and 1950 U.S. Senate candidate for Smith's Christian Nationalist Party; Arthur B. Cole of La Follette, Tennessee, founder in 1953 of that city's chapter of Hamilton's NCPA; Chicago's Joseph Beauharnais, jailed in 1950 for distributing racist leaflets, thus becoming a defendant in the first group libel case heard by the U.S. Supreme Court; Forrest Allen Mann, Jr., from Hinsdale, Illinois, where he published the Christian Patriots Crusade's newsletter, *The Revere,* and was arrested in July 1957 for distributing anti–Semitic pamphlets; and Peter Laurentius Norberg Xavier of Dayton, Ohio, former publisher of Henry Ford's *Dayton Independent,* and a member of that city's National Security League, described by the FBI as an "anti–Jewish, anti–Labor, anti–Negro front organization with ties to Gerald K. Smith and the American Firsters."[12]

Amidst that assemblage of fascists, the star of the show was special guest speaker John Kasper, released from federal custody on August 1. His coming-out party was a quiet affair after eight months inside, with only a handful of allies to greet him, including John Crommelin; Bill Hendrix; Catfish Cole; George Bright from Atlanta; and John Hamilton. Unfazed by his time in prison, Kasper called for a "return to Constitutionalism" via creation of a patriotic third party, since both Republicans and Democrats (outside the South) now favored integration, adding, "I used to think all our problems would be solved if every nigger killed a kike, but I find I overestimated the nigger mind." Joseph Beauharnais struck a similar note when he followed Kasper to the speaker's rostrum, preaching to the choir of dedicated segregationists.[13]

The fledgling NSRP chose Arthur Cole as its first national chairman, though its headquarters address was listed as a post office box some 180 miles from his Tennessee home, in Jeffersonville, Indiana. Edna Cowan of New Albany, Indiana—arrested in July 1958 while picketing in Louisville, on behalf of George Rockwell's National Committee to Free America from Jewish Domination—was named Vice-Chairman. Matt Koehl became the party's first National Organizer and Security Officer, while Ned Dupes was named first Secretary-Treasurer and Emory Burke served as a free-floating "advisor." The party's founding convention drafted John Crommelin as its prospective presidential candidate for 1960, and named Millard Grubbs as its standard bearer in Kentucky's 1959 gubernatorial race, but

Klan leaders Bill Hendrix (left) and James Cole (right) greet John Kasper on his release from federal prison, August 1, 1958 (Library of Congress).

despite that initial burst of enthusiasm, neither candidate sought those respective offices in the appointed years.[14]

The party's newsletter—titled *The Thunderbolt* after the old Columbians' publication—premiered in July 1958, edited by Dr. Fields. Three months later, it listed the following state officers[15]:

Edna Cowan, doubling as Vice Chairman and organizer for Indiana.
Harry Kirchman of Minneapolis as Minnesota state chairman.
The Rev. Dale J. Benjamin of Portland, Oregon's state chairman.
C. M. Baxter, Seattle attorney, state chairman for Washington.
Joseph C. Bryant, a Klansman jailed with brother Arthur in 1955 for mailing racist literature and illegal possession of dynamite, chairman of North Carolina.[16]
Don Hensley of Knoxville, Tennessee's chairman.
Kenneth Chester Griffin of Atlanta, Georgia's chairman.
F. Allen Mann, chairman for Illinois.
Dolores Fields, wife of Edward, chairperson for Kentucky.
James W. Bagwell of Greenville—Grand Dragon of the South Carolina Knights of the KKK before it dissolved in October 1957, then leader of a rival National Knights chapter—South Carolina's state organizer.[17]

Alabama's chapter and New York's had no officers named, operating from post office boxes in Birmingham and Manhattan, respectively. Ohio was described as "making very rapid progress," while Iowa Constitution Party members had "switched over to the stronger Racial platform of the NSRP and will announce officers soon."[18]

That shift of allegiance in Iowa highlights the fact that the NSRP was itself a merger of like-minded organizations. While some observers simply said the new group was "formerly known" as the United White Party, just as they claimed the UWP was a renamed version of Jesse Stoner's Christian Anti-Jewish Party, the NSRP actually combined multiple factions into one. *The Thunderbolt's* premier edition described the party as resulting from a merger of the UWP with "States Righters" under "the banner of the NSRP"—referring to the 1956 States' Rights Party (no relation to 1948's Dixiecrats) that ran T. Coleman Andrews for president. Even that claim from party headquarters is incomplete, however, as at least three other groups merged with the fledgling NSRP at, or soon after, its birth. Those included the National White Americans Party founded by Joseph Beauharnais in Chicago; Catfish Cole's North Carolina Knights of the Ku Klux Klan; and the Realpolitical Institute, founded in Chicago during 1954 by Ed Fields, Matt Koehl, Eustace Mullins, and Max Nelsen. In 1954 Nelsen phoned Chicago's FBI office, claiming to lead a huge right-wing underground army, prompting G-men to dub him a "mental case."[19]

The Realpolitical Institute, successor to Nelsen's Minneapolis-based Democratic Nationalist Party, used a thunderbolt symbol on its letterhead, with the slogan "Whiteman Awake—The Hour is Late!" and published a journal titled *Frontier*. One of its pamphlets, titled *Our American Destiny*, declared: "Our deep consciousness of being Whitemen and Whitewomen is as old and primitive as our hills. Forsake this precious bond and we will perish." Its platform, dated July 29, 1955, demanded "Immediate removal of all alien non–Whites, members of the disloyal Jewish Consensus, Pacifists, Communists, and Liberals from all local, State, and Federal Governments and the armed forces," coupled with "complete and officially enforced segregation of all alien non–Whites in our midst." A spin-off

Realpolitical  Institute

P. O. Box 1785 - Chicago 90, Illinois

Dear Sir:

We want your support of our group because you are a member of the Whiteman's Managerial Elite which has been made politically ineffective by the disloyal Jewish Consensus. You as a manager have produced the technological advances upon which our civilization is based, but a conspiracy has prevented you from fulfilling your political destiny as a Whiteman.

We have the answer to the Communist Manifesto. We work for an "implosion" . . . the internal release of the dynamic political energies of our own Whitefolk. We have our own revolutionary idea . . . the Whiteman's Managerial Revolution.

This is a personal opportunity for you to do something—will you give us your anonymous support? We shall be happy to meet you personally, here in Chicago, if you so desire. Write us today—the safety of your family and your future and perhaps your very life are at stake.

Administrative Staff.

WHITEMAN AWAKE—THE HOUR IS LATE!

Flier published by the Realpolitical Institute from Chicago, 1954 (author's collection).

Membership application for the National States Rights Party (author's collection).

from the Institute was the Committee to Free Ezra Pound, with members including Matt Koehl, Eustace Mullins, and New Jersey attorney Edward Albert Fleckenstein, who traveled widely in the 1950s, lobbying for Pound's release from custody. Despite the 36-year age difference between Koehl and Mullins, late movement insider Rick Cooper alleged (without supporting proof) that they enjoyed a longstanding homosexual relationship and that "In about 1955, Mullins, Koehl, and Fleckenstein were arrested in New York

State for sodomizing of a teenage boy in the back seat of a car on a country road." In the absence of police or court reports, will all of the accused deceased, that allegation must be taken with a hefty dose of salt, but it remains intriguing food for thought in light of the NSRP's stance on gays.[20]

Aside from racist outfits merging with the fledgling party in 1958, other individual members stand out. Brothers Richard and Robert Bowling, late of the Christian Anti-Jewish Party, quickly joined. So did Asa Carter, forging new political ties in Alabama.[21] Such extremists were drawn to the party's Nazi symbolism and the preamble of its constitution, which read, in part:

> We of the National States Rights Party believe in the Christian heritage of our people, the White Race and the Nation which the Whiteman created out of the wilderness of this continent...
> We believe in the principles laid down by our forefathers in the United States Constitution and the Bill of Rights contained therein...
> We will not allow the blood of our people to be polluted with that of black, yellow, or mongrel peoples...
> All that is patriotic, good, clean, and decent springs forth from the foundations of our White folk...
> We dedicate ourselves to the task of saving America and the White Race and the preservation of the pure blood of our forefathers, so that all future generations which come after us will be born as White children with a creative intelligence that will strengthen our civilized influence over the world for the good of all mankind.[22]

To achieve those goals, the party formed a National Repatriation Committee to oversee removal of minorities from the United States—blacks to Africa, Jews to Madagascar, and Asians to the Hawaiian Islands (not yet the 50th state).[23]

***

For all its extremism, the fledgling party held a unique position at the time of its formation. Not only standing firm in its defense of white supremacy, the NSRP's anti-Semitism marked it as the first fascist party to actively seek a place on state ballots since Pearl Harbor. Critics argue to this day as to whether the NSRP was a militant fascist movement or simply a group of "conservative populists," but forthcoming events would soon debunk one modern blogger's myopic claim that the party "proposed nothing more extraordinary than contesting elections." It would not only advocate violence, but also actively participate in mayhem time and again. Still, in an era when southern Democrats were condemned for even a remote connection to the national party, and Dixie's Republicans were paper tigers, neutered by association with Reconstruction, even a fascist clique could be invested with some semblance of credibility. Columnist Drew Pearson might dismiss them as a "dirty collar crowd," but Arnold Forster of the ADL described the NSRP's leaders as representing a "higher caliber than Klan elements and the membership [was] more articulate." Specifically, the men in charge—Stoner and Fields—qualified as professionals of the upper middle class, and future bombing defendant George Bright was labeled a "brilliant architect." Thus it was that even critical insider Rick Cooper noted that the NSRP "quickly became the largest White Nationalist organization in the country."[24]

One founder claiming that the party's "program is much more effective" than any rival group's still worried that the NSRP might sever its fascist roots. "We have 'watered down' the National States Rights Party to a rather dangerous level," he wrote. "This was done in order to allow the organization to become a truly mass movement, thus giving us one year to indoctrinate our following with the full meaning of the White Nationalist movement. Without *The Thunderbolt* we are just another Klan or White Citizens Council."[25]

Politics preoccupied the party, and John Kasper was first off the mark, entering Tennessee's 1958 gubernatorial race. On Election Day he placed last in a field of 10 candidates, polling only 17 votes out of 432,533 ballots cast.[26]

In California that same year, the NSRP found a strange ally in William Potter Gale, also seeking the governorship. Born in 1916, Gale was the son of a Russian Jewish immigrant, Charles Grabifker, who forsook his parents' religion, married a woman of English descent in North Dakota, then moved to California and raised their children as Christians after "Americanizing" the family surname. William Gale served in World War II under General Douglas MacArthur, retiring as a lieutenant colonel to work for Hughes Aircraft while fabricating a legend that he led Filipino guerrillas behind Japanese lines during wartime. Gale's future course was set in 1956, when he became a minister of Wesley Swift's Church of Jesus Christ—Christian.[27]

The cult had obvious appeal to white supremacists and anti–Semites such as Gale, attorney/preacher Bertrand Lewis Comparet, Klansman San Jacinto Capt, Connie Lynch, and Lockheed Aircraft engineer Richard Girnt Butler (a 1930s Silver Shirt), all inducted as pastors from its home base in Lancaster, California. With Gale and Comparet, Swift formed the Christian Knights of the Invisible Empire, a group enduring until 1964, and he was listed as a California member of the NSRP, with Connie Lynch and Neuman Britton, future head of the party's Golden State Security Division.[28]

The Thunderbolt endorsed Gale's independent gubernatorial bid in 1958. Despite that boost, he fell short of his goal, running third among six contenders with 2,301 votes out of 5,255,777 ballots cast statewide. Pressing on despite humiliation at the polls, Gale soon resuscitated Swift's dormant Christian Defense League, funded in large part by renowned Los Angeles haberdasher, John Birch Society member, and Swift supporter James Zera Oviatt. San Jacinto Capt signed on as a CDL officer, and remained in 1959 when Gale created the California Rangers as the CDL's paramilitary arm. Recruiting ex-servicemen from the Signal Hill American Legion post, where Swift and CDL loyalist George King, Jr., were members, Gale encountered trouble when police raided member William Garland's home in Cucamonga, seizing 100 rifles, eight machine guns, plus shotguns, pistols, and heavy-caliber rockets. Soon afterward, Swift complained that donations to the CDL were hurting contributions to his church, and Gale, while bitter, left his new brainchild to languish from neglect.[29]

Most observers viewed the fledgling NSRP as a crackpot, fly-by-night outfit spawned by the same unrest that launched a Klan revival in the latter 1950s, but their uninformed dismissal was distinctly premature. The party's thunderbolts would soon be heard and felt throughout the troubled South.

Chapter 4

Shock Waves

Racially motivated bombings were common to Dixie by 1958. In Birmingham, Alabama—nicknamed "Bombingham" for the frequency of blasts—Klansman and future NSRP member Robert Chambliss planted his first charge in August 1947, targeting a home lately purchased by blacks in a neighborhood soon to be christened "Dynamite Hill." Public Safety Commissioner Bull Connor personally issued a bomb threat to the pastor of the city's largest black church, Sixteenth Street Baptist, nine months later, warning that God, using Klansmen, would "strike the church down" if it continued hosting civil rights meetings. By the time Robert Chambliss carried out that threat in 1963, killing four young girls in Sunday school, he had earned the enduring sobriquet "Dynamite Bob."[1]

The South had lived with racist agitation since before the Civil War, but the 1954 *Brown* decision pushed some bigots over the line from tough talk to mayhem. At year's end, media reports claimed 195 racist bombings and arsons spanning the past 12 months, though few details were cited supporting the tally.[2] The drumfire of blasts and incendiary fires grew steadily, nearing a momentary peak in the latter 1950s, just in time for the NSRP's birth.

Clinton, Tennessee—scene of John Kasper's first riotous "triumph"—suffered eight bombings between September 1956 and February 1957, while 13 rocked Chattanooga, former home of Jesse Stoner, and another struck Knoxville's municipal auditorium during a performance by black musician Louis Armstrong. Other targets between January and May 1958, located in Alabama, Georgia, North Carolina and Tennessee, included African American homes, churches, a YMCA, and an integrated theater. More surprising, and of more concern to white southern leaders, were attacks on five Jewish targets between November 1957 and April 1958, spanning four states. On November 11, worshipers found an unexploded bomb during services at Temple Beth-El in Charlotte, North Carolina. February 9 saw another dud at Temple Emmanuel in Gastonia. On March 16 dynamite caused $30,000 damage to Temple Beth-El in Miami. That same day, another bomb exploded at Nashville's Jewish Community Center. Jacksonville's Jewish Community Center was bombed on April 28, while a janitor found dynamite with burned-out fuses at Birmingham's Temple Beth-El. In Nashville and Jacksonville, rabbis received phone calls from "The Confederate Underground," threatening further bombings and political assassinations.[3]

Violence against African Americans was commonly ignored in Dixie—or encouraged by officials such as Bull Connor—but many southern Jews were wealthy, influential, and considered "white" by all but the most extreme anti–Semites. To protect them, and secure their votes in forthcoming elections, action was required.

4. Shock Waves   53

***

On May 3, 1958, police from 21 southern cities met in Jacksonville to create a new investigative agency, the Southern Conference on Bombing. Segregationist mayor Haydon Burns chaired the meeting, and while J. Edgar Hoover refused to send FBI agents, a retired G-man working for the ADL furnished a list of the South's most notorious anti–Semites, including Florida Klansman Bill Hendrix, members of Ace Carter's defunct Original KKK of the Confederacy, Robert Chambliss, and—embarrassingly—Birmingham's Bull Connor. Connor's listing rated a hasty apology, citing a "clerical error," before the lawmen voted rewards totaling $55,700 for information leading to conviction of Dixie's modern dynamitards.[4]

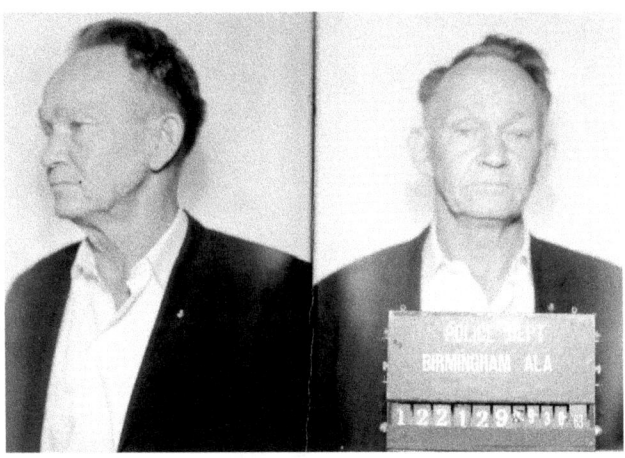

Robert "Dynamite Bob" Chambliss, longtime Klansman, NSRP member and serial bomber (author's collection).

Led on paper by Jacksonville's assistant chief of police, H. V. Branch, the SCB investigated groups such as Hendrix's Knights of the White Camellia and reportedly infiltrated the NSRP's founding convention at Louisville. For the moment, party ally Hendrix ranked as a prime suspect, condemned from his own lips. At one rally, he declared, "I don't advocate violence, but some people just plain need hangin'," proceeding to name Mayor Burns, Florida Governor Leroy Collins, and various black civil rights activists. At another meeting, Hendrix said, "Now, I don't want you good people to around blowin' up buildings or temples, but the next time somebody does blow up a temple, I sure hope it is filled with Jews."[5]

While SCB participants seemed sincere, and Mayor Burns declared in January 1959 that "the Conference has made excellent initial progress," no arrests resulted from the gathering and no one ever claimed the SCB's reward.[6] At least in Birmingham, however, that eventual defeat would not result from lack of trying.

Bull Connor returned from his embarrassment in Jacksonville determined to improve his public record on the bombing front. That signaled no diminution of his own racism, which remained a symbol of southern intransigence throughout the remainder of his career, highlighted by Connor blaming blacks for bombing their own homes and churches, while Klansmen caught in the act escaped prosecution entirely.[7] What he needed was a scapegoat, and one was already at hand.

No bigot in the South was better known for hating Jews than Jesse Stoner. SCB agents kept their eyes on Stoner, once searching his trash for evidence after he moved to Dublin, Georgia, working as a claims adjuster for State Farm Insurance, but they never built a case against him.[8] Bull Connor was convinced he could do better, and the help he needed came, ironically, from the Klan.

Three days after the SCB's creation, on May 8, longtime Klansman William Hugh Morris visited Connor's office, claiming Jesse Stoner was behind the bungled bombing

Bull Connor rouses a Citizens' Council audience to resist integration in Birmingham (Library of Congress).

of Temple Beth-El on April 28, as well as Jacksonville's blast the same day. "If he didn't do it," Morris added, "he is the kingpin who had it done." A Klan member since age 19, in 1924, Morris led Birmingham's violent Federated Ku Klux Klan in the 1940s and spent 67 days in jail during 1949, for refusing to give up a list of his members. Still in action a decade later, he offered Stoner to Bull Connor on a silver platter, and Connor took the bait.[9]

Aside from contract bombings, Morris charged that Stoner and his men were homosexuals. His "proof": Stoner was a bachelor with a "silly laugh," and he preferred 7-Up over "manly" colas. Connor hatched a scheme on the spot, proposing that Morris approach Stoner to solicit a Birmingham blast on behalf of local "steelworkers," to be portrayed by a pair of Connor's detectives. The prospective target: Bethel Baptist Church, led by black activist pastor Fred Shuttlesworth, who had accused Bull of alliance with the Klan. Previously bombed on Christmas Day 1956, Bethel Baptist made a perfect mark for terrorists. With any luck, Connor surmised, another blast might convince Shuttlesworth to "leave Birmingham and go up North where he belonged."[10]

Stoner drove to Birmingham on June 14, then parked his State Farm company car and borrowed one from Morris to visit Bethel Baptist. Stopping there, he asked to see Fred Shuttlesworth, but the minister was out. When asked his business, Stoner replied,

"I want him to pray for me. I'm in trouble." Afterward, Stoner allegedly offered to bomb the church for $2,000, knocking half off his standard fee if Morris's clients added a second target.[11]

A week later, Stoner returned to meet the "steelworkers"—Birmingham police Captain G. L. Pattie and Sergeant Tom Cook (known to FBI agents as Connor's liaison with the Klan). They spoke in Morris's car, while Connor watched and listened via microphone from another nearby vehicle, with FBI Special Agent in Charge (later Bureau director) Clarence Kelley. Connor and Kelley recorded the conversation, but later claimed their tape deck had "malfunctioned." Author Diane McWhorter suspects the tape was deliberately destroyed, leaving Captain Pattie's written statement as the meeting's only record.[12]

Referring to Stoner as "Mr. S" and Morris as "the informer," Pattie recounted a rambling conversation in which Stoner blamed Jews for the botched bombing of Temple Beth-El in April, then promised that Bethel Baptist would be "completely destroyed for $2,000." If the bomb failed to explode, he added, there would be no charge. Pattie told Stoner they would contact him through Morris in roughly two weeks, when they had collected the money. The statement includes no mention of assassinating Shuttlesworth, though Pattie claimed that Stoner "smiled" when reminding his clients of a previous bombing in Florida that killed an NAACP leader and his wife "several years ago" (on Christmas Day 1951).[13]

Fred Shuttlesworth stands before windows of his Bethel Baptist Church, shattered by a racist bomb on June 29, 1958 (Library of Congress).

On the night of June 29, a detective stationed at Birmingham's Greyhound bus depot saw Stoner disembark with future NSRP charter member Robert Bowling. Around 1:30 a.m. a pedestrian spotted a five-gallon paint can with a sizzling fuse attached, sitting beside Bethel Baptist. Alerted to the threat, guards from Shuttlesworth's Alabama Christian Movement for Human Rights moved the bomb before it detonated, blowing out church windows and damaging a nearby house. Captain Pattie and Sergeant Cook were the first responding officers, keenly aware that they might be in trouble for the bungled Stoner sting.[14]

Verging on panic, Connor headed for Washington, D.C., with Birmingham's assistant district attorney, surprising FBI headquarters with a plea for help in tracking Stoner. Bull told the Bureau:

We called our informer long distance and told him of the bombing and asked him if he thought Stoner had

had anything to do with it and he said no he didn't believe so. About twenty minutes later, our informer called back and said Stoner had just called him long distance and told him that they had bombed this church and he wanted him to get some money out of us for the job. Our man told our informer that we had never told him that we *would* give him any money to bomb any place or church. We said we *might* could get some people to give us some money. He [Morris] said he told Stoner that those people had not told him that we would give him any money to bomb this church.

There is no question in my mind after reading their statements and talking with my informer for eight hours Sunday that we have just about come to the end and we have got to have help from the FBI to catch him [Stoner] because he or his crowd do not live in the state of Alabama and we do not have men that we can put on to tail him 24 hours a day. I think this is one man who must be tailed every hour until he is caught or he and his crowd are going to do a lot of damage in the Southeast.[15]

Agents listened, then sent Connor home. According to the assistant D.A., "Bull's record had preceded him to Washington. I think they just didn't buy Bull." In July, Bureau headquarters ordered Birmingham agents "to hold contacts with Connor to a minimum in view of his unsavory background."[16]

Connor would never see his name cleared or the target of his clumsy sting indicted. By the time jurors convicted Stoner of bombing Bethel Baptist, 22 years had passed and so had Connor, killed by his second major stroke in 1973.[17]

***

While Stoner slipped through Connor's loosely woven net, southern bombings continued. On October 5, in a nod to John Kasper's finest hour, three dynamite blasts shattered much of Tennessee's Clinton High School. Even so, the bombers failed. Evangelist Billy Graham and columnist Drew Pearson funded the school's reconstruction, performed by local labor, and teacher Eleanor Davis later recalled, "We didn't miss a day of school because of the bombing."[18]

One week later, at 3:30 a.m. on October 12, 50 sticks of dynamite rocked Atlanta's Hebrew Benevolent Congregation, the city's oldest and richest synagogue, inflicting damage estimated at $200,000. The attack shocked even some of Georgia's hard-line racists, prompting the Citizens' Council to voice sympathy, while Council President Roy Harris falsely claimed, "We've got a hell of a lot of Jew members." *Atlanta Constitution* editor Ralph McGill won a Pulitzer Prize for his editorial on the bombing but failed to impress NSRP member George Bright. "Naturally he won the Pulitzer Prize," Bright said, "if you call that a prize. I don't. Pulitzer was just a Jew. It's a Jewish prize to all of the people who do good for the Jews."[19]

Within 15 minutes of the bombing, a man calling himself "General Gordon of the Confederate Underground" phoned United Press International, saying, "We bombed a temple in Atlanta. This is the last empty building we will bomb…. Negroes and Jews are hereby declared aliens." While Rabbi Jacob Rothschild viewed his congregation's role in civil rights promotion as "an extremely minor one," some local bigots clearly disagreed.[20]

And authorities did not have far to look for suspects in the case. On July 22 Jesse Stoner's Christian Anti-Jewish Party—still distinct and separate from the United White Party—had picketed the *Atlanta Constitution* with signs reading "Jews Control Press, Suppress News." Three of those pickets topped the suspect list: George Bright, Kenneth Griffin, and Luther King Corley, fingered by FBI informer Leslie E. Rogers, operating from inside the NSRP and the U.S. Klans. Within six days of the blast, police arrested those three, with Wallace Allen, Richard and Robert Bowling. All were soon identified as NSRP members, while Richard Bowling was also linked to Bill Hendrix's Knights of

Rabbi Jacob Rothschild (right) and Mayor William Hartsfield pose before Atlanta's Hebrew Benevolent Congregation synagogue, bombed on October 12, 1958 (National Archives).

the White Camellia. Corley was released for insufficient evidence, but a grand jury indicted the other five on October 17, based largely on Griffin's confession. Police searchers found minutes of a party meeting opened with a prayer: "Our heavenly father, we beseech thee to know that we will fight this battle to our last ounce of energy and to the enemy's last drop of blood. Amen."[21]

The NSRP and its allies went to work on their behalf at once. In Louisville, members

NSRP members charged with bombing the Atlanta synagogue. From left, George Bright, Wallace Allen, Luther Corley, Kenneth Griffin and Robert Bowling (Library of Congress).

Millard Grubbs, Dan Kurtz, Joseph Beauharnais, and Peter Xavier founded a Citizen's National Law Enforcement Commission to denounce further bombing investigations. A similar group—the National Committee to Secure Justice for the Atlanta Five—operated from Sandy Springs, Georgia, led by Wallace Allen's wife and William Scott Stephenson, publisher of *The Virginian,* a magazine that "focused on the Jewish Question." Cries of protest also came from George Rockwell's World Union of Free Enterprise National Socialists. In California, the *American Nationalist* trumpeted "Synagogue Bombing a Fraud," warning that "Jewish Groups Use Bomb Incident to Confuse Gentiles." The publishers offered a $250 reward for arrest of the "real synagogue bombers," doubled if those named "are revealed to be Jews, or in the pay of Jews." A flurry of calls from the Confederate Underground threatened death to grand jury members who indicted the five defendants.[22]

Kenneth Griffin, dubbed the party's "weakest link" by police, described by others as "feeble-minded" and "almost retarded-like," recanted his confession, but jailhouse snitch Jimmy DeVore stepped in to fill the gap, citing conversations with cellmate Richard Bright. Bail was denied, while prosecutors chose to try Bright alone as their first defendant. Klan attorney James Venable—who earlier secured release for the *Atlanta Constitution* pickets—led the defense and coached Kenneth Griffin through his recantation, grilling potential jurors on their religious affiliations until Judge Durwood Pye reminded him that "the Jewish race is not on trial in this case." When trial began on December 2, Venable struck a pose that other racist advocates would follow for the next decade, branding informer Leslie Rogers "a police pimp" and dismissing Jimmy DeVore as a felonious liar for hire. Against those accusers stood a list of "character witnesses," including U.S. Klans Imperial Wizard Eldon Edwards, Exalted Cyclops Wesley Morgan, Klan treasurer John Felmet, Arthur Cole ("I've got some awful good Jewish friends"), Edward Fields, and Matt Koehl, most reviling Rogers as a perjurer and all-around despicable character. Bright appalled some jurors with his ranting from the witness stand, but three held out for acquittal, forcing declaration of a mistrial on December 10.[23]

Determined to convict their suspects, prosecutors filed new charges against Bright two weeks after his mistrial. In the interim, flamboyant lawyer Reuben Garland, Sr., muscled Venable out of the case, first signing up Wallace Allen, then Bright and the Bowling Brothers. For starters, Garland struck potential jurors who were Jewish, "possibly Jewish," employees or neighbors of Jews, and those presumed "under Jewish Compulsion." In lieu of calling Klansmen to support his case, however, Gar-

Eldon Edwards, Imperial Wizard of the U.S. Klans and a defense witness at the first bombing trial of George Bright (Florida State Archives).

land promised to expose "who *really* bombed the Temple"—specifically, Leslie Rogers. His key witness, furnishing an alibi for Bright, was Marilyn Craig, on furlough from involuntary commitment to the Milledgeville State Hospital's psychiatric ward to testify during a brief "lucid interval." She placed Bright in her company when the bombing occurred, at an all-night pharmacy, and jurors acquitted Bright on January 24, after 35 minutes of deliberation. Prosecutors dropped all charges against the remaining defendants, prompting *The Thunderbolt* to cheer that "the Atlanta case was a triumph of concerted effort by the NSRP, together with allied patriotic groups."[24]

Officially, the crime remains unsolved, though opinions varied through the 1990s. Wallace Allen denied involvement until his death in 1995, while Richard Bright blamed Leslie Rogers in interviews with author Melissa Greene. Retired detective C. J. Strickland placed Jesse Stoner "in the background, where it all came from." In 1993 a friend of James Venable told Greene, "Everybody knows that Richard Bowling was involved," but by then both brothers were dead, Richard from alcoholism, Robert allegedly from AIDS.[25]

Only Jesse Stoner paid a small price for the Temple bombing, fired by State Farm over the resultant bad publicity and stripped of his company car. To replace it, he allegedly offered William Morris a new deal: his "boys" would target Dr. King next, and "would blow him up or do whatever was necessary, he or his family or anybody who was in the house."[26]

***

Still, party members faced ongoing legal problems. On February 12, 1959, Millard Grubbs phoned the FBI's Louisville office to render a "formal complaint" against G-men investigating "bombings and, etc.," declaring himself "completely unimpressed" with U.S. Attorney General William Rogers and challenging Bureau jurisdiction in civil rights cases. FBI headquarters logged the call in its file titled "Bombings and Attempted Bombings," noting that Grubbs was "carried as a general suspect in connection with investigations in the racial matters field." James Cole exhausted his appeals and entered prison on April 8, his Klan already shattered by news that he'd raised funds for treatment of his wife's nonexistent cancer. Soon afterward, on April 11–12, the NSRP staged its second national convention in Knoxville. John Kasper was back in custody on July 23, serving six months on outstanding charges from Clinton, Tennessee, with his appeal rejected in September.[27]

Jesse Stoner revived his Black Muslim obsession on August 6, 1959, with a letter mailed from Atlanta to New York City's police commissioner, signing himself as imperial wizard of the Christian Knights and arch leader of the Christian Party, for once omitting "Anti-Jewish" and any mention of the NSRP. It read (uncorrected):

Honorable Stephen P. Kennedy, Police Commissioner of New York City
CONFIDENTIAL AND TOP SECRET
New York, N.Y.
Re: the black Muslims
Dear Fellow Whiteman:

The Christian Knights of the Ku Klux Klan is composed of all loyal White people, both Catholics and Protestants, native born and foreign born, young and old. We are working to unite all of the forces of White Christendom in the struggle to Preserve the great White Race. The future of civilization depends upon the survival of the beautiful intelligent White Race—the bearer of Christian truth.

I have received a report from one of our Klansmen on the New York police force informing me that the nigger Muslims are in rebellion against White law and order. He reports that those blacks have no respect for you honest White Christian policemen. Therefore, in the interests of law and justice, I am offering you the support of the CHRISTIAN KNIGHTS OF THE KU KLUX KLAN.

I am an expert on the black Muslims and have kept up with their infidelic activities for many years. From my knowledge of them, I assure you that they are much more dangerous to White Christian rule in New York than you realize. You and I must join forces to stop the black Muslims now or they will soon drive every White person out of New York City. The largest city in the world will then be an all nigger city of black supremacy where White people will not be allowed to live. The only thing that can stop Elijah Muhammad and his black Muslims from conquering New York is for my Christian Knights and your New York police to join hands and work together to uphold White Christian Supremacy. Without the support of my Christian Knights, the Muslims will continue to force you to retreat until you and the great Mayor Wagner and all other White officials and judges will be ousted from office. Elijah Muhammad will then give your job to a nigger and put in a nigger as mayor of New York. Then he will only allow niggers on the N.Y. City Council and all judges and all policemen will be niggers. By then, the Muslims will have driven all White people out of New York, without exception. Don't let the black Muslim fool you when they demand entrance to schools in White neighborhoods or demand houses or apartments in White areas. They only wish to enter White neighborhoods and White schools so they can then proceed to drive all of the Whites out. Take my advice and we will put the niggers in their place instead of letting them take over New York City and all the national power that goes with it.

We need to put the black hoodlums out of business, but we must do it in a legal way with the police and the courts. As a Georgia lawyer, I insist on doing everything according to law. You know what I mean. It is urgent that you persuade the officials of the City and State of New York to immediately repeal all ordinances and laws that prevent Whites from discriminating against niggers because those evil laws constitute an open invitation to all the niggers in the South to move to New York City

NATIONAL STATES' RIGHTS PARTY

National Headquarters: POST OFFICE BOX 261   JEFFERSONVILLE, INDIANA

Dec. 24, '59

NATIONAL OFFICERS:

ARTHUR B. COLE
  Chairman

MRS. PETER COWAN
  Vice-Chairman

NED DUPES
  Secretary-Treasurer

MATT KOEHL
  Organizer

DR. EDWARD R. FIELDS
  Information Director

Address all mail to:
Corresponding Secretary
N. S. R. P.
P. O. Box 2161
Knoxville 1, Tennessee

My Dear Rev. Cole:

Seasons Greetings, and best wishes for what I know will be a good New Year for you, with all the blessings from God that are due you for all the undeserved suffering you have gone through. I know of no man that has done more for his country and fellow man then you have, only to be hounded and persecuted by those who fear the evils of communism, and hate folks with guts like you have, who expose, and speak out freely the true Gospel of Christ against communism and race-mixing. Bod Bless you Reverend.

Mr. Pennington, wrote me a nice letter, saying that he had visited you and that you were in good spirits, despite your un-constitutional incarceration. He seems like a good religious man, and I hope to have the pleasure of meeting him some day.

I understand that pressure was brought by those who hope to silence your right of free speech, and the parole board has not considered you freedom. Of course, I know that you would never accept a parole that would hinder your free exercise of free speech. Therefore, please let me know the present standing of your case, and the nearest date that you will be freed. I would like to come down with some of your friends to greet you when you are released, that will most certainly be a great day. Please write me and tell me just when you will be able to gain freedom and what we can do to help.

Also, thanks a million for the Christmas card, it sure made me feel good to receive it from a man who is as great a Patriot as you are. Keep up the good religious work with the souls around you, and I remain, faithfully:

Your Brother In Christ

Dr. Edward R. Fields
1737 Bardstown Rd.
Louisville 5, Ky.

Please note new house number.

HONOR–PRIDE–FIGHT!   SAVE THE WHITE!

A letter from Edward Fields to James "Catfish" Cole, consoling Cole on his failure to make parole in North Carolina for Christmas 1959 (author's collection).

where they will strengthen the Muslims and subject that giant metropolis to black supremacy. Those laws need to be replaced with laws that will help White Christians in New York to imitate us Southerners by keeping the darkies in their place. You might be interested in knowing that some Southern business men and farmers are complaining because their darkies are leaving their South and moving to New York where they can get higher pay. Wealthy Southern housewives are complaining because it is becoming harder to find colored maids and cooks who will work for a dollar per day; they want you to send them back and cut out those high wages for niggers in New York. They are moving to New York in large numbers to work for higher wages, on account of your laws against racial discrimination. Remember, every nigger who moves from the South to N.Y.C. makes the Muslims more powerful.

You need to learn more about that evil genius, Elijah Muhammad, or you will never stop him and his niggers from taking over your city. He claims to be the re-incarnation of that infidelic 7th Century prophet, Mohammad, who almost conquered the known world and he may be him because he is much more clever than the other niggers.

I think we need to put Muhammad out of business in a legal way and not use the criminal methods that the communist F.B.I. is using against him. I hear that the F.B.I. is hiring nigger pimps to join up with the Muslims so they can spy on them. They also start arguments in meetings so as to disrupt them. They also try to turn niggers away from Islam by accusing Muhammad and other Muslim officials of stealing money out of the Muslim treasury because the F.B.I. knows that most niggers will believe these kind of false charges without any proof. Even though I would enjoy seeing Muhammad hanged from a Harlem lamp post, I have to admit that he does not steal from his own followers. We are both familiar enough with red F.B.I. methods to know that the F.B.I. plans to frame the Muslims by having nigger F.B.I. pimps use violence and then blame it on the Muslims. Instead of using illegal F.B.I. police state methods, I suggest that we put the Muslims out of business with the White Christian methods that have worked so well in the South. Besides, any spies you put among the Muslims will probably be killed. Those Muslims are the meanest niggers in the world.

You need to realize that Muhammad has organized several hundred thousand niggers throughout America. His Muslim temples are springing up everywhere; he has several temples in my home city of Atlanta. If you were a student of Race, you would know that Christianity is the Whiteman's religion and has only been successful in White countries; whereas, the Muslim religion of Islam is a nigger religion which appeals to the nigger's black racial instincts. That is why the Muslims grow stronger every day even though every nigger that becomes a Muslim will go to hell when he dies. If we fail to stop the Muslims now, the 16,000,000 niggers of America will all soon be Muslims and you will never be able to stop them. Reports from Christian missionaries say that Islam is sweeping over all of Africa so don't underestimate the Muslims.

Up to and including its edition copyrighted in 1956, the Encyclopedia Britannica admitted under the heading of "Negro" that the nigger is close to the anthropoid ape than the White man in every respect except one. It also revealed the niggers to be natural born cannibals. For more information about the facts of Race, I suggest you read "Take Your Choice, Separation or Mongrelization" by the late U.S. senator Bilbo of Mississippi and "White America" by Earnest Sevier Cox. Both are in the library of Congress. Another valuable Race book is "The Cult of Equality" by Stuart O. Landry, 305 Chartres, New Orleans, La. Therefore, you can easily see that your problem is with black savages. We will help you put the blacks in their place before they turn all of your great city into a barbaric jungle.

The NAACP is a bad gang but I assure you that the Muslims are ten times more dangerous. The NAACP is a cream puff compared to black Islam. The NAACP likes White people so much that its members try to associate with us Whites every day, but the Muslims think they are better than us Whites even though everybody knows that we Whites are superior to the nigger coons. I guess you know that the NAACP is headed by a man who is not a nigger, but there is a bad nigger at the head of the Muslims.

I have had White Christian friends write to many magazines inciting them to denounce Muhammad and his Muslims so as to scare many cowardly niggers away from him. So far I have managed to "sic" both "Time" magazine and "U.S. News & World Report" on them.

Police Commissioner Kennedy, my dear friend, I now offer you the service of the Christian Knights of the Ku Klux Klan for the purpose of maintaining White Supremacy in New York City and for keeping New York niggers in their place. I think 5,000 Klansmen could clean up Harlem for you if you would give them police badges and N.Y. police uniforms to wear instead of their Klan uniforms. They will leave their Klan robes at home so the New York niggers won't know that your police reinforcements are White Christian Klansmen. You can use our Christian Knights as guards to protect every White business in Harlem and also in other New York areas where nigger customers are giving trouble to White business men. After all, how do the black jig-a boos expect to live without White business men to sell them what they need. You can also use our Klansmen to escort White salesmen into Harlem and other parts of New York City that are suffering from the black plague.

I will expect you to supply my Klansmen with police pistols (so they won't have to carry their own pistols). They will also require machine guns, riot guns, tear gas and big clubs. They will especially want some big sticks with iron inside the wood so they can crack hard nigger skulls. Niggers have thicker skulls and smaller skulls than we Whites. In your police uniforms, my Klansmen will teach New York niggers to respect White Christian policemen. I will send my Christian Knights to your rescue as soon as you call for them.

Do you want to keep these plans secret or make them public? If we give publicity to these plans, the yellow-livered, cowardly darkies would probably start shaking in their shoes and showing proper respect for White people before the arrival of the Ku Klux Klan. Please advise.

In case you decided to keep our plans secret, remember that the secret might leak out. In case of a leak, strongly deny that you have called for the support of the Christian Knights of the Ku Klux Klan. I want you to jump up and down and scream when telling the Newspapermen that we are not working together, in case our plans leak out. That will keep them from saying anything.

Tell your superiors to take their choice. You can either accept our support and have White Supremacy in your giant city; or, you can retreat and abandon New York City to Elijah Muhammad, his Muslims and black supremacy.

I know we will enjoy working together to roll back the black locusts. Together, my dear friend, we will save New York City for the White Race, the race that built civilization.

In the Christian bond of White racial brotherhood, I remain
Yours for Christ, Race and Country
J. B. Stoner[28]

Commissioner Kennedy ignored Stoner's offer, but it hardly mattered. Within a month, Stoner had found another target and was on the scene.

***

On September 29, 1958, Florida's Dade County Board of Instruction barred 14 African American students from admittance to the all-white Orchard Villa Elementary School. Shifting residential patterns had surrounded Orchard Villa with black residents, but board members held the color line until they faced an NAACP lawsuit spearheaded by state legislator John D. Orr, then named Orchard Villa a "pilot school" for gradual integration beginning on September 7, 1959.[29]

Any integration was too much for Jesse Stoner, who immediately traveled from Atlanta to Miami, interrupting a feud with Eldon Edwards of the U.S. Klans. Forewarned of his arrival, "respectable" Dade County segregationists warned their followers to shun him, whispering that he was a secret agent of the ADL or NAACP, but Stoner still found an ally in Fred Hockett, Citizens' Council organizer and cohort of John Kasper. Together, they picketed the school, haranguing white parents in a bid to spark a boycott with success amounting to a Pyrrhic victory. While most Dade County schools did not integrate until the late 1960s, Orchard Villa was all black by Christmas 1959.[30]

***

Although an early participant in the NSRP's foundation, George Rockwell went his own way in 1959, renaming his World Union of Free Enterprise National Socialists the American Nazi Party in December. While that ostracized Rockwell from most of his family, late movement insider Rick Cooper praised the ANP "not as a front group for Jewish scammers but [created] out of dedication and sincere belief." According to Cooper, many of Rockwell's recruits were "former NSRP people, and many of the new ANP

Jesse Stoner urges white parents to boycott Miami's newly integrated Orchard Villa Elementary School while reporters take notes, September 7, 1959 (National Archives).

financial supporters were former NSRP financial supporters," including "some of the most dedicated White Nationalists in the country and perhaps some of the kookiest too." Rockwell, meanwhile, addressed the problem of "kooky" members by saying of his Virginia headquarters, "There is a tendency for queers to come here, because to a queer, this place is as tempting as a girl's school would be to me." Emory Burke, now active in the Citizens' Council, served as informal liaison between that group and Rockwell's ANP.[31]

While praising Rockwell and his party, Cooper seemed to contradict himself, writing, "It was Jewish money that went to George Lincoln Rockwell's newly founded American Nazi Party until the Jews learned that Rockwell could no more be controlled than could Adolf Hitler in the 1920s when the Jewish bankers tried to control Hitler in a similar way."[32] Fascist sincerity notwithstanding, Rockwell's success at reaping headlines soon rubbed other far-right leaders the wrong way, igniting a feud with the NSRP that would simmer through the 1960s, landing both parties in court.

Chapter 5

Reading, Writing and Riots

Segregationists, like their slave-owning forefathers, often begged "more time" to let the plague of inequality resolve itself, yet they showed no inclination to advance the process. Eight years after *Brown,* in May 1962, journalist James Graham Cook found that only .01 percent of Dixie's African American Students—2,725 out of 2,482,170—had enrolled in formerly white schools. At that rate southern classrooms would be fully integrated by 9256—7,302 years after the Supreme Court issued its historic order. Border states across the upper South moved somewhat faster, predicted to comply with *Brown* by 6674.[1]

Even that glacial pace, however, was too swift for members of the fascist fringe.

Atlanta's Temple bombing and others that preceded it drove Congress to pass the Civil Rights Act of 1960, signed by President Eisenhower on May 6. That statute banned interstate or international flight to avoid prosecution for damaging or destroying any building or structure, or to avoid giving testimony in cases related to such offenses. Also banned was transportation or possession of any explosive with intent to perpetrate bombing. Maximum penalties included five years imprisonment and a $5,000 fine. During Senate debate on the bill, New York's Kenneth Keating documented 86 southern bombings since 1955, at least 16 of them theoretically linked to NSRP members.[2]

While that debate was underway, the party moved its headquarters from Indiana to a fieldstone building on Birmingham's Bessemer Road, near Asa Carter's former Klan lair, decorated by Ed Fields "to resemble a military headquarters." Among its first local recruits: Robert Chambliss, hosting Jesse Stoner at his home and drafting relatives to pass out party fliers. Almost simultaneously, on May 3, State Chairman Lee J. Crowder and Douglas Knowles, both of Opeleika in Lee County, named Arkansas Governor Orval Faubus as the party's presidential candidate for 1960, with previous draft choice John Crommelin demoted to serve as his running mate. That nomination followed a unanimous vote for Faubus at the party's national convention in March, held at the Midway Lodge outside Miamisburg, Ohio, with George Rockwell and three FBI informers attending. While Faubus ultimately waffled on collaboration with the NSRP, Ed Fields would later claim Ann Bishop—the party's National Vice Chairman, a Little Rock store clerk enriched overnight by oil speculation—was the governor's mistress, and Faubus "personally gave her permission to use his name as our Presidential candidate." Faubus biographer Roy Reed ignores Bishop, simply reporting that Faubus "snubbed" the NSRP.[3]

(Faubus certainly seemed to sympathize with white terrorists. On Labor Day 1959, second anniversary of local school integration, three racist bombings struck Little Rock targets. On September 9 police arrested two men: E. A. Lauderdale Sr., board member of the Capitol Citizens' Council, owner of a lumber company, and twice-defeated candidate for city office; and trucker J. D. Sims. Three more suspects joined them in jail the next day. At trial in November, one suspect confessed and evidence proved the bombings were planned at a KKK meeting, instigated by Lauderdale. Jurors convicted all five, resulting in three-year prison terms. Appeals left them free until February 1961, and Governor Faubus commuted their sentences five months later, personally refunding Lauderdale's $500 fine. Omitted from mercy: the only bomber who confessed, imprisoned for nearly two years.[4])

In Birmingham, party members adopted their first formal uniform, consisting of a white shirt, black pants and tie, with an armband bearing the thunderbolt version of a *Wolfsangel*—a German heraldic charge inspired by an actual wolf trap consisting of two metal parts and a connecting chain. An early symbol of the Nazi Party, later worn by certain units of the Waffen-SS, the *Wolfsangel* remained in use by several Nazi groups following World War II, although public display as a fascist symbol is outlawed in Germany. The party's banner was a version of the Confederate battle flag—the "Stars and Bars," *sans* stars—with a thunderbolt superimposed on the field. *The Thunderbolt*, climbing toward a peak paid circulation of 15,000, with thousands more printed each month as handouts and for street sales, drew inspiration in equal parts from Georgia Governor Eugene Talmadge and Third Reich propagandist Julius Streicher.[5]

One new recruit in 1960 was 21-year-old Royson Everett Frankhouser, Jr., a native

The *Wolfsangel* symbol, adopted for NSRP armbands.

Roy Frankhouser, Jr., compulsive joiner of fascist groups, distributes Nazi literature ca. 1960 (House Committee on Un-American Activities).

of Reading, Pennsylvania, who quit high school as a sophomore to work full-time for racist causes, collecting Nazi uniforms and memorabilia. Frankhouser spent one year in military service before an honorable discharge, met George Rockwell in 1958, then joined both the NSRP and Rockwell's ANP in 1960, along with the paramilitary Minutemen. In 1961 he spent two months at Max Nelsen's Institute of Biopolitics. Described by ADL's Irwin Suall as "a thread that runs through the history of American hate groups," Frankhouser—"Riot Roy" to his friends—would serve for many years as Pennsylvania's Klan grand dragon, further attaching himself to the National Renaissance Party, the Citizens' Council, and the Liberty Lobby, among other groups. Over the course of his career, Frankhouser logged 142 arrests and at least three federal convictions, on charges including obstruction of justice and trafficking stolen explosives.[6]

***

Perhaps disappointed by relegation to the role of presidential running mate in 1960, John Crommelin tried his hand at a separate race, once more challenging Alabama Senator John Sparkman in May's primary. NSRP members Matt Koehl and Eustace Mullins moved into the basement of Crommelin's Wetumpka home, campaigning for the self-styled "white man's candidate" who branded Jews the enemies of "white Christian Alabamians," puppeteers of the NAACP. Some voters agreed, but not enough. On May 3, Crommelin ran second in a field of three contenders, logging 51,571 votes to Sparkman's 335,722.[7]

Two months later, at 12:30 a.m. on July 12, FBI agents acting on an informer's tip caught two men—Emmett E. Miller and Robert Lloyd Parks, both from West Memphis—lighting the fuse on a bomb containing 40 sticks of dynamite, placed beneath a dormitory staircase at Little Rock's all-black Philander Smith College. While police booked the pair, explosions in Little Rock damaged a public school warehouse and two African American homes. Later on July 12, G-men arrested Hugh Adams of Bassett, Arkansas, as an accomplice to the Philander Smith attack, filing a complaint that said four agents watched Miller and Adams collect the dynamite from Memphis, Tennessee, on July 8 and deliver it to Parks at home. The case seemed airtight, but it never went to trial. In January 1961 a local grand jury indicted Miller on a misdemeanor charge—"attempting to commit a felony"—but refused to charge Parks or Adams. Federal prosecutors indicted all three under the new Civil Rights Act, then dismissed their case in May to protect the FBI's anonymous informer, whereupon the case collapsed. Within a year, *The Thunderbolt* named Emmett Miller as Arkansas Vice Chairman of the NSRP.[8]

In August 1960 John Kasper emulated John Crommelin, entering Tennessee's Democratic senate primary against incumbent Estes Kefauver. Endorsed by the NSRP, he fared no better than Crommelin, running last in a field of three candidates with 4,867 votes out of 718,051 ballots cast.[9]

A heart attack killed U.S. Klans leader Eldon Edwards on August 1, 1960. His successor, Robert "Wild Bill" Davidson, soon renamed his faction the United Klans of America, publicly dissociating it from the likes of Kasper, the NSRP, and George Rockwell. He told the press, "I don't get myself connected with any fanatical movement. I can't go around lambasting Jews, Negroes, and Catholics and expect to get a national following." Within a year, that attitude saw Davidson exiled, his UKA merged with Robert Shelton's Alabama Knights.[10]

In late October 1960 the American Jewish Committee adopted a "quarantine" strategy toward anti–Semites such as Crommelin and Rockwell, lobbying to restrict media coverage of the NSRP, ANP, and similar groups, while simultaneously promoting community education programs to foster racial and religious tolerance. An AJC report concluded, "In the long run, the most effective defense against unsound ideas is more speech and more ideas, in the certain knowledge that ultimately truth will triumph." That policy eclipsed litigation to restrain fascist gatherings, following a path adopted by black civil rights activists—namely, recognizing that censorship was more likely to rebound against minorities than fringe extremists. While a reasonable proposition, it had little or no impact on the outpouring of bile from far-right groups.[11]

Adolf Eichmann, defended by the NSRP and other fascist groups after his May 1960 kidnapping from Argentina (Library of Congress).

A case in point was that of Otto Adolf Eichmann, Third Reich SS-*Obersturmbannführer* (lieutenant colonel) and a major architect of Hitler's "final solution." Briefly detained by Allied forces at war's end, Eichmann escaped to Argentina and was traced there by Israeli agents, kidnapped from his home in a Buenos Aires suburb on May 11, 1960, and smuggled to Jerusalem for public trial. Convicted in August and sentenced to death in December, Eichmann mounted the gallows in the predawn hours of June 1, 1962. While Argentine diplomats condemned Israel's invasion of their territory, the NSRP formed an Adolf Eichmann Trial Facts Committee, soliciting "emergency donations" to support the cause, and police jailed Matt Koehl for brawling at one of its rallies.[12] Speaking on behalf of that committee, Ed Fields wrote:

> If spies, traitors, and Communists were executed in Germany during the war—SO WHAT? Are we going to crawl in the dirt in the name of Jewry, and beg the Jews to forgive the White Race because a Whiteman once meted out Justice to the Jews? I say NO, A THOUSAND TIMES NO! We are going to fight these greedy, scheming Jews, who seek to destroy our Race, Nation, and Faith and everything we hold dear. Whatever the final solution to the Jewish problem turns out to be, it will be the Jew who will bring it upon himself. The wrath of all the peoples is upon his head.[13]

***

Presidential politics dominated party affairs through summer and fall 1960. Matt Koehl and Eustace Mullins remained at John Crommelin's Alabama home as campaign strategists until—if we believe National Socialist Vanguard founder Rick Cooper—Crommelin "booted them off his property" for engaging in homosexual activity. Cooper's third-hand "proof" is a comment from ANP Deputy Commander Karl Allen, relayed to party member Christopher Bailey, and thence to Cooper in the early 1980s. At that time, neither Crommelin nor Allen answered Cooper's registered letters; Ed Fields *did* reply to Cooper, but denied any knowledge of gay liaisons—a claim Cooper found "not believable [since] these guys all know each other going back at least two decades!"[14]

Arkansas Governor Orval Faubus (reading statement). Nominated for president by the NSRP in 1960, he commuted the sentences of convicted racist bombers linked to the party (Library of Congress).

Whatever happened in Crommelin's basement, if anything, the campaign continued. Most scholars today call Orval Faubus the party's unwilling candidate, and while it's true he never campaigned, Ed Fields insists the governor approved his nomination. John Kasper did his part, warning Klan rallies across the Upper South that if Massachusetts Catholic John Kennedy were elected he should be "impeached before the sun rises."[15] Minutemen founder and biochemist Robert Bolivar DePugh also gave his pitch for the party at various rallies, and John Crommelin, distributed fliers reading:

> The ultimate objective of the Communist-Jewish conspirators is to use their world-wide control of money to destroy Christianity and set up a world government in the framework of the United Nations, and erase all national boundaries and eliminate all racial distinctions except the so-called Jewish race, which will then become the master race with headquarters in the state of Israel and in the United Nations in New York, and from these two communication centers rule a slave-like world population of copper-colored human mongrels.[16]

Even with such extremist views on full display, the NSRP earned ballot slots in several southern states, including Florida, which Edward Fields recalls as "our strongest state." There, Bill Hendrix publicly endorsed the party's ticket, prompting rival William Griffin to support GOP candidate Richard Nixon, thereby planting a time bomb that detonated during Nixon's third televised debate with JFK. Before that program aired, however, Faubus had his name removed from Florida's ballots. As Fields recalls: "John F. Kennedy was concerned that our vote could cost him the state and the election itself. Kennedy contacted Gov. Faubus and asked him to remove his name from the ballot. He

Supporters of NSRP candidates in 1960's presidential campaign (Library of Congress).

[Faubus] then told Mrs. Bishop the he could not be in a position where it would be said that he had cost Kennedy the election. He told her he would have to remove his name from the state's ballot but would allow it to remain in the other states. At the time the liberal media made it appear as [if] he had repudiated the NSRP. Nothing could have been farther from the truth."[17]

Faubus wound up endorsing JFK, though not the Democratic Party's civil rights platform. On November 8, the NSRP received 44,984 votes out of 68,840,889 ballots cast in America's second-ever closest presidential election (after 1880), coming from Alabama, Arkansas, Delaware and Tennessee. Faubus, more concerned with retaining his governor's seat, won a fourth term with 73 percent of the popular vote and would serve a total of five before his defeat in 1970.[18]

***

Next, a crisis erupted in New Orleans, where influential Catholic Archbishop Joseph Francis Rummel had proclaimed segregation "morally wrong and sinful" in 1956. Louisiana oilman and political kingmaker Leander Perez fought Rummel bitterly for six years, until Rummel finally excommunicated him, and Perez's fury reached its peak on November 14, 1960, when two elementary schools in New Orleans's Lower Ninth Ward opened with orders to desegregate classes. A white boycott left young African Americans virtually alone at both schools, with jeering mobs outside, but Perez remained unsatisfied. "Fantastic as it may appear," he told reporters, "the social aim is a negroid South."[19]

Shortly before the Crescent City's baptism of fire, Perez served as state finance chairman and a presidential elector for the Louisiana States' Rights Party, backing future Governor David Treen and flamboyant far-rightist Kent Howard Courtney until Treen abandoned the LSRP, branding it "anti–Semitic." On November 15 Perez staged a rally of 5,000 persons, including "pro-segregationists from all over the South." NSRP members and the local Citizens' Council distributed copies of *The Thunderbolt* with a front-page photo of Perez under the headline "Perez Turns Spotlight on the Enemy." Eliminating any doubts of who that might be, Perez warned his audience, "Don't wait for your daughter to be raped by these Congolese. Don't wait until the burrheads are forced into your schools. Do something about it now."[20]

On November 16 police dispersed hundreds of whites from the Orleans Parish School Board office, but mayhem spread citywide, with white attacks on African Americans sparking retaliation. Officers jailed 194 people for loitering, 27 for vandalism and 29 for carrying concealed weapons, while firefighters doused the flames of random firebombings. After the initial outbreak, white women dubbed "The Cheerleaders" laid siege to integrated schools, while authorities dickered over the slow advance of desegregation. Many white families fled the Lower Ninth Ward for nearby St. Bernard Parish, reducing the ward's white population by 77 percent. Despite Archbishop Rum-

Louisiana kingmaker Leander Perez collaborated with the NSRP to foment violence in New Orleans in November 1960 but dismissed its hopes of third-party relevance (Library of Congress).

New Orleans housewife "cheerleaders" oppose school integration in November 1960 (National Archives).

mel's private fervor, local Catholic schools remained strictly segregated until September 1962. As for Perez, stung by his recent failed foray into states' rights politics, he dismissed the NSRP out of hand, saying, "I don't think any third party has any hope of success."[21]

On November 26–27 the party convened in Chattanooga to elect national officers, using a lodge that doubled as Dixie Klans headquarters, doors still plastered with "Faubus for President" stickers. Fifty delegates from 10 states chose Ned Dupes as National Chairman; Ann Bishop as vice chairman; Florida's W. B. Burch, assistant chairman; Bernice Settles of Knoxville, secretary; Matt Koehl, security officer; and Ed Fields, information officer. Relative fledgling Roy Frankhouser became National Organizer, ironically rejecting proposed gray-shirt uniforms because he was "opposed to any neo–Nazi movement." Still a member of the ANP and NRP, Frankhouser's rise highlights his skill at doubletalk.[22]

John Kennedy's inauguration marked the onset of what some would call Dixie's "Second Reconstruction." Mobilizing for the challenge, Edward Fields addressed a Chicago rally staged by Max Nelsen on April 3, 1961, addressing 35 persons including members of the ANP and its new front group, the Fighting American Nationalists. On April 16, in Macon, Georgia, police arrested Joseph Beauharnais during a hectic ANP rally. Meanwhile, the NSRP, while outwardly pledged to "peace and friendship with all other right-wing movements but entangling alliance with none," joined the Northern European Ring in company with Rockwell's ANP, Sweden's *Nordiska Riksparteit* (Nordic Reich Party) and Britain's National Party, forged in 1960 by merger of the National Labour Party and the White Defence League, two splinters of the League of Empire Loyalists. Leader John

Bean, a disciple of Sir Oswald Moseley's wartime British Union of Fascists, welcomed the NSRP to his party's "circle of friendship and cooperation."[23]

***

On April 10, 1961, Jesse Stoner addressed his last known letter to Elijah Muhammad in Chicago. It read (uncorrected):

Black Devil:

You Black Muslims claim that you will take America away from us Whites by 1970, but you are dead wrong. Instead, I am going to put you Congo jungle bunnies out of business in 1961, or by the end of 1962 at the latest. America was discovered, settled and developed by White men for their own White posterity only and you stinking niggers have no place in this Whiteman's country. Your ape ancestors were brought over here as slaves only for the purpose of picking cotton. Now that we have mechanical cotton pickers, we don't need you coons any more.

You know I can put you Black Muslims out of business because my secret agents are mobilizing Christian darkies against the infidelic niggers. I pressured the Pittsburgh Courier into dropping your weekly column and I forced them to fire their managing editor for being too friendly to you. I have hired many niggers to put pressure on the Chicago Defender, The Afro-American and other nigger papers to expose you and scare Christian darkies away from you Muslims.

Behind the scenes, I have pulled strings to get White newspapers and magazines to expose you black infidels. Bask in that publicity while you can, because the purpose of it is to set you Muslims up as clay pigeons. Then, it will be easier for me to get the cops to prosecute you. I will fill the jails with Black Muslims.

We Christian Knights of the Ku Klux Klan don't like the way you Black Muslims have come into our White city of Atlanta to establish your mosque and open a grocery store. We know that you Black Muslims are rapidly taking over New York, the world's largest city, but Atlanta belongs to us Whites and we will never surrender it to you cannibals. That's all niggers are, cannibals! Savages from the jungles of Africa. Most Atlanta niggers are staying in their place, so we want you Muslims to leave them alone.

Completely within the law, I am going to run you Black Muslims out of Atlanta. I am launching a boycott against your Muslim grocery store in Atlanta. That will be easy because most darkies know that niggers don't know how to operate a store or how to keep it clean and sanitary. Only White people know how to efficiently run a store.

Beginning April 13, Christian Knights will begin phoning Atlanta's White housewives and telling them to tell their nigger maids and cooks to stay out of the Muslim mosque at 4444½ Edgewood Avenue, N.E., and to BOYCOTT your Muslim grocery store. Also we are going to call on Atlanta's White merchants and tell them to tell their nigger employees to stay away from your mosque and BOYCOTT your Muslim store. Niggers couldn't get along without White stores, so they must smarten up and BOYCOTT the nigger Muslim store.

As soon as it is printed, we will send an appeal to all of Atlanta's colored Christian preachers calling upon them to join in the Christian BOYCOTT against the mosque and store of the Muslim infidels. I feel sure that all of Atlanta's Christian darkies will support the Klan's BOYCOTT of your mosque and store because they know that you Black Muslims are heathen infidels trying to drag them down into hell. You Black Muslims are the meanest niggers in America, but you will meet your Waterloo in Atlanta.

You know what I have done to you Black Muslims in the past, such as inciting nigger newspapers against you bad niggers and having your column removed from the nigger press. Here in Atlanta, I have spies in about every nigger organization to BOYCOTT you Muslims until you have to leave town. You know as well as I do that the good Christian darkies will stand with the Klan against you White-hating Mohammedan infidels.

I am writing this letter to try to persuade you to sell your mosque and store in Atlanta and pull all of your Muslim invaders out without delay. That way you would avoid a financial loss and the Klan would no longer have to worry about you Black Muslims taking over Atlanta. If you are ready to withdraw your heathen forces from Atlanta, notify me immediately and I will call off the Klan boycott of your mosque and store. You know that you dumb niggers can't win against the Klan. Your early reply is awaited.

If you Black Muslims don't pull out of Atlanta, we Christian Knights will drive you out, legally, of course. The Christian Knights of the Ku Klux Klan intend to maintain Atlanta as a Christian City under White rule. Islam is an infidelic nigger religion, so we don't intend to allow it. You Black Muslims should be ashamed of yourself for trying to lead Atlanta's Christian darkies down into hell with your false religion of Islam. You know your religion is no good because there are no White people in it. Christianity is the one and only religion that can get you into Heaven.

Black Muslims! Black Infidels! Take your choice! Sell your mosque and store now and pull out of Atlanta, or be driven out by the Klan BOYCOTT. The Christian Knights of the Ku Klux Klan have spoken.

With many wishes for the failure of the Black Muslims in America, I remain,
Yours for Christ, Race, & Country
Archleader J. B. Stoner, Imperial Wizard[24]

***

Foreign friendships and poison-pen letters intrigued party headquarters, but a new "menace" threatened Dixie. The U.S. Supreme Count had twice ruled segregated buses unconstitutional, in a pair of Virginia cases from 1946 and 1960, but southern states ignored those decisions and Washington took no steps to enforce them. Likewise, all concerned dismissed a 1955 ruling from the Interstate Commerce Commission explicitly banning "separate but equal" seating on interstate buses. Finally, in 1961, the Congress of Racial Equality moved to challenge southern intransigence with integrated "freedom rides," the first leaving Washington on May 4 and scheduled to reach New Orleans on May 17, anniversary of the *Brown* ruling.[25]

CORE expected trouble and was not disappointed. Arrests began in North Carolina on May 8, and a Klansman punched rider John Lewis in Rock Creek, South Carolina, on May 9, but the real danger waited in Alabama, where the Klan and NSRP joined hands to stop the buses cold on May 14—Mother's Day. By then, the integrated team occupied two buses, one Greyhound and one Trailways. Stopping in Anniston, the Greyhound passengers entered the realm of Kenneth Lamar Adams, notoriously violent leader of the local Alabama Knights and Calhoun County spokesman for the NSRP, who led the 1956 attack on Nat "King" Cole. Surrounded by racists who slashed their tires, the riders drove on a few miles, then had to stop, whereupon pursuers firebombed the bus and held its doors closed, hoping to kill the passengers, until an undercover highway patrolman repelled them at gunpoint. Next came the Greyhound, swarmed by armed rioters, its passengers beaten, then ordered on toward Birmingham, where matters went from bad to worse.[26]

Fully recuperated from the Stoner sting, Bull Connor stood ready to greet invaders three years later. He continued working with the Klan through Alabama Knights Grand Titan Hubert Page, but ignored a letter of praise from Edward Fields in January 1961. On May 11, armed with details of the freedom ride itinerary, Connor issued orders from his office facing Birmingham's Greyhound depot, conveyed to Eastview Klavern 13 by Detective W. W. "Red" Self and Sergeant Tom Cook. Those officers declared, "Something big is coming to Birmingham, some freedom riders in buses. We want some people to meet them and beat the shit out of them." Cook added that Klansmen would have 15 minutes without police interference. "You can beat 'em, bomb 'em, kill 'em, I don't give a shit," he said. "There will be absolutely no arrests. You can assure every Klansman in the country

"Freedom Ride" Trailways bus burned by NSRP members and Klansmen rallied by Kenneth Adams outside Anniston, Alabama, May 14, 1961 (Library of Congress).

that no one will be arrested. We don't ever want another freedom rider coming through Alabama again. I want it to be something they remember for the rest of their lives." Page later told his knights of Connor's personal order: to provoke a fight and leave the riders looking "like a bulldog got hold of them." More specifically, "niggers" should be stripped, permitting their arrest for public nudity. FBI informer Gary Thomas Rowe, Jr., alerted his Bureau handlers, who took no action.[27]

Connor excluded party members from his conspiracy, hoping to arrest some at the scene on May 14, but Ed Fields learned of the plan and phoned visiting CBS newsman Howard K. Smith at his motel on May 13, advising, "Be sure to be at the bus station tomorrow, because you're going to see action." Smith and other newsmen showed up early, but police were scarce, warned by dispatchers to ignore disturbance calls and steer clear of a six-block radius around the two depots, four blocks apart. Red Self and other detectives loitered at the Trailways station as observers, while a plainclothesman assigned by Tom Cook kept a pay phone clear for emergency calls to the Klan. Robert Shelton and Hubert Page saw Dr. Fields and Jesse Stoner on the scene, threatening their competitors. Page told Stoner, "Get your goddamned people out of here. When we get through whippin' ass here, we're going to whip yours too." Stoner demurred, saying his men "had been invited" to participate. Page phoned Tom Cook, reporting the development, and Cook, despite his plan to jail the party members, said, "You boys should work together."[28]

News of the Anniston attacks prompted a rush to the Greyhound depot, where the second freedom bus arrived at 4:15 p.m. Chaos ensued, with mass assaults on the protesters, journalists, and random civilians. In the confusion, some Klansmen struck each other. Ed Fields appears in one photo, observing while others—including FBI spy Gary Rowe—beat bystander George Webb, leaving him badly injured. Police obeyed their hands-off orders, and when Patrolman Floyd Garrett—nephew of Robert Chambliss—saw Klansmen attacking radio newsman Clancy Lake in his car, he radioed headquarters to say, "Nothing to it." Still high on violence when police told them to "go home and get a good night's sleep," Gary Rowe and others roamed the streets, attacking African Americans until one would-be victim stabbed Rowe in the throat, requiring eight stitches from a Klan-allied doctor.[29]

Rowe fudged that story, claiming he was wounded at the Greyhound depot, and his handlers were impressed enough to pay him $265 for his "service" in the riots—until a photo surfaced of him beating Webb, albeit with his back turned to the camera. Coached by Agent Barry Kemp, Rowe filed a false report denying he committed any violence, naming Webb's assailant in the photo as Eastview knight and NSRP member Charles "Arnie" Cagle. Rowe further blamed Fields and "his boys" for instigating the riot. On May 15, Tom Cook phoned Rowe to congratulate him on doing "a goddamn good job down there. People always love you for it." When Montgomery Klansmen mimicked Birmingham's riot against freedom riders on May 20, Governor Patterson reluctantly sent National Guardsmen to disperse the mob, boasting he had "showed the world that this state can and will continue to maintain law and order without the aid of federal force."[30]

Despite Bull Connor's promise, six Klansmen *were* arrested for their roles in the Trailways riot: three from Tarrant County received 30-day jail terms and $30 fines; two others saw their charges dropped for lack of evidence; the sixth escaped three mistrials before his accidental death canceled a fourth. In Anniston, on May 22, FBI agents charged Ken Adams and eight cohorts with firebombing the Greyhound bus. Three received a year's probation in January 1962, while jurors acquitted a fourth and prosecutors dropped charges against the rest. Jesse Stoner represented Adams and one other defendant. (*The Thunderbolt*'s take on that case: "'Freedom Riders' Burn Bus While Bobby Kennedy Blames 9 Innocent White Alabamians.") In a sideshow to that trial, one juror faced perjury charges for falsely denying Klan membership, and Fields flirted with a contempt citation for harassing jurors by phone. The NSRP went unmentioned when DOJ attorneys filed an injunction against the Alabama Knights and U.S. Klans, barring future interference with interstate buses. Gary Rowe remained an FBI informer until his involvement in a notorious 1965 murder case, then vanished into the Federal Witness Protection Program, incredibly resurfacing as deputy U.S. marshal "Thomas Neil Moore" before his death in May 1998.[31]

The FBI suffered repercussions for its handling of Rowe in 1983 and '84, when riot victims Walter Bergman and James Peck sued the Bureau for negligence in failing to protect the freedom riders. They sought damages of $1 million and $500,000 respectively. Both won their cases, separate judges awarding Bergman $35,000 and Peck $25,000. Questions persist about Rowe's role in other crimes, including the fatal bombing of Birmingham's Sixteenth Street Baptist Church in September 1963.[32]

***

Overlooked in May's freedom ride turmoil, Atlanta's school board announced its acceptance of applications from African Americans hoping to attend white schools. George Rockwell threatened demonstrations, Klansmen published the applicants' names, and Jesse Stoner agitated "around the fringes of the scene," but no mobs formed until August 30, when four newly integrated schools opened for business. That day, 20-year-old Jerald Quillan Dutton—a fourth-generation Klansman who' founded the Knights of the Confederacy at his high school—led voluble protests, then turned up at a Labor Day

Klan rally led by James Venable, spending time with the Bowling brothers before he mounted the stage to join Roy Frankhouser (lodging with George Bright). Frankhouser logged the first of his 142 arrests there, for kicking Captain R. E. Little's shin and "screaming like a banshee." Arrested for assaulting an officer and disorderly conduct, he posted $150 bond.[33]

The NSRP moved on to new adventures. Max Nelsen hosted Edward Fields at Chicago's LaSalle Hotel on August 19, 1961, but their audience shrank by 20 percent from April's gathering. The party's national convention met in New Orleans on Labor Day, September 4, and Jesse Stoner addressed an Anniston rally the following day, where Attorney General Robert Kennedy and FBI Director Hoover were burned in effigy. On October 11, police in Fairfield, Alabama, arrested Fields and Robert Lyons for distributing *The Thunderbolt* despite an injunction obtained by Mayor Claude Smithson. Both received five-day jail terms and $50 fines, precipitating a legal fight that ultimately reached the U.S. Supreme Court.[34]

In December 1961 Martin Luther King chose Albany, Georgia, as his first target for single-stroke desegregation of a whole community. The campaign saw more than 1,000 African Americans jailed within a single week, including King, but he ultimately left town declaring the effort a failure, largely due to Police Chief Laurie Pritchett. Whereas other southern lawmen brutalized protesters and unleashed vigilantes upon them, Pritchett surveilled Klansmen and exiled Nazis, supervised mass arrests with discretion and sometimes even prayed with King's protesters. The media soon tired of Albany, and while violence sputtered elsewhere in southwestern Georgia— four black churches burned and a home-invading Klansman slain in self-defense—sensational headlines were lacking. Albany's main contribution to the civil rights movement was SNCC—the Student Nonviolent Coordinating Committee—founded during the campaign, soon spreading across the South.[35]

A question mark still dangling over Albany is the involvement of NSRP "official policy speaker" Connie Lynch, reported by journalist Trevor Armbrister as present on the scene, and previously during Little Rock's disorders in 1957–59. Inquiries to both cities for this volume found

Charles "Connie" Lynch, the NSRP's "official policy speaker," in action, rousing a racist crowd ca. 1964 (Florida State Archives).

no evidence of Lynch, but he was drawn to racial flashpoints of the era, traveling alone or with girlfriend Marie Calabria in his coral-pink Cadillac, sporting a Confederate battle flag vest as he harangued racist rallies. Texas born in November 1912, Lynch drifted to California as a lemon picker, then joined the army as a cook in World War II, later boasting of his imaginary prowess as a "Jap killer." In 1956 he logged his first arrest for non-support of his spouse, and soon afterward became a "traveling parson" for Wesley Swift's Church of Jesus Christ—Christian, explaining, "I like to go where the challenge is." Swift praised Lynch as "a constructive organizer" with "a fine moral background." When donations flagged, Lynch worked as a plasterer for California NSRP members Neuman and Rufus Britton, and in early 1962 became the party's Golden State organizer, also a member of the Minutemen and William Gale's Christian Defense League. Armbrister quotes Ed Fields as saying Lynch "raised more money than any other man we ever had, but he was too extreme. He scared away the more substantial elements of the community. He organized his group with black belts, boots and helmets. This was not authorized," forcing Fields to demand his resignation. An alternate version, published by California's attorney general, has Lynch demoted as State Organizer but still affiliated with the party. Today Fields flatly denies any conflict with Lynch, whom he describes as a loyal party activist until his death in 1972, a claim borne out by Lynch's unbroken association with Jesse Stoner and *The Thunderbolt*.[36]

California's party was eternally in flux. James P. Thornton served as State Organizer in 1962, replaced by Lynch in 1963 with Thornton's elevation to State Director. He lured Robert Lee Lewton from Rockwell's ANP to edit California's party newsletter, *The Attack*, and serve as Deputy Director. Robert Barber was Director for Kern County, while Neuman Britton doubled as District Director of San Bernardino County and Security Division Chief of Staff. Lynch and Britton gained infamy for their impassioned rants against blacks and Jews, while Thornton tried a more low-key approach. After a violent incident in San Bernardino (see Chapter 6), Thornton left California—replaced by State Chairman Terrel R. Eddy of San Diego—to work at Birmingham headquarters, then left with other defectors to form a rival splinter group in 1964[37]

***

Nineteen sixty-two brought prominent new members to the party, cost the party one, and raised another opportunity for action. The defector was Matt Koehl, who resigned in March to join Rockwell's ANP, exacerbating a feud between the two groups. Around the same time, in Louisville, Fields warned Rockwell of a suspected *agent provocateur* in their midst. Rockwell immediately phoned FBI agents, whom he greatly admired, to report their conversation, convincing Fields that Rockwell himself was a spy. In May, Fields attacked Rockwell in *The Thunderbolt* as an FBI collaborator on the Jewish payroll, laying groundwork for a bitter libel suit. August's issues blared: "Proof Rockwell Cooperates with Drew Pearson and ADL" and "FBI Counterspy Says Rockwell Sabotages Right Wing."[38]

While that drama played out, Gordon Winrod joined the NSRP for a six-month stint as National Chaplain, proceeding from there to lambaste Jews as "anti–Christs" in various publications and radio broadcasts. *The Thunderbolt* announced John Kasper's forthcoming marriage in February 1962, followed three months later by Hollywood's release of *The Intruder*, with William Shatner portraying thinly veiled "Adam Cramer" as he whips a fictional southern town into vigilante madness. Emory Burke formally

Matt Koehl (left) with George Rockwell after his defection from the NSRP. Deputy Commander Alan Welch stands to the right (National Archives).

joined the party in August 1962, honored with membership card No. 1 for his years of service to fascism. Bombing suspect Robert Bowling had left the NSRP to form his own National White Americans Party, but merged it with the Fields-Stoner group in 1962, while heading the Remember Mary Phagan Committee to commemorate Atlanta's 1913 murder victim and the lynching of alleged Jewish slayer Leo Frank two years later. Another new recruit, integration protester Jerry Dutton, had briefly served as the National White American Party's Information Director before following Robert Bowling into the NSRP and becoming its Youth Leader. James Warner came to party headquarters from the ANP, formerly denounced as a "profiteer," now welcomed with the priceless mailing list he compiled as Rockwell's National Secretary, using it to enhance *Thunderbolt* circulation when he became the newspaper's associate editor. From Florida, Oren Potito—another minister of Wesley Swift's church, president of its Eastern Conference, publisher of the *National Christian News*—signed on as National Organizer.[39]

Politics remained the party's ostensible *raison d'être*, and 1962 was another election year. John Crommelin challenged Senator Lister Hill again in May's Democratic primary, with Oren Potito serving as his campaign manager, and failed again, running last in a field of three contenders with 56,822 out of 495,290 votes cast. William Gale fared worse a month later, in his second bid to become California's governor: he ran last in a field of four, with 17,369 votes out of 1,694,298 recorded. From Canada came more encouraging news in June: the conservative-populist Social Credit Party had gained 30 seats in Parliament, establishing itself as the nation's major third party and inspiring dreams of similar success for the NSRP.[40]

A dark horse candidate in Alabama that November was James Chester Robinson—called simply Chester in *The Thunderbolt* and "James George Robinson" in mistaken federal reports. Montgomery County's party chairman, he owned Chester's Restaurant on Mobile Highway, purveyor of "the world's best food," where the party met each Monday night for shoptalk and entertainment by the Harmony Boys Quartet. Oren Potito managed Robinson's at-large campaign for a seat in Congress, to no avail: in November he ran last among 12 contenders, with 32,446 votes out of 5,326,026 ballots cast.[41]

The year's best news for racists was George Wallace's gubernatorial election. Recalling his 1958 vow to "out-nigger" future opponents, Wallace hired Ace Carter as his chief speechwriter and fundraiser, forged "the most intimate terms" with Robert Shelton, and gave Birmingham's Eastview Klavern $7,500 to buy a new van, for distribution of *The Thunderbolt* and campaign fliers. Wallace's personal pilot, Albert J. Lingo, was an ex-highway patrolman and future chief of Alabama's Department of Public Safety, known as "hell on niggers" and a "good friend" of the Klan. Wallace led a field of seven rivals in the May 1 primary (Bull Connor placing fourth), and four weeks later trounced his remaining opponent with 56 percent of all votes. Six months later he scored a landslide, claiming 96 percent of the popular vote against 4 percent for his Republican opponent. Vigilantes had another friend in the governor's mansion.[42]

***

On September 2, 1962, the party held its national convention in Montgomery, where attendees dined at Chester's Restaurant the night before, then cheered Minutemen founder Robert DePugh's speech next day—rated a "great success" by *The Thunderbolt*. Also announced was local construction of a Patriotic National Center and School for Racial Studies and Leadership, opening that month as headquarters for each unit's youth section, including classrooms and dorms.[43]

While the conventioneers dispersed, trouble arose in Mississippi, with the latest challenge to segregation at the state university in Oxford. Clyde Kennard was first to attack the Magnolia State's color line at Mississippi Southern College ("Southern Miss") between 1956 and '59, ending with a frame-up that sent him to prison, where he contracted terminal cancer. Two years later, 29-year-old James Meredith fixed his sights on "Ole Miss," launching a legal fight that culminated with a court order to enroll him in September 1962. Governor Ross Barnett vowed that "no school will be integrated in Mississippi while I am your governor," and state legislators passed a special law excluding Meredith based on alleged "false voter registration" in Jackson County. When a federal court invalidated that statute, racists nationwide rallied to support Barnett's defiance of the *Brown* decision and subsequent court orders.[44]

Calls to arms went nationwide. From Montgomery, James Robinson wired Barnett, suggesting creation of a state militia to arrest integrationists and pledging NSRP members would "place our lives and fortunes at the disposal of your supreme authority as governor." Ken Adams sent a telegram from Anniston, saying hundreds of men "are on a stand-by alert waiting for your call to protect the sovereign state of Mississippi." Seven Mississippi congressmen cabled the White House, warning JFK of "a holocaust in the making," while

Top: Mississippi Governor Ross Barnett (with flag) and his wife enjoy a football game before the integration of Ole Miss, September 29, 1962 (Library of Congress). *Bottom:* James Meredith arrives at the University of Mississippi, flanked by Assistant Attorney General for Civil Rights John Doar (right) and Chief U.S. Marshal James McShane (left) (Library of Congress).

Louisiana's Citizens' Council offered Barnett "10,000 volunteers." In Miami, Fred Hockett pledged 1,500 combatants and Earl Linder phoned William Somersett, a member of the Florida States' Rights Party (and police informer), inviting Somersett to join him in Oxford. Klan-friendly Sheriff Jim Clark offered to rally his "special posse" in Selma, while Robert Shelton contacted Klansmen by phone and CB radio, predicting, "This could be another War Between the States." In Georgia, UKA Grand Dragon Calvin Craig promised, "A volunteer force of several thousand men would be on its way to Mississippi straight off." Elsewhere in the Peach State, Jerry Dutton told a Decatur Klan rally that "carloads" of men were bound for Oxford, and Melvin Bruce—ex-chauffeur for George Rockwell—packed his Mauser rifle after wiring Barnett: "I volunteer my services, arms and munitions to you as a combat infantryman." Kansas City broadcast a radio bulletin rallying all available Minutemen. John Doar, First Assistant Attorney General for Civil Rights, named Meredith's chief opponents as the Citizens' Councils, NSRP and KKK, plus "various related groups and subgroups." Among the NSRP's "most important leaders" he listed ex–Marine Lieutenant Colonel Ervin Robert Whitman, a vocal critic of "Jewish supremacism" who set off from St. Petersburg with Oren Potito and Robert O. Perrow. Before leaving Florida, Potito told a party meeting in Pinellas Park that he had four men in the audience "who would do anything he requested," alerting them to active duty.[45]

Potito may have been referring to "guerrilla warfare cells" operating from his St. Petersburg church and other Identity congregations. As he described them, "These 'survival groups' are designed to defend the country in case of a take-over. We have regular rifle practice, and our members go on maneuvers in jeeps and boats in different places in different states."[46]

Amidst that furor, the chief civilian agitator was Edwin Anderson Walker, a decorated ex–major general who led troops integrating Little Rock's Central High School in 1957, then decided he was "on the wrong side." Forced from the army in 1961 for bombarding his troops with extremist propaganda and telling them how to vote, Walker plunged full-time into far-right politics. His speeches ranged from furious to incoherent, once urging the Citizens' Council to prepare for "war in the fourth dimension." An open letter to JFK warned that without a Cuban blockade, public opinion "could rebel in revulsive repudiation of its traditional bounds against the untraditional escalation of intrusive and compulsive accommodation." Sharing a stage with Ross Barnett in December 1961 he told Mississippians, "We are at war. Man your weapons and attack." Five months later Walker floundered in the Texas gubernatorial primary, placing last among six rivals with 9.56 percent of the vote. Unfazed, he broadcast a message from Shreveport on September 26: "It's time to rise. Rally to the cause of freedom. Bring your flag, your tent and your skillet."[47]

Thousands responded to such calls. FBI informers reported Hubert Page and 700 Klansmen in Oxford by September 24. Five days later, as Walker landed in Mississippi, Fred Hockett phoned Jackson and spoke to Ed Fields, allegedly backed by 1,800 men. Jesse Stoner was en route with Ken Adams, Emory Burke, the Bowling brothers, and Jerry Dutton. Stoner and Adams met Walker in Oxford on September 30, while John Crommelin huddled with Captain Richard Touart, professor of naval science at Ole Miss, "grilling" him and talking "psycho-politics," leaving copies of the *Protocols* and W. V. Reedy's *The Coming Red Dictatorship*. William Gale rendezvoused with Oren Potito, and Wesley Swift considered flying east but decided against it. A team of UKA observers reported to Robert Shelton, while 2,000 Citizens' Council members rallied at the governor's mansion on September 30, led by William James Simmons, Council chief and Governor Barnett's speechwriter. Oxford air traffic controllers refused Robert Shelton's plane permission to land, sending him off to seek another airfield. Al Lingo was more fortunate, dispatched by George Wallace with colleague Hunter Phillips to observe the proper crafting of a campus crisis.[48]

Rioting began with nightfall at Ole Miss, an estimated 3,000 bigots besieging U.S. marshals at the Lyceum with gunfire, bottles, rocks, and firebombs, once rushing their lines with a stolen fire truck. Based on the number of outsiders present, author William Doyle called the uprising "the beginnings of a Ku Klux Klan rebellion." Most witnesses agreed that Edwin Walker led a charge against the Lyceum, repulsed by tear gas. Two men died in the fighting: French reporter Paul Guihard, shot execution-style at point-blank range, and a campus employee slain by a seeming stray bullet. Both crimes remain unsolved today. Federal troops arrived on October 1 to relieve the marshals. Authorities detained 300 rioters, one-third of them students, then released all but 12 on October 2, while scattered violence continued. Two of those caught with guns in their car but released were Oren Potito and Robert Perrow. Robert Shelton appeared with 23 aides on October 1, staying at a home near Oxford "provided by associates of Ross Barnett" and keeping "in regular contact" with the governor. A total of 166 marshals suffered wounds (30 shot), along with 48 soldiers, three highway patrolmen, and eight students. Troops seized hundreds of guns, including seven from the Sigma Nu fraternity run by future Senate Majority Leader Trent Lott. Robert Kennedy ordered Edwin Walker detained for 90 days' psychiatric

The aftermath of riots at Ole Miss, October 1, 1962 (Library of Congress).

Edwin Walker (hat in hand) returns to Dallas on October 7, 1962, following release from a federal psychiatric hospital (Library of Congress).

evaluation in Springfield, Missouri, but a doctor's protest freed him after five, while James Warner and two other party members picketed the hospital.[49]

Controversy surrounds Connie Lynch's role at Ole Miss. Trevor Armbrister claims he was present during the riot, but no local source confirms it. According to the DOJ, Lynch announced plans to visit Oxford on October 1, but his next public appearance was delivering an "anti–Jewish speech" at a UKA rally with Robert Shelton in Bessemer, Alabama, 12 days later. In Mississippi, Ross Barnett called U.S. marshals—who shot no one during the riot—"trigger-happy" and accused them of "instability and unwarranted brutality against unarmed youths." A local grand jury indicted no civilians, but charged Chief U.S. Marshal James McShane with "inciting" the riot; a federal judge dismissed that charge in 1964. Federal grand jurors indicted Edwin Walker and 16 others for obstructing court orders, all but three released by July 1963. Of the remainder, Jesse Stoner won acquittal for Melvin Bruce, who later published an article titled "Oxford Victim Tells Story." Hugh Cunningham—Ross Barnett's law partner, future defender of assassin Byron De La Beckwith—secured acquittals for the other two, both Alabamians. A federal court fined Barnett $10,000 for contempt, overturned on appeal. Meanwhile, James Meredith remained under constant guard, graduating with a degree in political science in August 1963.[50]

Edwin Walker enjoyed a checkered career after Oxford, addressing audiences from the NSRP, the Klan and it's front, Americans for Preservation of the White Race. He sued the Associated Press for libel and won $800,000 in June 1964, then saw his triumph overturned three years later when the Supreme Court ruled him a "public figure." In April 1963 Walker survived an alleged assassination attempt at his home by Lee Harvey Oswald. Six months later he was linked to a Dallas attack on United Nations Ambassador Adlai Stevenson, then sponsored infamous "Wanted for Treason" handbills against JFK in November. In 1965 he told a Birch audience in Atlanta, "There will be a KKK in the USA longer than there will be an LBJ." Police jailed him twice for public lewdness in 1976 and '77, the first time for fondling an undercover officer in a restroom. The army quietly restored Walker's pension in 1982, and he died from lung cancer in 1993. Thirteen years later, the anonymous *DeGuello Report* deemed Walker "a sincere American Nationalist and strong anti-communist," but accused him of gay trysts with various men including right-wing evangelist Billy James Hargis and ex–Lieutenant Colonel Archibald Roberts, a Liberty Lobby board member.[51]

The NSRP finished 1962 without looking back at Ole Miss. On December 14, member Tom Blanton, Jr., bombed the Bethel Baptist church in Birmingham. *The Thunderbolt* expanded circulation with mailing lists acquired from Klansman Evall Johnston's *Georgia Tribune* (30,000 subscribers), William Stephenson's defunct *Virginian*, and James Warner's *Action*. New articles praised the ANP-breakaway American National Party, founded by Dan Burros and John Patler (né Patsalos), and called for JFK's impeachment, airing his secret first marriage and listing 15 examples of "treason." Soon, *The Thunderbolt* ranked among the far right's most successful publications.[52]

With notoriety, rumors proliferate. On the fascist fringe, they frequently include charges of homosexuality and/or Jewish lineage. One such target was American Nazi and future New York king kleagle Daniel Burros—in fact, the son of Jewish parents, whose sexuality remains undocumented. A decade after his death, the anonymous *DeGuello Report* claimed Burros had "confided to his 'girlfriend' James Warner that like himself, Ed Fields was a Jew. Actually, Fields is the 'poor relative' of two very wealthy Chicago Jewish families." According to the unknown author, "On his father's side [Fields] is related to the Jewish Fields dry goods family and on his mother's side to the Jewish Morrell meat packing family. Warner was able to use this information to blackmail Fields into dropping his expose [of Warner] and into actually taking him into his own headquarters." In fact, there is no "Jewish Fields dry good family." Marshall *Field,* a descendant of Puritans who immigrated to Massachusetts in 1650, founded the famous Chicago-based department store chain. His wives were Nannie Scott and Delia Spencer, neither of them Jewish. George Morrell and son John were Irish Catholic immigrants who began curing hams in 1830, settling in *Iowa* by 1877. No evidence connects either family to Edward Fields, born to a family of Chicago Catholics. Fields's father *did* work as controller for a meatpacking firm, but it was Armour, founded by a 19th-century robber baron and sold to Boston Catholic Frederick Pierce in the early 1920s.[53]

CHAPTER 6

Mayhem

January 1963 began a year of mixed blessings for the NSRP. *The Thunderbolt* peaked at 50,000 copies printed per month—absorbing the mailing list of *The Rebel,* published by H. G. Jones—and Ace Carter penned George Wallace's inaugural address for January 14, declaring, "In the name of the greatest people that have ever trod this earth, I draw the line in the dust and toss the gauntlet before the feet of tyranny, and I say segregation now, segregation tomorrow, segregation forever." Birmingham police watched the party, noting a headquarters visit by one "Captain X" from Bakersfield, California, sporting a tailored Nazi riding uniform with spike-heeled jackboots, riding crop, rouge and mascara. Oren Potito and "Dr." Kenneth Goff lectured a Montgomery meeting, and Californian Bob Lewton published a "Security Division Creed." Some reports claim Emory Burke quit the party after quarreling with Gordon Winrod, then surfaced in Virginia three months later, sharing a stage with George Rockwell for Hitler's birthday. Youth Leader Jerry Dutton launched an Atlanta "dog corps." James Robinson moved to Dallas, logging an arrest on January 25 for cross-burning, and another five months later for assault.[1]

Connie Lynch returned to California in early 1963, for a recruiting drive launched from Wesley Swift's churches and George Rigler's Bible Foundation Church in Bellflower. *The Thunderbolt* called Rigler "one of the best speakers on the Israel Identity Message." On February 8, Swift addressed a party meeting in Los Angeles, telling his audience the NSRP "paid no attention to laws; it would decide which meetings would be broken up, and that no one could ever break up a National States Rights meeting." San Bernardino police felt otherwise two weeks later, after Lynch and four companions wearing "uniforms of the storm trooper variety" left a local church and visited a diner, where teenagers objected to their shouts of "Kill the Jews!" In the resulting brawl, one youth suffered wounds from a pellet gun in Nazi hands. On March 21, jurors convicted Neuman and Rufus Britton of assault and disturbing the peace. They also found Lynch guilty on the latter charge, imposing fines of $1,200.[2]

A short time later, conservative columnist David Lawrence—founder of *U.S. News & World Report* in 1933—accused the NSRP of taking communist money to foment disorder. The John Birch Society followed Lawrence's lead, after liberal lawyers helped two party members win a free speech case. The society's unsigned editorial read: "We don't recall the ACLU, the NAACP, or the Justice Department coming to the rescue of General Walker when he was illegally incarcerated in a mental hospital. But two degenerate agitators with fat FBI files, the contents of which would make your hair curl, go scot-free to keep agitating for the Party. Which Party? You can guess." NSRP headquarters sued both offenders. Birchers settled their case with an apology, while a judge dismissed the Lawrence's case.³

Other members rating mention in *The Thunderbolt* included Roy Frankhouser, fighting restaurant integration along U.S. Route 40 in Baltimore, and from Florida, the team of Dewey McKinley Taft and Robert Ervin Whitman. Taft, the party's State Director, published *The American Digest* and was jailed with Kenneth Goff in 1951 for ripping down a Soviet flag in a Denver United Nations display. Whitman, an ex–lieutenant colonel in the Marine Corps, ranked as a former military officer "opposed to Jewish supremacism." On April 1 Atlanta police jailed Robert Bowling for robbing city parking meters.⁴

***

Birmingham heated up in March, as residents faced a potential change in city government, Bull Connor running for mayor against moderate rival Albert Boutwell. Billy Hargis and Edwin Walker arrived to help Connor with "Operation Midnight Ride," drawing cheerleaders Ed Fields, Ace Carter, Robert Shelton and Bob Chambliss on March 18, and bombers struck another black home six days later. Voters rejected Connor on April 2, but he clung to office with Mayor Arthur Hanes, Sr., until court rulings removed them. Rumors spread of couriers from Washington, D.C., dispensing cash to Stoner, Shelton, Al Lingo and others, but FBI men found no evidence.⁵

Evangelist Billy James Hargis supported Bull Connor for mayor of Birmingham in 1963 (Library of Congress).

Backstage, Robert Shelton quarreled with members of his Eastview Klavern, driving some into the NSRP. When Robert Kennedy visited Governor Wallace on April 25, John Crommelin led party demonstrators at the capitol, bearing signs that read "No Kennedy Congo Here," "Kosher Team: Kennedy, Kastro, Krushev [*sic*]," and "The Giant, Jew-Communist Race Mixing TRAINED NIGGERS Road Show and Traveling Circus." Police jailed 17 protesters but spared Crommelin, who posted appeals bonds for 10, including Jerry Dutton and James Warner, fined $100 each with Jesse Stoner representing them.⁶

Blood spilled in Alabama on April 23, when a Klansman's "stolen" rifle killed lone civil rights marcher William Lewis Moore near Attalla. Police detained the gun's owner, then

William Moore, nephew of NSRP member Charles Cagle, was murdered by an Alabama Klansman during a one-man "freedom walk," on April 23, 1963 (Library of Congress).

released him without charges. Prior to setting out from Baltimore to Jackson, Mississippi, Moore wrote to an aunt in Birmingham, wife of Klansman and NSRP member Charles Cagle. He asked to stay overnight at their home and was refused, Aunt Helen citing "the motive you have in mind." She added, "When I was a young girl I did the best I could to help Mama and Daddy take care of you, and we tried to raise you right. And this is the thanks we get." After Moore's slaying, the Cagles grudgingly retrieved his corpse for shipment home. Helen spurned reporters, saying, "Too much has been said already. We don't want to read any more about him."[7]

Birmingham's tensions continued in May. Party members hung a large effigy of Dr. King outside party headquarters, and James Warner broke a hand assaulting demonstrators. On the night of May 11–12, UKA Exalted Cyclops Robert Creel sent NSRP member William "Jack" Cash—owner of a diner favored by Klansmen, jailed in 1957 for beating Fred Shuttlesworth—with other Eastview Knights to smash Jewish shop windows downtown, while bombers struck the Gaston Motel (missing Dr. King) and the home of King's brother, Alfred.[8]

Edward Fields (left) and an unidentified NSRP member sit below the effigy of Dr. Martin Luther King outside the party's Birmingham headquarters in May 1963 (National Archives).

In Anniston on May 12, gunfire blasted an African American church and two homes. Police charged Ken Adams on May 20, and jurors convicted him on two counts five days later, imposing a one-year sentence and $200 fine. A separate panel acquitted him of the church shooting on April 8, 1964.[9]

June reminded voters of Wallace's vow to "stand in the schoolhouse door," blocking integration of the state university in Tuscaloosa, scheduled for June 11. One week earlier, the NSRP staged a Birmingham rally, distributing fliers that read: "White Men, Unite. Back Governor Wallace. Help us stop negro mixing at the University of Alabama." At a nocturnal meeting, Jesse Stoner taught attendees to build time bombs using candles; Sgt. Tom Cook watched and dropped a dollar in the collection plate. Next morning, Al Lingo warned Klansmen that any found in Tuscaloosa on June 11 would be jailed. Bull Connor repeated that warning to Tuscaloosa's Citizens' Council on June 7, and Ace Carter took time from writing Wallace's crisis speech to visit NSRP headquarters. Fields recalls he "requested that we not go down to Tuscaloosa and hold any type of demonstration. He said it would be best for us to leave the entire event to the Governor."[10]

Some racists listened; others did not. On June 8 Eastview's knights met at Cash's Barbecue, preparing to ignore the governor. Ostensibly bound for a UKA rally outside Tuscaloosa, they loaded two cars with weapons and took off, after Gary Rowe warned G-men of his orders to "tear the school apart." While agents did nothing, state troopers stopped the cars en route, seizing the arms along with Rowe, Jack Cash, brother Herman, Charles Cagle, and three others. A reluctant officer blamed Lingo, saying, "Jesus Christ, we sure hate to bust you when you come down here to help us keep the goddamn niggers away from the school." All missed the Tuscaloosa rally, but a judge who lent his courtroom to Klansmen for meetings soon released them, saying, "I want to congratulate you on being an outstanding American. Take your weapons and use them well." Only Cagle suffered for the incident, losing his welder's job as a result.[11]

Bomb damage at the Gaston Motel, May 12, 1963 (National Archives).

Wallace's stand against desegregation fizzled with admission of two black students, and the action shifted to Mississippi on June 12. Hours after JFK delivered a televised message demanding equal rights for African Americans, future NSRP member and Klansman Byron De La Beckwith murdered NAACP Field Secretary Medgar Evers in Jackson, dropping his rifle at the scene. Prosecutors tried Beckwith twice in early 1964, defended by Ross Barnett's partner Hugh Cunningham, while Barnett and Edwin Walker visited Beckwith in court and Jesse Stoner became Beckwith's friend. Neither jury reached a verdict, leaving Beckwith at liberty for 30 years. Elsewhere, on the day Evers died, Montana Senator Lee Metcalf contacted Postmaster General Edward Day, seeking a mail ban on *The Thunderbolt* and similar hate sheets, but his request was denied on First Amendment grounds.[12]

***

In July the party deemed Barry Goldwater "too liberal," leaning toward Strom Thurmond as its 1964 presidential candidate, but South Carolina's senator showed no interest. Publication of "Birmingham Daily Bulletins" began with 5,000 copies on July 22, reporting integration of various stores and urging a white campaign of "selective buying." Dutton logged another arrest for complaining of "two communists" lurking at party headquarters. The offenders proved to be FBI agents, whereupon officers jailed Dutton for filing a false report. Those struggles paled, and bulletin publication dropped from daily to weekly, as Fields looked forward to September's opening of integrated city schools.[13]

On July 17, in a rare show of cooperation, Jerry Dutton joined Robert Shelton and Bob Chambliss to disrupt a meeting called to mobilize support for school integration. Five days later, Fields and Warner led a rally in Anniston, warning of the latest peril. Afterward, a plainclothes state trooper led them to a nearby motel where his boss sat

Medgar Evers's driveway in Jackson, Mississippi, scene of his June 12, 1963, assassination by future NSRP member Byron De La Beckwith (Library of Congress).

waiting. Fields recalled, "Colonel Lingo told me that if we waged a boisterous campaign against the integration of the schools and petitioned the Governor for the closing of such schools and held demonstrations in front of those schools on opening day, that this would give Governor Wallace reason enough to close mixed schools." Fields readily agreed.[14] Before schools opened, though, the SCLC had prepared a masterstroke to take its message nationwide.

Birmingham's first sit-ins occurred on July 23, with Dr. King joining in one week later.

Albert Lingo, head of Alabama's State Police under Governor George Wallace, a "good friend" of the KKK and coordinator of NSRP demonstrations at Birmingham public schools in 1963 (National Archives).

That afternoon, police arrested Fields, Warner, Jerry Dutton and visiting Georgia organizer Albert DeShazo for parading without permits around those stores, bearing Confederate flags and placards reading "This Store Serves Negroes."[15]

***

On August 1 Dr. King joined leaders of five other national civil rights groups to announce a March on Washington for Jobs and Freedom, scheduled for the 28th. William H. Hoff Jr., New York's NSRP organizer and future King Kleagle of the UKA, broadcast plans for a counterdemonstration by 40 delegations, leading one of them himself, but none materialized and the ANP's small protest passed almost unnoticed.[16]

Three days later, Ed Fields led a caravan of some 100 cars and pickups from Birmingham to Montgomery, carrying the promised petition to Governor Wallace. A no-show, Wallace left Fields a letter reading: "I want to assure you that my not being here is because of a previous engagement of longstanding." He promised "an extensive private audience" with two "personal representatives," but in fact Fields met four—Al Lingo, executive secretary Earl Morgan, and two other aides—spending an hour with them after delivering a rant against "Martin Luther Coon" from the Capitol steps.[17]

On August 10, Charles Cagle and prison guard Levie Yarbrough burned St. James Methodist Church in Warrior, 24 miles northwest of Birmingham, target of a failed arson attempt in November 1962. Five days later, Albert DeShazo—son and nephew of committed mental patients, a deserter from the army with arrests for burglary and robbery—tear-gassed Loveman's, a newly integrated Birmingham department store. On August 19 a new klavern, the Cahaba River Group, held its first meeting with NSRP members including the Blantons, Robert Chambliss and others, choosing Troy Ingram as their exalted cyclops.[18]

As with the Columbians before them, the NSRP's relationship with America's largest Klan remained in flux. Abandoning his enmity from 1961, Robert Shelton confessed, "there is not too much difference in philosophy" between the party and his UKA. Still, it galled Shelton to watch Fields court the governor. NSRP members joined Klansmen in the new United Americans for Conservative Government, including factions from the UKA, Citizen's Council, and John Birch Society. Worse yet was party infiltration of Eastview Klavern 13, where prominent members included Bob Chambliss, Charles Cagle, the Cash brothers, Thomas "Pop" Blanton and his son. Cagle participated in the first bombing of Birmingham attorney Arthur Shores's home on August 20. Later that month, Shelton branded the Blantons "undesirables" and expelled them from the UKA when they refused to sever ties with Fields and company. Shelton also forbade his knights from attending speeches by Connie Lynch—jailed for a disturbance at Gadsden that summer—but had trouble separating himself from the party's firebrand: Shelton shared the stage with Lynch in Spartanburg, South Carolina, on August 17, 1963, joined by UKA grand dragons Calvin Craig, James Jones, and Robert Scoggin. Shelton also banned affiliation with Rockwell's Nazi Party and the Minutemen, whom he hinted were communist spies, but had no luck enforcing the rule: his own King Kleagles in Pennsylvania, New York, and New Jersey—Roy Frankhouser, William Hoff, and Frank Rotella, Jr.—belonged to all three proscribed groups. Throughout Shelton's empire, *The Thunderbolt* remained as popular with Klansmen as the UKA's own *Fiery Cross*.[19]

***

Racists inspired by the NSRP protest scheduled integration at a Birmingham high school, September 1963 (Library of Congress).

6. Mayhem

Labor Day meant the advent of school integration in Birmingham, and the NSRP inflated its ranks by absorbing two smaller groups, the National White Americans Party and the Conservative Party of America—although the former would remain contentious. By September 1 the party had an office in the Redmont Hotel, close to the target schools, handing out reams of literature while Fields reportedly told his troops to "break through police lines" and storm school buildings on opening day. On September 2, Detective Marcus Jones attended a speech by Governor Wallace in Ensley Park, where he found Bull Connor huddled with party leaders and the park "full of Klansmen." Wallace invited Fields onto the stage, while Connor railed against "Bobby-socks Kennedy" and "lying foreign owned-newspapers." Wallace spoke next, vowing he'd take "whatever action is necessary to maintain segregation," but urging the crowd to "let law and order handle the situation in Birmingham." He alluded to "secrets for Birmingham and other places. I'm not going to tell any of my plans up here, but I've got plans. We've always got plans in Montgomery." One such was his arrangement, dating back to June, for the NSRP to lead protests at various schools.[20]

As Wallace seemed to adopt the party, a web of Byzantine proportions formed in Birmingham. NSRP headquarters hired a covert agent, South Carolina Klansman Phillip Thomas Mabry (code-name "Mockingbird") to liaise between Jesse Stoner and Ace Carter (aka "Ace-Deuce"), as if the men were not established friends. On the sly, Mabry also kept Al Lingo informed of Carter's actions, in case Ace went rogue and exceeded his brief from the governor's office. Exactly who was serving whom remains unclear.[21]

On September 3 the party staged two rallies, drawing crowds of 600 and 2,000 in preparation for opening day resistance. The next morning, 150 members picketed West End High School, then drove to Graymont Elementary, where two black students had registered and departed. Frustrated, the troops charged police lines, shouting, "Hang Albert Boutwell!" before swinging clubs drove them back. James Warner went to jail for hitting Marcus Jones with a brick. Next, 60 drove to Ramsey High School—still all-white—lobbing bricks and striking officers with picket signs before they were routed again, four more arrested. Bob Chambliss eluded police and rushed off to buy a case of dynamite from Klansman Leon Negron's construction supply store. Back at the Redmont, Ed Fields complained of "Gestapo tactics" by "Boutwell's storm troops." Despite warning Klansmen to shun the party's demonstrations, Robert Shelton dropped by and promised help "compiling reports from various areas of police brutality against women and children." A police informer taped party member

Jesse Stoner (right) with Atlanta journalist Al Kuettner at the scene of an NSRP school demonstration, September 1963 (National Archives).

Edward Ramage saying Fields "talked to Governor Wallace just before the meeting" and Wallace "promised that Al Lingo would have the State Troopers at the schools in the morning to see that the people were not manhandled by the police." He did better, issuing an executive order that barred integration "for the sole and expressed purpose of preserving the peace." On the nightly news, Wallace proclaimed white rioters were "not thugs—they are good working people who get mad when they see something like this happen. It takes courage to stand up to tear gas and bayonets" (neither of which were used).[22]

That night, Bob Chambliss, Charles Cagle and Klansman John Hall bombed the home of Arthur Shores again, touching off a black riot. Chambliss admitted his role in the bombing to relatives, and witnesses saw Cagle's car at the scene. Ninety minutes later, Cagle and Hall met Chambliss at home, retrieving a case of dynamite from his car and hiding it in a kudzu patch off Highway 31 en route to Gardendale, for future use.[23]

When party members gathered for another fracas on September 5, they found the target schools closed, but they regrouped to picket the empty buildings next day. On September 7 Governor Wallace addressed a UACG fundraiser at Birmingham's Thomas Jefferson Hotel, with Ed Fields and his top aides holding front-row seats. Fields later waffled on whether his invitation came by phone or from a state trooper who stopped his car on the highway, but it hardly matters. Fields basked in the limelight and, he recalls, "At the end of his speech, Governor Wallace walked down the steps to our table and shook hands with all four of us. We considered this to be our reward for helping him in the struggle against the integration of the Birmingham public school system."[24]

Home of black attorney Arthur Shores, bombed for the second time on September 3, 1963 (Library of Congress).

Nor was the party finished "helping" yet. While the banquet went on, Herman Cash joined Gary Rowe and others to bomb the Tarrant, Alabama, home of black hotelier A. G. Gaston. On September 11 party-trained youths led a walkout protesting admission of two black students at West End High School; one trainee treated strikers to a bugle rendition of "Dixie" on the football field. The next day, an NSRP procession of 150 cars circled the target schools, ending when Jack Cash was arrested with two guns, a razor, and a baling hook in his vehicle. Police also stopped Bob Chambliss, seizing his Confederate flags. Five days later a federal grand jury indicted Cash for weapons violations; Fields, Warner, Jesse Stoner, Birmingham member Barney Carmack and Chicagoan Ralph W. Lewandowski faced conspiracy charges. Soon after posting bail, Fields met with Robert "GG" Gafford—a UACG officer, Chambliss confidant and future four-term state legislator—who offered to arrange future party meetings at the National Guard's armory. Field's chaired a defense fund with party treasurer Carl Ridout and Hugh F. Delenne. Matthew Hobson Murphy, Jr., doubling as the party's lawyer and James Venable's successor as UKA Imperial Klonsel, secured dismissal of the indictments in February 1964.[25]

While Birmingham captured headlines, Mobile had problems of its own. With Murphy High School scheduled for desegregation, student Thomas Albert Tarrants III joined a protest demonstration, facing disorderly conduct charges with 54 classmates. Suspended for 10 days, Tarrants phoned Governor Wallace's office, warning of more trouble ahead if integration proceeded. After that, his mother said, Tarrants "became more and more engrossed in the Bible. He used to read his Bible day and night.... His whole personality changed, in that he thought communists were taking over the country." He also stopped watching TV, convinced that "it was poisoning people's minds against democracy."[26] His next step would be violence, with the party's help.

***

At 10:22 a.m. on Sunday, September 15, 1963, a bomb rocked the Sixteenth Street Baptist Church, killing four young girls, blinding a fifth in one eye, and injuring 22 other persons. The previous day, a niece of Robert Chambliss heard him tell his wife, "You just wait 'til after Sunday morning. They'll beg us to let them segregate." That said, Dynamite Bob seemed shocked by TV news of the mass murder, muttering, "It wasn't meant to hurt anybody. It didn't go off when it was supposed to."[27]

Decades elapsed before the heinous crime's solution, if indeed it has been solved. Today we know the bombers made a trial run past the church on September 2. Those involved were all from the Cahaba Group, including Chambliss, Tom Blanton, Jr., Herman Cash, and Bobby Frank Cherry. On September 8 John Crommelin visited Birmingham for a secret meeting with like-minded racists. On September 13 a diner at Cash's Barbecue heard Jack Cash on the pay phone. He asked for "Joe" and said, "Leave the case at the Powderly church." Next day, Robert Shelton flew to Birmingham, met by Chambliss at the airport. Ace Carter arrived the same day, as did Jesse Stoner, his car seen parked at Ed Fields's home. Investigators collected witness testimony placing Chambliss, Herman Cash and Tom Blanton, Jr., in a car near Sixteenth Street Baptist, in the predawn hours of September 15, waiting for Bobby Cherry to plant the explosives.[28]

The bombing sparked another riot that claimed two more lives. Police shot 16-year-old Johnnie Robinson in the back, allegedly for stoning a carload of whites waving racist banners. At NSRP headquarters, teenage Eagle Scouts Michael Lee Farley and Larry Joe Sims—both participants in the party's earlier school protests—bought a Confederate flag

DENISE MCNAIR CYNTHIA WESLEY ADDIE MAE COLLINS CAROL ROBERTSON

THEIR LIVES WERE TAKEN BY UNKNOWN PARTIES ON SEPTEMBER 15, 1963 WHEN THE SIXTEENTH STREET BAPTIST CHURCH WAS BOMBED.

"MAY MEN LEARN TO REPLACE BITTERNESS AND VIOLENCE WITH LOVE AND UNDERSTANDING" and went searching for prey aboard Michael's motor scooter. Soon they spied black brothers James and Virgil Ware bicycling toward home, and Sims fired a pistol, killing Virgil instantly. Impressed by their lawyer's plea for "these two raw, grieved untutored boys who have had this unfortunate thing come into their lives at their age," a judge sentenced Sims to six months' juvenile detention and placed Farley on probation.[29]

On September 17, calling the church blast a "blackening sin against humanity," Judge Clarence Osgood convened a special session of the federal grand jury charged to indict anyone involved in obstructing desegregation of Birmingham's schools. That all-white panel ignored the obvious suspects, Governor Wallace and Al Lingo, indicting only their tools from the NSRP (none of whom would serve time). Wallace Malone, a Dothan banker and architect of the 1948 Dixiecrat revolt, posted bail for those charged.[30]

Meanwhile, FBI agents compiled a list of suspects, building a case they dubbed "BAPBOMB." Agents questioned Ed Fields on September 23; he denied any knowledge of the crime, then reportedly filed suit against them. G-men interviewed Jerry Dutton on September 24, but he refused to answer questions, referring them to attorney Jesse Stoner. Stoner was a prime suspect himself, thinly disguised as "Mr. X" by newsman George McMillan in a June 1964 article for the *Saturday Evening Post*, described as "an out-of-state man" who had "probably been involved in more bombings than any one individual in the South." He possessed "a distinguishing physical characteristic and he always tells his buddies it's too dangerous for him to be seen, that he would be noticed, marked and remembered." Nonetheless, police said, "Invariably that bastard is in the general area when a bomb goes off." His conviction of murder, McMillan vowed, was only a matter of time.[31]

On September 19 bombers struck a black man's home in North Birmingham. Police grabbed a neighbor who reported it, drove him to an isolated spot and beat him, then charged him with drunkenness. Three days later Chambliss, the Blantons and other prime suspects joined Robert Gafford for a "kiss-of-death" meeting on the Cahaba River Bridge, joining hands as they vowed silence on the BAPBOMB case under pain of execution. George McMillan implied that "Mr. X" was present for the ceremony. On September 23 a double blast jolted a black neighborhood on Center Street. The first explosion drew police; the second, loaded with shrapnel,

"BAPBOMB" suspects hastily arrested on orders from George Wallace. From left, John Hall, Charles Cagle, Robert Chambliss (National Archives).

Opposite, top: Bomb damage to the Sixteenth Street Baptist Church, killing four young girls and wounding 23 other persons on September 15, 1963 (Library of Congress). *Bottom:* A plaque dedicated to the "BAPBOMB" murder victims before any convictions in the case (author's collection).

was designed to kill them but failed. "Bombing matters," as the Bureau dubbed them, had gotten out of hand.[32]

While G-men toiled and their director ultimately closed the case without arrests, fearing "embarrassment" if another white jury released racist killers, Governor Wallace worked in secret to humiliate the DOJ. On September 29 Al Lingo summoned Robert Shelton, John Hall, Bobby Cherry, and other Klansmen to a meeting at the home of UACG President Bill Morgan. The topic: selection of scapegoats to placate the media. Bypassing local police and the FBI, Lingo (with Shelton) arrested Hall, Bob Chambliss, and Charles Cagle. Matt Murphy signed on to defend the trio as Wallace crowed, "We certainly beat the Kennedy crowd to the punch."[33]

But where was the dynamite they had possessed? Tipped by an informer, FBI agents searched the kudzu patch near Gardendale and found nothing. On October 1, while Matt Murphy prepped for a *habeas corpus* hearing, Al Lingo took Cagle from jail to the site already scoured. This time, troopers found a sack with 2½ sticks of dynamite—and then, 100 yards away, a case of 130 sticks, with 10 missing. Tracing the TNT was simple: manufactured on August 28, it sold to Leon Negron on September 3, then to Chambliss one day later. That afternoon, a judge formally charged all three suspects with a misdemeanor count of possessing explosives, then released them on $300 bond.[34]

In related events, Tom Blanton, Jr., failed an FBI polygraph test on October 1. Agents raided his home three days later, seizing guns and charging him with assault when he pulled a knife. Bobby Cherry allegedly passed his test on October 9, rushing to tell Jesse Stoner and Ed Fields that he "beat the lie detector." Between those tests, on October 6, the Cahaba Group met, hearing Chambliss curse and threaten Robert Shelton and UKA investigator Don Luna, whom he blamed for "framing" him to collect rewards totaling $92,000.[35]

Chambliss, Cagle and Hall faced trial on October 8. A judge convicted all three the next day, fined each $100, and suspended 180-day jail terms pending appeal. A higher court later dismissed their case on jurisdictional grounds, since the dynamite was found outside Birmingham's city limits. Hall turned informer for the FBI on October 29 but failed to advance the case. Herman Cash became the Bureau's "prime suspect" in May 1965, but was not charged. Twelve more years passed before Chambliss faced trial for murder, 24 more before grand jurors indicted Bobby Cherry and Tom Blanton, Jr. When state investigators trailed Cherry to Texas in 1977, he immediately phoned Robert Gafford. No murder charges stuck to "Mr. X."[36]

While hiding evidence against Blanton, Chambliss and Cherry for years, the FBI considered other suspects. A Miami report to Hoover dubbed George Wallace a close friend of William Gale, adding, "Gale is responsible for the church bombing in Birmingham on September 15, 1963." Judge Seymour Gelber's diary records a conversation between Joseph Milteer and William Somersett, stating, "Before they parted, Milteer confided to Somersett he was certain that Dixie Klan Imperial Wizard Jack Brown either placed the bomb, or engineered the act, which caused the death of four children in the Birmingham church bombing." G-men checked, finding that Brown was in Tennessee on September 15. Another suspect, present in Birmingham when the bomb exploded, was Robert Pittman Gentry, a member of the United Florida KKK indicted five months later for bombing a Jacksonville home.[37]

A month after the church blast, George McMillan exposed a "new" terrorist cell in Dixie called "Nacirema"—"American" spelled backwards—in *Life* magazine. Omitting names, he said members of the bombing clique came from various Klans and the NSRP, seeking thrills other groups denied them. Most, McMillan wrote, possessed a criminal record, a physical deformity, or both. Two years later congressional investigators learned that "Nacirema Inc." existed by July 1961, offering demolition classes led by UKA members William Anderson and William Crowe, including a session attended by Robert Shelton and Calvin Craig in October 1961. Crowe's criminal record dated from 1941; police jailed Anderson with others for running an Atlanta brothel in March 1963.[38]

The NSRP's rejoinder came at a "White Rally" in Gardendale, Alabama, on October 19. There, after aides hanged JFK, Dr. King and Fred Shuttlesworth in effigy, Jesse Stoner lectured the 150-person audience on "Jewish control" of the FBI and blamed G-men for bombing Sixteenth Street Baptist. Stoner's FBI rap sheet lists two arrests during this period: one for "conspiring against [the] U.S. government" on September 25, no disposition listed and apparently dismissed; the other states no charge but claims he paid a $30 fine to Birmingham police on October 15.[39]

Chapter 7

"It happened like I told you"

By spring 1963, JFK ranked as the president most hated by southern racists since Abraham Lincoln. Aside from his liberal Catholicism, he openly advocated expansion of black civil rights, backed by intervention in the freedom rides and at Ole Miss. Despite the rage in Dixie, he seemed likely to be reelected in November 1964, particularly if Republicans nominated Arizona's far-right Senator Barry Goldwater.

The NSRP had a personal stake in deposing Kennedy by any means available. Aside from racial politics, party members were involved—with Klansmen and Minutemen—in training Cuban exiles for attacks on Fidel Castro's Cuba, ostensibly canceled by JFK after the disastrous Bay of Pigs invasion in 1961. Two years later, an FBI report disclosed that—

> Captain ROBERT KENNETH BROWN, The School Brigade, Fort Benning, Georgia, advised that he has been active in Cuban matters for several years and during the spring of 1963, in connection with anti–Castro activity, he was in contact with the National States Rights Party in Los Angeles, California.
>
> In connection with this, he contacted Dr. STANLEY L. DRENNAN, 375 Wonderview Drive, North Hollywood, California, who was active in the National States Rights Party. Brown stated that once while a guest in Dr. DRENNAN's home, DRENNAN stated that he could not do it, but what the organization needed was a group of young men to get rid of KENNEDY, the Cabinet, and all members of the Americans for Democratic Action and maybe ten thousand other people. BROWN stated that he considered the remarks as being "crackpot"; however, as DRENNAN continued the conversation, he gained the impression that DRENNAN may have been propositioning him on this matter.[1]

Secret Service agents interviewed Dr. Drennan on June 14, 1963, but took no further action. Born in 1916, he survived unmolested by law enforcement until his death in Idaho, in September 2008. His sole recorded court appearance occurred in February 1971, when the U.S. Secretary of Health, Education and Welfare joined Blue Shield of California to accuse him of overcharging aged convalescent patients more than $60,000 since 1969. In 1979 a federal appellate court ordered reimbursements to Drennan for one monthly visit per patient, excluding the remainder he billed as excessive.[2]

Three months after Secret Service agents questioned Brennan, an FBI informer tipped his handlers to the activities of Klansman G. Clinton Wheat, who hosted meetings of the American Nazi Party, Christian Defense League, and Church of Jesus Christ—Christian at his Los Angeles home. The spy described speakers delivering "classic examples of the hate-monger sermons," including William Gale's claim that "I can show you top-secret documents that prove that the six million Jews Hitler was supposed to kill are right here in America." In September 1963 talk allegedly shifted to JFK's murder, and a neighbor recalled Wheat making a hasty trip to Dallas that autumn, borrowing $400 for the road. Witness Lawrence Howard identified Wheat's home as a place "where paramilitary organizations held meetings and prepared ammunition." In 1967, after New Orleans District Attorney Jim Garrison sought to subpoena him, Wheat fled into hiding, first in Oregon, then in northern California.[3]

***

Between October 18 and 20, 1963, the far-right Constitution Party convened in Indianapolis. Founded in July 1952—with participants including Conde McGinley, Elizabeth Dilling, Eugene Sanctuary, Merwin K. Hart, Joseph Beauharnais, John Hamilton, and Oliver Kenneth Goff (Colorado's state chairman, born an albino)—the party had nominated ex–General Douglas MacArthur for president, polling 17,205 votes that November, mostly from Texas. In 1956 the party nominated T. Coleman Andrews, calling itself the States' Rights Party in Virginia and several other states. In 1960 it fell even further, choosing retired Marine Corps Brigadier General Merritt B. Curtis with running mate Curtis Bean Dall from the Liberty Lobby.[4]

By October 1963 the Constitution Party had degenerated to a group of hard-core bigots, if it was ever anything else. Delegates in Indianapolis included William Gale; Curtis Dall; Richard Cotten, then editor of *The Conservative Viewpoint*; ex–Marine Corps Lieutenant General Pedro del Valle; ex–Lieutenant Colonel Archibald "Arch" Roberts, forced to retire from the army for collaborating with General Edwin Walker's indoctrination program in 1961, later a Liberty Lobby board member; Kenneth Goff from Soldiers of the Cross, a Minutemen affiliate; Joseph Adams Milteer, representing the NSRP and Georgia's Citizens' Council; covert police informant William Augustus Somersett from Miami; plus Klan leaders Jack Brown and James Venable.[5]

Pedro del Valle, anti-Semite activist and member of the Constitution Party in 1963 (National Archives).

Some conspiracy theorists suggest the Indianapolis meeting occurred primarily to plot removing JFK from office before 1964. True or not, attendees variously cheered Kennedy's assassination in November 1963 or hastened to blame communists. Goff, writing for *The White Sentinel* in December 1963, alleged that accused assassin Lee Harvey Oswald "called me, before a meeting in a Dallas hotel about a year ago. He poured out his pro–Communist venom…. His Red record was no secret to those fighting Communism in the Texas area." Why a supposed devotee of Castro's Cuba would place such a call to Goff, whom Oswald never met, is anyone's guess.[6]

***

Midway through the Indiana convention, on October 19, the NSRP staged a "White Rally" at Olive Ball Park in Gardendale, Alabama, near the site of NSRP's secret dynamite stash. Chambliss, under close surveillance since the Sixteenth Street Baptist bombing, mocked pursuers and trailed one of their unmarked cars to the rally, later telling Detective Marcus Jones that he enjoyed taunting FBI agents. Jesse Stoner lectured the crowd of 100 to 150 racists on "Jewish control" of the FBI, which be blamed for the Birmingham blast. Afterward, participants hanged and burned effigies of Dr. King, Fred Shuttlesworth, and Attorney General Robert Kennedy.[7]

Before October's end, William Gale and Wesley Swift created the Christian Knights of the Invisible Empire, inducting 38 members at their first meeting. The new Klan's founders considered it a "Third Front" of their growing structure that included Swift's Church of Jesus Christ—Christian as the "First Front," something called the AWAKE Movement as their "Second Front," with the Christian Knights "which will have the outward impression of a political-religious group not interested in violence." More militant Klansmen would comprise for an "Inner Den" pledged to guerrilla warfare. Gale said, "Leaders in our country might have to be eliminated to further the goals of the CKIE" and "God will take care of those who must be eliminated." By Christmas, Gale and Swift parted ways after a violent quarrel, Gale assuming command of the Christian Knights, while Swift led the declining CDL. Gale later blamed the split on Swift, telling biographer Cheri Seymour Swift "took some money from some widows ... two elderly ladies. That's the official version. Nothing to do with the Church."[8]

On October 30, 1963, the police chief of Denton, Texas, told Secret Service agents a local man had boasted, "We have something planned to embarrass President Kennedy during his visit to Dallas." Agents questioned the man, still unidentified. He denied making any threats but admitted being "a former member of the 'Klan' in Arkansas and the National States Rights Party, and [being] a member of the John Birch Society.[9]

Two weeks later, on November 14, a man detained on federal auto theft charges told FBI agents a similar story. According to that report—

> he is a member of the Ku Klux Klan.... During his travels throughout the country, his sources have told him that a militant group of the National States Rights Party plans to assassinate the president and other high-level officials. He stated that he does not believe this is planned for the near future, but he does believe the attempt will be made.[10]

Secret Service agents closed their file on that report without further investigation, accepting the FBI's opinion that "the subject was trying to make some sort of deal with them for his benefit," and that there was "no information developed that would indicate any danger to the president in the near future or during his trip to Texas."[11]

JFK was killed in Dallas eight days later.

***

Enter William "Willie" Somersett, an FBI informer whose work for the Bureau began in the 1950s, while serving time in Atlanta's federal prison for violation of the 1910 White-Slave Traffic Act. His work as a "snitch" earned Somersett early release, and he continued serving through the late 1960s. Beginning in February 1962, Somersett also informed for the Miami Police Department. According to local handler Charles H. Sapp—described in various accounts as a sergeant, lieutenant, and captain in charge of Miami PD's Intelligence Unit—Somersett dealt with police when he began to mistrust Hoover's agents.[12]

Aside from labor and underworld ties, Somersett was a dues-paying member of the NSRP and the Klan, furnishing information on his racist contacts across the South—

including the aforementioned Joseph Milteer. FBI files describe Milteer as a native of Quitman, Georgia, born on February 26, 1902, who stood five-feet-four in adulthood, bespectacled, further depicted as "heavy waisted, small round shouldered, nearly always unshaven, short gray stubble with around two days growth, shabby dresser, wears old fashioned clothes, hunting type cap, tan in color, short legged, most of height from waist upwards." A high school graduate, Milteer had been arrested once—on suspicion of burglary in Valdosta, Georgia—then released without charges. In 1963 he lived part-time with Mrs. C. C. Colfield of Valdosta, labeled a prostitute in Bureau files, and often drove her Volkswagen instead of his registered Volvo. When not immersed in fascist politics, Milteer sold novelty items by mail and bootlegged wine at home, earning enough to rank as "independently wealthy."[13]

Joseph Adams Milteer, NSRP member suspected by some theorists, including former FBI agents, of participation in the JFK assassination (National Archives).

On November 9, 1963, while Jesse Stoner led a Klan rally in Jacksonville, Somersett met Milteer at Somersett's home on North Miami Avenue, where a tape recorder planted in a closet by Detective Everett Kay secretly recorded their conversation. A six-page transcript, labeled "Interrogation by Sgt. Everett Kay," reads as follows (uncorrected):

SOMERSETT: Now we are going to, you are going to have to take, Kenney, what do you call his last name?
MILTEER: Kenneth Adams
SOMERSETT: Yeah, you are going to take him in, he is suppose to be one of the hard core of the underground, are you going to invite him into that, too? What about Brown, now are you going to invite Brown in? You are going to have Brown in it?
MILTEER: Yeah.
SOMERSETT: Now, I will tell you between me and you, because we are talking, we aren't going to talk to everybody like we are talking here. Now, you know this, I like Brown, he is a good fellow, you know him, now here is something, when we was in his house, now, he knows me and you, but he didn't know Lee McCloud, well I think he done too much talking in front of a man he didn't know. Brown trusts a lot of people, he figures everybody is good.
MILTEER: Yeah.
SOMERSETT: And you know when he was telling or him (not legible) her about blowing up all those churches and, you know, I don't think he should have said all that in front of McCloud.
MILTEER: That is exactly the way I feel about it, too. And I didn't talk about it any more after we left there.
SOMERSETT: No, I see you didn't you see, these things come to my mind, I don't know McCloud well, and Brown never seen him before in his life, that I know of, now you seen this boy, Jackie, didn't open his mouth, he just sit there and listened. Jack Caulk (phonetic) he is a very quiet boy, Brown it just seems, well, he, I guess he has gotten by with so much he just don't care. He come out with all that about going over to Atlanta carrying that stuff, and showing them how to operate, I didn't want to say anything to him, but I don't think it is a good idea for people to discuss things like that in front of strangers. What do you think about it?
MILTEER: No, I think he should operate that, the same as he does the rest of it.
SOMERSETT: That's right, damn right that is right. Now you take like the Birmingham... (Milteer breaks in)

MILTEER: Any conclusion they come up with, that's them, not him.
SOMERSETT: That is true.
MILTEER: He didn't give them anything.
SOMERSETT: Well, he didn't give them nothing.
MILTEER: Just like me at home there folks want to know, "Joe, where do you get all of your information? Well, I get it, that is all you are interested in," and that is as far as it goes, see. And the same guy will turn around and give me some information, but he doesn't know where I am getting my information. The same guy who asks me where I get my information, will turn around and give me information.
SOMERSETT: We, sure, of course, I realize that.
MILTEER: That is the way you have got to operate.
SOMERSETT: Well, that is what I say, if you are going to take Brown in, and Brown is going to be one of the head men, the man behind you, then you have got to talk to Brown a little bit, and tell him, you know, "You have got to be a little more conscientious, especially on these bombings, and killings," after all he comes right out with it.
MILTEER: We have got to let him understand that that is his operation, and not ours.
SOMERSETT: Yeah, that is true. We don't care, if he wants to go to Birmingham and blow up a church, let him.
MILTEER: If he wants to blow up the National Capital, that is alright with me. I will go with him, but not as a party though, as an individual.
SOMERSETT: Well, if you want to go with him and help him blow it up, that is not the party, it is an individual, you are going to have to make him understand that.
MILTEER: There is a party movement, and there is also an individual movement.
SOMERSETT: Yeah, that is right.
MILTEER: And they are distinct and separate.
SOMERSETT: Well, you are going to have to make him understand that, right there, he didn't exactly admit it, but Jesus Christ, he intimated, he indicated right there, he backed the bombings of killing the Negroes in Birmingham, well, you know damn well we don't want anybody talking like that.
MILTEER: Can't afford it.
SOMERSETT: Well, you know damn well that is bad talk especially to somebody he don't know. He could have said that to me, and you would have been alright, it would have been between you and me then.
MILTEER: That is true.
SOMERSETT: But to go ahead and say it in front of Lee McCloud, what that hell (Milteer breaks in)
MILTEER: Well, I think he thought that he would not have been with us, if he had not have been alright. But that is still not enough.
SOMERSETT: No, hell no, that is no good, at least before he made all those statements, he should have called you outside, or consulted about this man a little bit.
MILTEER: You have to have reservations, you know.
SOMERSETT: That is right. Hell, he didn't say these things in any way to try to get us in trouble, because the only one who could be in trouble would be him, he was confessing on his damn self, he wasn't confessing on us, because we hadn't done a damn thing.
MILTEER: You and I would not get up there on the stand and say that he told us a cotton picking thing either.
SOMERSETT: Well, he knows that, but how about the other man.
MILTEER: Well, that is what I say.
SOMERSETT: Yeah, hell yes. I tell you something, you take Kenneth Adams over there, he is a mean damn man, like Brown was saying, the guy he was sending him to, well Kenneth is real mean, and the way Brown indicated they (not legible) the Negroes, well, we don't care anything about that. I would rather he wouldn't tell us those stories.
MILTEER: You sure can't repeat them.
SOMERSETT: Yeah. That is the set-up we are in now, I mean, we have to work with them, but let them operate their grollings (phonetic), like you say, if you want to go with them, that is your opinion, you go with him up to Washington and blow with him, if you want to go (Milteer breaks in)

7. "It happened like I told you"

MILTEER: I have a man who is the head of his underground of his own up there in Delaware, and since I worked on the Supreme Court, he wanted me to give him the lay-out there so they could go over there and do some things there, you know. But he called it off, I don't know why, I didn't even ask him why. That was his affair, but he called it off. But it was ready to go with him. I gave him the damn information he wanted.

SOMERSETT: You worked on the Supreme Court.

MILTEER: Yeah, three and a half years.

SOMERSETT: Well, that is why he wanted you to go, then, well, them things have got to be done, but outside the Party, we have got to be mighty careful who the hell we let know anything. Now, here is one thing you have got to realize, transporting dynamite across the state line is a Federal Offense, well you better let them know that.

MILTEER: Well, there is a way to beat that, you know. All you have to do is pull up to the state line, unload it there, slide it across the line, get in the car and load it again, and they can't accuse you of transporting it then, because you didn't do it. I have done the same thing with a woman. I had one, then I had a woman frame me on it. I got to the state line, and I said, "Listen, toots, this is the state line, get out, and I will meet you over there" she got out walked across the line, got in my car in the other state, I didn't transport her, there wasn't a fucking thing she could do about it, I had her ass for a long time.

SOMERSETT: I was talking to a boy yesterday, and he was in Athens, Georgia, and he told me, that they had two colored people working in that drug store, and that them, uh, they went into the basement, and tapped them small pipes, I guess that they are copper together, and let that thing accumulate, and blowed that drug store up. He told me that yesterday, do you think that is right?

MILTEER: It could have happened that way.

SOMERSETT: Well, that is what he told me, and he is in town right now.

MILTEER: Does he know who did it? Do they think these Negroes dit it?

SOMERSETT: Oh, no, they killed the Negroes, because they had two Negroes working in the place, that is what he told me. He is in town now, he is from Chattanooga. He knows Brown, he knows all of them, his uncle is in the Klan there. He is a young boy, he has been in the Marines, and he really knows his business. He went there, he went down and looked, and he told me that is what happened. So he has been involved in quite a little but of stuff, according to his story about Nashville, Chattanooga, and Georgia. I have no reason not to believe him, because he told me too much about Brown's operation, that is the reason I (not legible)

MILTEER: Yeah. You take this boy, Connor McGintis (phonetic) boy up there in Union, N.J., of course he doesn't go to anything like that, but he is on our side, he is the one that puts out that Common Sense. He is an ex–Marine. He is all man, too.

SOMERSETT: Now, you see, we will talk to these other people, you have made up your mind that you are going to use the Constitutional Party as a front.

MILTEER: Yeah, Constitutional Party States Rights.

SOMERSETT: Yeah, and it will strictly be secret, and nobody will be exposed except you.

MILTEER: Yeah.

SOMERSETT: Because when we talk to them today, you want to know exactly what to tell them, how it operates.

MILTEER: Yeah, and we have got to set up a little fund there to get it operating.

SOMERSETT: Oh, yeah, sure.

MILTEER: And I am going to devote my time to it, I don't have any idea of getting elected to that City Commission, but I am just making it cost them bastards, it cost them as it is, it cost them between $1,500 and $2,000 to beat me before, so I want to make it cost them another couple of thousand dollars. If they want to get rid of me, they can buy my fucking property, and I will get out of the damn town. In other words, they will save money. I am going to put that out in one of the damn bulletins there, see. We put, the way I operate, put out these little bulletins, like a typewriter page, eight and a half by eleven, and brother don't you think they ain't waiting for them, when I don't put them out, "Joe, where is the bulletin?" Bill, that could go all over the country the same way. That was just a trial proposition, if it will work in a little stinking town like that, it will work anywhere.

SOMERSETT: I don't know, I think Kennedy is coming here on the 18th, or something like that to make some kind of speech, I don't know what it is, but I imagine it will be on the T.V., and you can be on the look for that, I think it is the 18th that he is suppose to be here. I don't know what it is suppose to be about.

MILTEER: You can bet your bottom dollar he is going to have a lot to say about the Cubans, there are so many of them here.

SOMERSETT: Yeah, well he will have a thousand bodyguards don't worry about that.

MILTEER: The more bodyguards he has, the easier it is to get him.

Somersett: What?

MILTEER: The more bodyguards he has the more easier it is to get him.

SOMERSETT: Well how in the hell do you figure would be the best way to get him?

Milteer: From an office building with a high powered rifle, how many people (room noise tape not legible) does he have going around who look just like him? Do you know about that?

SOMERSETT: No, I never heard that he had anybody.

MILTEER: He has got them.

SOMERSETT: He has?

MILTEER: He has about fifteen. Whenever he goes any place they (not legible) he knows he is a marked man.

SOMERSETT: You think he knows he is a marked man?

MILTEER: Sure he does.

SOMERSETT: They are really going to try to kill him?

MILTEER: Oh, yeah, it is in the working. Brown himself, Brown is just as likely to get him as anybody. He hasn't said so, but he tried to get Martin Luther King.

SOMERSETT: He did.

MILTEER: Oh yes, he followed him for miles and miles, and couldn't get close enough to him.

SOMERSETT: You know exactly where it is in Atlanta don't you?

MILTEER: Martin Luther King, yeah.

SOMERSETT: Bustus Street (phonetic)

MILTEER: Yeah 530.

SOMERSETT: Oh Brown tried to get him huh?

MILTEER: Yeah.

SOMERSETT: Well, he will damn sure do it, I will tell you that. Well, that is why, look, you see, well, that is why we have to be so careful, you know that Brown is operating strong.

MILTEER: He ain't going for play you know.

SOMERSETT: That is right.

MILTEER: He is going for broke.

SOMERSETT: I never asked Brown about his business or anything, you know just what he told me, told us, you know. But after the conversation, and the way he talked to us, there is no question in my mind about who knocked the church off in Birmingham, you can believe that, that is the way I figured it.

MILTEER: That is right, it is about the only way you can figure it.

SOMERSETT: That is right.

MILTEER: Not being there, not knowing anything.

SOMERSETT: But just from his conversation, as you and me know him, but if they did it is their business, like you say (Milteer breaks in)

MILTEER: It is up to the individual.

SOMERSETT: That is right. They are individual operators, we don't want that within the party. Hitting this Kennedy is going to be a hard proposition, I tell you, I believe, you may have figured out a way to get him, you may have figured out the office building, and all that I don't know how them Secret Service Agents cover all them office buildings, or anywhere he is doing, do you know whether they do that or not?

MILTEER: Well, if they have any suspicion they do that of course. But without suspicion chances are that they wouldn't. You take there in Washington, of course it is the wrong time of the year, but you take pleasant weather, he comes out on the veranda, and somebody could be in a hotel room across the way there, and pick him off just like (fades out).

SOMERSETT: Is that right?

MILTEER: Sure disassemble a gun, you don't have to take a gun up there, you can take it up in pieces, all those guns come knock down, you can take them apart.

SOMERSETT: They have got damn, this boy was telling me yesterday about, they have got an explosive that you get out of the army, it is suppose to be like putty or something, you stick it up, induse a small fuse, you just stick it like that, he told me, and I think that is what happened in the church in Birmingham, they stuck this stuff somebody stuck it under the stens with a short fuse, and went on home. This boy is pretty smart, demolition is that what you call it?

MILTEER: Demolition, that is right.

SOMERSETT: I am going to talk with him some more.

MILTEER: Yeah I would.

SOMERSETT: I am going to talk with him some more, and find out a lot more about his operation, because he knows a hell of a lot.

MILTEER: You need a guy like that around, too. Where we can put our finger on him, when we want him.

SOMERSETT: Yeah. Well, you have got somebody up there in that country now, if you need him.

MILTEER: Well, we are going to have to get nasty first (not legible)

SOMERSETT: Yeah, get nasty.

MILTEER: We have got to be ready, we have got to be sitting on go, too.

SOMERSETT: Yeah, that is right.

MILTEER: There ain't any count down to it, we have just got to be sitting on go. Count down is alright for a slow prepared operation, but in an emergency operation, you have got to be sitting on go.

SOMERSETT: Boy, if that Kennedy gets shot, we have to know where we are at. Because you know that will be a real shake, if they do that.

MILTEER: They wouldn't leave any stone unturned there no way. They will pick up somebody within hours afterwards, if anything like that would happen just to throw the public off.

SOMERSETT: Oh, somebody is going to have to go to jail, if he gets killed.

MILTEER: Just like that Bruno Hauptman in the Lindberg case you know.

(Dials telephone)

SOMERSETT: "Hello, is Jim there?" "Has he gone to the office?' "Un hun, well, is he coming back home?" "Alright, I will do that, thank you." He has gone out to one of his apartment houses, and he will be back later. We will go see whatamacalit, he closes at 1:00 o'clock. We will go up and see Andres, and we will double back to Jim's (room noise)

MILTEER: Actually the only man we are interested in up at that place (room noise—not legible—door closes)[14]

The "Brown" discussed above was Jack William Brown, co-founder with brother Harry Leon Brown of the Tennessee-based Dixie Klans in October 1957, a month after Imperial Wizard Eldon Edwards expelled their Chattanooga klavern from the U.S. Klans based on its "alleged uncontrollable proclivity for violence." Jack Brown—who died from a heart attack in October 1965—was also an NSRP member, his followers suspected of killing black housewife Mattie Green with a bomb at her Ringgold, Georgia, home in May 1960. Lee McCloud, an Atlanta racist, had traveled with Milteer and Somersett to the Constitution Party's Indianapolis convention in October 1963. The garbled mention of "Connor McGintis" clearly referred to longtime anti–Semite Conde McGinley Sr., publisher of *Common Sense* from 1947 to 1972. "Jack Caulk," if that was his name, remains unidentified.[15]

The alleged bombing murder of two black employees at an Athens, Georgia, drugstore never happened, but two vaguely similar cases are known from Georgia history. The more recent happened on October 31, 1963, in Marietta—future site of NSRP national headquarters and the place where Columbians founder Emory Burke toiled at the Bell Bomber Plant during World War II. At 6:24 on Halloween night, an explosion shattered

Atherton's Pharmacy in Marietta, Georgia, following a gas explosion on October 31, 1963 (Library of Congress).

Atherton's Drug Store, killing six persons and injuring 50, disrupting a costumed parade on the city square. Six years earlier—on December 5, 1957—another gas leak was blamed for the explosion that killed 12 persons, wounding 20, in and around a Berry's Pharmacy at Villa Rica. In that case, three members of the town's municipal gas board were repairing a leaky basement pipe when it exploded. In neither case were any of the victims African Americans.[16]

Contradictory reports exist of how police and federal agents responded to Somersett's conversation with Milteer. Several accounts claim Secret Service agents canceled JFK's upcoming motorcade in Miami, while a 1976 memo to Senate investigators from James T. Burke, Assistant Director of the Secret Service (Protective Intelligence), denied any Miami motorcade was ever scheduled. Somersett later claimed Milteer phoned him from Dallas at 10:30 a.m. on November 22, 1963, saying JFK would "be there later that day and will not be visiting Miami again." Researchers allege Milteer then joined the crowd watching JFK drive to his death on Elm Street, captured for posterity in a snapshot taken from across the street. The House Select Committee on Assassinations gave that photo to a panel of experts, who discounted any serious resemblance based on calculations of Milteer's height and receding hairline.[17]

Somersett and Milteer met again on November 23, in Jacksonville, before traveling to a Klan rally in Columbia, South Carolina.[18] Upon his return to Miami, Somersett briefed his police contacts as follows:

> During the journey he told me that he was connected with an international underground. He said there would be a propaganda campaign put on how to prove to the Christian people of the world that the Jews, the Zionist Jews, had murdered Kennedy. He was very happy over it and shook hands with

me. He said, "Well, I told you so. It happened like I told you, didn't it? It happened from a window with a high-powered rifle." I said, "That's right. I don't know whether you were guessing or not, but you hit it on the head pretty good." He said, "Well, that is the way it was supposed to be done, and that is the way it was done." From the impression he gave me, and what he told me, the Oswald group was pro-Castro. This group was infiltrated by the patriot underground who arranged from there to have the execution carried out and drop the responsibility right into the laps of the Communists. I don't think there was any agreement with this little flimflam organization that Oswald belonged to.... I don't believe Milteer did it, but it might be a possibility that he knows who engineered it. The impression I get from him, I think the thing was set up to kill Mr. Kennedy in the South, in some southern state ...Milteer is too much enthused about it, before hand and after, not to know something about it.[19]

A separate FBI report states that Somersett met Milteer at Jacksonville's railroad station at 4:25 on November 23, before driving to Columbia. According to that document, Somersett—labeled a source of prior reliable information—described Milteer as "very jubilant over the death of President KENNEDY. MILTEER stated, 'Everything ran true to form. I guess you thought I was kidding you when I said he would be killed from a window with a high powered rifle.' When questioned as to whether he was guessing when he originally made the threat regarding President KENNEDY, MILTEER is quoted as saying, 'I don't do any guessing.'" En route to Columbia, Milteer also described visiting Imperial Wizard Robert Shelton at the UKA's Tuscaloosa headquarters on September 14, the night before Birmingham's deadly church bombing.[20]

Florida authorities planned on luring Milteer and Jack Brown to Miami after JFK's murder, hoping to catch both men on tape, but the plan went awry on December 4, when Somerset phoned Milteer in Georgia, learning that FBI agents had questioned Milteer and Brown concerning any knowledge they possessed of recent violence. A diary kept by Seymour Gelber—a circuit judge and one-time mayor of Miami Beach—noted: "Somersett is extremely concerned about this turn of events. Milteer did not accuse him of being an FBI informer, but inasmuch as the questioning appeared to be based on the statements made to Somersett, suspicion would inevitably rest on him.... There is no chance of getting Milteer and Brown to Miami now and there is a possibility they will show considerable caution in future conversations in Somersett's presence. I wonder why the FBI picked these people up after the President's assassination rather than before the act? All this manages to do is jeopardize the safety of our undercover agent. Based on the Milteer tape, I had anticipated such government action prior to the President's visit to Miami.... I did not expect it as an afterthought.... There is nothing of substantial value to be gained by this dramatic move except to scare hell out of Milteer, Brown and a few others.... It ruins our investigation and further weakens the effectiveness of the undercover agent, not only for us, but also for the FBI."[21]

In fact, Milteer was not "picked up" for questioning. An FBI report dated December 3, 1963, states that agents Donald Adams and Kenneth Williams interviewed Milteer at his home on November 27. Milteer "emphatically denied" making any threats against JFK or participating in the assassination, simultaneously claiming ignorance of Birmingham's September church bombing. Beyond that, Milteer freely discussed his travels to far-right conclaves: a New Orleans jaunt to attend a national meeting of the Congress of Freedom in April; a June trip to Dallas, asking radio propagandist Dan Smoot to run as the Constitution Party's vice presidential candidate in 1964; and the October trip to Indianapolis with Somersett and Lee McCloud, at the personal invitation of Curtis Dall. Milteer characterized himself as a "non dues paying member" of the Constitution Party,

Congress of Freedom, and Atlanta's Citizens' Council, while failing to mention the NSRP or the Klan.[22]

Somersett shed further light on Milteer's travels and connections during that same period. He spoke with Milteer after the Congress of Freedom rally in April, quoting Milteer's observation that "If the Congress of the U.S. doesn't cut the UN out, if it continues that way for twelve months, there has got to be some violence. You could tell if you had been there and stood around and seen the people, the expression on their faces, heard the way they talked. Those people are people of means, financially, and educationally. They are not there just for an ice cream party. This can't continue on, with the people financing these things, something must happen. I will bet my head on a chopping block there will be some people killed by this time next year and it will be in high places." In October, before visiting Indiana, Somersett met Milteer in Vero Beach, Florida, where Milteer vowed, "The National States Rights Party is going to move in Miami fast." In Indianapolis, serving as a director of the Constitution Party, Milteer persisted in calls for violence, formulating "plans to put an end to the Kennedy, King, Khrushchev dictatorship over our nation." At that same meeting, Somersett and another informer, Stanley Pospisil, described Jack Brown's admission of involvement in Birmingham's Sixteenth Street Baptist bombing, "virtually bragging about this role there." After hearing Somersett's report from Indiana, Miami police hatched their plan to capture Milteer's remarks on tape.[23]

Investigative journalists subsequently learned that Milteer had opened a bank account in Provo, Utah—more than 1,500 miles from his Georgia home—on July 31, 1963, in the name of his "common-law wife," Mrs. C. C. Cofield. His initial deposit of $5,000 was followed by two others, for $5,000 and $2,000 respectively, on August 20 and September 24. How that account might benefit Mrs. Cofield in Valdosta is anyone's guess. On January 31, 1964, someone closed the account, withdrawing all $12,000.[24]

William Somersett died on May 7, 1970, in Goldsboro, North Carolina, near his birthplace. At 3 a.m. that day, his best friend in Miami, one George Brackett, received a call from an anonymous stranger claiming to be at Walter Reed Hospital in Washington. The caller reported Somersett's death and claimed he was calling Brackett because a card in Somersett's wallet listed Brackett as an emergency contact. In truth, Somersett never visited Walter Reed, dying 272 miles south of that facility. The caller remains unidentified today, his motive unexplained.[25]

Milteer's death in Quitman, occurring on February 28, 1974—two days after his 72nd birthday—is equally shrouded in mystery. Officially, he died from "severe third degree burns on both lower extremities," suffered when a gas heater exploded in his bathroom on February 9. Authorities performed no autopsy, but mortician Marion Maxwell opined that the burns he saw on Milteer's corpse were partly healed and not severe enough to kill him. Compounding that riddle is a letter Milteer wrote on January 27, two weeks before the alleged explosion, describing an eerily similar injury. It read: "I had an accident wherein I knocked over a sauce pan of hot water on the floor into which I fell and the hot water burned the small of my back."[26]

After Milteer's death, his home was ransacked several times by unknown burglars. Once, a neighbor told Judge James R. Knight that several men in a truck bearing Texas license plates removed numerous boxes from the house in broad daylight. Miami journalist Dan Christensen reports that several days after Milteer's death, "a small cache of arms and ammunition was uncovered in his car." In 1976, while Milteer's property languished in probate with no living relatives to claim it, Christensen visited the house, recovering little of interest besides some fragments of unfinished correspondence.[27]

***

While J. Edgar Hoover adopted the "lone-nut assassin" line before Lee Oswald was charged with killing JFK, pressuring his agents—and later the Warren Commission—to adopt that tunnel-vision view of the case, actively suppressing evidence of Oswald's contacts with the Texas FBI, agents in the field pursued other leads. Connie Lynch rated interest, G-men reporting that he had been "speaking at Ku Klux Klan rallies during the last two months," in Jacksonville, Florida. Whether or not that absolved him of a trip to Texas on November 22, it must be acknowledged that Lynch generally limited his activism to rabble-rousing, letting others take the risks involved with direct action.[28]

Other rumbles of a potential threat had reached FBI ears as early as April 1963, when informant George Harding told agents of an eight-man team created to assassinate 300 officials in high government offices. The resultant memo says, "Harding claimed that the leaders in the group were Dr. Wesley Swift, James Shoup and others.... The second in command was a Colonel William Gale ... who was supposed to have been the youngest intelligence officer under MCARTHUR [sic]." Four months later, a Secret Service memo noted the arrest of Gale associate George King, Jr., for sale of illegal firearms. The report described King as "extreme right wing, hates Jews.... Emotionally unstable." Gale was also under surveillance, described in a Miami FBI memo dated October 27, 1963, as being "on the east Coast in the Southern part, exact location not given on important business." One day later, a garbled Miami police report quoted William Somersett as saying that "KENNETH GULF [sic, "Goff"] and COLONEL GALE are coming to Florida in an attempt to stir up the people down here; probably on the lower east coast. His information is that they want to train and recruit men for physical action." That trip was in progress when Somersett recorded Milteer's threats against JFK on November 9.[29]

On the very afternoon of JFK's assassination, a police officer in Richardson, Texas, phoned Dallas FBI agents with the name of a possible suspect: "Jimmy George Robinson, and other members of the white supremacist National States Rights Party because of their open hatred for President Kennedy." Oswald would not be charged with Kennedy's murder until 11:25 that night, but G-men ignored the lead, penning a comment on the Richardson lawman's report that read, "Not necessary to cover as true suspect located."[30]

Of course, "Jimmy George Robinson" was James *Chester* Robinson, born in 1939, formerly chief of the NSRP and owner of Chester's Restaurant in Montgomery, Alabama, listed as a resident of Garland, Texas, during 1963 and 1964, where he ran a small gas station between arrests for cross-burning and assault. The latter charge cost him $25 and court costs in June 1963. By early 1965 he was back in Alabama, assaulting Dr. King and two FBI agents at Selma.[31]

***

Once Lee Oswald was formally charged as JFK's lone assassin, the problem of trial and conviction briefly arose, settled—at least officially—when transplanted Chicago gangster Jack Ruby shot Oswald on live television, during Oswald's transfer from Dallas police headquarters to a safer lockup. The officer in charge of that bungled transfer—Lieutenant George Butler of Dallas, born in 1907—knew Ruby personally as a "friend" of law enforcement who furnished officers free drinks and "dates" with dancers at his notorious Carousel

Jack Ruby (right) shoots Lee Harvey Oswald in the Dallas Police Department's basement on November 24, 1963. Lieutenant George Butler reacts, standing to Oswald's right (Library of Congress).

strip club. In 1946 Butler confronted other Chicago mobsters invading Dallas, though reports vary as to whether he accepted bribes or was the point man for a Dallas P.D. sting against the gangsters. Either way, the mob endured, with Ruby branded the police department's "payoff man." By 1959 Butler had founded the Dallas Police Association, whose headquarters is named in his honor. More pertinent is Butler's reported affiliation with the Klan. In 1961, according to *Midlothian Mirror* publisher Penn Jones, Jr., Butler visited his office and "offered me the job of printing a regional newspaper under the auspices of the Ku Klux Klan. He told me that half of the Dallas police were members of the KKK."[32]

While Jones died in January 1998, and 1960s Dallas police involvement with the Klan is presently impossible to verify, we know Klansmen dominated Dallas life and politics during the 1920s, with the highest per capita Klan membership of any American city. At least 13,000 men joined the Dallas Klan, from a population of 160,000, while some 800 women joined the order's ladies' auxiliary. Congressional investigators found no klaverns based in Dallas during 1967, whatever that may prove, but paramilitary action by the Klan continued in the Lone Star state through the 1980s.[33]

As for Butler, history records he was suspended from duty for 30 days in 1941, for beating a black youth in custody. He was also a confidant of oil tycoon Haroldson Lafayette Hunt, and "handled personal investigative assignments for Hunt Oil" while drawing his police paychecks. Students of the JFK assassination note that Hunt's son, Nelson Baker Hunt, joined Edwin Walker to finance and distribute the notorious fliers branding JFK "Wanted for Treason" immediately prior to his assassination. While in charge of Oswald's transfer on November 24, 1963, Butler told colleagues, "He'll never make it to the street." Admiring journalists tout such prescience as "the kind of insight that made George Butler a legend." Skeptics view it as more evidence of a conspiracy.[34]

In passing, we should also mention that Roy Frankhouser, an NSRP stalwart and the UKA's Pennsylvania grand dragon, claimed he was subpoenaed to testify before the Warren Commission, concerning his alleged acquaintance with Oswald intimates Michael and Ruth Paine in Texas. That subpoena, Frankhouser alleged, was quashed by FBI headquarters on "national security grounds," shortly after two G-men visited his home and warned him, "If you release information on the Paines or the Commission, you'll be in deep trouble with the FBI."[35]

***

In 2012, nearly half a century after JFK's murder, ex–FBI agent Donald Adams—coauthor of the December 1963 memo in which Joseph Milteer "emphatically denied" threatening the president—published a book on the assassination, naming Milteer as a prime suspect. Among the revelations in that volume, titled *From an Office Building with a High-Powered Rifle*, we read that five hours after JFK's death, Atlanta's Special Agent in Charge James McMahon wired J. Edgar Hoover, as well as the Bureau's Dallas and Miami field offices, reporting Milteer's threats of November 9, then added, without attribution, that "Milteer's whereabouts at Quitman, Ga. [were] this date ascertained." Author Adams disputes that exoneration, noting that he personally visited Milteer's home at 4 p.m. on November 22, 1963, and found him absent. Neither was Milteer at any of his other "known haunts" in southern Georgia, until Adams finally traced him to his lover's house in Valdosta on November 27.[36]

Adams also disagrees with those—including the House Select Committee on Assassinations—who disregard an alleged photo of Milteer in Dealey Plaza, watching JFK's motorcade approach the murder site. While critics quibble over calculations of Milteer's height and placement of his hairline, Adams wrote, "I stood next to the man. I interviewed him and spent hours with him. There is no question in my mind. As soon as I saw that picture I almost fell off of my feet." Unfortunately, Adams did not see the photo until 1992, a decade after his retirement from the FBI. When he filed his report on Milteer with Agent Williams in December 1963, Adams also didn't know that Milteer's Miami remarks—so "emphatically denied" in person—had been recorded by police. Today Adams believes Joseph Milteer, while clearly not a triggerman in the assassination, was a key figure in the conspiracy leading to JFK's murder.[37]

***

Aside from the hated president's sudden elimination, NSRP headquarters had further cause for celebration as 1963 drew to a close. On December 16, represented by attorney Melvin Wulff—with support from the ACLU and the NAACP Legal Defense and Educational Fund—Edward Fields and Robert Lyons won their appeal against the city of Fairfield, Alabama, for banning a party rally there in October 1961. Liberal supporters argued, and the high court agreed, that injunctions against racist rallies would undoubtedly rebound against civil rights activists in the South.[38] The legal path was thereby cleared for action in the years to come, and the party took advantage of that triumph as the 1960s escalated into ever greater violence.

Chapter 8

A "segregated superbomb"

St. Augustine, Florida—America's oldest continuously occupied city—stands rooted in racial and religious violence. French Protestants came first, 244 slaughtered in 1865 by Spaniards who left a placard reading: "Hanged, not as Frenchmen, but as Lutherans and heretics." Their successors retaliated in 1567, executing 200 Spaniards and raising a sign: "Hanged, not as Spaniards, but as traitors, robbers, and murderers." Between those massacres and afterward, European explorers decimated Native American tribes. Francis Drake razed and looted the city in 1568—but always, survivors rebuilt and endured.[1]

St. Augustine's quadricentennial celebration loomed in 1965, preceded by years of preparation. The Kennedy administration donated $6 million ($46 million today) toward renovation of 70 historical landmarks, including a plaza some still called the Old Slave Market, and therein lay the rub. Black St. Augustinians looked back through history, and they were not amused. First, they asked JFK to withhold federal funding for the quadricentennial, since the money would be used "to celebrate 400 years of slavery and segregation in America's oldest city." Failing there, they struggled on at home.[2]

Dentist Robert Hayling moved to St. Augustine in 1960 and assumed leadership of its NAACP Youth Council in 1963. That June he allegedly told reporters, "We are not going to die like Medgar Evers. Passive resistance is no good in the face of violence. I and others of the NAACP have armed ourselves and will shoot first and ask questions later." (Hayling later denied saying it; white newsmen affirmed their reports.) Shooting began on July 1, wounding four blacks; the white youth who shot them was released on July 17 for "lack of evidence." Meanwhile, Sheriff Lawrence Davis, in office since 1949, and Police Chief Virgil Stuart, on the force since 1934, began arresting demonstrators. On August 3 Hayling wrote Washington again, complaining of "police state tactics."[3]

Though seemingly aloof, Washington listened. On August 16 the Florida Advisory Committee to the U.S. Commission on Civil Rights found widespread discontent among St. Augustine's blacks, no lines of communication with all-white officials, and a "repressive" atmosphere. The panel recommended cutting off quadricentennial funds and suspending federal contracts if segregation continued, and condemned discrimination by national unions. Closing, it dubbed St. Augustine a "segregated superbomb aimed at the heart of Florida's economy and political integrity—the fuse is short." Mayor Joseph Shelley countered, lamenting "the failure of the leaders of our nation [who] seek the minority vote by calling the [white] majority names."[4]

***

Into that atmosphere strode Connie Lynch. The Klan preceded him, two rival factions joined in June 1961 as the United Florida KKK, represented in St. Augustine by Klavern 519, aka the Ancient City Gun Club. The rival UKA arrived in early 1963. Despite warnings from Robert Shelton, Klansmen widely hailed Lynch as "a springboard to get where we want," known for "putting teeth" into white resistance. On July 17 he spoke at the first in a series of UFKKK rallies around Jacksonville and St. Augustine, led by Eunice "Gene" Fallaw, veering northward on August 17 to share a stage with Shelton and his dragons at Spartanburg, South Carolina. Congressional investigators later determined that Fallaw sought to join the UKA with a phalanx of defecting UFKKK members.[5]

On September 18, Lynch and Fallaw were back in Florida, staging a rally outside St. Augustine. Fallaw welcomed 400 attendees with a prayer—"Help us to be ready to fight, to shed blood if necessary, to maintain our way of life"—before Lynch sketched the "glorious history of the Klan," then segued to typical attacks on "Jew bastards from the Anti-Defamation League," "cotton-pickin', half-witted preachers" who claimed Jesus was Jewish, and integration ("if you mix ice cream and axle grease, you don't hurt the axle grease much at all, but you play hell with the ice cream"). Next he turned to Birmingham's recent church bombing.[6]

> I'll tell you people here tonight, if they can find those fellows, they ought to pin medals on them. Someone said, "Ain't it a shame that them little children was killed?"
>
> Well, they don't know what they are talking about. In the first place, they ain't little. They're 14 or 15 years old—old enough to have venereal diseases, and I'll be surprised if all of 'em didn't have one or more.
>
> In the second place, they weren't children. Children are little *people,* little *human beings,* and that means white people. There's little dogs and cats and apes and baboons, and there's also little niggers. But they ain't children. They're just little niggers.
>
> And in the third place, it wasn't no shame they was killed. Why? Because when I go out to kill rattlesnakes, I don't make no difference between little rattlesnakes and big rattlesnakes, because I know it is the nature of all rattlesnakes to be my enemies and to poison me if they can. So I kill 'em all, and if there's four less niggers tonight, then I say, "Good for whoever planted the bomb." We're all better off.[7]

Bringing his message home, Lynch railed, "I'll tell you something else. You've got a nigger in St. Augustine ought not to live ... that burr-headed bastard of a dentist. He's got no right to live at all, let alone walk up and down your streets and breathe the white man's free air. He ought to wake up tomorrow morning with a bullet between his eyes. If you were half the men you claim to be you'd kill him before sunup." Moments later, rally lookouts raised the cry of "Niggers!" dragging four black men from the shadows at gunpoint. Surrounded, Dr. Hayling, James Hauser, James Jackson and Clyde Jenkins watched Lynch leap from his stage, grab a pistol from his Cadillac and pass it to another Klansmen, before the mob closed in, interrogating and beating its captives. Observer Irwin Cheney, associate director of the Florida Council on Human Relations, slipped away to call authorities, and sheriff's deputies arrived to find Klansmen dousing their prisoners with gasoline. City apologists claimed the officers "rescued" Hayling's party and arrested four whites; in fact, they also jailed the victims, and only Hayling was convicted—on October 26, fined $100 for "assaulting" his attackers—while jurors acquitted the Klansmen. White politicians gloated that "very few" of the Kluxers "could be identified as citizens of St. Augustine."[8]

Klan fever gripped the area. When Lynch staged a second rally on September 19, he drew 2,500 spectators. Beginning on September 27 the *St. Augustine Record* announced every impending Klan meeting. Lynch moved on, landing in California by November, where he joined William Gale's CDL, leaving St. Augustine to the United Florida Klan and its Ancient City Gun Club.[9]

Reportedly founded in 1952, the club was led in 1963 by Holsted "Hoss" Manucy, a hog farmer and convicted bootlegger released that year from federal prison. Manucy denied Klan membership on grounds that he was Catholic, but congressional investigators disagreed and Jesse Stoner admitted there was "some overlap" in membership between the club and Klan. Both groups held meetings at the local Surfside Casino, or at Sheriff Davis's county jail, where four Klansmen served as full-time deputies and a reserve of "special" officers encompassed most of the gun club, including its ex-convict leader.[10]

After Connie Lynch moved west, Manucy's men began armed patrols of Lincolnville, the city's black ghetto, sometimes firing randomly. On October 22, nightriders firebombed homes of three black families whose children had integrated county schools. Three days later return fire killed vigilante William Kinard as he rode with others, shotgun in hand, a block from the home of NAACP officer Goldie Eubanks, Sr. On October 28, white gunmen shot up two black nightclubs, a market, two homes, and several cars. Lynch returned next day, officiating at Kinard's funeral with Klan pallbearers, then led another rally, followed by more drive-by shootings and a hand grenade thrown at the Harlem Club. Prosecutors jailed Eubanks, his son and a neighbor in connection with Kinard's death, but later dropped the charges. Mayor Shelley complained of reporters giving his town a "raw deal," adding, "We are about as desegregated as we can get. And things are very quiet."[11]

And so it continued. On December 16 a grand jury blamed "two outside militant elements, the Ku Klux Klan and Negro civil rights workers," for all local violence. On January 21, during a PTA meeting, arsonists torched a car owned by Charles Brunson, whose son attended a formerly white school,. A second family's house burned on February 7, and gunmen riddled Goldie Eubanks's home the next night, killing his dog. The segregationist *St. Augustine Record* opined that it was "high time" for some law enforcement, but officials kept mum while terrorists burned a black minister's car.[12]

***

On February 16 the spotlight shifted north to Jacksonville, where United Florida Klansmen and a Hoosier transplant, William Rosecrans, bombed the home of six-year-old Donald Godfrey, recently enrolled at a white school. Prosecutors indicted Rosecrans and five local Klansmen: Barton Griffin, Robert Pittman Gentry (present in Birmingham when Sixteenth Street Baptist was bombed), Jacky Don Harden, Donald Eugene Spegal, and Willie Eugene Wilson (doubling as Jacksonville's NSRP leader). Rosecrans fled to St. Augustine, where terrorists knew they could trust the police: Sheriff Davis hired Klansmen (including four Godfrey defendants), attended their rallies and hosted meetings in his jail, and also loaned cars to visiting knights (including Gentry, Griffin and Spegal). With his fourth election approaching, Davis bragged, "I went out to Elk's Rest to talk with those niggers. Niggers, that's what I called them. I told them I didn't want a single nigger vote, because I didn't want to beholden to them [sic] for any election." Virgil Stuart was no better. Police chief since 1958, he lived by the same racist code as St. Augustine's other white civic fathers.[13]

Rosecrans ran out of luck on February 26, when dynamite derailed two freight trains on the strike-bound Florida East Coast Railway. Craving a reward offered for the bomber's arrest, a confused Hoss Manucy fingered Rosecrans for FBI agents. Rosecrans passed a polygraph on that crime, but implicated himself in the Godfrey bombing, naming conspirators from Jacksonville's Robert E. Lee Klavern. The accused retained Matt Murphy and Jesse Stoner to defend them, while brother Klansmen schemed to kill Rosecrans. They failed, but his confession earned him seven years in prison.[14]

On May 3 Klansmen paraded through Jacksonville, protesting a new civil rights bill that had passed the House and moved on to the Senate. Afterward, Jesse Stoner led a rally north of town, sharing the dais with Bart Griffin, whose home had been firebombed days earlier. Critics suspected Griffin, staging a bid for sympathy, but Stoner had other ideas: "I suspect that niggers bombed it with FBI consent or the FBI bombed it itself. Even if they didn't, they set him up as a target." As for blacks in general, Stoner said, "People in other parts of the county like to think of niggers as human beings because they have hands and feet. So do apes and gorillas have hands and feet. If a nigger has a soul I never read about it in the Bible. The only good nigger is a dead nigger."[15]

***

In the Ancient City, Dr. Hayling knew he needed help. On March 6 he met Martin Luther King at an SCLC conference in Orlando, requesting aid. "Spring Project" volunteers began arriving on March 23—a "mass invasion" in white terms—and arrests escalated. Klansmen rallied at Vilano Beach on May 15, and Dr. King arrived three days later, promising a "long, hot summer" for the city he called "a small Birmingham." Blacks staged their first night march from the Old Slave Market on May 28, attacked by club-wielding whites while police kept their distance.[16]

Chaos spiraled from there. Drive-by gunmen peppered Dr. King's beach cottage on June 8, whereupon authorities banned night marches and Sheriff Davis called for all "law abiding and responsible men" to become "special" deputies. Blacks stoned police cars and smashed a "white" grocery's windows. On June 9, federal judge Bryan Simpson overturned the ban on nocturnal demonstrations. Two days later, integrationists "tested" the Monson Motor Lodge by leaping into its pool; "under great stress and excitement," owner James Brock doused them with (harmless) muriatic acid and the swimmers went to jail, along with Dr. King.[17]

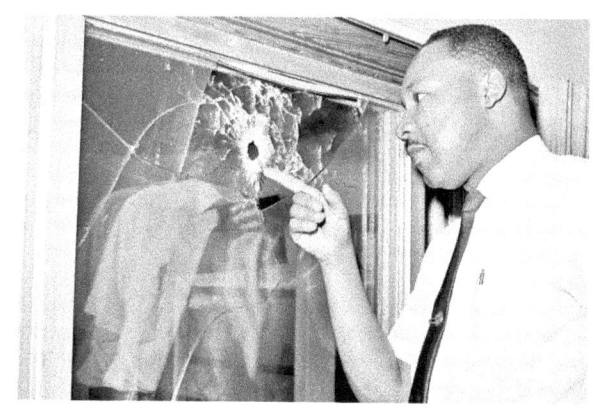

Dr. Martin Luther King, Jr., indicates gunfire damage inflicted by nightriders on his SCLC beach cottage in St. Augustine. The house was later set afire by terrorists (Library of Congress).

Stoner and Lynch appeared the same day, organizing a white protest march into all-black Lincolnville on June 12, declaring, "We're not gonna be put in chains by no civil rights bill, now or any other time!" ("Respectable" racists accused them of "perfectly coordinating" actions to aid Dr. King.) On June 15, Governor Farris Bryant invoked emergency powers to create a "Special Police Force" from six state agencies, superseding Sheriff Davis and city police. Whites attacked "wade-in" demonstrators at a public beach. On

James Brock, proprietor of St. Augustine's embattled Monson Motor Lodge in 1964, pours muriatic acid into the pool during an integrated "swim-in" on June 11, 1964. He later desegregated the motel, whereupon white terrorists firebombed it (Library of Congress).

Jesse Stoner (with UKA Grand Dragon Don Cothran) rouses a racist crowd in St. Augustine, Florida (Florida State Archives).

June 18, grand jurors called for a 30-day moratorium on black protests "to demonstrate good faith," refused by Dr. King. Two days later, Governor Bryant defied court orders, banning night marches again.[18]

June's *Thunderbolt* headline—"Gov. Farris Bryant, Liar and Betrayer"—unnerved Florida party chairman Dewey M. Taft of Tampa. Addressing reporters, Taft said his appointment was temporary, expiring on December 31, and stressed "that I accept no responsibility for the policies of the National States Rights Party which are set by the national officers in Birmingham, nor for anything appearing in *The Thunderbolt*, the party's organ published in Birmingham."[19]

St. Augustine approached a state of all-out war. Beach attacks proliferated, some led by Neuman Britton, recently arrived from California. When police clubbed a white rioter, Hoss Manucy moaned, "I can't understand why any white citizen would want to protect niggers against white people." On June 22, Judge Simpson ordered Governor Bryant, Sheriff Davis, and others to appear four days hence, explaining why he shouldn't hold them in contempt. The city's worst riot to date came on June 25, when Lynch advised, "If it takes violence to preserve the Constitution, I say all right. I favor violence to preserve the white race anytime, anyplace, anywhere. Now it may be some niggers are gonna get

St. Augustine's triumvirate of terrorism hold a press conference on June 25, 1964, promising more violence to come. From left, Jesse Stoner, Holsted "Hoss" Manucy and Connie Lynch (Florida State Archives).

killed in the process, but when war's on, that's what happens." Afterward, Stoner, Lynch, and Manucy staged a press conference, Hoss promising, "Violence will continue as long as Negroes continue to use the public beach, which has been used by whites for hundreds of years." Governor Bryant dispatched more Special Police, bringing the force's strength to 235 in "a very explosive and very tense situation." Next day, racists beat a white Miami youth who jeered Jesse Stoner. On June 30, Governor Bryant sought a truce by falsely announcing creation of a biracial committee to study local problems, and a telegram arrived from former Black Muslim Malcolm X, reading: "We have been witnessing with great concern the vicious attacks of the white races [sic] against our poor defenseless people there in St. Augustine. If the Federal government will not send troops to your aid, just say the word and we will immediately dispatch some of our brothers there to organize self-defense units among our people and the Ku Klux Klan will then receive a taste of its own medicine. The day of turning the other cheek to those brute beasts is over."[20]

After spiking in late June, mayhem slowly declined. SCLC leaders left St. Augustine on July 1, and Governor Bryant created a real biracial commission, one day before President Johnson signed the Civil Rights Act of 1964. Demonstrations and white assaults resumed on Independence Day, while whites picketed newly integrated establishments. Alonzo Manucy, nephew of Hoss, marched outside the Monson Motor Lodge with a sign reading: "Niggers ate and slept here, would you?" Jesse Stoner told James Brock he ordered the picket, smirking, "We're just trying to get you some nigger business." Daily Klan rallies convened at the City Baking Company on State Road 207. Someone firebombed Brock's motel on July 24, while police jailed Stoner, Lynch, and three others—Klansmen Paul Cochran, Bill Coleman, and Bart Griffin—for illicit cross-burning. Cochran faced an additional charge of wearing an illegal mask. Stoner's FBI rap sheet lists no disposition, suggesting dismissal of the charge.[21]

Things went badly for Hoss Manucy in Judge Simpson's court. Grilled about harassment charges on July 25, Manucy pled the Fifth Amendment 33 times. On August 5, Simpson enjoined Manucy and his gun club from discouraging integration "by any threat or action." On October 14, Simpson ordered Hoss to produce a list of club members, then jailed him for contempt nine days later, when Manucy refused. Scattered shootings and assaults continued through early December, but the worst had passed, leaving Florida's "segregated superbomb" more or less intact, at least physically.[22]

***

In Jacksonville, Klansmen faced trial for the Godfrey bombing, defended by Jesse Stoner and UKA Imperial Klonsel Matt Murphy (also an NSRP member). Informer Gary Rowe later said that beforehand, UKA leaders offered to kill witness William Rosecrans for the UFKKK, nominating three Alabama knights later convicted of slaying a white civil rights worker in 1965. That effort failed, but they need not have worried. With *The Thunderbolt* branding the trials a "conspiracy against Jacksonville whites," Rosecrans earned praise for recanting his confession, claiming FBI coercion, and jurors acquitted one defendant on July 5, 1964, followed by the other four on November 25. Rosecrans went on to serve his time alone, living in fear of reprisals, while the rest went free.[23]

And officialdom began rewriting history. On July 31, 1964, a preliminary report from Florida's Legislative Investigating Committee accused the NSRP of playing a key role in recent violence (true), broadly hinting that it secretly served Dr. King (entirely unsubstantiated). The panel deemed Connie Lynch "accomplished at whipping a crowd into a riotous condition," and recommended prosecution for perjury when he applied for a Florida driver's license, denying prior traffic accidents when he had been convicted of a hit-and-run in California. Dewey Taft dodged a committee summons, but the panel proceeded without him, writing: "The committee calls to your [the legislature's] attention the activities of one organization whose name we believe to be misleading, and whose principles we believe to be contrary to the precepts of good citizenship. Today's hawkers of hate have made capital of hiding behind the facade of conservatism and waving the banner of anti-Communism. With their bigotry thus cloaked, they have made converts who unwittingly serve to undermine the very causes in which they devoutly believe."[24]

Closer to home, on September 27, the *St. Augustine Record* decried "the lash of federal judicial infringement on the rights of citizens and the constitutional powers of local and state courts." Specifically, Judge Simpson had removed the trials of 500 black protesters to Jacksonville, on grounds that they could not obtain fair trials in St. Johns County. On January 7, *Record* editor A. H. Tebault Jr., blamed all his city's troubles on "national publicity." Two months later, Chief Stuart sent a report to the state legislature, marginalizing Dr. Hayling as a Svengali of "young negro [*sic*] troublemakers" and "hoodlum followers," while blaming last spring's "invasion" on the National Council of Churches. He was especially incensed that "young teen-age white girls began to show up dating and mixing socially with negro male students from Florida Memorial College." The state's Legislative Investigating Committee agreed in August, noting that FMC's student body furnished the SCLC "a ready and enthusiastic supply of pickets and demonstrators who already had gained considerable experience during the summer of 1963." Most distressing were "imported young white girls strolling through the Plaza arm in arm with Negroes or imported white men escorting Negro women," whose appearance provoked a few "inexcusable" attacks. As for the other violence, the panel blamed Judge Simpson.[25]

St. Augustine would grudgingly desegregate, but change came slowly. Sheriff Davis held office until 1970, when Governor Claude Kirk removed him based on allegations of brutality. Jurors cleared him at trial, and state legislators "exonerated" him in a separate hearing, but his time had passed. Running for reelection in 1972, Davis lost to a rival and vanished from public life. Chief Stuart remained as chief of police until 1981, each day donning a badge whose inscription read: "Commemorating the triumph of the white primary."[26]

And as the smoke cleared, Connie Lynch and Jesse Stoner moved to other battlefields.

CHAPTER 9

Dirty Wars

St. Augustine was not the party's only field of action during 1964. In January, FBI agents monitored a "right-wing meeting" chaired by Max Nelsen at Chicago's Fort Dearborn Hotel. Nelsen warned attendees, "We are today in the same position that the American Indian was in 100 years ago. We are fighting for the survival of a way of life, and we are now doing it in the same stupid way that the Indian did, and he lost." Delegates hoped to unite Ed Fields and George Rockwell as allies, prompting a Chicago meeting of the parties on January 12. With Rockwell absent, unity fell through, but Fields appeared, delivering what an informer called "the same old story" on blacks and Jews. G-men placed Fields in Chicago through mid–February, vainly seeking an Illinois party chairman.[1]

Ironically, party unity of a sort *was* forged in Chicago, without either leader's input. Informers claimed the NSRP's Chicago chief and "all members" belonged to the ANP, doing little on their own. Spies reported that the local NSRP "does not function as an organization. If, in fact, it does exist, its make up is most informal and its activities are unscheduled and most irregular."[2]

The same could not be said elsewhere. From headquarters, Fields published *What World Famous Men Said About the Jews,* and 200 delegates gathered in Louisville on February 29, cheering keynote speaker Matt Murphy. With Ned Dupes—"a sincere but slightly senile old man," in one critic's estimation—presiding on March 1, members chose John Kasper as their presidential candidate, with Jesse Stoner as his running mate.[3]

Later in March, California State Organizer James P. Thornton, recent author of *The Real Hate Mongers,* replaced James Warner as associate editor of *The Thunderbolt.* The anonymous, unverifiable *DeGuello Report* claims "Warner talked one of Fields' secretaries into thinking that he planned to marry her. The two disappeared from the NSRP headquarters (along with a copy of Fields' mailing list) and the next thing Fields heard about it was a phone call from his secretary saying that Warner had left her stranded and asking for bus fare home." Warner landed in California, founded the "marginally profitable" Sons of Liberty, briefly joined Willis Carto to publish Carto's *Washington Observer* newsletter, helped anthropologist Roger Pearson edit Carto's *Western Destiny,* then worked on Pearson's quarterly magazine *The New Patriot* before allegedly stealing Pearson's mailing list. Soon, Warner joined Wesley Swift's Christian Defense League, helping produce its *CDL Report* and *Christian Vanguard.*[4]

After his 1963 high school suspension in Mobile, Thomas Tarrants sought scapegoats, listening to tapes from Wesley Swift and poring over *The Protocols of the Learned Elders of Zion.* After joining the John Birch Society, he visited John Crommelin at home and shifted to the NSRP, frequenting its local office. On June 11, 1964, police caught him with member Robert M. Smith, carrying an illegal sawed-off shotgun in their car. Tarrants claimed the weapon, pled guilty, and received probation, taking one step closer to a career in terrorism. He next founded a tiny Christian Military Defense League, hatching plots that ranged from "distributing the dismembered body of a key black leader around the black community to setting booby traps in the black communities of Mobile." Police seized another shotgun from Tarrants in August, during a fight with a black gas station attendant in Prichard, but they pressed no charges. After he daubed a synagogue with swastikas and made threatening calls to a rabbi, his mother took him to see a psychiatrist, worried that Thomas was "something less than sane."[5]

Around the same time, judging Birmingham to be a burnt-out battleground, the party moved its headquarters to Marietta, Georgia. Identified leaders included National Chairman Ned Dupes, National Vice Chairman Ann Bishop, National Organizer Oren Potito, National Coordinator Robert Bowling, Information Director Ed Fields, and Secretary-Treasurer Bernice Settles. Marietta was a providential choice: seat of Klan-friendly Cobb County, home to Jesse Stoner, site of Leo Frank's 1915 lynching, and the place where Emory Burke built army bombers during World War II.[6]

Party Youth Leader Jerry Dutton skipped the move, quit the party with *Thunderbolt* associate editor James Thornton and Alabama State Director James Robert McDaniel Jr., stayed in Birmingham, and revived his former National White Americans Party as the American States Rights Party, publishing *The White American* and adopting the slogan "Racial Purity is America's Security." FBI reports say Georgia organizer Albert DeShazo followed Dutton's example, leaving the NSRP with "many local members" around the same time. At first, the defectors blamed their move on Ed Fields and his "defeatist attitude, saying he "had no intention of actually organizing a political party capable of winning control of America away from the Jews." Later, they cited his "illegal" sex life, perhaps referring to unfounded rumors of homosexuality or tales that Fields's "second wife" had followed him from Louisville to Birmingham with their illegitimate daughter. The party's budget topped out at $3,892.41 in 1965, nearly all spent on print propaganda. In spring 1966 the ASRP reclaimed its old NWAP title, Dutton rivaling Fields in rank as its Information Director, failing in his bid to join the Alabama House of Representatives. In June 1967 Dutton's group rejected a proposed merger with Rockwell's ANP. Despite initial qualms among NSRP leaders, the new party never caught on and dissolved by 1970.[7]

***

April 1964 brought an order for NSRP members to sever all ties with the Minutemen. Founded in June 1960, by 10 Missourians who tired of endless talk from the John Birch Society, the new paramilitary group stockpiled arms and drilled against the coming "communist invasion" of America by Chinese troops concealed in Mexico. Leader Robert Bolivar DePugh, born in April 1923, studied *Mein Kampf* in high school and opposed U.S. entry into World War II, but joined the army in 1942, then was discharged for "medical" reasons in 1944.[8] More specifically, the report read:

> Soldier is unable to perform duty due to anxiety, nervousness and mental depression. This condition is chronic and for three years has been attended with vague auditory hallucinations and mild ideas of reference. Patient has had vague hallucinatory experiences for the past three years. In a crowd he seems to hear someone call "DePugh," but can't identify the caller.... There is a paranoid trend to his thinking.... Diagnosis: psychoneurosis, mixed type, severe, anxiety and depressive features, schizoid personality and incipient schizophrenia.[9]

DePugh, an acquaintance of William Gale, patterned his group on Gale's California Rangers, which made it appealing to Klansmen and Nazis. In 1961 a meeting occurred at the Little Rock home of a national NSRP leader, to found a Minutemen chapter. DePugh appeared as a featured speaker at the party's national convention in September 1962, touting the urgency of guerrilla training, but the relationship soured 19 months later, when party headquarters warned all members to quit the Minutemen on grounds that "the right wing must come to power by use of the ballot box." DePugh's publication, *On Target,* calling the party "pseudo–Nazi," led by "a bunch of tin-horn Hitlers," and replied: "For the information of the NSRP leaders, we have no desire to 'come to power.'"[10]

Some party members, like compulsive joiners Roy Frankhouser, Frank Rotella, and Connie Lynch (Minuteman #C41412), ignored the April order. When Minutemen western regional coordinator Troy Houghton sought to delay a jail sentence in November 1964, party associate Bertrand Comparet represented him in court. Two years later, when New York state police jailed 20 Minutemen on conspiracy charges in October 1966, seizing an arsenal of weapons and explosives, one of those detained was longtime Klansman Robert Bagwell, bearing the NSRP's thunderbolt tattoo. As late as October 1969, Jesse Stoner tried to visit DePugh at Leavenworth prison—held for firearms violations and conspiracy to rob banks—but officials rebuffed him, as Stoner wasn't DePugh's lawyer of record.[11]

***

The Arkansas party held its small 1964 state convention at the home of Thomas J. Bardin, nominating grocer Kennedy Hurst as its gubernatorial candidate. In August Hurst told reporters, "I won't put out no steam until September, but by that time, I'll know which way the wind is blowing and I'll really start to huff." In fact, his steam ran out, and by September's end he'd quit the race.[12]

John Crommelin lowered his political sights in May 1964, challenging 13-term incumbent congressman George Grant in Alabama's 2nd District. Although defeated, polling 21,469 ballots out of 69,125 cast in the two-man race, Crommelin wounded Grant badly enough that GOP rival William Dickinson unseated him in November.[13]

In June, William Gale opposed Edwin Reineke in the Republican primary, seeking a seat from southern California's 27th congressional district. Defeated once again, with 12,092 of 38,609 votes cast, Gale channeled his energy into reactivating the CDL, "in limbo" since 1959. Incorporating officers included former Silver Shirt Richard Girnt Butler as president; Bertrand Comparet, vice president; American Committee to Free Cuba board member Steven Foote, western regional director; and John Crommelin, eastern regional director. Wesley Swift maintained a guiding hand until his death in 1970. Butler decamped to Idaho three years later, to lead the Aryan Nations, leaving James Warner to head the CDL.[14]

Far-right voters staked their main hopes on 1964's presidential race. While some admired the NSRP's ticket, more leaned toward George Wallace, embarking on his first run for the White House as a dark horse Democrat. Wallace had announced his plan to oppose incumbent JFK at a Dallas convention, days before Kennedy's assassination, and maintained his resolve when Lyndon Johnson occupied the Oval Office. Eyeing Democratic primaries, Wallace said, "If I ran outside the South and got 10 percent, it would be a victory. It would shake their eyeteeth in Washington." In fact, he did much better, winning one-third of the vote in Wisconsin, almost 30 percent in Indiana, and 43 percent

A demonstration against GOP presidential nominee Barry Goldwater following a Klan endorsement of his candidacy (Library of Congress).

in Maryland—where Wallace said, "If it hadn't been for the nigger bloc vote, we'd have won it all." Overall, he banked 672,984 primary votes (10.8 percent) against 1,106,999 for incumbent LBJ.[15]

Still, Wallace realized he could not actually win the race. Before Republicans nominated Barry Goldwater in July 1964, Alabama's governor tried to learn if Goldwater, as president, would seek repeal of the 1964 Civil Rights Act (which he voted against in the Senate), and offered to change parties if Goldwater would take him on as running mate. Instead, Goldwater chose former New York congressman William Miller, earning a standing ovation at the GOP convention when he said, "I would remind you that extremism in the defense of liberty is no vice. And let me remind you also that moderation in the pursuit of justice is no virtue." That alone won Goldwater Robert Shelton's endorsement, despite Goldwater's Jewish ancestry and Miller's Catholicism. (Rejected by his presidential choice, Shelton huffed, "That's his privilege.") Many southern Democrats followed the Klan's lead in November, deserting their traditional Democratic roots to hand Goldwater Alabama, Georgia, Louisiana, Mississippi and South Carolina, but the only other state he carried was his native Arizona. Johnson crushed him.[16]

Lost in the LBJ landslide, Kasper and Stoner polled a mere 6,953 vote—all from Arkansas and Kentucky—out of 70,629,884 ballots cast on November 3. Even so, Stoner struck a familiar tone, telling an Anniston rally that when it came to blacks, "the only good ones are dead ones." In Montana, Butte carpenter Jack Gunderson ran for the state's lone congressional seat on the NSRP ticket, losing a three-way race with 644 votes out of 120,908 cast. Humbled by defeat, John Kasper retired from politics and public life, began calling himself "Fred," and divorced twice, after siring several children.[17]

On November 28–29, 1964, the NSRP convened in Mobile, at the Admiral Semmes Hotel, to elect new national officers. Around the same time, George Rockwell wearied of his feud with Ed Fields and *The Thunderbolt*, filing a defamation suit against his rivals. Matt Murphy represented Fields in an exchange of letters, warning Fields that a trial would cost him at least $2,500, win or lose. Rockwell settled out of court for a retraction of various accusations against him, plus $1,000 in damages.[18]

***

Unnoticed in the heat of politics and litigation, the FBI prepared its own guerrilla war against the racist right. Launched on September 2, 1964, as "COINTELPRO—WHITE HATE GROUPS," the program targeted 17 Klans and nine affiliated organizations: the Mobile-based Alabama States Rights Party; Rockwell's ANP; Miami's Council of Statehood, aka "Freeman"; Baltimore's Fighting American Nationalists; the NSRP; the National Renaissance Party; Miami's United Freedom; Tampa's Viking Youth of America; and Chicago's White Youth Corps. Director Hoover demanded field office recommendations for potential action "on or before" October 15.[19]

COINTELPRO—Bureau shorthand for "*Counter Intel*ligence *Program*"—was not a new idea. Launched in 1956 against the Communist Party USA, it expanded to include the Socialist Workers Party in 1960. The lawless programs included FBI standards such as warrantless wiretaps and bugging, with wholesale theft of mail, plus other "dirty tricks" including frame-ups, anonymous letters and phone calls designed to spark tension within target groups, and insertion of *agents provocateur* to foment criminal violence. One of Hoover's strangest efforts was "Operation Hoodwink," trying in vain to provoke lethal violence between American Communists and the Mafia. It failed, but similar efforts targeting black militants produced several murders across the county.[20]

While the FBI devoted only 15 percent of its total COINTELPRO efforts toward the "White Hate" program, reserving most of its energy for "leftists" and minorities, Hoover still demanded urgent action from his men (there were no female agents at the time). The program's inaugurating memo read:

> The purpose of this program is to expose, disrupt and otherwise neutralize the activities of the various Klans and hate organizations, their leadership and adherents. The activities of these groups must be followed on a continuous basis so we can take advantage of all opportunities for counterintelligence and also inspire action in instances where circumstances warrant. The devious maneuvers and duplicity of these groups must be exposed to public scrutiny through the cooperation of reliable

FBI Director J. Edgar Hoover (addressing Congress, with second-in-command Clyde Tolson) ordered an illegal FBI "counterintelligence campaign" against white hate groups in September 1964 (Library of Congress).

news media sources, both locally and at the Seat of Government. We must frustrate any effort of the groups to consolidate their forces or to recruit new or youthful adherents. In every instance, consideration should be given to disrupting the organized activity of these groups and no opportunity should be missed to capitalize upon organizational and personal conflicts of their leadership.[21]

To that end, the FBI paid infiltrators, planted or fabricated news items, stole records and mailing lists, circulated defamatory rumors, produced mocking cartoons, encouraged its civilian spies to destroy marriages by seducing the wives of target group members, and indulged in childish pranks such as canceling hotel reservations for scheduled conventions. Some entire klaverns were led by FBI "moles," producing mass defections from various Klans. In the worst cases, far-right terrorists were spurred to violence against "leftists" by the Bureau, and at least one Klansman falsely accused of informing was murdered in Mississippi.[22]

COINTELPRO—WHITE HATE began in the Magnolia State, under pressure from President Johnson, after Klansmen murdered three civil rights workers—two of them white northerners—in June 1964. From there, it spread nationwide, suspected by Ed Fields and Jesse Stoner, while George Rockwell seemingly remained oblivious. To the end of his life, Rockwell remained enamored of the "patriotic" Bureau, writing: "ONLY the Federal Bureau of Investigation [stands] between America (and therefore the World)—and Communist total victory! Heil Hoover!" That stance spawned his feud and ultimate lawsuit against the NSRP, whose leaders branded him a Bureau stooge. Meanwhile, Stoner and sidekick Connie Lynch incessantly denounced the "Federal Bureau of Integration," deriding Hoover's agents as "nigger babysitters and haters of white men." Unable to punish Lynch with federal charges, G-men settled for telling local police that his driver's license had expired.[23]

Within a few short years, the Bureau's efforts would advance to bribing turncoats in the party, landing some members in prison, while guerrilla war between the feds and fascists claimed at least one life. On occasion, G-men sent data on black militants to NSRP headquarters, heedless of what action might result against them. In Mississippi, they also mailed Klan literature and "any other literature that can be obtained from organizations having an extreme hatred of black people" to black activists. By 1969 surveillance expanded to include "informant coverage of the Klan, White Hate Groups, and white ghetto areas," opening files on "unaffiliated white racial extremists" and "neighborhood groups" in suburbs of large cities, particularly if "these groups are known to sponsor demonstrations against integration and against the bussing of Negro students to white schools." At the same time, Bureau headquarters sympathized with their white targets, advising field offices that since such groups operated "on principles of fear rather than hate," investigation must remain "discreet." Hoover revealed his bias in March 1965, telling reporters, "White citizens are primarily decent, but frightened for their lives. The colored people are quite ignorant, mostly uneducated."[24]

CHAPTER 10

Ballots and Bullets

St. Augustine took its toll on both sides. Connie Lynch returned to California, preaching at Wesley Swift's church and promoting the Christian Defense League. In February 1965 he and Neuman Britton applied to use San Bernardino's Civic Auditorium for a joint rally of the CDL and NSRP, taking advantage of the party's latest recruiting drive. California's attorney general called the party "largely a one-man project" (Ed Fields), but the state's Senate Factfinding Subcommittee on Un-American Activities took a contradictory view, saying: "This organization is, in our opinion, more potentially dangerous than any of the American Nazi groups, as it is interested in activities that are far more vigorous and direct than the picketing that has become so popular in this country during the past few years."[1]

In June the California party issued a leaflet pleading the case of Frank Lollar Britton, publisher of *The American Nationalist* newspaper from Inglewood since 1952, serving one year to life at Folsom on the "insignificant charge" of trying to bribe a policeman. That case allegedly sprang from Britton's arrest for "a minor street infraction," later dismissed in court. Furthermore, "The last parole officer to review his case was a Negro, who turned Britton down." Jesse Stoner promised a speaking tour to aid Britton and promote statewide recruiting, but the party's main boost came from Los Angeles, where the Watts riot raged from August 11 to 17, leaving 34 persons dead (most shot by police), 1,032 injured, and 3,438 arrested, with property damage exceeding $40 million. Two months later, writing in *The Thunderbolt*, Neuman Britton claimed "rapid" party growth, gloating that white Californians "are more against negroes than are the people of the South."[2]

***

Recuperating after Florida, Dr. King cast his eyes toward Alabama once again. There, young SNCC volunteers, working with the Dallas County Voters League, pressed white authorities to register black voters in Selma, birthplace of Bull Connor and the state's first Citizens' Council. They faced Sheriff Jim Clark, an ex-rancher appointed by Governor James Folsom in 1955 to replace an incumbent who died in office. Elected on his own in 1958 and 1962, Clark wore a "Never" button to announce his stance on civil rights and filled his "special posse" with Klansmen and NSRP members, à la Sheriff Davis in St. Augustine.[3]

Barely 2 percent of Selma's African American majority was registered to vote when King arrived on January 2, 1965, determined to provoke passage of new voting rights legislation. Police Chief Wilson Baker, Clark's bitter rival, sought to emulate Laurie Pritchett's style from Albany, but Clark and Judge Thomas Werth Thagard preferred clubs and cattle prods. King's first attempt to register new voters, on January 18, met stony opposition at the county courthouse, where George Rockwell appeared, challenging King to a public debate. Politely rebuffed, Rockwell faced taunts from NSRP member James Robinson, who called out, "Let's have some vaudeville, Rockwell?"—a reference to Rockwell's stage-performing parents—then accused Rockwell of working for the Jews and FBI. Later, as King's party registered at the Hotel Albert, Robinson attacked King from behind, punching him twice and kicking him in the groin. Charged with assault, Robinson paid a $100 fine and received a 60-day jail sentence.[4]

NSRP member James Robinson (hand raised) interrupts a confrontation between George Rockwell and Martin Luther King in Selma, January 15, 1965 (National Archives).

James Robinson (facing camera) attacks Dr. King (in hat) at Selma's Albert Hotel, January 15, 1965 (Library of Congress).

Aside from King's scuffle, reporters paid little attention to Selma before February 18, when state troopers attacked demonstrators in nearby Marion, fatally wounding marcher Jimmy Lee Jackson. (In 2010 his killer pled guilty to manslaughter and served five months in prison.) With Dr. King back in Atlanta, SNCC and SCLC officers tried to lead a march from Selma to Montgomery on March 7, protesting black disfranchisement and police brutality. Al Lingo's troopers and Sheriff Clark's posse stopped them on the Edmund Pettus Bridge, hurling tear gas, beating marchers with clubs and whips, trampling some with horses, sending 56 victims to the hospital (one with a fractured skull).[5]

Behind the officers and fleeing marchers came white vigilantes, spoiling for action. FBI agent Thomas Doyle, stood with reporters, photographing three men beating a black victim—taking no steps to intervene—when one of the assailants rushed him, brandishing a rubber-coated cable with a metal clamp at one end. Doyle identified himself as a G-man, but the attacker plowed into him, both falling to the pavement. Other whites surrounded them, one snatching Doyle's camera, while his attacker escaped in the confusion. Later that day, police detained "Jimmy George Robinson" on assault charges, fining him $27 dollars. A federal grand jury subsequently charged Robinson and two others—Noel D. Cooper and Thomas Randall Kendrick—with assaulting a federal officer. Kendrick faced an additional charge of stealing government property (Doyle's camera), but those cases never went to trial. State police records identify Robinson's two accomplices as "associates" of the NSRP.[6]

Television coverage of "Bloody Sunday" shocked the world. A second attempted march two days later—"Turnaround Tuesday"—ended with King and 2,500 protesters praying, then retreating, although troopers stood aside to let them pass. On March 16 federal judge Frank Johnson, Jr., approved a march to Montgomery, enjoining Governor Wallace and law enforcement from any interference. Next day, LBJ sent voting rights legislation to Congress. On March 20 police arrested members of Jerry Dutton's American States Rights Party for "desecrating the Confederate flag" (overlaying it with a lightning bolt on their armbands). Party leaders blamed Governor Wallace and bitterly turned against him. Dr. King's demonstration proceeded on March 21, reaching Montgomery four days later, with a crowd of 25,000 massed on the capitol steps. That night, March 25, Klansmen shot and killed Detroit housewife Viola Liuzzo as she ferried marchers from Montgomery back to Selma.[7]

In that case, arrests came swiftly. FBI informer Gary Rowe was in the murder car and named his three companions: William Orville Eaton, Eugene Thomas, and Collie Leroy Wilkins. According to Rowe, Thomas drove and furnished a pistol to Wilkins, who, with Eaton, fired the fatal shots. Rowe merely "waved" his own gun out the window without firing. Authorities accepted his version, resulting in state murder charges against the accused, backed by federal indictments of civil rights deprivation. (Thirteen years later, ABC News reopened the case with startling results: Thomas and Wilkins named Rowe as Liuzzo's killer, both passing polygraph tests; Rowe failed his test when denying their charges. A murder indictment followed, but a federal court blocked Rowe's prosecution.)[8]

Collie Wilkins faced trial first, on May 3, 1965. Ed Fields joined Klansmen in the Hayneville courtroom, passing out copies of *The Thunderbolt* to spectators before Matt Murphy launched his rambling racist defense. He attacked Mrs. Liuzzo, branded Rowe a "pimp" and "Judas" traitor to the Klan, roped in the Jews and the United Nations, managing to leave the all-white, all-male jury deadlocked for a mistrial. *Life* magazine put

Murphy on its cover, on May 21, and Murphy autographed a copy "To my friend Ed Fields, Best wishes."[9]

Prosecutors scheduled Wilkins's retrial for October, but Murphy wouldn't be there. At 3:45 a.m. on August 20, driving drunk from Birmingham to Tuscaloosa, he rear-ended a tanker truck and died instantly. (The UKA claimed murder.) Ex-mayor Art Hanes, Sr.—a friend of Murphy's since college, named by Gary Rowe as a "card-carrying Klansman—stepped in to defend Wilkins, winning acquittal for his client on October 22. Klan cars sprouted bumper stickers reading "Open Season," but celebration was premature. Federal jurors convicted all three defendants of civil rights violations on December 3, resulting in 10-year prison terms. Eaton died while free on bond, pending appeal; Thomas and Wilkins served six years.[10]

***

One day before James Robinson attacked Dr. King in Selma, Millard Grubbs became embroiled in convoluted legal problems in Louisville, Kentucky. The matter involved condemnation of an elderly local's property by the city's Urban Renewal and City Development Agency, which Grubbs opposed as "national chairman" of the tiny National Law Enforcement Committee, operated from his home. Grubbs and company prepared a "citizen's arrest warrant" which NLEC members John T. Gover and Paul Boyd Wright served on one H. A. Lewis, accused of "false swearing" to legal condemnation documents. A grand jury surprised the vigilantes on February 2, indicting Gover and Wright for false arrest, further charging Grubbs, James E. Finch, and Walter H. Mullikin as accessories for "aiding, abetting and counseling" the illegal action.[11]

Free on $500 bond, Grubbs visited the Louisville FBI office on February 15, lodging a civil rights complaint on behalf of himself and his four comrades. Agents interviewed Grubbs five times, collecting various documents and assuring him his case would be reported to the DOJ, then logged their memos in the NLEC's growing file, tagged "Racial Matters." Gover and Finch missed a court appearance on April 2, whereupon Judge Frank Ropke revoked their bail. Judge J. Miles Pond issued bench warrants for the pair when they also skipped their trial on November 30, pushing the case into January 1966. Wright pled guilty to an amended charge of assault and battery on Kelly, while jurors convicted the rest on January 25, sentencing Grubbs to five years, Mullikin to three, Gover to two, and Finch to one year. Wright received a one-year suspended sentence. Thus ended the NLEC.[12]

In California, William Gale continued his Identity "religious" work, forming a Ministry of Christ Church to compete with ex-mentor Wesley Swift. At the same time, he published a booklet titled *Racial and National Identity,* allegedly drafted at the request of "a bunch of military officers" including John Crommelin, Pedro del Valle, and former colonel Ben Von Stahl. Gale described his publication as "a little Identity magazine," proposed by his ex-military friends on grounds that "the people should know a little bit about this law, Posse Comitatus." Passed by Congress in 1878, the Posse Comitatus Act bans use of federal troops to enforce domestic laws "except in such cases and under such circumstances as such employment of said force may be expressly authorized by the Constitution or by act of Congress." Far-rightists calling themselves Posse Comitatus later invoked the statute in opposing virtually any law enforcement they opposed by agencies above the county level—and also threatened local sheriffs who refused to do their will.[13]

***

Jesse Stoner continued his sporadic trips to Birmingham in 1965, coinciding with a series of successful and attempted bombings. On March 21, during Mass, police defused a bomb containing 50 sticks of dynamite at Our Lady Queen of the Universe Catholic Church. An identical bomb targeted A. D. King's home the same day, but failed to explode. On April 1 bombers struck the Crowell home in one of Birmingham's black districts, injuring a 13-year-old boy. Later that day, bombs containing 38 and 50 sticks of TNT, respectively, were found and disarmed at the homes of racial "moderates" Mayor Albert Boutwell and City Council member Nina Miglionico. The attacks remain officially unsolved today.[14]

***

The next major civil rights battleground was Bogalusa, Louisiana. Once a logging town, by the 1960s Bogalusa was virtually owned by Crown-Zellerbach Corporation (CZ), whose paper mill employed 40 percent of the town's population. Most of those were whites opposed to integration, joining the KKK in such numbers that Bogalusa earned the nickname "Klantown," while Washington Parish and adjoining Pike County, Mississippi, across the Pearl River, were lumped together as "Klan Nation." Organized racist violence dated from 1919, when black laborers tried to found a biracial union and management fought back with the all-white Self-Preservation and Loyalty League, burning homes, torturing union organizers, and murdering four persons in a raid on union headquarters. In 1960, 40 percent of Bogalusa's residents were African Americans, but only 10 percent could vote, thanks to a Citizens' Council purge of voter rolls, enforced by Klan terrorism.[15]

Into that oppressive atmosphere stepped the Bogalusa Voters & Civic League, aided by CORE. In 1963 CZ integrated its plant's cafeteria, then closed it during a white boycott. Patrons in a local bank applauded news of JFK's assassination, while loss of 500 factory jobs left blacks outnumbered six to one by white racists. Cross-burnings began in January 1964, and police declined to intervene when 800 Klansmen rallied in masks, violating state law. Near year's end, the BVCL sought help enforcing the 1964 Civil Rights Act from the Federal Community Relations Service, created to ease racial tension. In turn, the FCRS invited former Arkansas Congressman Brooks Hays, now one of its officers, to address an integrated dinner at a local church—canceled by telephoned bomb threats.[16]

January 1965 brought white CORE workers Bill Yates and Steve Miller to Bogalusa, while the BVCL chose black union activist A. Z. Young as its new president, with Robert Hicks as vice president, hosting Yates and Miller in his home. Klan-friendly police chief Claxton Knight warned the outsiders to leave town, but they declined, and armed neighbors rallied to guard Hicks's house. On February 3, Klansmen chased Yates and Miller from the union hall to a black-owned café, beating them until bystanders intervened. With phone service mysteriously blocked, police and vigilantes besieged Hicks's home until Governor John McKeithen dispatched state troopers. Black demonstrations proceeded, while the Klan received a new nonprofit charter as the Anti-Communist Christian Association, escalating violence against African Americans. In response, Ernest Thomas and F. D. Kirkpatrick founded a local chapter of the Deacons for Defense and Justice—created in Jonesboro seven months earlier—taking their cue from North Carolina's Black Armed Guard of the 1950s. Thomas told recruits, "It takes violent blacks to combat these violent whites. It takes nonviolent whites and nonviolent Negroes to sit down and bargain whenever the thing is over and iron it out."[17]

White reactions to the Deacons were predictable: J. Edgar Hoover called them a "national threat" and marked them for "intensified attention," while reporters branded them "a black Ku Klux Klan" composed of "kill-whitey" radicals. Black self-defense—a revolutionary concept in 1965—produced its first violence on April 6, when nightriders faced gunfire during an attack on Robert Hicks's home. On April 9 police stood by while racists battered protest marchers and reporters observing the demonstration. As Selma dropped out of headlines, media interest in Bogalusa increased. Mob assaults on blacks at Cassidy Park and elsewhere brought state troopers back on May 29, maintaining tenuous order.[18]

Sheriff Dorman Crowe took a conciliatory step in 1964, hiring military veterans Oneal Moore and Creed Rogers as Washington Parish's first black deputies, assigning them as partners to patrol African American districts. They had served for almost exactly one year by June 2, 1965, when they turned for home and were ambushed by gunmen riding in a dark-colored pickup truck with a Confederate flag decal on its bumper. Moore died instantly from gunshot wounds, but Rogers, blinded in one eye, remained conscious long enough to radio a description of the murder vehicle to headquarters. An hour later, Mississippi police stopped an identical truck driven by CZ worker Ernest Raphael McElveen—"Ray" to his friends—who carried membership cards for the NSRP, UKA

Funeral for Deputy Oneal Moore in Bogalusa, Louisiana. Prime suspect Ernest McElveen, an NSRP member and Klansman, escaped prosecution (Library of Congress).

and Citizens' Council, along with a .45-caliber pistol. Another card identified him as a "special agent" of Louisiana's Public Safety Department, signed by Director Thomas Burbank. Congressional investigators also later pegged him as a member of the Louisiana-based Original Knights of the KKK.[19]

Mixed reactions followed Moore's murder. Mississippi's White Knights donated $500 to McElveen's defense fund, while other Klan units posted rewards for capture of "the real killers." Klansman Saxon Farmer posted McElveen's bond, as Governor McKeithen raised a $25,000 reward for conviction of the slayers, denying the Klan existed in Bogalusa even as he secretly negotiated with its leaders. On June 5 drive-by gunmen shot up the home of an officer investigating the ambush. McElveen never faced trial due to "lack of evidence." Specifically, Moore and Rogers were shot with a rifle and shotgun, neither found in McElveen's truck at his arrest. Despite sporadic reinvestigations, the case remains unsolved today, presumably stymied forever by McElveen's death in February 2003, at age 79. Jack Gremillion, Louisiana's attorney general since 1957, ruled widow Maevella Moore ineligible for state employee survivor benefits because her husband was not slain "while engaged in the direct apprehension of a person." Years later, Sheriff Robert Crowe—Dorman's son—told reporters, "The KKK killed that officer, that's definite."[20]

Marches, beatings and arrests (of blacks only) continued through June, into July. After one roundup, Chief Knight told prisoners, "You niggers ain't gonna rule this town." On July 8 a hurled rock injured marcher Hattie Mae Hill. Deacons Henry Austin and Milton Johnson rushed her to an aid station run by the Medical Committee for Human Rights, since local hospitals refused African American patients. On arrival, whites dragged Johnson from the car, beating him until Austin shot and wounded Alton D. Crowe, whereupon police jailed Austin and Johnson, ignoring their attackers.[21]

Jesse Stoner with supporters in Bogalusa, July 1965 (National Archives).

That night, Jesse Stoner and Connie Lynch arrived to stiffen white resistance, Stoner raging to his audience of 1,500, "The nigger is not a human being. He is somewhere between the white man and the ape.... What the nigger really wants is our white women. We don't believe in tolerance. We don't believe in getting along with our enemy, and the nigger is our enemy." Two days later, federal judge Herbert Christenberry ordered Bogalusa police and Washington Parish deputies to guard protesters and to cease their own "violence, harassment, intimidation, verbal abuse, unnecessary force, and unlawful arrest." Stoner and Lynch addressed 2,000 racists on July 10, and led a march by 500 white counter-protesters on July 11. John Doar observed six mob attacks on black protesters at the Pine Tree Plaza on July 16, while local and state police stood idle. Three days later, the DOJ filed separate civil and criminal contempt charges

Bogalusa police escort a white protest march led by Connie Lynch (in Confederate flag vest) and Jesse Stoner, July 11, 1965 (National Archives).

against Chief Knight and his boss, Bogalusa Public Safety Commissioner Arnold Spiers. Judge Christenberry convicted both officials on July 30, fining them $100 daily until they obeyed his previous orders. As a result, violence briefly shifted elsewhere, with two black churches torched at Slidell on August 2 and a Baton Rouge motel housing civil rights workers bombed the following day.[22]

Stoner and Lynch were gone by then, headed back for another round of action in Alabama. On December 1, the U.S. 5th District Court of Appeals enjoined the Klan and its front group, the ACCA, against further pursuit of "a violent design to prevent Negro efforts to achieve equal rights." Identical injunctions faced a Washington Parish deputy charged with brutality and segregated Bogalusa restaurants that still defied the 1964 Civil Rights Act. Even then, old habits died hard. Black army captain Donald Sims suffered gunshot wounds in a Bogalusa phone booth on March 11, 1966. Claxton Knight arrested white suspect Thomas Bennett. Ernest McElveen and Saxon Farmer raised Bennett's $10,000 bond, before the case evaporated without trial. Four months later, on July 30, police found CORE associate Clarence Triggs shot dead in his car at roadside. Chief Knight told reporters the murder was "definitely not racial," but offered no other motive. Fingerprints led to suspects John W. Copling Jr., and Homer Richard Seale. White jurors acquitted Copling, and prosecutors dropped Seale's charges.[23]

***

Black protests and white reaction continued in Alabama when national attention strayed to Bogalusa. On May 9, Ed Fields addressed a UKA rally in Anniston, apparently reversing Robert Shelton's ban on group collaboration when he said, "We look forward to even greater rallies and future cooperation with our fellow white fighters in the Ku Klux Klan." Afterward, the party furnished signs and Confederate flags for a Klan parade. Connie Lynch followed Fields to Anniston on July 15, telling his audience, "If it takes killing to get the Negroes out of the white man's streets and to protect our constitutional rights, I say, yes, kill them."[24]

That time, his words drew blood. Rally attendees Clarence Lewis Blevins, Johnny Ira DeFries, and Hubert Damon Strange went looking for trouble and found it when they spotted black 37-year-old foundry worker Willie Brewster, Sr., driving home after his shift, on Alabama State Route 202. Strange fired a shotgun primed with 550-gram "pumpkin ball" slugs, fatally wounding Brewster, and afterward bragged of the shooting to brother-in-law Bill Rozier, who accompanied Strange to the scene and observed Brewster slumped in his car. (Brewster died three days later, at an Anniston hospital.) Arrests followed on August 14, and the defendants retained Jesse Stoner, who predicted acquittal or, at worst, a mistrial.[25]

Before that trial convened, more action awaited. In the predawn hours of August 20, Matt Murphy died in his car, bound from Birmingham to Tuscaloosa. Later that morning, FBI agents arrested Ken Adams on charges of receiving explosives stolen from Fort McClellan. (Jurors acquitted him in January 1966). Finally, before day's end, Klansman and "special deputy sheriff" Tom Coleman shot two white civil rights workers in Hayneville, killing Episcopal seminarian Jonathan Daniels and critically wounding Catholic priest Richard Morrisroe. Al Lingo rushed to the scene, driven by Coleman's state trooper son, with a Klan bondsman to procure Coleman's release. Laughing jurors acquitted Coleman of all charges on September 30. Three weeks later, another panel in the same courthouse cleared Collie Wilkins of killing Viola Liuzzo.[26]

In that atmosphere, most observers shared Stoner's prediction of acquittal for his Anniston clients—until witness Jimmie Glenn Knight came forward, seeking the $20,000 reward offered for conviction of Brewster's slayers. On the night Strange shot Brewster, Knight was drinking beer with Bill Rozier and the defendants joined them, boasting, "We got us a nigger." Knight accompanied them to the shooting scene, where Strange said, "I had to lean half way out the window to get a shot at him." Judge Robert Parker was assigned to hear the case over FBI objections, since he had once successfully defended Ken Adams on charges of assaulting a black couple near the site of Brewster's murder, but Parker declined to step aside. Before the trial convened, Strange attacked Jimmie Knight and they shot each other, neither fatally. To nearly everyone's amazement, jurors convicted Strange of second-degree murder on December 2, imposing a 10-year sentence."[27]

No one was more astonished than Jesse Stoner, grumbling to reporters, "I was surprised that a jury of 12 so-called white men would convict an innocent person on such a flimsy case." Jimmie Knight's testimony convinced jurors, but several observers blamed Stoner for the verdict. "J. B. Stoner wasn't a good lawyer," Judge Parker said, decades later. "Oh, he used some rudiments of the law, but he didn't do a very good job." Defense witness Bill Rozier agreed, saying, "The lawyer for my brother-in-law got him convicted.

J. B. knew the law, but he had no presence in the courtroom, he couldn't tell a story. He wasn't persuasive." Nonetheless, a fresh jury acquitted Johnny DeFries in February 1966, whereupon prosecutors dismissed all charges against Clarence Blevins. Hubert Strange never served his prison time: while free on bond pending appeal, he engaged in another of his habitual shooting scrapes at an all-white "private club," and died from his wounds on November 5, 1966. Alabama's Supreme Court belatedly dismissed his appeal in February 1967.[28]

Surprise jury verdicts were only the tip of the iceberg in Alabama. Congress passed the Voting Rights Act of 1965 on August 4 and LBJ signed it two days later, taking immediate effect. Federal registrars fanned out across the South. Jim Clark sought reelection in 1966, briefly doffing his "Never" button, but 9,000 new black voters rejected him. He worked selling mobile homes and kept a low profile until 1978, when federal jurors convicted him of smuggling marijuana, whereupon he served nine months in prison. Al Lingo resigned as Alabama's top cop in September 1965 and sought election as Jefferson County's sheriff, once visiting a black church, but he fooled no one. Defeated in April 1966, he survived three more years before heart disease killed him in August 1969, at age 59. Clark outlived his old comrade, reaching age 84 before he passed in June 2007.[29]

***

While Dixie seethed, the party also planted northern flags. On June 20, 1965, the *St. Louis Post-Dispatch* reported that "several small groups of businessmen" had allied themselves with the NSRP to block further civil rights advances in suburban South St. Louis and Wellston. Allen O. Kern, state party chairman, told the paper that other entrepreneurs in North and East St. Louis, Belleville, Collinsville and Cahokia were also interested, and several had discretely joined the party with promises of "strong financial support." "Generally speaking," Kern said, "we don't even mail any material to them. Mostly it is hand-carried to them, and if anything is mailed there is nothing on it to indicate it came from the National States Rights Party." In retaliation for his efforts, Kern alleged, his committeeman at Local 325 of the United Auto Workers had warned Kern of attempts to have him fired. In May, he'd also received calls and letters "threatening to blow me to hell or otherwise kill me."[30]

In Cincinnati, Ohio, police raided the party office on May 8, 1965, arresting local chapter boss Jerrold Black and seizing literature under the state's criminal syndicalism law. Jesse Stoner came to defend Black on February 2, 1966, but his case was postponed for "two or three weeks," then dropped out of print. Four years later, the U.S. Supreme Court ruled Ohio's law unconstitutional in another race-related case, overturning the conviction of Klansman Clarence Brandenburg.[31]

Black's case was not the first that drew Stoner to Cincinnati, where party official Eloise Witte doubled as "Grand Empress" of James Venable's National Knights. A young associate, Daniel Wagner, penned a 10-page letter describing his relationship with Mrs. Witte, subsequently landing in a witness chair before the House Committee on Un-American Activities. According to Wagner, Mrs. Witte proposed a string of violent acts during spring 1965, including the assassinations of President Johnson, Vice President Humphrey, Dr. King (a contract job, for $25,000)—and her own husband, who had threatened to "have her committed" unless she quit all racist groups to become a full-time wife and mother. She canceled that mariticide when Stoner visited to "legally straighten out" her husband, but added NSRP State Chairman R. D. Eldridge to the hit list for having "grown too independent," missing a rally without explanation. Wagner also named National Knights Klaliff (vice president) William Morris as a murder target, *and* as the "head of shipments" for dynamite sent from Georgia, to bomb the NAACP office in Columbus. Witte quit the Klan in November 1965, pleading illness, and left Venable seeking compensation for trips to Ohio.[32]

Florida was quiet by comparison, except for the work of FBI agents. In August 1965, when the party held a joint rally with the Klan at Vero Beach, featuring Fort Lauderdale Exalted Cyclops Charles Riddlehoover, G-men furnished Dade County authorities and newsmen with details of Riddlehoover's conviction on a firearms violation. That COINTEPLRO trick nearly cost Riddlehoover his job, and curtailed local Klan activity with fear of additional exposure.[33]

CHAPTER 11

Un-American

In his televised address of March 26, 1965—after announcing the capture of Viola Liuzzo's killers—President Johnson called for a congressional investigation of the Ku Klux Klan. Southern members of the House Committee on Un-American Activities were happy to oblige, embarrassed by the black eye racist violence had given "decent" segregationists. Four days later, the committee voted to investigate the Klan, NSRP, and various associated groups, dispatching field investigators and issuing subpoenas for executive and public hearings carried out between September 29, 1965, and February 24, 1966. HUAC's final report to the nation, with five volumes of testimony, appeared on December 11, 1967.[1]

While officially tasked to propose legislation suppressing "un-American" groups and activities, HUAC, from its beginning in 1930 under Congressman Hamilton Fish III, relied more on exposure and public censure—blacklisting of "red" Hollywood actors and writers, etc.—to crush the menace of the moment. The vast majority of its hearings were red-baiting rituals, in which witnesses who claimed their Fifth Amendment freedom not to testify were pilloried with presumptions of guilt. Few, if any, of its proposed bills spanning 45 years passed Congress to become law, typically because their terms ignored the basic Bill of Rights.[2] Probing the NSRP and the Klan, HUAC began with hearings to identify the players and embarrass them with prior criminal records and tales of financial chicanery. The final round focused on violence, seeking to prove, in the words of Alabama member John Hall Buchanan, Jr., that—

> Their record seems to be one of staggering hypocrisy. Claiming to be champions of the South, they have brought down upon the fine people of the South, who, in overwhelming majority, are not racial bigots and who deplore terrorism and violence, the scorn of the world and the wrath of the Nation. The Klan itself has thus proved the wellspring of unjust and punitive legislation against the South. Claiming to be anti-Communist, the Klan has played into the hands of atheistic communism, fulfilling Communist goals for racial strife and turmoil in our Nation, punctuated by acts of violence, and providing grist for the Communist propaganda mills all over the world.[3]

Thus might segregation be absolved of any criticism, and its ill effects—including lynching, nightriding and riots—dumped at the Klan's doorstep alone, exonerating racist politicians, police, and the "respectable" Citizens' Councils.

HUAC investigators touched upon the NSRP chiefly where its members were also Klansmen or rallied with Klans. Notwithstanding Robert Shelton's order for his knights to shun the party, UKA Pennsylvania Grand Dragon Roy Frankhouser was a member, as were King Kleagles Frank Rotella, Jr. (in New Jersey) and William H. "Wild Bill" Hoff Jr. (New York). Robert Hudgins, Imperial Kladd ("conductor" in charge of initiations) and holder of a federal firearms license, got his start in James Cole's North Carolina Knights and attended early NSRP meetings in 1958. Eloise Witte, a Tarheel transplant to Ohio, doubled as the party's Cincinnati leader and "Grand Empress" of James Venable's National Knights. Willie Wilson, indicted for the 1964 Godfrey bombing, led the party's Jacksonville chapter and Robert E. Lee Klavern No. 508 of the United Florida KKK. Jesse Stoner personified the bonds between various Klans and the NSRP, shifting from one group to another, self-proclaimed imperial wizard of his own Klan in the 1950s, never straying far from the hooded order throughout his career. In his attorney role, Stoner represented 17 HUAC witnessed: 13 UFKKK members, Militant Knights Imperial Wizard Donald Joseph Ballentine, and three Florida UKA officers: Grand Klabee (treasurer) Leon Aspinwall, Grand Titan Charles Riddlehoover, and Exalted Cyclops Jack Harold Grantham, Sr. Without exception, Stoner's clients followed his advice to plead the Fifth Amendment under questioning.[4]

NSRP members subpoenaed by HUAC included Roy Frankhouser, who refused to deliver UKA documents and pled the Fifth Amendment 28 times. Byron De La Beckwith, represented by White Knights attorneys Travis Buckley and Charles Blackwell, denied possession of any Klan records despite his role as a kleagle and took the Fifth 14 times, while committee members refrained from mentioning the Evers murder. Willie Wilson, advised by Stoner, refused to deliver UFKKK documents collected as exalted cyclops and pled the Fifth 26 times. Eloise Witte missed her first appointment with the committee on February 11, 1966, pleading illness, but appeared three days later to spar with interrogators, ducking some of their questions with vague and evasive answers. Other questions—concerning accusations that she plotted to kill LBJ, Vice President Hubert Humphrey, Dr. King, Klansman William Morris, NSRP National Organizer R. D. Eldridge of Dayton (called "E. D." in HUAC transcripts) and her own husband, then bomb an NAACP office—she seemed to answer openly and scornfully. Her accuser, Daniel Wagner, was "a psychopathic case," she said, scrawling a statement filled with utter fabrications. The plot against Morris, in particular, amused her: "We both laughed about it. It was so ridiculous." Morris concurred in nearly identical terms, then hedged: "I don't know if she in so many words denied it. It was not necessary."[5]

HUAC saved the best—or worst—for last, calling Jesse Stoner on February 24, ending its final day of public hearings. Representing himself, Stoner declined to answer 44 questions, ranging from his date and place of birth to his education, on through various activities associated with his sundry racist groups from 1942

Byron De La Beckwith declines to answer questions posed by the House Un-American Activities Committee in 1966 (National Archives).

through early 1966. Unwilling to explain himself, he sat and listened while the panel recited his history, introducing various newspaper items spanning 14 years. Texas Representative Joe Pool seemed eager for a fight, noting that Stoner had submitted a petition to Congress on September 27, 1965, calling for HUAC's censure on grounds of abusing his client, Florida Klansman Robert Gentry, during an executive session. The problem: Gentry had not testified until September 29, two days *after* Stoner's complaint. "There have been many false statements in this petition," Pool said, "and you know that and you signed it, and your signature is on here. You knew it because the man had not even testified."[6]

Another sore point was the February 1966 *Thunderbolt*, headlined "Flash-Bulletin: Un-American Rats Subpoena Atty. J. B. Stoner in Giant Smear Campaign." Midway through that article, Stoner attacked HUAC chairman Edwin Edward Willis of Louisiana, asking, "Is Willis an Ape?" It went on: "The Thunderbolt has received a report that nigger-loving, Edwin E. Willis, chairman of the red, hatchet-job, un–American committee is part ape. We call upon Louisiana readers who have the detailed facts to rush them to us." Closing, it warned readers that Willis "hates all White people, both Catholic and Protestants." Taking the bait on Willis's behalf, Pool pointed out that the chairman *was* a Catholic, "and he does not hate anyone." Furthermore, raged Pool, "The 'rats' are the Ku Klux Klan and the National States Rights Party, not Congress."[7]

Unchastened, Stoner wrote in April that HUAC "was once a great Committee and it did much good patriotic work when it was dominated by the late Congressman John Rankin. Now, the committee is packed with leftwing pro-communist race-mixers and political quacks ... [who] openly endeavored to insult and entrap patriotic White witnesses.... The committee, acting as pimps for the Federal Bureau of Integration called me before the committee in an effort to entrap me; to assassinate my character and also to besmirch my reputation by reading into their record the lies of paid FBI pimps who falsely accuse me of being responsible for most of the racial violence and killings in the South ... [Representative] Pool gave instructions to the Committee staff to find the identities of all witnesses' employers and get them fired if they work for Jews. FBI agents went to Bart Griffin's job in Jacksonville and tried to get him fired. When the NSRP eventually wins political power, we will prosecute, imprison and execute all of those devils who persecuted us and worked with the Communist-Jewish conspiracy to destroy our religion, our race and our nation."[8]

***

Fascist gadfly Daniel Burros never received his HUAC subpoena. On October 29, 1965, he met *New York Times* reporter John McCandlish Phillips for an interview in Queens, New York, reciting details of his career and hatred of Jews until Phillips said, "Your parents were married by the Reverend Bernard Kallenberg in a Jewish ceremony in The Bronx." Livid, Burros threatened to kill Phillips, then stormed out. The *Times* published its exposé on Halloween, including details of Burros's bar mitzvah. He drove to Roy Frankhouser's Pennsylvania home, raging and kicking furniture before he found a .32-caliber pistol, turning to Frankhouser and his girlfriend. "I've got nothing to live for," he said, and shot himself in the chest. Still standing, he gasped, "This will do it" and fired a second shot into his head.[9]

On November 12 the UKA held a memorial rally for recent "martyrs" Burros and Matt Murphy at Rising Sun, Maryland, burning a large cross for Murphy and a smaller

Daniel Burros (facing camera, with glasses) committed suicide at Roy Frankhouser's Pennsylvania home in October 1965. He is shown with the American Nazi Party's "Hate Bus," trailing Freedom Riders in May 1961 (Library of Congress).

one for Burros. William Hoff was present, replacing Burros as New York's king kleagle, while Roy Frankhouser supervised recruitment. Delaware Grand Dragon Ralph Earl Pryor described Frank Rotella pacing around the dais, talking to himself, until Frankhouser urged him to calm down. Mounting the stage, Rotella "sputtered and muttered incoherently," comparing the "tragedy" of Burros's suicide with another in New Jersey: the reelection of Democratic incumbent Richard J. Hughes as governor. Frankhouser took the microphone next, sporting a new eye patch after a brawl with "a gang of unidentified Jews" in Reading, telling the audience of 2,000 that he respected "good Jews" and separatist Black Muslims, but liberal Jews who fomented integration would soon "face another Dachau." He blamed the "Jew York Times" for killing Burros, adding that the martyr's parents were not Jews, but simply married in a Jewish ceremony "for some unknown reason." William Hoff closed with a promise of "avenging" Burros's death.[10]

Unknown to his audience, Hoff had as much reason to fear exposure as had Burros. Brooklyn born in 1934, third of six children, he was himself part African American, living in a racially mixed neighborhood where new immigrants frequently landed. William Hoff, Sr., hailed from South Carolina and changed the family's surname from "Huff" in the 1930s.[11] Years later, son Sheldon Hoff discovered the family's secret. As he explained:

> We found out that my [father's side of the] family were mulattos. In some censuses, like in 1910, our family is listed as black; in others, they were white, but all the families around them were black. My forefather, Emanuel Rodriguez, came to this country in 1640 as a slave. He came to Virginia with an

owner from Barbados, Frances Pott, and married a white indentured servant here. People would say, "Hey, 'Driguez, hey, 'Driguez," and soon they were just calling him Driggers. You can see documents where people are swearing that a relative of mine is white—"I swear that so-and-so Driggers is a white person and I know them," and so forth. That name is a corruption, but it stuck, right up to now. If you go to Moncks Corner today, you'll see stores and everything with the name Driggers. Anyway, he was eventually able to buy freedom for himself and a couple of his children.[12]

When Sheldon broke the story to his brother, he recalled, William Jr. "brushed it off" and continued his career as a fascist.[13]

***

In Florida, after he dodged bombing charges and stood mute before HUAC, Willie Wilson got back to party politics. Looking forward to state primaries in May 1966, Wilson told readers of the October 1965 *Thunderbolt*—

> We will make every effort to elect our candidates to both houses of the Florida legislature.... Also, we hope to elect a Congressman in this district [Baker, Duval, and Nassau Counties]. All of our candidates will speak in plain words so that everybody who is against the Jews, negroes and communists will know to vote for our candidates. Far from being subtle, in this forthcoming election campaign, we will call a spade a spade, a dog a dog, a Jew a Jew, a cannibal a cannibal and a communist a traitor who is controlled by the Jews.[14]

Despite those bold assertions, the only NSRP candidate found on a Florida ballot (for state legislator) polled 13,600 votes—2,500 short of making the vital runoff. John Crommelin made the now-traditional run against Senator John Sparkman in Alabama that June, placing third in a field of four contenders, with 114,622 votes out of 663,945 ballots case. Statewide, four other party candidates sought seats as city commissioner, school board members, and a state legislator, all defeated. Elsewhere, journalist Robert Sherrill found the party "maintaining a weak but stubborn foothold" in Durham, North Carolina, and enduring "an almost comic opera existence" in Arkansas, where 20-year-old organizer Norman K. Anspach announced his intent to "revitalize" the party, which had "fallen into disrepair." He denounced George Rockwell as a puppet of Jewish interests, declaring, "He says he's an anti–Semite, but yet he's had Jewish lawyers. The National States Rights Party is the most extreme anti–Semite group in the country." Sherrill deemed the Razorback party "virtually moribund," noting that its support for segregationist gubernatorial candidate James Douglas "Justice Jim" Johnson "must be taken on faith." (Johnson lost to Winthrop Rockefeller, Arkansas's first Republican governor since Reconstruction.) In what may be the only error in his national assessment, clearly refuted by subsequent mayhem, Sherrill added: "The National States Rights Party, judging from the pervading ignorance of its existence, seems to have no foothold in Mississippi whatsoever."[15]

Georgia's gubernatorial race was the most controversial of 1966, eclipsing Alabama's landslide selection of Lurleen Wallace to serve as husband George's placeholder until he could legally run again in 1970. Six men entered the Democratic primary in June: ex-governor Ellis Arnall; Lieutenant Governor Garland Byrd; James H. Gray Sr., from Albany; aging five-time contender Hoke O'Kelley; future governor (and president) Jimmy Carter; and Lester Garfield Maddox, Sr., an Atlanta restaurateur best known for driving blacks from his Pickrick chicken joint at gunpoint. Most strident of the lot, Maddox had shared a stage with George Wallace and Grand Dragon Calvin Craig in July 1964, at a rally where whites beat black observers with metal folding chairs. Republicans held no Georgia primary, but candidate Howard "Bo" Callaway Sr., nearly doubled the number of petition signatures required to place his name on the ballot opposing whichever Democrat emerged victorious. Arnall topped Maddox in the September 14 primary, forcing a runoff two weeks later, in which Maddox rallied to win by a margin of 70,051 votes. On November 8, Callaway topped Maddox by a slim plurality of 3,059 ballots, while Arnall—running as an independent—claimed some 51,000 votes, leaving the final choice to Georgia's Democratic-dominated General Assembly. That body chose Maddox on its first ballot, prompting a court challenge that struck down Georgia's constitutional provision for gubernatorial selection, then was reversed by the U.S. Supreme Court, ensconcing Maddox in the governor's mansion.[16]

Interviewed by Robert Sherrill afterward, Jesse Stoner claimed credit for putting Maddox over the top. *The Thunderbolt* urged all Georgia readers to support Maddox, and Stoner claimed, "We'd kick anybody out who didn't vote for Maddox," further noting that "the Callaway family has given millions of dollars to niggers." ADL monitors reported party headquarters mailing Maddox literature during the campaign, and while other observers still claim Maddox once refused to share a rally stage with Stoner, no one seems able to pinpoint the date or location. Ed Fields, writing in 2015, could recall no such snub, adding that Lester's brother, Allen B. "Pat" Maddox Sr., "was a lifelong subscriber to our paper and told me he regularly shared it with Lester who agreed with it."[17]

***

In spring 1966 the breakaway American States Rights Party reverted to its original identity as the National White Americans Party, still operating from impoverished headquarters in Birmingham and using a version of the NSRP's lightning-bolt insignia. Subsisting on less than $4,000 per year, the NWAP spent most of its cash on print propaganda, produced erratically. Three printing companies dropped its newspaper, *The White American*, for lack of payment, missing five consecutive issues before the party acquired its own small press. A typical issue, from July, "exposed" media mogul Samuel Irving Newhouse, Sr., absentee publisher of the *Birmingham News* and *Huntsville Times*, among other newspapers, as "The N.Y. Jew Who Rules Alabama." Branching out, the party also produced *Night Riders: The Inside Story of the Liuzzo Killing*, billed as offering "64 pages and 66 pictures that will shock even the most hardened right wing patriot." Cover adorned with a police photograph of Viola Liuzzo dead in her car, the booklet also promised "Exclusive Statements by Accused Klansmen!" (who emerge as heroes of the piece.)[18]

Financial straits notwithstanding, the NWAP vowed to capture to capture at least a few state legislative seats in 1966 but failed. The only candidate of record, Jerry Dutton, was denied permission for a booth at Alabama's State Fair and claimed only 728 votes out of 125,041 ballots cast in November. Fifteen years later, reunited with the NSRP, he reportedly led a coup against Edward Fields that shattered the party.[19]

***

Summer brought new opportunities for NSRP agitation outside the South. Connie Lynch toured the West Coast in early 1966, doubling back to Baltimore in July, in time for real action. An inmate revolt against brutal guards at Baltimore's Maryland State Penitentiary set the tone on July 8, 1966, leaving 36 prisoners indicted for arson, burglary and rioting. Coincidentally, CORE held its national convention in Baltimore over the long weekend of July 1–4, triggering open housing protest marches by local black activists. Initial white response came from Charles Luthardt, Sr., chairman of the local Fighting

11. Un-American

An issue of *The White American,* published by the National White Americans Party in 1966 (author's collection).

American Nationalists chapter and a hopeless gubernatorial candidate, but even with swastika banners flying along Eastern Avenue, toward Broadway from Patterson Park, Luthardt clearly needed help.[20]

Connie Lynch arrived in the last week of July, accompanied by Maryland State Coordinator Richard Berry Norton, Youth Director Joseph Carroll, William Brailsford (running for the House of Delegates from Dundalk), Robert Lyons, and two Baltimore troopers, Paul Cardel and Edwin Hendel. Posing as members of "The Citizens for Brailsford Committee," they obtained permits for political rallies in Patterson Park on July 25, 27, and 28, using a sound truck with amplifiers. Carroll opened on the 25th, saying, "The time has come for all white youths to unite and fight for white power. Let's smash this nigger revolution here and now. I guarantee you we are the loudest bunch of hate mongers in the entire State. Are we going to let these vile black beasts to run wild, pillage, rape our white people? The time has come for us to fight and that is exactly what we are going to do. How about you?" Norton followed, telling his audience, "Connie Lynch on the subject of violence is a moderate. I know he is a moderate. Connie Lynch personally told me he favors just enough moderate violence to get the niggers the hell out of America." Thus introduced, Lynch railed, "Let me tell you, let me remind all of you niggers and you nigger lovers, whatever you be, whether you be politicians and what have you, you're just beginning to see and hear a little bit of what you're going to see and hear in the very near future and you can be sure of that. Niggers are going to be hanged. More than ever been hanged before in any country or in any nation in all the world. Certainly I believe in violence. Anybody ask you to believe in non-violence to defend what you believe is right you tell him 'Hell, yes you believe in violence.' How you folk feel about it? We are going to kill all the niggers if it takes that to keep us white. How do you folks feel about that?"[21]

July 27, like all party rallies, replayed the same themes, speakers appearing in the same order. Carroll advised a larger audience, "Most of these nigger lovers are sick in the mind. They should be bound, hung and killed. If they want violence we'll give it to them. White man, that is the time to get your gun and kill your share of niggers. We'll never, never have any racial peace and there can be no peace until the nigger hangs from every lamppost. White man fight!" Referring to CORE, Norton opined, "I know when they open up you white folks are going to beat the hell out of them." Lynch's prescription was simple: "Rise up and unite white man and fight." He promised to lead his audience of 600 in a "clear-cut race riot." Six white youths who took Lynch at his word faced arrest for raiding a black neighborhood.[22]

Realizing the party's deception—no mention of Brailsford at either rally so far—and the potential for violence, Baltimore's Park Commissioner canceled the standing permit on July 28. In fact, fighting had already occurred, requiring police to escort CORE observers away from the first two rallies. Undeterred by official sanctions, Lynch and company moved their sound truck a short distance, to the edge of Patterson Park, and greeted their largest audience yet, estimated at 2,000. Joe Carroll began by saying, "The white people aren't going to tolerate any more of this, they are going to riot. There is only one way. I want you to watch me. Raise your right fist and shake it. White man, fight!" Richard Norton asked the mob rhetorically, "Are you ready to fight?" Lynch beamed, "I know you are enthused with fight," then attacked Mayor Theodore McKeldin as "a super-pompous jackassie nigger lover." He closed raging, "To hell with the niggers, and those who don't like it, they can get the hell out of here!"[23]

Thus "enthused with fight," hundreds of white youths spilled into a nearby African American neighborhood, assaulting residents who hadn't ducked inside their homes. Some stayed to battle the invaders, throwing bricks and bottles, until police arrested 10 persons, most of them white. Another group of whites attacked Dennis Alexander, a 16-year-old black youth walking his dog through Patterson Park, beating him and tying a rope around his neck before officers intervened. On July 29, Judge William O'Donnell granted an injunction barring the NSRP from staging further local rallies for the next 10 days. That afternoon, a grand jury indicted Lynch, Carroll and Norton on charges of inciting a riot. Earl Poorbaugh, the mayor's press secretary, told reporters the defendants had targeted Baltimore "because they figured the white people here would have gotten tired of the CORE program." Major General George M. Gelston, Maryland's Adjutant General, National Guard commander and acting police commissioner, concurred that recent violence was "caused by the segregationists and not by the Negroes."[24]

The indicted party leaders wasted no time posting bond: $5,000 for Lynch, $2,500 each for Carroll and Norton. Temporarily banned from rousing Baltimore's rabble, they moved downstate to Princess Anne, seat of Somerset County and site of Maryland's last lynching, where officials granted permission for an August 6 meeting outside the courthouse. Captain Paul J. Randall, Troop Commander of State Police for the Eastern Shore District, permitted use of a sound truck, stipulating only that speakers omit any mention of two pending rape cases involving black offenders and a white victim. Jesse Stoner readily agreed and the rally proceeded, opening with strains from a song by Klan-friendly singer Clifford "Johnny Rebel" Trahan: "Move Them Niggers North."[25]

Joe Carroll spoke first, at 7:15, declaring the event a rally designed to promote white aspirations, while opposing "mongrelization," "black terror," and the pervasive "Communist conspiracy," vowing resistance by all legal means to block further encroachments by "niggers" and "Martin Lucifer Coon." Taking his theme from the rally's opening song, Jesse Stoner advised, "If we only hire whites and we move the blacks out legally, in accordance with the law, up to New York or some place like that, we won't have niggers down here to mix up with."[26] Connie Lynch cast racial violence in terms of self-defense:

> Whenever they make demands into our white society, when they say they're going to invade our white communities, we are told we can't do anything about it, they have a right to come into your communities. But they're coming in there non-violently. Reminds me of someone coming to my house, knocking on my door, saying, "Now look-a-here, I'm coming into your house, but I'm not coming in there violently; I'm coming in with a non-violent manner." Then when he says, "Now I see your wife there, non-violently I want your wife. And I see you got a beautiful daughter over here, with no violence, but non-violently I want your daughter." Well, I've got an answer to it tonight. I'm willing now and I'll be willing tomorrow and I'll always be willing to fight. Yes, hell yes, any way it takes to fight to stop this invasion of our white communities. How do you white folks feel about it out there, huh?[27]

Buoyed by applause, Richard Norton took center stage, bemoaning the fact that local schools must integrate or forfeit "LBJ's Judas thirty pieces of silver" in federal aid.[28] While observing Stoner's deal with Captain Randall, Norton case his eye back across three decades of history.

> In 1933 a nigger grabbed a 75-year-old white woman in this town and brutally raped her, brutally raped her. What did they do? Did the people go out and say that nigger was a victim of discrimination and that's why he raped her? No. Let me tell you what happened. I am not advocating this but I am just recounting a bit of history. Three thousand people from this town rose up, took that beast out and hung him. You know what the Baltimore papers said? You know what they said? They called it Eastern Shore barbarism, Eastern Shore barbarism. Now a lot of old-timers here tonight remember the stickers you all had on your cars and windows: "I am an Eastern Shore man and damn proud of it." You folks proud of it?[29]

Ringing cheers drove Norton on to recount the past week's violence in Baltimore, closing with this advice: "We always urge white people to get their gun, always have a gun, know how to use it, always have a good supply of ammunition. I will tell you, friends, you are going to have to use it. It's no use hiding; you can't bury your head in the sand like an ostrich. The problems aren't going to go away. The time is come. You are going to have to stand up and face it. You are going to have to face it."[30]

On August 7 the Circuit Court for Somerset County issued an order banning further NSRP rallies for 10 days, followed on August 30 by an interlocutory order extending the ban for 10 months. The party appealed, beginning a legal process that saw the temporary injunction affirmed by Maryland's Court of Appeals on November 19, 1968, while the interlocutory order was reversed. Two years before that symbolic victory—on November 18, 1966—Baltimore jurors convicted Lynch, Carroll and Norton of inciting a riot, conspiracy to riot, disorderly conduct, and violating park rules. On November 21, Judge J. Gilbert Prendergast gave all three two-year prison terms, plus concurrent 30-day terms in the local House of Correction; Lynch and Norton also received $1,000 fines, while Norton's $50 fine was suspended. Jesse Stoner took their case to Maryland's Court of Appeals, which affirmed the verdicts on December 6, 1967. Further appeals kept Connie Lynch at liberty until October 1968, released from prison in November 1969.[31]

Unknown to Lynch and company, FBI agents played a role in the party's Maryland travails, collaborating with Baltimore police, feeding city officials information that buttressed the July injunction and indictments. Under Bureau prodding, local media also agreed to curtail coverage of the NSRP's activities, as trials and appeals depleted party finances. Pressing ahead, the party's *White Marylander* newsletter carried Robert Norton's message: "Right now, begin to build up a good private arsenal. Many fine surplus military weapons are available at low cost in the area. There should be at least three weapons to each white household." Even in temporary defeat, Robert Sherrill granted that "Stoner and Lynch stand high and apart in the pantheon of violent racist demagogues today."[32]

***

Before the trials in Maryland, Chicago beckoned. Local activist Albert Raby's Coordinating Council of Community Organizations began agitation for open housing in July 1965, opposed by powerful Mayor Richard Daley. Raby invited Dr. King to lead a Windy City demonstration that summer, but another year would pass before King marched in Chicago. He *did* announce plans for a Chicago Freedom Movement on January 7, 1966, declaring that "the moral force of SCLC's nonviolent movement philosophy was needed to help eradicate a vicious system which seeks to further colonize thousands of Negroes within a slum environment," and later that month moved his family into a ghetto apartment. When critics panned that move as a publicity stunt, SCLC responded by founding Operation Breadbasket, led by Jesse Jackson, aimed at abolishing racist hiring practices by companies active in African American neighborhoods.[33]

Mass marches finally began in July 1966, met with white resistance increasing daily. On August 5, leading 700 demonstrators to Marquette Park on Chicago's Southwest Side, King faced a mob hurling rocks and bottles, waving placards that included the message "King would look good with a knife in his back." One stone struck King in the head, dropping him to his knees, while 30 others were also injured. Stunned, King told reporters, "I have seen many demonstrations in the South, but I have never seen anything so hostile and so hateful as I've seen here today."[34]

Clearly, Chicago was ripe for action by white "outside agitators." Connie Lynch arrived in the third week of August, as did George Rockwell and a retinue of ANP stormtroopers. Both addressed separate rallies in Marquette Park on August 21, and while Rockwell went unmolested by police, officers arrested Lynch and companion Evan Lewis—identified in FBI files as representing James Venable's National Knights of the KKK—on charges of "addressing a group without a permit." Their arrest sparked a white protest march by several hundred rally attendees, bound from Marquette Park to Police District 8. A downpour dispersed that mob, but some returned to the arrest site an hour later, blocking traffic and sidewalks. Police detained six more adults and three juveniles for rock-throwing, then freed all nine without bond. Lynch and Evans posted bail but never faced trial, likely because the charge was deemed unconstitutional.[35]

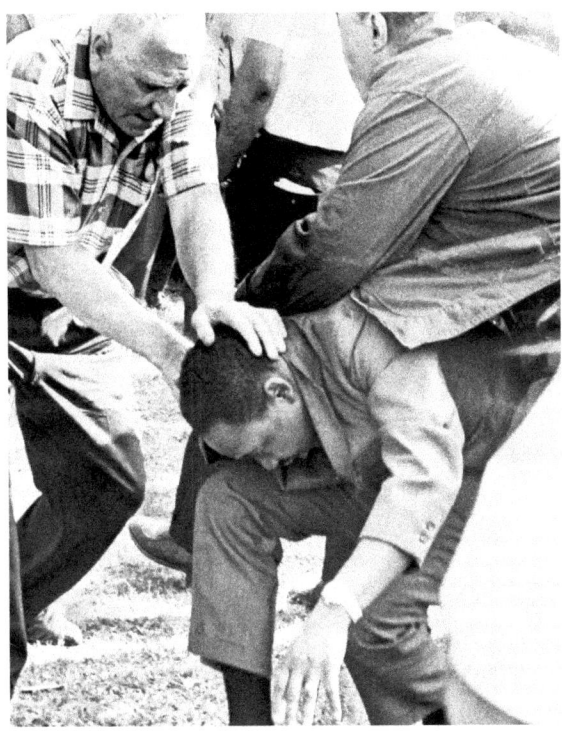

Dr. King, felled by a rock during an open-housing march in Chicago on August 5, 1966 (Library of Congress).

Some civic leaders in Baltimore blamed Lynch and the NSRP with stalling open housing there until a new Fair Housing Act passed Congress in April 1968, but Mayor Daley took full credit for Chicago's blockage of the movement, floating a program of accommodation in early 1967 that Dr. King later called "a sham and a batch of false promises." Aside from banning racial discrimination in real estate rentals and sales, the 1968 Fair Housing Act also made it a felony for any person to "travel in interstate commerce ... with the intent to incite, promote, encourage, participate in and carry on a riot." J. Edgar Hoover eyed the statute's future use against black militants, while civil libertarians decried it for "equating organized political protest with organized violence."[36]

***

Fascist agitators felt more at ease in Dixie, despite publication of HUAC's report and claims that membership was dwindling in the aftermath of public hearings. Evidence of that was visible in the Sunshine State, where observers deemed the United Florida KKK "inert" by September 1966, despite assists from the NSRP. Two Jacksonville rallies featuring Connie Lynch drew paltry crowds of 35 and 37 listeners, respectively. Edward Fields and Albert T. Massey attracted 150 of the curious on October 15, but when Massey and Willie Wilson tried again, two days later, their following dropped to 75.[37]

Alabama seemed more promising, though George Wallace had severed his ties to the party and NSRP headquarters had decamped to Georgia. In January 1966, four months before May's gubernatorial primary, doctors diagnosed surrogate candidate Lurleen Wallace with cancer. George hid it from the public to ensure her victory—54 percent of the primary vote, 63.4 percent in November's general election—and a hysterectomy failed to stop the malignancy's spread, eventually killing Mrs. Wallace barely halfway through her term. On inauguration night, while George and Lurleen attended various celebratory balls, a strategy session convened at Montgomery's Woodley Country Club to plot Wallace's next presidential campaign.[38]

That meeting echoed one held four years earlier, less than 24 hours before George's inauguration as governor and his famed "Segregation Forever" tirade. On that occasion he huddled with right-wing Virginia newspaperman John Synon and others, to hear Synon's scheme for electing the next southern president. Impressed by 1960s statistics—so close that electoral votes from Alabama, Arkansas, Georgia, Louisiana, Mississippi and South Carolina might have determined the victor—Synon devised a scheme for boosting "favorite sons" from key southern states—Wallace, Ross Barnett, Strom Thurmond, and Virginia's Harry Byrd, Sr.—to see which one Americans found most palatable.[39] The plan didn't work out for Wallace in 1964, but primary results had been encouraging enough for him to try again in 1968.

Selma's Jim Clark and Ace Carter issued invitations to the Woodley gathering. Four years as the governor's gray eminence had neither mellowed Ace nor curbed his thirst for alcohol: a few months earlier, drunk and raving, he'd threatened to "beat the shit out of" a local detective unless said officer stopped questioning Klansmen about a recent church bombing. Now, in answer to the siren call, there came a group that one attendee dubbed a *Who's Who* of "super-patriot leaders": John Synon, Ross Barnett, Leander Perez, William Simmons from the Citizens' Council, plus spokesmen for the John Birch Society, Carl McIntyre's American Council of Christian Churches, Australian Fred Schwartz's Christian Anti-Communism Crusade, the Christian Crusade of Billy James Hargis, Edgar Bundy's Church League of America, and Willis Carto's Liberty Lobby. In advance of the Woodley meeting, Carto and Carter had printed a pamphlet titled *Stand Up For America: The Story of George C. Wallace*, hailing Wallace as the only person capable of stopping "Blacky" and the Jew-Communist dominated federal government. The Liberty Lobby mailed 175,000 copies to its subscribers, holding 150,000 in reserve for Wallace's use as a future campaign tool.[40]

From those tainted beginnings grew a movement that would secure two more gubernatorial terms for Wallace and launch him twice more upon the White House campaign trail.

CHAPTER 12

Night Terrors

Nineteen sixty-seven began with an FBI investigation of the NSRP over a threat to kill Robert F. Kennedy, elected to the Senate from New York in 1964. Hated and burned in effigy at party rallies since the freedom rides, now with rumors of a coming presidential bid, RFK had riled one fascist enough to plot his murder. Word came to the Bureau from Chicago informer "CG T-2," describing a conversation between the would-be killer (name excised from declassified reports) and two other party members. Said to be a Hoosier transplant to the Windy City, Mr. X carried a pistol in his car and raged against all "Kennedys" for "controlling Massachusetts with their money." Agents coordinated with police, but files contain no mention of the suspect being found or interviewed. Kennedy survived another 18 months, until his televised assassination in Los Angeles.[1]

Chicago's chapter proved elusive, operating without office space, holding only one formal meeting between February and September, while other activities were "limited mainly to contacts between members." One recruit in suburban Berwyn, also tied to the Klan and Minutemen, performed "investigative checks" on local residents for Robert DePugh's private army. Chuck O. Farris, identified as chairman of Chapter 49, appeared on the Alan Douglas radio talk show in April. Three other members drove to Milwaukee, counter-demonstrating against marchers from the NAACP Youth Council. Elsewhere, members staged a fish fry at Jacksonville, Florida, in June and returned two months later for their national convention. In Savannah, informer "SV T-16" furnished records on the party's executive committee from Liberty National Bank and Trust, showing that Ed Fields had received three checks totaling $649.49, Jesse Stoner got one for $150, and Connie Lynch claimed two totaling $175.[2]

In Milwaukee, one of the North's most segregated cities, Lynch "helped stir things up" in 1967. Trouble had started the previous summer, when Klansmen bombed an NAACP office and stoned demonstrators from the NAACP Youth Council, requiring deployment of National Guardsmen. Another march on Kosciuszko Park in August 1967, protesting the Common Council's refusal to pass an open housing ordinance, brought some 4,000 whites into the street, fired by Lynch's rhetoric, hurling stones and bottles at the demonstrators led by white Catholic priest James Groppi. Lynch escaped arrest that time and failed to halt the rising tide, as protests continued through winter, until passage of the 1968 Fair Housing Act. Even so, while denigrating the party's overall numbers, Robert Sherrill admitted, "When racial trouble breaks out, the spokesmen for the NSRP can be expected to show up and to operate effectively. They are masters of *ad hoc* violence."[3]

Senator Robert Kennedy, target of many NSRP protests and an alleged death threat in January 1967 (Library of Congress).

Sherrill visited the party's new headquarters that year—"two small, very rundown rooms" in an Augusta, Georgia, office building—to interview Jesse Stoner. Business was slow, overall. Ed Fields had lately addressed a rally at Birmingham's Thomas Jefferson Hotel, but only 30 listeners turned up. Sherrill concluded, "In Alabama, once its kingdom of splendid terror, the NSRP now has no influence at all, and if not there of all places, much less than nothing in other southern states."[4] That judgment, as we'll see, was premature.

***

In its 1967 report, HUAC listed 18 rival Klans with a combined membership of "approximately" 16,810, some 15,075 pledging allegiance to the UKA. (It offered no tally for the NSRP.) More objective Klan watchers pegged peak membership around 50,000, suggesting that congressional tales of violence actually spurred short-term recruiting.[5] Whatever the true statistics, Klansmen and their party allies were about to enjoy a brutal revival in Mississippi.

White Knights Imperial Wizard Samuel Bowers maintained headquarters in Laurel, but most of 1967's action occurred around Meridian and Jackson. Meridian's chapter was the party's flagship in Mississippi, led by Klansman Raymond Roberts, with his sister-in-law as secretary, meeting at a barbershop. Raymond's brother, Alton Wayne Roberts, was also a member, indicted with 18 others on federal charges for the 1964 "Mississippi Burning" murders of three civil rights workers. In his free time, Raymond stalked white lawyer Lawrence Rabb, from Meridian's Committee of Conscience, and followed Rabb's wife home from college night classes. On June 11, Raymond attended a party rally in Jackson with White Knights bomber Joe Daniel "Danny Joe" Hawkins and infamous bomb-maker Laude E. Matthews (later a suspected FBI informer). There, another Bureau spy heard an unidentified man invite Matthews to a second rally on the 14th, south of Laurel. When the NSRP planned a public meeting near Meridian, G-men urged police to visit the landowners, resulting in the rally's cancelation.[6]

That kind of COINTELPRO interference irked the party, but did not retard its plans. By June, many White Knights held joint membership in the NSRP, as well as the Klan's front group, Americans for Preservation of the White Race. Their rage manifested in serial arson and bombing attacks. On January 21 fire leveled an African American church in Collins, used as a Head Start center for poor children. One week later, 15 days after a federal grand jury indicted the "Mississippi Burning" lynchers, a car bomb killed NAACP secretary Wharlest Jackson, recently promoted to a "white man's" factory job in Natchez. On March 4 fire damaged the Vincent Chapel African Methodist Episcopal Church in Grenada, used as SCLC headquarters. (Police Commissioner Paul McKelroy, whose officers failed to protect black children enrolled at formerly white schools from mob attacks in September 1966, deemed the fire "definitely not arson.") Three days later, bombers struck Jackson's Blackwell Real Estate office, whose owner welcomed black buyers. On March 13 a bomb severely damaged the Head Start office in Liberty, serving three counties.[7]

FBI agents suspected Klansmen Joe Denver Hawkins and son Danny Joe in most of those incidents, branding the clan—with matriarch Johnnie Mae and daughter-in-law Kathy—"one of the meanest and most violent families" in Mississippi. (A grand jury indicted Danny Joe for the Blackwell bombing, based on an accomplice's eyewitness confession, but an all-white jury acquitted Hawkins in August 1968, then congratulated him with handshakes.)[8] The family would soon have new accomplices, but first, another notorious racist claimed headlines.

***

On February 14, 1967, Klansman and NSRP member Byron De La Beckwith announced his campaign to become Mississippi's lieutenant governor. Running on the slogan "He's a straight shooter," Beckwith billed himself as "a candidate whose political position has already been established," telling voters, "I wish to express my heartfelt gratitude to the fine Christian people of Mississippi who have sustained and sheltered me in times past." Sam Bowers supported Beckwith and assigned aide Delmar Dennis—an FBI informer—to "take care" of Beckwith on his visits to Meridian. Asked about his murder of Medgar Evers, Beckwith said, "I don't think it will hurt me. Everybody knows how I feel about racial matters. Everybody knows what my platform is. It's absolute white supremacy under Protestant Christian rule. I'm not trying to please everybody. I don't want the nigger vote."[9]

Extreme as he was, when primary ballots were counted on August 8, Beckwith claimed 34,598 votes out of 665,738 cast for lieutenant governor, 5.21 percent of white voters. He ran fifth in a field of six rivals, losing out to Clarksdale attorney Charles L.

Top: NSRP chapter leader Raymond Roberts (with flag) demonstrates outside the federal courthouse where his brother faced trial for the "Mississippi Burning" murders. *Bottom:* Remains of Wharlest Jackson's truck after a car bomb killed him on February 27, 1967 (both photographs, National Archives).

Sullivan, a 1960 failed contender for president on the Constitution Party ticket.[10] Disenchanted with politics, Beckwith soon relapsed into his insular world of race hatred and violence.

***

Thomas Tarrants III took his act on the road that summer. Supporting himself by armed robbery, he first visited Robert Shelton in Tuscaloosa, then drove to Laurel, Mississippi, offering his services to Sam Bowers. By daylight, he worked at the Masonite plant, soon embroiled in a bitter strike sparked by automation and reduction of the labor force. Strikers battled "scabs," killing one security guard, while bombs wrecked the plant's water line and railroad tracks. Management broke the strike by firing all involved, replacing them with college students on a temporary basis, then luring black replacements with claims that Klansmen instigated the strike.[11]

Through the White Knights, Tarrants soon met Danny Joe Hawkins and newly married Kathryn Madlyn Ainsworth (née Capomacchia), born July 1941 in Chicago and raised in Miami by her second-generation Hungarian immigrant mother, while her Mexican father traveled as a juggler with the USO. Kathryn graduated with honors from Coral Gables High School, with scholarship offers from several Florida colleges, but her mother's bitter racism had already infected her. She chose segregated Mississippi College in Clinton, enthralled by the teachings of Dr. W. M. McCaskey, a hard-line white supremacist and advisor to Governor Ross Barnett. There, Kathryn roomed with the daughter of serial bombing suspect Sidney Barnes, often visiting his home to hear Wesley Swift's tape-recorded lectures. Degree in hand, Kathryn began teaching fifth grade at Jackson's Lorena Duling Elementary School, where few colleagues knew of her after-hours involvement with the NSRP, Klan, and Americans for Preservation of the White Race. Kathryn's mother knew and approved; husband Ralph Ainsworth—married to Kathryn in August 1967, with Sidney Barnes giving the bride away—knew but failed to dissuade her. They honeymooned at Christ of the Ozarks, Gerald L. K. Smith's Arkansas theme park and headquarters, then returned to Jackson, where Ralph ran health clubs, Kathryn dividing her time between school and nocturnal fascist rallies. Upon meeting Tom Tarrants she recognized a soulmate.[12]

Kathryn Ainsworth, mild-mannered schoolteacher by day, rabid racial terrorist by night (National Archives).

In early September, Tarrants warned Sam Bowers to establish an ironclad alibi for the night of Monday the 18th. At 10 o'clock that evening, Tarrants and Ainsworth bombed Rabbi Perry Nussbaum's Temple Beth Israel in Jackson, effectively destroying the synagogue. Structural and psychological damage aside, the blast's effects must have disappointed Tarrants. Three days later, spokesmen for the Greater Jackson Clergy Alliance organized a "Walk of Penance" to express the group's "sorrow and support for the Jewish community." Created in July, by 60 ministers from 10 denominations, the alliance was

Mississippi's first racially integrated association of Catholics, Protestants and Jews. As a coordinated federal, state, and local manhunt began, the Reverend Thomas Tiller, alliance president, told reporters, "By default, we may have contributed to a climate of opinion which gives rise to terrorism. What concerns us, and others like us, is that we may not have been zealous enough in protecting our God-given freedoms."[13]

***

The fresh investigation coincided with acceleration of the FBI's COINTELPRO—WHITE HATE program. Agents wrongly suspected Danny Joe Hawkins of bombing Temple Beth Israel, but despite increasing its number of paid Klan informers, the Bureau had no clue that Tom Tarrants or Kathy Ainsworth existed. As part of their broader campaign, G-men planted an article in the *Tampa Tribune,* linking Klansmen to the NSRP. They also furnished information to Miami TV station WKCT, naming UKA Exalted Cyclops Richard Hampton Farley as chairman of the party's Hollywood chapter and the "No. 1 man of the NSRP in Florida." Baltimore agents chipped in with material on the party's role in that city's 1966 riots, and newsman Wayne Ferris took it from there, producing a 30-minute documentary titled *Thunderbolt on the Right.*[14]

Aired to an estimated audience of 150,000 viewers on September 9, 1967, the program included clips of violent speeches by Connie Lynch and Neuman Britton, an interview with Broward County resident and party Youth director Joseph Carroll, coupled with remarks from Jesse Stoner on the "Federal Bureau of Integration," branding its agents "mangy dogs" and its director a "Jew-dominated" homosexual, and calling Hitler "too moderate." Ex-convict Robert Quarterman appeared, printing party literature on a press he shared with Broward County UKA Exalted Cyclops Fred Kiefer. Dr. Granville Fuisher, professor of psychiatry at the University of Miami, analyzed the party's motives, declaring that its "hate, violence and a destructive attitude" toward "scapegoats" constituted "venting" of an emotional response to "frustration" over its members' low social status. Florida's Republican Party state chairman requested a special screening for his staff and ADL officials, while public schools sought copies for use in their classrooms.[15]

Newspapers piled on next, with John Powell telling readers of the *Tampa Tribune* such "extremists" should be permanently silenced. "[They are] insane radicals," he wrote. "You and I had to fight a war because of them.... Hitler only had 20 percent of the German people. It can happen here.... Most have prison records.... These men are just as great a danger to our way of life as are the Rap Browns who holler for death and violence against white people... [They are] a definite threat to our national security and our families."[16]

Within a few months of the documentary's airing, Broward County's three NSRP chapters folded—ironically, as Klansmen elsewhere shifted to the party's ranks. In North Carolina, informers within UKA Guilford College Unit No. 156 logged complaints about increasing dues, with comments that the NSRP "had something better to offer than the Klan." Similar grumbling emanated from klaverns in Atkinson, Mount Holly, and Sanford. Money was so tight, in fact, that rebellious knights spoke of deposing Grand Dragon James Robert Jones.[17]

***

Party associate-turned-adversary George Rockwell renamed his ANP the National Socialist White People's Party in January 1967, seeking to broaden its appeal without abandoning the Nazi trappings. Five months later, on June 28, he survived a murder attempt near party headquarters in Arlington, Virginia, catching a glimpse of two assailants as they fled. Local authorities ignored his request for a gun permit, and Rockwell was unarmed when a gunshot claimed his life on August 25, outside an Arlington laundromat. Police soon arrested ex–ANP member John Patler, expelled in March 1967, and convicted him of Rockwell's murder, while Roy Frankhouser blamed an ADL conspiracy. Sentenced to 20 years, Patler won parole in 1975 but soon violated terms of his release, spending another six years in prison.[18]

Jesse Stoner shed no tears for Rockwell, once a party founder, later a bitter enemy. "He phoned me in 1966," Stoner told Robert Sherrill, "and suggested I cooperate with the FBI to get them off my back. I told him to go to hell."[19]

Rockwell's death elevated Deputy Commander Matt Koehl to lead the NSWPP, with an estimated 300 members and 3,000 financial supporters nationwide. Membership soon declined, however, a circumstance Nazi historian Rick Cooper blames in equal parts on Koehl's personality and his alleged "homosexual background [which] was no secret within the NSWPP membership, especially among the old timers." While some defectors left the fascist fringe forever, others drifted into what Cooper dubs "sneaky Nazi" groups, such as the NSRP. In November 1982 Koehl moved headquarters to his native Milwaukee, renaming his shrunken party the New Order, a "spiritual," rather than political movement, though still influenced by Rockwell's writings.[20]

***

On October 6, 1967, Tom Tarrants bombed the home of Dr. William T. Bush, a white dean at mostly–African American Tougaloo College, seven miles north of Jackson. Rumors claimed that Bush lived with a black woman, and Tougaloo itself was deemed a hotbed of communism for its civil rights activities. FBI agents entered the case, linking it to their Temple Beth Israel investigation, but still had no viable suspects.[21]

One day later, the trial of 19 "Mississippi Burning" defendants convened in Jackson, before notoriously racist federal judge William Harold Cox. JFK reluctantly appointed Cox in 1961, as a trade-off with Senator James Eastland for Thurgood Marshall's appointment to the U.S. 2nd Circuit Court of Appeals, Eastland advising Robert Kennedy, "Tell your brother that if he will give me Harold Cox, I will give him the nigger." Three years later, Cox derided black witnesses in his court as "a bunch of chimpanzees," prompting calls for his impeachment, and he dismissed the original Neshoba County conspiracy indictments in February 1965, only to have the Supreme Court reinstate them in March 1966. Sam Bowers and company expected favorable treatment from Cox, but their attitude—and muttered threats to bomb the courthouse—irked him to the point that he warned defense attorneys, "I am not going to allow a farce to be made of this trial." Jurors convicted seven of the nine defendants on October 20, acquitting nine, and failing to reach verdicts on three more. Three months later, Cox imposed prison terms ranging from three to 10 years, with the maximum penalty handed to Bowers and NSRP member Alton Roberts. Afterward, Cox told reporters, "They killed one nigger, one Jew, and a white man. I gave them all what I thought they deserved." (In fact, both white victims were Jewish.)[22]

The Jackson verdicts severely damaged Mississippi's Klan. In November the Memphis *Commercial Appeal* counted 700 Klansmen in the Magnolia State, 200 loyal to Bowers, most of the others in Robert Shelton's camp. Despite those losses, the December

Alton Wayne Roberts (right) decks a newsman during a break from his October 1967 trial on civil rights charges (National Archives).

Rabbi Perry Nussbaum and wife Arene amidst the ruins of their home, bombed by Thomas Tarrants on November 21, 1967 (National Archives).

sentencing left Bowers and company free on bond pending appeal of their convictions, some of them itching for action. On November 19 Tarrants and Ainsworth bombed the Jackson home of Robert Kochtitzky, a layman active with Rabbi Nussbaum and others on the Committee of Concern. Two nights later they struck again, blasting Rabbi Nussbaum's residence. On December 20, nine days before his sentencing in court, Sam Bowers went riding with Tarrants, planning to strafe the Clinton, Mississippi, home of a black man who allegedly shot at police. A night marshal saw their car, bearing Alabama license tags, and stopped them, quickly spotting a .45-caliber submachine gun on the front seat, partly hidden by a sweater. Bowers escaped further punishment, denying knowledge of the weapon, but prosecutors charged Tarrants—whose probation on the sawed-off shotgun charge had recently expired—with another federal firearms violation.²³

***

Free on bond, Tarrants returned to Alabama in January 1968 and enrolled at Mobile College (now the University of Mobile). In March he drove to California, visiting Wesley Swift and procuring a rifle with which he hoped to kill Martin Luther King. "That was my ambition," Tarrants later wrote. "I hated Dr. King." Back in Mobile on March 23, he found FBI agents waiting at his home and narrowly escaped, fleeing to North Carolina, where "survivalist" Swift disciples sheltered him.²⁴ There, he penned a memo reading:

Thomas Albert Tarrants III, indoctrinated by the NSRP in high school to pursue an adult guerrilla war of terrorism in the South. This mug shot followed his arrest with Imperial Wizard Sam Bowers on December 22, 1967 (National Archives).

> Gentlemen,
> Please be advised that as of March 23, 1968, I, Thomas Albert Tarrants III, was forced to go underground or be arrested and imprisoned on framed Federal charges of violation of the Federal Firearms Act and other misc. charges. My decision to make this announcement was in part influenced by a similar announcement by that great patriot Robert DePugh of the Minutemen. In that my situation is very similar to his I have decided to make public this announcement.
> I will further state that I have always believed in military action against the common enemy. I have committed myself totally to defeating the communist jew conspiracy which threatens our country—any means necessary shall be used. On March 23, 1968, I was forced to go underground or face framed federal charges of possession of a submachine gun in Collins, Mississippi, on 21 December 1967 [sic].
> Please be advised that since March 28, 1968 I Thomas Albert Tarrants have been underground and operating guerrilla warfare.²⁵

Nor was Tarrants alone. During his absence from Mississippi, in January and February 1968, bombers struck three black churches in Meridian, all carefully ignored by the *Meridian Star*. On February 8 arsonists burned the local grocery owned by ex-policeman, ex–Klansman, and federal prosecution witness Wallace Miller. On February 22 they set fire to New Hope Baptist Church, site of a Head Start program and civil rights activities, causing minor damage. One night later, fire destroyed the parsonage of Newell Chapel Methodist Church—another Head Start center—and terrorists fired shotgun blasts into the home of Head Start bus driver J. R. Moore. Another drive-by at the home of black dentist Dr. Robert Kornegay wounded his daughter with flying glass. The attacks had their desired effect to some extent, forcing certain churches into what author Michelle Simmsparris calls "social incapacitation." Congregants at Meridian's First Union Baptist feared bombing so much, they refused use of their building to Head Start promoters.²⁶

Throughout the reign of terror, Meridian Police Chief Roy Gunn fought back in kind, fielding a "blackshirt squad" of officers who harassed known Klansmen, detonated small explosive charges in their yards, and fired shots into their homes. Anonymous callers responded by threatening Gunn's family. In a Kiwanis Club speech, Gunn brandished a shotgun and received a standing ovation when he said, "I pray to God to spare my life long enough that I can be a pallbearer to these people's funeral, so as to send them to hell where they belong." FBI agents joined the campaign, Agent Frank Watts dubbing the terrorists "animals," while other G-men threatened reluctant informers with death. Ray Roberts made hay in the midst of chaos, recruiting more ex–Klansmen for his NSRP chapter.[27]

The stage was set for bloodshed. All it needed was a spark—and Thomas Tarrants would provide it soon.

CHAPTER 13

Dream Killers

From the 1955 Montgomery, Alabama, bus boycott onward, Martin Luther King, Jr., was arguably the prime target of racists nationwide, marked for death on multiple occasions. Klansmen bombed his Montgomery home on January 30, 1956, and solicited J. B. Stoner to kill King two years later, in Birmingham. In May 1963 they bombed Birmingham's Gaston Motel but missed King again. Four months later, John Crommelin joined William Gale, Noah Jefferson Carden, and suspected serial bomber Sidney Crockett Barnes in Birmingham to discuss King's murder. November 1963 brought William Somersett's report of NSRP member Joseph Milteer naming Klansman Jack Brown as a "likely" King assassin who had made prior murder attempts. Another Somersett report, from May 1964, identified a former Florida housepainter as planning to murder King on the 10th anniversary of the *Brown* ruling. Around that same time, racists rallied by Stoner and Connie Lynch shot up King's beach cottage in St. Augustine. In July 1964, leaders of Mississippi's White Knights solicited outside criminal help to kill King, continuing those efforts at Selma in January 1965. One month later, police arrested Nazi Keith Gilbert for stockpiling explosives, allegedly to kill King during a speech at California's Hollywood Palladium. June 1965 produced tales of James Venable's Klan, led by NSRP member Eloise Witte, plotting to murder King in Ohio. One year later, Mississippi's "Cottonmouth Moccasin Gang" killed sharecropper Ben Chester White, hoping to lure King within rifle range. In 1967 White Knights offered an "open contract" on King's life. On April 3, 1968—as he left Atlanta to lead a protest march in Memphis—a bomb threat delayed King's aircraft.[1]

One day later, at 6:01 p.m. on April 4, a sniper's bullet killed Dr. King at the Lorraine Motel in Memphis. Over the next week, ghetto riots erupted in 125 cities nationwide, leaving 46 persons dead, 2,600 injured, and 21,270 jailed, while property damage topped $45 million. By encouraging "white flight" from major cities to the suburbs, the so-called "Holy Week Uprisings" strengthened residential segregation and arguably tipped the scales for "law and order" presidential candidate Richard Nixon in November.[2]

Strong suggestions of conspiracy in King's death surfaced in Memphis on April 4 and spread internationally over the next two months, as prime suspect "Eric Starvo Galt"—later identified as escaped convict James Earl Ray—fled to Canada and then to Europe, financing his travels by means still unknown. FBI agents investigated various ranking bigots, including Jesse Stoner, but soon abandoned their hunt for anyone except a "lone nut assassin." In Stoner's case, agents learned that he addressed a Mississippi NSRP rally on April 4 and thereafter discounted him, never surmising that he might have had accomplices.[3]

Washington, D.C., was one of 125 cities scarred by race riots after Dr. King's murder. NSRP spokesmen hailed that violence as the onset of a race war (Library of Congress).

William Somersett allegedly developed another lead on King's assassination. According to a memo from Miami police lieutenant Charles Sapp, delivered to Chief Walter Headley on April 25, 1968, Somersett attended a National Labor Relations Board meeting in Washington on April 1, where he overheard members of the Longshoremen's Union and the Sanitation Workers' Union discussing King's interference in the Memphis garbage workers' strike. One spokesman allegedly said, "When Martin Luther King returns to Memphis, we don't have any alternative but to kill him," since King had "stopped being a preacher and is interfering as a labor organizer." Somersett warned his Miami handlers on April 3 and visited Atlanta the next day, where garage owner Frank Love predicted King would be murdered that night. Love, now deceased, and one of his employees "reluctantly verified" the conversation to Lieutenant Sapp on April 25. Florida Assistant Attorney General Seymour Gelber forwarded Somersett's information to U.S. Attorney General Ramsey Clark on April 9, 1968, but he got no response from anyone at the DOJ. Miami police reports on the King threats subsequently "disappeared," and were unavailable when the House Select Committee on Assassinations reviewed King's murder during 1976–79, concluding that Somersett's information was "without substance."[4]

Authorities finally identified "Eric Galt" as James Earl Ray on April 18, 1968, but he had given them the slip, fleeing through Canada to Britain and on from there to Portugal before returning to London. British police arrested him at Heathrow Airport on June 8, when Ray returned from Lisbon and presented false identification at the passport desk. Soon afterward, Ray received a letter from Jesse Stoner's "Patriotic Legal Fund," offering to represent him, but he declined in favor of ex–Birmingham mayor and perennial Klan defender Arthur Haynes, Sr. Harry Avery, Tennessee's Commissioner of Corrections, later said that Ray's brother, Jerry, claimed Stoner had represented him and James "two years before the assassination," but James was imprisoned at the time and congressional investigators were "unable to find evidence to support this allegation."[5]

Art Hanes flew to London on June 19, but a British judge barred him from seeing Ray and Hanes returned to Birmingham two days later. A second trip on July 5 proved more successful, Hanes advising Ray to give up his fight against extradition and return for trial in Tennessee. By then, Hanes had struck a lucrative deal with Alabama author William Bradford Huie, whose literary coups included purchasing and publishing confessions from the acquitted murderers of black teenager Emmett Till in *Look* magazine. Their contract gave Hanes

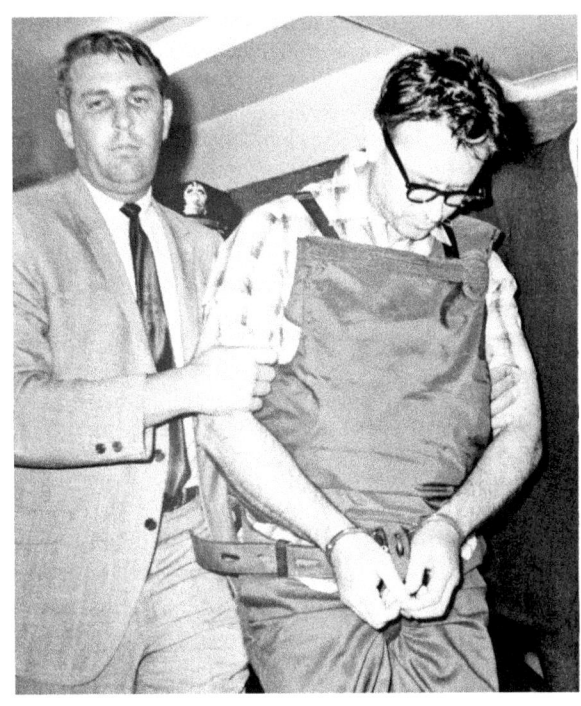

James Earl Ray in the custody of Shelby County Sheriff Bill Morris, following his extradition from England (National Archives).

$40,000 plus 60 percent of all future royalties on Huie's publication of Ray's tale, while granting Huie "absolute and exclusive rights" to the story. Ray initially opposed the deal, then reluctantly signed off while Hanes and son Arthur Jr., began their investigation. Meanwhile, Ray claimed, Huie personally offered him $12,000 to refrain from testifying at any future trial, thereby protecting the story from other authors. On November 8, four days prior to Ray's first scheduled trial date, brother Jerry phoned Texas celebrity attorney Percy Foreman—defender of some 1,500 murderers, who'd won acquittals for 1,439—to take over the defense. Foreman met Ray two days later, agreeing to replace Hanes for a fee of $150,000. His retainer: title to Ray's former car and the alleged murder rifle.[6]

Today, we know Foreman did next to nothing on Ray's case, spending less than an hour with Ray during his first 70 days on the job. He hired no investigators, and during a November 1969 civil suit admitted he had never heard the names of the state's key witnesses. He *did* collect $5,000 from Huie "for defense purposes," while devoting a month to a Florida divorce case, but otherwise proved elusive. Instead of defending his client, Foreman told Ray that a guilty plea "would be in [Ray's] financial interest." On the side, Foreman loaned money to Jerry Ray, telling James the loan was "contingent on the plea of guilty going through on March 10, 1969, without any unseemly conduct on your part in court." Presiding judge W. Preston Battle accepted that plea, later admitting that he feared Ray might have been acquitted otherwise.[7]

Huie, meanwhile, was hot on the trail of conspirators. His first salvo, appearing in *Look* four months before Ray's guilty plea, told readers:

The outline of the plot to kill Dr. King now begins to become visible to me. It may not be visible to my readers because, until Ray has been tried, I cannot reveal all that I have found to be true. But from what I know, what I have learned from Ray, and from my investigative research some of the features of the plot were:

* Dr. King was to be murdered for effect. His murder was planned, not by impulsive men who hated him personally, though they probably did hate him, but by calculating men who wanted his murder to trigger violent conflict between white and Negro citizens.

* He was to be murdered during the election year of 1968.

* Since he was to be murdered for maximum bloody effect, he was to be murdered, not while he was living quietly at his home in Atlanta, but at some dramatic moment, at some dramatic place where controversy was raging…

* He was to be murdered by a white man, or white men, who would be described as "Southerners" and "racists." …

* There was no necessity, after the murder, for the murderer or murderers to be murdered to prevent a trial—because a trial or trials could yield extra dividends of hatred and violence.

Therefore, in this plot, Dr. King was the secondary, not the primary target. The primary target was the United States of America.[8]

Ray's guilty plea in March 1969, coupled with government denials of conspiracy, scuttled Huie's plans for an explosive book-length exposé. Instead, a month after Ray's plea, Huie reversed his previous claims, asserting that Ray killed King on his own, in hope of gaining "criminal status."[9] What of the conspirators he'd mentioned earlier? Huie wrote:

Well, there are large conspiracies and little conspiracies. In large conspiracies, rich and/or powerful men are involved. Small conspiracies involve only little men…. I believe that one or two men other than James Earl Ray may have had foreknowledge of this murder, and that makes it a little conspiracy. But if there was a conspiracy, I now believe that James Earl Ray was probably its leader, not its tool or dupe.[10]

Remarkably, while posing as a longtime friend and confidant of Dr. King, Huie passed the next 17 years, until his death in 1986, with no attempt to name or otherwise identify the "little men" involved in King's murder. To explain his waffling on the case in *Skeptic* magazine, Huie claimed he "had agreed that *only after Ray had been tried and sentenced* would I publish *my account* of how and why Dr. King had been murdered. *Before* the trial I would publish only what Ray wanted published. *After* his trial and sentencing I would publish only the truth as I saw it."[11] Alas, Huie's contract with Hanes and Ray, long since made public, contains no such provision.

In 1976, a year before Huie lied in *Skeptic*, journalist George McMillan did his bit to paint Ray as a lone, racist assassin. As evidence, he wrote: "In 1963 and 1964 Martin Luther King was on TV almost every day, talking defiantly about how black people were going to get their rights, insisting that they would accept with nonviolence all the terrible violence that white people were inflicting on them, until the day of victory arrived, until they did overcome.

Ray watched it all on the cellblock TV at Jeff City. He reacted as if King's remarks were directed at him personally. He boiled when King came on the tube. He began to call him Martin 'Lucifer' King and Martin Luther 'Coon.' It got so that the very sight of King would galvanize Ray. 'Somebody's gotta get him,' Ray would say, his face drawn with tension, his fists clenched. 'Somebody's gotta get him.' "[12]

Bill Armontrout, associate warden at Jefferson City, Missouri's prison during Ray's tenure and after, says no TV sets were permitted on prison cellblocks until November

1970, three years after Ray's escape and two years after King's assassination. McMillan's crucial scene was a total fabrication.[13]

***

While James Earl Ray tried to dodge Tennessee's electric chair, and Jesse Stoner schemed to take over Ray's case, the NSRP was preoccupied with other violent events. Thomas Tarrants returned to Mississippi from North Carolina several times, huddling with Sam Bowers and other colleagues. On May 28, 1968—"Restoration Day" at white churches fund-raising for repairs to black churches damaged by terrorists—Tarrants and Danny Joe Hawkins bombed Meridian's Temple Beth Israel, causing $50,000 damage. Informers tipped FBI agents and Mississippi police that a terrorist from out of state, known only as "The Man," was responsible for most recent bombings in Meridian and elsewhere. Suspicion soon focused on Tarrants and Hawkins. In early June, Roy Gunn and Meridian Mayor Al Key visited wealthy ADL activist Adolph Botnick in New Orleans, opening negotiations for $36,500 to buy information leading to their suspects' capture. Although dedicated NSRP and Klan members, Alton and Raymond Roberts agreed to betray their comrades in exchange for cold cash. On June 24 the brothers reported that Tarrants and Hawkins were back in Meridian, planning to bomb the home of Jewish activist Meyer Davidson four days later. Police staked out the house but no one showed.[14]

On June 29 Tarrants met the Roberts brothers, accompanied by Kathryn Ainsworth, joining Tarrants for the Davidson attack while her husband spent two weeks training with the National Guard. Police lay in wait when the couple arrived and a gunfight ensued, killing Ainsworth, badly wounding Tarrants, a policeman, and a bystander. Tarrants survived to receive a 30-year prison term in November, while the NSRP denounced prosecution witnesses at his trial and parallel cases involving the White Knights as "FBI pimps." Tarrants briefly escaped in 1969, was recaptured, and later became a "born-again Christian" before his release in 1976.[15]

After the ambush, while eulogizing Ainsworth as a "martyr," the NSRP began raiding White Knights membership. Speakers drew 70 persons to a Jackson meeting, but FBI agents and police prodded a building inspector to seek code violations at their venue, forcing later meetings into private homes. G-men also sent a letter to the *Jackson Daily News*, signed by "one of the silent majority," protesting the influx of "radicals" and "rabble-rousers." Public meetings ceased in early 1970, with attendance at private gatherings shrunken to a handful.[16]

Ainsworth, deceased, was later mentioned as a suspect in two major 1968 assassinations. Her own mother claimed that she and Tarrants were in Memphis on April 4, crediting them with a CB radio hoax that diverted police from James Ray's escape route. Police reject that theory, blaming the "prank" on a youth who was never criminally charged. Other theorists claim Ainsworth was the mysterious "girl in a polka-dot dress" seen at the Ambassador Hotel in Los Angeles, accompanied by confessed assassin Sirhan Bishara Sirhan shortly before he allegedly killed presidential candidate Robert Kennedy. Seconds after that shooting, witnesses described the still-unidentified woman fleeing from the scene, shouting, "We killed the senator!" L.A. police insist that no such girl existed, and they pressured witnesses to change their stories with threats of potential prosecution.[17]

***

Two months before Tarrants faced trial in Mississippi, on September 1, Connie Lynch led an NSRP rally at Berea, Kentucky. Similar gatherings had passed without incident on July 20 and August 23, but this one sparked lethal violence. The rally was concluding at 4 p.m., when three carloads of African Americans rolled up to the site and furious words were exchanged. Gunfire erupted, killing local party Sergeant-at-Arms Elza Rucker and black assailant Lenoa John Boggs. Police charged seven blacks with killing Rucker, and jailed seven whites on suspicion of killing Boggs. Those held included Lynch, Peter Xavier, Jerry Pope, and four members from Ohio: Charles Eldridge, R. D. Eldridge, Dallas Hale, and Dudley Hughes, Jr.[18]

Berea's city council met on September 3, passing a resolution that condemned the violence and promised to investigate legal means of banning future "inflammatory gatherings," further suggesting creation of a human rights group to resolve the city's racial tension. A grand jury indicted 12 of the 14 suspects on riot charges. Six of the African Americans pled guilty to reduced charges of unlawful assembly and received nine-month jail terms. Following a two-day trial in March 1969, jurors convicted NSRP defendants Xavier, Pope, Hale, Hughes, and R. D. Eldridge on charges of disorderly conduct. All received $500 fines, while Xavier, Hughes and Eldridge also faced short jail terms. Lynch escaped punishment but entered Maryland's state prison in October, remaining there until November 1969. Party leaders treated victim Elza Rucker to a martyr's funeral, although his slaying went unpunished. Jesse Stoner seized the opportunity to tell CBS News that the party's goal was "a white Christian America without Jews or niggers."[19]

***

Stoner finally gained access to James Earl Ray on September 28, 1968, visiting him for 90 minutes at the Shelby County Jail in Memphis. Deputies logged their observation that "Mr. Stoner brought a note out of A Block with him which Ray had given him," but they had no clue to its contents beyond noting that the conference "involved a legal matter." Eleven years later, the HSCA reported that Ray and Stoner discussed a possible lawsuit against the Time Inc. news empire to prevent pretrial publicity.[20]

Three days after his March 1969 guilty plea, Ray penned a letter to Judge Battle, declaring, "I wish to inform the Honorable Court that famous Houston attorney Percy Fourflusher is no longer representing me in any capacity.... I intend to file for a post conviction hearing in the very near future." Soon afterward, Ray mailed another letter to Battle, saying, "I would respectfully request this court to treat this letter as a legal notice of an intent to ask for a reversal of the 99-year sentence petitioner received in this aforementioned court." A clerk found Battle dead in his chambers on March 31, killed by a heart attack. His head lay on his desk, atop Ray's letter and another defendant's plea for retrial. Tennessee law at that time required automatic granting of retrials if a judge died while considering the pleas, yet Ray's bid was denied, while the other inmate's was duly granted.[21]

Angered by Tennessee's violation of its own statute, Ray formally hired Stoner in April 1969, to press his plea for a retrial. Stoner failed, and his case was not officially reopened until Congress tried to solve the mystery a decade after King's death. Ray maintained his claim of innocence for the rest of his life, until complications from a chronic hepatitis C infection killed him in April 1998.[22]

13. Dream Killers

***

Politics distracted NSRP headquarters in 1968. John Crommelin entered Alabama's Democratic senatorial primary in May, polling 10,926 votes out of 535,362 ballots cast, placing fifth in a field of six contenders. His entry in New Hampshire's Democratic presidential primary was even more embarrassing, producing a mere 186 votes. In southern California, William Gale sought to represent the state's 27th congressional district, but he polled only 3,371 votes out of 75,602 cast in the Republican primary, placing last in a three-man race.[23]

Meanwhile, George Wallace's presidential campaign garnered support from racists nationwide, bolstered by reactions to the riots after Dr. King's assassination. Wallace's vehicle was the American Independent Party, founded by Californian William Kennedy Shearer and wife Eileen in 1967. From day one the AIP was a conglomerate of far-right racist groups, including the Citizens' Councils, John Birch Society, KKK, Minutemen, and others. When the party chose Wallace as its presidential candidate, John Crommelin helped Willis Carto found a Youth for Wallace group in Washington, D.C. Jesse Stoner told reporters, "Our slogan is the same as in 1964: Governor George C. Wallace—Last Chance for the White Vote!" Maryland's Klan leader wired Wallace his "100 percent support" and Ace Carter remained Wallace's favorite speechwriter, paid by a third-party corporate backer. When Wallace addressed cheering supporters at Madison Square Garden in October 1968, journalists identified various delegates as Klansmen, Minutemen, and American Nazis sporting "I Like Eich" buttons. In St. Louis, John Larry Ray—brother of James—distributed AIP campaign literature from his saloon. Cash seemed plentiful: Texas oilman Nelson Bunker Hunt personally delivered a suitcase containing $250,000 and watched Wallace stuff $18,000 into his coat pocket. The net result, while far from triumphant, was still encouraging for bigots. On November 5 Wallace and the AIP received 13.5 percent of the national popular vote—some 9.9 million ballots in all—and won 46 Electoral College votes from Alabama, Arkansas, Georgia, Louisiana, and Mississippi.[24]

Interviewed by Robert Sherrill after the election, Jesse Stoner claimed the party "indirectly could swing 20,000 votes in Georgia," but offered no proof. He described the party as "growing rapidly," but a financial report to the House of Representatives showed expenditures of $40,000 yearly exceeding income by $5,000. Headquarters circulated 25,000 copies of *The Thunderbolt* monthly, but few went to paying subscribers. In summation, Stoner said, "We are a white racist extremist organization. We take an anti-nigger stand. Some Klans we work with and some we don't. The ones we don't are controlled by the FBI."[25]

On November 15 Willis Carto used his Youth for Wallace mailing list to create a new National Youth Alliance. Formally incorporated in March 1969, the NYA published a newsletter titled *ATTACK!* that focused on denigration of Jews and nonwhites. Its board of advisors included John Crommelin and four fellow anti–Semites: ex–Bircher and *National Review* cofounder Revilo Pendleton Oliver; sometime radio commentator Richard Berkley Cotten, best known for telling listeners, "Freedom is not free; Free men are not equal, and equal men are not free"; ex–Marine Corps lieutenant general Pedro del Valle; and German-American scholar Austin Joseph App, a Holocaust denier and frequent contributor to Gerald Smith's *The Cross and the Flag*. In 1970, NSWPP defector William Luther Pierce joined the NYA, penning articles for *ATTACK!* as "Luther

Williams," later chafing at Carto's domination and leading a dissident NYA faction to become his own National Alliance.²⁶

The AIP faced its own changes after Wallace's defeat. In 1969 delegates from 40 states established a new American Party to supplant the AIP, while remnants of the parent organization clung to life across the landscape, nominating presidential candidates in the next four elections, finally merging with other far-right parties after 1980.²⁷

***

Today, thanks to investigative journalists, we know at least one NSRP member plotted Dr. King's assassination for a full year in advance, beginning with King's speech against the Vietnam war in New York, exactly one year to the day before his death. Joseph Milteer, with comrade Hugh R. Spake and two others, spent most Fridays in 1967 at Atlanta's General Motors plant, collecting payday contributions from the factory's Klan and Citizens' Council employees. At the time, an estimated 80 percent of Atlanta's United Auto Workers' members belonged to the Council, with some 5,000 doubling as Klansmen. Ostensibly, the money went to forestall integration at the plant; in fact, most of it was invested in a contract on King's life, while the remainder purchased mountain woodland acreage in North Carolina, later home to far-right "survivalist" groups.²⁸

In autumn 1967 a threat to Dr. King emerged from Atlanta, later judged "credible" by the HSCA. A man known only as "Ralph" approached house-painting brothers Claude and Leon Powell in a local bar, displaying $25,000 in a briefcase and promising another $25,000 when King was dead. When the brothers hesitated, Ralph departed and they never say him again. Claude reportedly passed an FBI polygraph test, while Leon's was "inconclusive." The DOJ filed its report and took no further action.²⁹

Dixie Mafia boss Carlos Marcello employed Klan members as "muscle" and confessed involvement in the JFK assassination to prison cellmates. Some theorists believe he also "brokered" the King assassination for profit and personal pleasure (National Archives).

Authors Lamar Waldron and Thom Hartmann conclude that Milteer conspired to kill Dr. King with Carlos Marcello—boss of a powerful Mafia family spanning the South, whose interest in King spanned his involvement in refuse collection (targeted by Dr. King in Memphis during 1968) and his bitter racism, including donations to the Klan and employment of Klansmen as "muscle" in labor disputes. Also a prime suspect in JFK's assassination, Marcello confessed his role in that crime to a prison cellmate shortly before his death. He was also deeply involved with Jimmy Hoffa's Mafia-dominated Teamsters Union in states where Marcello held sway. Marcello's acquaintance with NSRP members dated from his days funding right-wing exile raids on Cuba for the CIA during the early 1960s.³⁰

More crucial yet is the revelation that James Ray telephoned Hugh Spake in Atlanta on the morning after King's murder. Spake in turn called Milteer, who drove 230 miles from his Quitman home to Atlanta in time for Ray's arrival there on the evening of April 4. Milteer's presence in Atlanta is confirmed by a letter from fellow Constitution Party member Woody Kerns, of West Virginia, who wrote to Milteer on April 19: "Looks as though you and the hunted suspect were in the capital area about the same time. They found a car there—they say." The car in question was Ray's Mustang, parked at the Capitol Homes housing project. Curiously, while nonsmoker Ray allegedly traveled alone, FBI agents found the Mustang's ashtray brimming with cigarette butts, while the passenger's side of its floorboard bore muddy footprints.³¹

As G-men shuffled evidence to support their director's lone-assassin verdict, informer William Somersett traveled widely in search of clues to Dr. King's assassins. His memo filed with Miami police on June 11, 1968, reported visits to South Carolina, Alabama, Tennessee and Mississippi, "circulating around in order to obtain information in regards to the assassination of Martin Luther King." In Memphis he met alcoholic Charles Quitman Stephens, the only prosecution witness who could place Ray at the murder scene and thus secure his extradition from England. Somersett reported that Stephens "said he had lied to the police and FBI, saying he knew something about it, whereas he did not." Other witnesses, ignored by the state, described Stephens as passed out drunk when the shooting occurred. In a second memo, dated August 29, Somersett quoted a rabid racist Miami housepainter and friend of NSRP member Thomas Tarrants as blaming Tarrants for the CB radio hoax that diverted Memphis police on April 4 and saying that he—the painter—"allowed Tarrants to stay at his home a week or ten days after the killing of Martin Luther King."³²

The HSCA's final assassinations report of 1979 makes no mention of Tarrants or Milteer as suspects in Dr. King's death. Milteer *was* briefly mentioned, albeit anonymously, in regard to the JFK case, but he was spared interrogation by his death in February 1974. Sometime between 1971 and 1976, the Dade County state's attorney's files on Milteer vanished from a North Miami warehouse, according to Judge Seymour Gelber. Hugh Spake lived on until January 5, 2006, but no one showed any interest in questioning him. As authors Waldron and Hartmann note, "[T]here may be no one left to prosecute for Dr. King's murder, but authorities should at least explore the possibility."³³

***

The 1960s ended with a flurry of activity by NSRP members and allies. In April 1969 Edward Fields addressed 100 students at Chicago's Bogan Junior College (now Daley College), advocating "repatriation" of black Americans to Africa. That same month, informers reported Chicago party members mingling with United Patriots International, a self-described "militant anti–Communist group" that had harassed members of Students for a Democratic Society in February, at the University of Chicago. Leader Emile Vedrine published the UPI's *Battle Cry* newsletter from suburban Englewood. In May, informers reported 25 Dayton, Ohio, members meeting at the home of organizer R. D. Eldridge.³⁴

The party held its national convention in Jacksonville, Florida, on June 7–8, cheering Norman Anspach when he said, "I won't be satisfied until every damn nigger in the state of Arkansas wants to shoot me." Jesse Stoner told attendees, "Our old friend Connie Lynch is up in the penitentiary in Baltimore, Maryland, but we hope to have him out this coming week. There is so many Jews on the parole board and so many niggers working in the offices, that they can't keep their faces straight, especially when it comes to dealing with a white face. Now, Connie Lynch up in Baltimore has been very happy in the penitentiary up there and [it] has been a good rest for him and he's expecting to get out and go back to fighting Jews and niggers again as soon as he can." Two weeks later, headquarters printed an "Open Season on Whitey" handbill for distribution in Chicago.[35]

On September 15 the party sent a three-page ultimatum to New Jersey legislators, opposing sex education in public schools. It read, in part: "At present we are engaged in a warfare between two diametrically opposed forces. Spiritually, pagan Talmudism is waging war on Biblical Christianity.... If you Men of State do not heed the will of the People who grant you your Power; if you do not protect the Integrity of Our Children, then your blood will be upon your hands and upon your children for you will ultimately have to answer to us, the MEN of the THUNDERBOLT, THE NATIONAL STATES RIGHTS PARTY. *SO HELP U.S. GOD.*" Signatories of the letter included Jerome E. Heinemann, John A. Goble, and Thomas F. Whorokowski. On September 28, Roy Wake, editor of the party's *Prairie Fire* newsletter, attended a Chicago meeting dominated by local UKA members.[36]

G-men were watching when Edward Fields, his wife and three children went nightclubbing with Chicago party members on December 20, 1969. One spy reported to headquarters that "Fields enjoys night clubs and is an avid dancer knowing all the latest steps." The next day, NSRP pickets protested the annual Israel Man of the Year dinner at Chicago's Conrad Hilton Hotel.[37]

In California, during 1969, party ally William Gale founded the paramilitary United Christian Posse Association, soon copied by retired dry cleaner and ex–Silver Shirt Legion member Henry Lamont Beach of Portland, Oregon, who plagiarized Gale's manifesto to charter units of his own anti–Semitic Posse Comitatus, which declared that no public officials above the rank of county sheriff held any legitimate authority. According to the Posse's literature, "Our nation is now completely under the control of the International Invisible government of the World Jewry."[38]

Meanwhile, on the far side of the country, NSRP spokesmen became embroiled with Klan politics in North Carolina. Contempt of Congress charges had placed UKA Imperial Wizard Robert Shelton in prison, along with Tarheel Grand Dragon James Robertson Jones. In Jones's absence, on July 4, 1969, Klansmen rallying at Swan Quarter, in Hyde County engaged in a shootout with hostile African Americans, leaving one black girl and two highway patrolmen wounded, plus one police car riddled with bullets. The incident curtailed open-air Klan rallies in North Carolina and turned a spotlight on dissension within UKA ranks. Acting Grand Dragon Joseph Bryant—identified as the state's NSRP chairman in 1958—was among 17 Klansmen arrested on charges of inciting a riot. While UKA headquarters hired lawyer Arthur Haynes, Sr., to defend most of those charged, Bryant retained his own attorney and later pled guilty. Titan E. J. Melvin called on statewide leaders to depose Bryant as grand dragon, and Tuscaloosa headquarters issued a report branding Bryant a government *provocateur*. The report included a letter from Edward Fields, alleging that Bryant "is an FBI pimp from way back.... He was kicked out of the NSRP in 1961 for being a paid pimp of the FBI." On September 15, 1969, Bryant and fellow UKA defectors nailed their membership cards to a cross before setting it afire and forming their own break-away faction, the North Carolina Knights of the Ku Klux Klan.[39]

The year ended badly for William Hoff in New York. Indicted for plotting to detonate explosives in a roomful of civil rights workers, he pled guilty to conspiracy and weapons charges, serving six years in Attica Prison.[40]

CHAPTER 14

Rumors of War

FBI agents had the NSRP under their microscope as 1970 began, noting in January that Chicago's chapter "does not appear to have any members willing to provide the funds or work to increase the low level of activities." In February an informer reported that a party member joined two UKA Klansmen meeting with "three civic leaders" at a Cicero bowling alley to discuss vigilante "civilian patrols" against street criminals.[1]

February's *Thunderbolt* announced Jesse Stoner's return from a visit to England, pictured in front of Westminster Abbey. Noting more than one million nonwhites in the country, he warned readers, "Unfortunately, most Englishmen, the whites, that is, practice birth control and only have small families. On the other hand, the Jewish-controlled Government pays the blacks and browns to have large families. The horrible result is that one child out of every five born in England is a negro. Inter-racial breeding, along with a high negro birth rate, will change Britain from a White nation into a mongrel dark nation in only a few generations unless all nonwhites in Britain are settled outside that country."[2]

In April 1970 G-men reported that *The Thunderbolt* had 800 Illinois subscribers, but when they pursued rumors of an active cell in Paradise, California, they found it defunct for over a year. On April 4 party members joined far-right radio preacher Carl McIntyre's Vietnam "Victory March" on Washington, where he proclaimed, "We are challenging the moratorium march and the entire hippie concept of immediate and total withdrawal—and that is surrender." Virtually lost among 50,000 protesters, the NSRP still claimed one of the march's largest delegations, gloating that police stopped them chasing hippies from the National Mall.[3]

Spies tipped the Bureau in advance to the NSRP's national convention in Newport, Kentucky, on June 20–21, 1970. Edward Fields initially said the gathering would be held at the lodge of an Italian with "Mafia connections," but its 200 delegates, drawn from across the USA and Canada, convened on Saturday at the Grandview Gardens Restaurant. One pilgrim from British Columbia touted Hitler as "a good man," while an "alcoholic former member" of the UKA and Minutemen sought sponsorship to become the party's Indiana organizer. Two other Indiana Minutemen suggested merging their group with the Hoosier NSRP and Indiana's UKA klavern. John W. Miller, Louisville's district chairman of the American Party, turned up "as an observer" with three colleagues, and several young men arrived by bus from Chicago. Registered speakers included Fields, Jesse Stoner, Ned Dupes, Ken Adams, Willie Wilson from Florida, Neuman Britton and Bob Barker (no relation to TV's *The Price is Right* host) from California, Jerome Heinemann from New Jersey, R. D. Eldridge from Ohio, and Roy Wake, publisher of the party's Chicago

NSRP members joined a Vietnam "Victory March" led by Carl McIntyre (with megaphone) in Washington, D.C., on April 4, 1970 (Library of Congress).

Prairie Fire newsletter. Eldridge told the cheering crowd that only "skunks" supported integration, while Wilson vowed to kill as many Jews and "niggers" as he could when the time came, adding, "And you'd better believe it!" Stoner gave the longest speech, hyping his Georgia gubernatorial campaign while blasting "niggers, Jews, and the Federal Bureau of Integration." Its agents were homosexual "Jew pimps," he said, and if elected he would "run all the niggers out of Georgia." Following collection of $600 for his race, a secret "top level" meeting was announced for midnight at the Gateway Motel. On Sunday, a pilgrimage was organized to Elza Rucker's Berea gravesite, but only three carloads of mourners turned out. Fields closed the meeting with a plea to recruit new members. Afterward, *The Thunderbolt* billed the convention as the party's "most successful ever."[4]

A month after the Newport gathering, on July 22, Roy Wake married Patricia Britton, Neuman's daughter. They divorced in December 1972, whereupon Wake moved back to Chicago from Arkansas.[5]

Candidate Stoner promised Georgia voters that if elected governor, he would reduce taxes to eliminate welfare and busing, repeal the state's compulsory education law, grant tuition for students in private white schools, freeze hiring of African Americans, impose a "special high tax on National Banks" to lower the sales tax, "stop the Jew-negro voting bloc in Atlanta from dominating Georgia elections," and "smash the Hippie and Black revolutionists in Georgia." Despite those vows, while panning Jews as "vipers from Hell" and claiming Hitler was "too moderate," Stoner still billed himself as the "candidate of love." "I love white people and white children," he proclaimed. Stoner sought in vain for major public forums, while the *Atlanta Constitution* opined that his true danger lay in the fact that he "makes all the other white racists look good." After WAGA-TV criticized Stoner, campaign manager Ed Fields pled for funds to broadcast "a message so dynamic that people will remember it 100 times longer than any Jew propaganda diatribe." The cash did not materialize, and as September's Democratic primary approached, Fields admitted, "We have run out of money." Stoner received 17,763 votes out of 794,982 ballots cast, easily defeated by liberal Jimmy Carter. Afterward, party treasurer Peter Xavier reported to Congress that the NSRP had received $39,434.5 in donations, while spending $40,298.14.[6]

A sideshow to the main event involved Stephen Donald Black—"Don" to his friends—a campaign volunteer at NSRP headquarters. While ostensibly serving Stoner, Black undertook a secret mission for Robert Lloyd, a leader of the NSWPP, to steal the NSRP's mailing list. On July 25, three days before Black's seventeenth birthday, live-in sentry Jerry Ray caught him in the act and shot him. Although near death, Black managed to survive, return to high school, and later rise to prominence in Klan affairs. Ray faced charges of aggravated assault, but jurors acquitted him in November. Before year's end Black met and befriended rising Klansman David Ernest Duke, who credits his racial "awakening" to *The Thunderbolt*. There, he later wrote: "Dr. Fields carefully documented Jewish control of America's three major television networks, NBC, ABC, and CBS."[7]

Jerry Ray (left), brother of James Earl Ray, with Jesse Stoner at NSRP headquarters, where he shot Don Black for trying to steal party files on July 25, 1970 (National Archives).

In other 1970 elections, NSRP member Lou Hennes sought a school board seat in Evanston, Illinois (while G-men tracked his spending), another party member tried in vain for Skokie's school board, and loyalist Bill Brailsford lost his bid to become the sheriff of Maryland's Baltimore County. In Alabama, John Crommelin ran for lieutenant governor, polling 7,678 votes out of 815,978 cast, running last in a field of four contenders.[8]

Sad news reached headquarters on October 8, when Wesley Swift died in California. Party alumnus Matt Koehl also faced hard times as chief of the NSWPP, when one Wilfried Kernbach approached William Pierce—holder of a Ph.D. in physics, who left his job at the aircraft division of Pratt & Whitney to work at ANP headquarters in 1966—bearing files purportedly proving Koehl was gay, allegedly stolen from the home of an ADL member who had infiltrated the NRP ten years earlier. Confronted with the "evidence," Koehl refused to step down, whereupon Pierce left the NSWPP in December to join the National Youth Alliance, rising to dominate that group, ultimately squeezing out founder Willis Carto and renaming it the National Alliance.[9]

14. *Rumors of War* 177

Roy Frankhouser faced his own travails in 1970, as FBI agents raided a Minuteman camp near his Pennsylvania home and "church." First publicized in *Playboy* magazine the previous year, the camp became a target after Frankhouser showed it to author Eric Norden, saying, "We've got hundreds of bunkers like this all over the country ... all of them packed with machine guns, mortars and automatic weapons—and that's in addition to the caches of arms we wrap in plastic and bury underground." Luckily for Frankhouser, by 1970 he was a paid informer of the ATF, recruited by Agent Edward Slamon. Affiliation with the feds would not spare Frankhouser from Nazi critics, though, as they accused him of expulsion from the UKA based on his homosexuality. (In fact, Frankhouser remained the UKA's Pennsylvania grand dragon as late as 1998).[10]

In January 1971 an FBI informer reported that the NSRP and Minutemen were stockpiling "bomb balls"—primitive grenades called "Blue 26 bomblets"—stolen from the Joliet Army Ammunition Plant in Illinois. The spy told G-men he was confident the two groups would consolidate for their convenience "if he made the suggestion." Two months later, burglars from the Citizens' Commission to Investigate the FBI looted COINTELPRO files from a field office in Media, Pennsylvania, subsequently publishing the lot and inspiring a series of congressional investigations. The Bureau's illegal harassment programs supposedly died with J. Edgar Hoover in May 1972, when countless secret files vanished from headquarters, but documents later released under the Freedom of Information Act

The Joliet Army Ammunition Plant, where party members allegedly stole explosives in January 1971 (Library of Congress).

prove that agents continued spying on the NSRP at least through 1974, noting cancellation of a rally planned in Berwyn, Illinois; the merger of Chicago's chapter with "the Northern NSRP group"; gatherings in Baltimore and Chicago; Stoner's travels to Texas, Arizona, and New Mexico; arrests of three Youth Corps members for defacing traffic signs in North Riverside, Illinois, slapped with $100 fines and one year's probation; contacts with Chicago's Klan; and widespread literature mailings.[11]

James Warner founded the Identity-based New Christian Crusade Church in early 1971 and resettled in California, publishing the *Christian Vanguard* newsletter while simultaneously chairing the Sons of Liberty publishing house and leading the seemingly contradictory Odinist Religion & Nordic Faith Movement. Ed Fields mailed a four-page "personal newsletter" to *Thunderbolt* subscribers in February, claiming that the party "gives you more action and more results than any other group," then spent the last half begging funds for a permanent headquarters. Jesse Stoner continued his defense of James Earl Ray, joining Memphis attorney Richard Ryan to sue Percy Foreman, William Huie and Art Hanes, Sr., before the Sixth Circuit Court of Appeals. A district court had already rejected Ray's plea for injunctive relief, and the Sixth Circuit affirmed that judgment in April 1971.[12]

While Stoner pursued Ray's appeals, North Carolina's Klans were in turmoil, overshadowed in 1971 by the more militant Rights of White People, whose members shot up homes and burned school buses around Wilmington. Black militants retaliated in kind, resulting in two shootout deaths. In May 1973 jurors convicted ROWP member Leroy Gibson of bombing a Maoist bookstore, thereby making him a movement martyr and winning support from the NSRP. Meanwhile, in February 1972 the party sponsored a protest outside the White House, condemning President Nixon's decision to recognize Communist China. The 10 participants included Jesse Stoner, William Pierce from the NYA, and members of David Duke's short-lived National Party. Duke also led the White Student Alliance at Louisiana State University in 1972, and was arrested with three fellow members—including future wife Chloe—for embezzling $500 from George Wallace's third presidential campaign. Klan leader James Lindsay persuaded the Wallace camp not to press charges.[13]

David Duke, Nazi and KKK leader, credited Edward Fields and *The Thunderbolt* for his "awakening" to the global "Jewish conspiracy" (National Archives).

Presidential politics were volatile in 1972. Aside from Nixon's "dirty tricks" campaign, climaxed by Watergate, George Wallace made another White House run, this time as a Democrat. (He had triumphed over incumbent Albert Brewer in 1970's gubernatorial race, vowing to stay off the White House trail and be a "full-time governor," then announced his next presidential campaign the day after his reelection.) Wallace's campaign ended in Laurel, Maryland, on May 15, 1972, when would-be assassin Arthur Bremer shot him five times and left him a paraplegic. Even so, he won primaries in Maryland,

Michigan, Tennessee and North Carolina, earning a speaker's slot at the Democratic National Convention. Without Wallace to carry its banner, the AIP nominated California congressman John Schmitz, an outspoken Bircher, and polled 1,100,868 votes—1.42 percent of the national total.[14]

Jesse Stoner set his sights on a U.S. Senate seat in 1972, entering Georgia's Democratic primary despite the state party's official rejection of his candidacy. His television ads—approved by the Federal Communications Commission in August, after complaints from the ADL and NAACP—declared: "I am the only candidate for U.S. Senator who is for the white people. I am the only candidate who is against integration. All of the other candidates are race mixers to one degree or another. The main reason why niggers want integration is because the niggers want our white women. I am for law and order with the knowledge that you cannot have law and order and niggers too. Vote white." The final count on September 9 showed 40,675 votes for Stoner out of 668,968 ballots cast, placing him seventh in a field of nine contenders.[15]

Victory was not the point, however. As Ed Fields told his readers: "Stoner spent only $10,000 for 40,675 votes.... Everyone knew we could not win, that our main goal was to reach the public with our message. The senate race was an ideal vehicle for the broadcasting of our views.... It resulted in $1 million worth of publicity for this cause." As for the future, he added: "What is required? Every Jew who holds a position of power or authority must be removed from that position. If that does not work, then we must establish [the] Final Solution!"[16]

One month after the primary, freshman Michael Fraase arrived in Carrollton, Georgia, to begin study at West Georgia College with a double major in psychology and philosophy. At the city limits, a billboard greeted new arrivals, decorated with photos of Stoner and Lester Maddox, warning black travelers to vacate Carroll County by sundown.[17]

The NSRP lost its foremost firebrand when a heart attack killed Connie Lynch on September 30, 1972, while he bathed at a friend's home in Starke, Florida. No one since John Kasper had roused mobs like Lynch, and the party would not see his like again. An ex-grand dragon was among the friends who bore him to his rest on Saturday, October 7. Don Black claims Lynch and friend Bob Barker left the party in summer 1970, but if so, Jesse Stoner harbored no hard feelings. Reminiscing, he told author Patsy Sims, "Connie and I had a lot of fun." Dr. Fields denies their defection outright.[18]

Roy Frankhouser kept busy in 1972, marching down Manhattan's Fifth Avenue in an NRP uniform to test the city's ban on Nazi regalia, embarking on a Klan speaking tour, offering to serve as an FBI informer against sundry terrorist groups (headquarters declined), and spinning tales for his ATF handlers about a Black September cell in Canada. In the process, he rubbed shoulders with Dr. Mohammed Taki Mehdidi, an Iraqi living in Manhattan, who had published an apparent apologia for Robert Kennedy's assassin four years earlier. Roy's career as secret agent "Ronnie" soured in February 1973, when he complained that the ATF was "cheating" him and they belatedly discharged their worthless spy. Despite exposure of his turncoat role, Frankhouser still attended the Liberty Lobby's third annual Policy Convention and National Strategy Seminar in October 1973, honoring paroled Minutemen founder Robert DePugh.[19]

Elsewhere in 1973, FBI informers followed the party's Chicago progress (five members with no office, bank account or funds) and noted a rally at Kilbourne Park; logged the March purchase of a house in Marietta, doubling as headquarters and Jesse Stoner's home; tabulated a national membership of 50 to 75, with 2,500 "mail-type members" receiving *The Thunderbolt*; found two small Indiana chapters distributing Klan and Minutemen pamphlets; noted an "operating group" in Villa Park, Illinois, dubbed the American Independent Youth Alliance; and observed Stoner traveling from Garland, Texas, to Tampa, Florida, and Richmond, Virginia. On August 30–28 months after COINTELPRO's "official termination"—the Albany field office wrote to Director Clarence Kelley, offering "suggested predication of investigation of leaders and activities" under various federal conspiracy and civil rights statutes.[20] That memo read:

> As the NSRP has engaged in provocative demonstrations apparently intended to create a confrontation with established authorities and/or opposing political groups, all activities should be subject to a full field investigation. In the case of a person attending an NSRP function where the particular function and/or participation involves a possible violation of the Federal law, the person attending the function should be considered an activist and the predication for the investigation of this individual is the one set forth above.[21]

In California, William Gale quarreled with disciple Richard Butler and they split, Butler subsequently migrating to Kootenai County, Idaho, erecting a fortified compound at Hayden Lake for his offshoot Aryan Nations, Church of Jesus Christ—Christian.[22]

A new face on the Nazi scene, as yet unrecognized, was that of James Clayton Vaughn, Jr., a Mobile, Alabama, native born in 1950, victim of a severe head injury at age seven, later a high school dropout. Vaughn stole a copy of *Mein Kampf* at age 15 and joined the American Nazi Party three years later, equally obsessed with Charles Manson's "helter skelter" race war in Los Angeles. At 20 he began stalking interracial couples, logging his first arrest—for carrying a concealed weapon—in 1972. He joined the NSRP in 1973 and peddled *The Thunderbolt* on street corners, then joined Atlanta's Klan three years later, but soon defected when the order proved too tame. That same year, he mailed a threatening letter to president-elect Jimmy Carter, legally changed his name to "Joseph Paul Franklin"—after Third Reich Minister of Propaganda Paul Joseph Goebbels and American founding father Benjamin Franklin—and attacked a mixed couple with chemical mace in Maryland. Already dangerous, his most flamboyant headlines lay ahead.[23]

Mississippi Klansman and assassin Byron De La Beckwith had joined the NSRP and befriended Jesse Stoner around the time of his 1964 mistrials for killing Medgar Evers. In 1973 he appeared as featured speaker at the party's national convention, then faced arrest in Louisiana on September 26, while carrying a time bomb, various other weapons, and stolen license plates to New Orleans, intent on blasting the home of ADL Director Adolph Botnick, who orchestrated the Tarrants-Ainsworth ambush five years earlier. Tracked by ATF agents and state police from a luncheon meeting with Klan bomb maker Laude Matthews, where he received the explosive device, Beckwith made bail on October 20 and flew home on the private plane of an unnamed "concerned patriot." Mississippi's UKA promised $50,000 for Beckwith's defense but could only raise $5,000, while David Duke called Beckwith a "penniless victim of government illegality and crime." Despite those efforts and a rousing defense by Klan attorney Travis Buckley, jurors convicted Beckwith of conspiracy to commit murder on August 1, 1975. Still free on bond pending appeal, he joined Stoner and 1,000 other Nazis for the September 1976 World Nationalist Conference at New Orleans, then resigned his Methodist affiliation in October, becoming a member of James Warner's New Christian Crusade Church. On January 2, 1977, the Rev. Buddy Tucker—founder of National Emancipation of the White Seed—ordained Beckwith as an Identity minister in Knoxville, Tennessee. Beckwith's appeals ran out in April 1977, and May found him caged at Louisiana's Angola State Prison, where he languished until January 1980. Stoner visited Beckwith in jail, as did James Warner's wife, while imprisoned Klansman and NSRP devotee Robert Schepff greeted Beckwith as an "old friend." Upon release, Beckwith rejoined his "jolly band" including Stoner, Edward Fields, retired lieutenant colonel Gordon "Jack" Mohr, and John Standring's paramilitary Christian Guard.[24]

Beckwith's legal problems were a sideshow to the party's main events in 1973 and '74. International relations burgeoned as Canadian Klansman John Ross Taylor addressed the party's 1973 convention, and Jesse Stoner returned the favor, speaking at a banquet of the Western Guard a year later. FBI agents kept watching the party through summer 1974, collecting copies of *The Thunderbolt* with headlines reading "Jews Control Pornography Rackets," "Study of African Reactions to Solar Eclipse," "Shocking Truth of FBI 'COINTELPRO' Plot," and "Married Women Urged to Keep Maiden Names!"[25]

A major focus of the party and the Bureau was Jesse Stoner's campaign to succeed Lester Maddox as Georgia's lieutenant governor, detailed in the July 1974 *Thunderbolt*. Controversy ensued when Macon mayor Ronald "Machine Gun Ronnie" Thompson ordered Stoner's campaign signs removed from city buses, sparking accusations of censorship and conspiracy. Stoner personally retaliated with a tongue-in-cheek call for blacks to support Thompson in the Republican primary. While neither candidate won his race in August, Stoner's 73,449 votes out of 790,217 ballots cast placed him fourth among 10 Democratic contenders—and his vote alone surpassed all votes cast for the GOP's four gubernatorial primary candidates.[26]

During that hectic Georgia race, Stoner was distracted by a lawsuit in Jacksonville, Florida, arising from the city's refusal to let the NSRP meet at its Civic Auditorium's Little Theatre "so long as [the] Party's membership policies discriminate on the basis of race or color." A federal district court issued the injunction and Stoner appealed on behalf of local party leader Willie Wilson, while a group of African Americans sued for permission to join the rally. In July 1974 the Fifth Circuit Court of Appeals declared, "The case, simple enough to state, presents awesome problems as First and Fourteenth Amendment rights collide." Finding that the city leased the Little Theater to all applicants on a first come, first served basis, three justices voided the injunction while permitting blacks to pursue their claim against the city. It was a victory of sorts for both sides, but the meeting's date had long since passed and it was not rescheduled.[27]

On February 21, 1974, FBI agents arrested Roy Frankhouser on suspicion of leading an explosives theft and smuggling ring. The pilferage occurred between January and July 1973 at the Reading Anthracite Company in Schuylkill County, where thieves stole dynamite, 960 pounds of black powder, hundreds of electric blasting caps, and thousands of feet of detonation cord. The arrest blew Frankhouser's ATF cover and left handlers scrambling to deny that he involved himself in the conspiracy at their behest, though Agent Edward Slamon granted under oath that many of Roy's travels and activities were approved by Jack Caulfield, an ATF assistant director mired in the Watergate scandal. Charles Edward Sims, a former bodyguard for Klansman Robert Miles in Michigan, claimed Frankhouser had shipped 240 pounds of dynamite to the Wolverine Klan. Miles, in turn, gloated when "Thor in heaven threw down some of his plumbing from Valhalla" on October 13, 1974, leaving Sims brain-damaged at a federal lockup in Terre Haute, Indiana. Witnesses against Frankhouser suffered a run of grim luck: shotgun blasts killed two, in March and June 1975, while conviction on burglary charges rendered a third's testimony worthless. That September, Frankhouser pled guilty on two reduced charges, receiving a sentence of "unrestricted one-year probation" in exchange for recantation of his accusations against the ATF.[28]

While the NSRP stood aloof from Frankhouser during his trial, it openly heralded the 1974 return of white supremacist Gerald Russell Carlton, founder of the National Christian Democratic Union, from self-imposed European exile. David Duke, rising to command Louisiana's Knights of the KKK after founder James Lindsay's still-unsolved murder, recruited Don Black and other NSWPP members to the fold and visited James Warner's North Hollywood home in 1974, where he met New Christian Crusade Church member and future California grand dragon Tom Metzger. The first issue of Duke's *Crusader* newsletter advertised Warner's church, and Warner moved to Louisiana in 1975, joining the Klan. Duke also solicited aid for Robert Miles and Byron De La Beckwith, while praising slain Mississippi terrorist Kathryn Ainsworth as "an innocent, pregnant Christian girl." In 1976 the anonymous *DeGuello Report* by supposed Nazi insiders accused Warner of supporting himself and his church via mailing lists stolen from the NSRP, ANP, Willis Carto, and Wesley Swift. It also branded Warner and Duke as gay lovers, describing Warner "following Duke around, holding hands with him in public bars and casting long loving glances his way." Needless to say, both Warner and Duke deny all such charges, while the *DeGuello Report*'s anonymity precluded libel actions.[29]

Frazier Glenn Miller became "obsessed" with white supremacy after reading *The Thunderbolt* in 1974, embarking on a lifelong course of racial terrorism (National Archives).

In North Carolina, active-duty Green Beret Frazier Glenn Miller read an issue of *The Thunderbolt* in summer 1974, and "within two minutes of browsing.... I knew I had found a home within the American White Movement. I was ecstatic." He ordered more literature from Marietta headquarters, including *Mein Kampf*, and soon joined the party at age 34, aided by Tarheel organizer Ken Poole. After his first rally in Rocky Mount, Miller described himself as "obsessed, totally, completely, and unashamedly, and I stayed that way for the next 12 years," until his imprisonment on federal conspiracy charges—and, as we shall see, for long years afterward. While never breaking fully with the NSRP, Miller switched his formal membership to Harold Covington's National Socialist Party of America in February 1976, then formed his own Klan in 1980. Throughout those years, Miller writes, "I also continued to send money to the National States Rights Party, ordering thousands of copies of their newspaper, which I continued to distribute all over the state." Covington accompanied Miller to NSRP rallies, including one in 1978 where a new recruit got drunk and terrorized a store near Rocky Mount at gunpoint.[30]

Farther north, in May 1975, a spokesman for the party's Chicago chapter attended a UKA meeting at a motel in Kankakee, Illinois. Before an audience of 25, including 10 members of the Devil's Advocates Motorcycle Club, he announced a Windy City meeting for the next week. Two recruits sworn in as new Klansmen were paid investigators for the Illinois Legislative Investigating Commission.[31]

Media exposure of widespread crimes committed by the FBI and CIA prompted formation of the U.S. Senate Select Committee to Study Governmental Operations with Respect to Intelligence Activities in January 1975. Commonly called the Church Committee, after chairman Frank Church of Idaho, the 11-member panel held extensive hearings, interviewing federal officials, their informers, and the targets of various government harassment campaigns. Gary Rowe emerged from the witness protection program to testify in a crude white hood, detailing flagrantly illegal orders from his Bureau handlers and their suppression of evidence linking Klansmen to violent crimes. Volume 6 of the panel's report, published in April 1976, included 1,000 pages of documents on FBI misbehavior, tracing J. Edgar Hoover's criminal behavior back to 1939. The DOJ adopted new guidelines for investigation, but later revelations indicate they were more honored in the breach than in observance, with abuses still reported to the present day. In April 1976, concurrent with publication of the committee's report, Attorney General Edward Levi ruled that the NSRP posed no threat and canceled any further surveillance. Jesse Stoner's FBI file claims investigation and informer coverage ended in 1975, yet G-men still logged his passport application a year later.[32]

David Duke formally chartered his Knights of the KKK in August 1975, recruiting NSRP alumnus Jerry Dutton as acting grand wizard, but they soon parted ways. As he had left the NSRP to create his own National White Americans Party, Dutton quit Duke's Klan in November 1976 to join rival Bill Wilkinson's Invisible Empire Knights. In transit, he published a pamphlet, *The Truth About David Duke,* that pegged Duke's total membership around 300; branded Duke "a liar"; revealed Duke's pseudonymous authorship of a sex guide for women and a martial arts manual for black militants; and accused Duke of mishandling Klan funds. John Crommelin saw no problems with Duke, however, assuming duties as the *Crusader*'s editor in 1976.[33]

September 1976 saw the World Nationalist Congress, also called the International Patriotic Congress, convened at Duke's base in Metairie, Louisiana. Aside from Duke, attendees included Jesse Stoner, James Warner, Byron De La Beckwith, Jerry Dutton, Richard Cotten, Louisiana Klansman Rene LaCoste, plus Identity preachers Dan Gayman, Buddy Tucker, and Joseph Dilys from Warner's New Christian Crusade Church. Delegates from 35 foreign countries included Manfred Roeder from West Germany, with Canadian Nazis Wolfgang Droege, James McQuirter, and John Taylor. Warner's *Christian Vanguard* billed the meeting as "a worldwide Anti-Jewish Congress" and "the first step in 40 years of Right-wing organizations to form a united front against the Jews." Police arrested Duke and Warner for inciting a riot and failure to disperse after a confrontation with counter-demonstrators. Jurors convicted both in May 1977, resulting in a six-month jail sentence and a $250 fine for Duke, while Warner got off with three months and $150. A new judge reconsidered Warner's case in July, permitting a reduced guilty plea to disturbing the peace and suspending his jail term. Duke collected more than $10,000 for appeals and secured a second trial in August. Although convicted once again, his jail term was suspended in favor of one year's probation, while his fine doubled to $500.[34]

Presidential politics dominated headlines in 1976, but the race offered little to white supremacists. Lester Maddox claimed the AIP's nomination in August, leading a field of four contenders, but fellow Georgian Jimmy Carter swamped him in November, leaving

Maddox with 170,531 votes out of 81.6 million ballots cast, running fifth in a field of fourteen rivals.[35]

James Warner emerged from his near-miss conviction as Duke's grand dragon for Louisiana and soon revived the dormant CDL, buying an ad in *The Spotlight* on September 26, 1977, that warned: "The Zionists have managed to take prayer out of your schools. They have managed to integrate MAJORITY schools while keeping theirs segregated on 'religious grounds.' They have forced manufacturers of food products to put their 'K' and 'U' symbols on food and passed this Kosher Tax on to you. If you are fed up and want to fight back then write to: CHRISTIAN DEFENSE LEAGUE." When that movement failed to prosper, Warner led a campaign protesting NBC-TV's miniseries *The Holocaust* in April 1978. Socially, David Duke served as a witness to Warner's marriage when Warner tied the knot with Debra Coleman—daughter of "Dr." John Coleman, false claimant of former ties to British intelligence agencies, best known for his fantastic exposés of Zionist conspirators he dubbed the "Black Nobility." In spring 1978 the *Baton Rouge Morning Advocate* reported Deborah's demand for three prime-time TV hours, granting the CDL an opportunity "to present their version of what happened to Jews in Europe during the period just before and during World War II." She also opposed the East Baton Rouge Parish school board's use of a study guide linked to *The Holocaust,* preferring that students read *The Six Million Swindle* and *The Hoax of the Twentieth Century*. "Let's keep history that's fact," she said. "I don't think we should constantly be reflecting on things in the past." Asked her opinion of the Holocaust's reality, she sniffed, "How is that relevant?"[36]

Nineteen seventy-six closed with issuance of the anonymous *DeGuello Report,* a 40-page booklet mailed to selected members hailed as "person[s] whose integrity is highly regarded among Nationalists in the United States." Drawing its name from a bugle call, named for the Spanish verb *degollar* ("throat-cutting") that symbolized no quarter, the original Deguello is best known for its employment at the Alamo in 1836. Specifically, the 1976 broadside warned fascists of their movement's alleged infiltration by Communism sporting "three faces": Socialism, Judaism, and "homosexuality." Beginning with Karl Marx, it condemned the John Birch Society (whose "considerable financial strength comes through secret transfer of money from Jewish individuals and/or organizations in the amount of $300,000 to $800,000 yearly"); Conde McGinley ("completely duped by a Jew named Benjamin Freedman, who pretended to have turned against his own people"); Bertrand Comparet and his followers ("deeply infiltrated" by Jews); Jesse Stoner (named as gay, an ADL informer, and "an especially destructive Jew infiltrator into the U.S. Nationalists movement," whose "specialty is running for political office so as to gain public exposure where he spews forth a stream of such venomous hatred toward the negro [sic] race as to convince most fair minded citizens that the typical leader of an American Nationalist organization must be totally insane"); James Madole of the NRP (an "aging homosexual" financed by Jews); and a long list of additional reputed gay traitors including Roy Frankhouser, James Warner and "girlfriend" Dan Burros, Oren Potito, William Pierce, Edwin Walker, and David Duke (absurdly described as a leftist who "overflowed with sympathy for the negro [sic] people"). In fact, the report declared, "Within the United States, the Nationalist movement has been infiltrated by homosexuals to an extent that is almost incredible." Edward Fields made the list, falsely linked for the first time to Chicago's Marshall Field and the Morrell meat-packing firm.[37]

While echoes from the *DeGuello Report* reverberated through the racist right, the NSRP continued its bid to go international. In 1976 Fields, Stoner, and Warner joined

David Duke in Diksmuide, Belgium, for a rally with the *Vlaamse Militanten Orde* (Order of Flemish Militants), whose members fought with Hitler's troops against their countrymen in World War II. (Stoner used his new passport, acquired in Miami on May 21.) Also present were members of Britain's League of St. George, a self-described umbrella group for Nazis of all ages, linked to anti–Catholic terrorists of the Ulster Defense Association in Northern Ireland. Observers note that Fields and Stoner also "traveled regularly" to Great Britain, addressing rallies of the blatantly racist National Front. After one such trip, Fields informed *Thunderbolt* readers, "To thundering cheers from the throng I told the patriots that the Jew is the common enemy of all the white nations of Europe.... I also warned that colored immigration and foreign workers threatened to pollute and destroy all the white countries of Europe." Later, at another Diksmuide rally, futile plans were hatched for breaking Jesse Stoner out of prison, where he'd landed on a bombing charge.[38]

In 1977, after a short stint with Alabama's National Guard, Joseph Paul Franklin launched a one-man reign of terror with his first bank holdup in Atlanta. From there, on July 25, he bombed the Maryland home of Morris Amitay, executive director of the American Israel Public Affairs Committee, killing the family dog. Four days later Franklin struck again, bombing a Chattanooga synagogue. On August 7 he robbed a Wisconsin bank and killed an interracial couple, Alphonse Manning and Tony Schwenn, at a nearby shopping mall. Before year's end, Franklin robbed more banks in Arkansas and Ohio, then killed black St. Louis victim Gerald Gordon in October, wounding companion William Ash. In February 1978 he killed Johnny Brookshire and paralyzed Brookshire's white girlfriend, Joy Williams, in Atlanta. The following month, he wounded *Hustler* publisher Larry Flynt and lawyer Gene Reeves outside a Georgia courthouse, leaving Flynt a paraplegic. Later that year, Franklin robbed banks in Georgia, Kentucky, and Alabama, then killed Bryant Tatum and wounded his white girlfriend, Nancy Hilton, in Chattanooga. Married for the second time in Georgia during 1979, Franklin capped his honeymoon by killing Harold McIver at a fast-food restaurant that July, then drove to Virginia for another restaurant slaying, of Raymond Taylor, in August. Franklin broke his wedding vows with teenage prostitute Mercedes Masters in December 1979, then killed her when she admitted "dating" black clients.[39]

Joseph Paul Franklin, NSRP member and Klansman, launched a one-man reign of terror against minorities nationwide in 1977, killing more than 20 victims before his final capture (National Archives).

While Franklin remained unidentified, NSRP member Frederick William Cowan made bloody headlines in New Rochelle, New York, on St. Valentine's Day 1977. Born in 1943, a graduate of Catholic schools and an ex-army sharpshooter—court-martialed twice, for going AWOL and leaving the scene of a car accident—Cowan came back to his parents' home, decorating his room with Nazi regalia and his body with Nazi tattoos. A 250-pound bodybuilder, he worked 10 years for Neptune Moving and Storage before Jewish supervisor Norman Bing suspended him in January 1977, citing rudeness to customers. Cowan returned with guns blazing on February 14, killing Bing and four coworkers—three black, one a recent immigrant from India—and wounding five more. When police arrived, he killed one officer and wounded three, then shot himself. Neighbors recalled him as "a nice man" but "real prejudiced," who spent his leisure time with boys and "did not seem to like women particularly." When one youth asked if he would rather have a girl or a gun, Cowan "said he didn't need girls," adding, "If you want to be a man, get a gun." Sometimes he called himself "the second Hitler." Aside from the NSRP, journalist Maury Terry documented Cowan's friendship with local resident Jack Cassara, landlord of "Son of Sam" serial killer David Berkowitz.[40]

James Warner tried to revive the moribund CDL in early 1977, calling on father-in-law John Coleman for his alleged expertise. Gunshot survivor Don Black toured the country as David Duke's right-hand man, introduced by Duke to one New York audience as the "new breed of Klansman, young, articulate, educated," but when he tried using the Klan as a launching pad for his 1979 Birmingham mayoral race, Black polled only 1,786 votes out of 60,398 ballots cast, running sixth in a field of seven contenders. Meanwhile, Black's near-killer, Jerry Ray, still lived at party headquarters in Marietta through 1977, into 1978.[41]

Jesse Stoner had problems of his own. In Alabama, Attorney General Bill Baxley reopened Birmingham's racist bombing cases in 1977. Herman Cash and Gary Rowe allegedly passed polygraphs; John Hall and suspect Ross Keith both died of cirrhosis before their tests. Baxley secured testimony from Elizabeth Cobbs with a promise to charge uncle Robert Chambliss, Jesse Stoner, Robert Shelton, and unnamed Birmingham police with the BAPBOMB explosion. Instead, Chambliss faced indictment alone, while Stoner was charged on July 26 with bombing Bethel Baptist in 1958. A year before the grand jury handed down those indictments, Edward Fields wrote to Baxley, accusing him of pursuing the cases for private political gain.[42] Baxley's reply, penned on official stationery and dated February 28, 1976, was succinct.

Dear "Dr." Fields:
   My response to your letter of February 19, 1976 is—kiss my ass.
Sincerely,
Bill Baxley
Attorney General[43]

Stoner surrendered in Cobb County on July 28. Governor Wallace signed an extradition order eight days later, but Stoner won a delay on December 20. Anticipating a courtroom defeat, Stoner launched another gubernatorial bid in February 1978, planning to shield himself from extradition if elected. He faced incumbent George Busbee, who had angered racists in March 1978 by signing the Georgia Fair Employment Practices Act. Calling Busbee "one of the worst race-mixing governors in the history of Georgia," Stoner promised to repeal that statute, adding that if Busbee won a second term he would celebrate by passing more laws that "take from the whites and give to the niggers." Despite a petition from Atlanta NAACP leader Julian Bond, the FCC reaffirmed Stoner's right to free speech, including TV spots repeating, "We cannot have law and order and niggers too." On August 8 primary voters gave 37,654 votes to Stoner out of 695,911 ballots cast, placing him third in a field of six rivals, while Busbee easily won reelection. Georgia opened extradition hearings on September 20, but Cobb County judge Howell Ravan rejected Alabama's petition on November 29. Georgia appealed, but Ravan stood firm until the state's supreme court overruled him in July 1979. The same court refused to hear Stoner's appeal, and in November he filed a last-ditch plea with the U.S. Supreme Court.[44]

While working toward a conclusion that both JFK and Dr. King died at the hands of conspirators, the House Select Committee on Assassinations considered many suspects in King's death, including Jesse Stoner, various Klans, and the Minutemen.[45] Stoner received his subpoena on January 31, 1978, and appeared on April 18, denying any knowledge of plots against King, but told committee members that Klansman Hugh Morris had offered him $25,000 in the late 1950s, to find a sniper who would murder King. Stoner refused, he said, but admitted spoofing Morris with an offer to kill King with dynamite, for an up-front payment of $5,000 he planned to bank without following

The House Select Committee on Assassinations found evidence of conspiracy in the JFK and King assassinations but ignored critical evidence from both cases (Library of Congress).

through. Later, Stoner said, Morris approached Ace Carter with his $25,000 offer. Carter denied it, and the panel found no evidence supporting Stoner's claims. Morris, for his part, said Stoner hoped to discredit him prior to his appearance for the state at Stoner's bombing trial.[46]

The HSCA made light of informant William Somersett's several reports to Florida police and federal agencies concerning both assassinations, and managed—awkwardly—to summarize his remarks without naming Joseph Milteer, killed in suspicious circumstances in February 1974. While completely ignoring Milteer's prescient remarks on JFK's impending death, and fudging the dates of Somersett's first reference to Dr. King by four years, the committee dismissed his report of a plot against Kennedy and its aftermath, while minimizing his investigation of King's death. Reports doled out selectively from FBI and Secret Service headquarters alleged that Somersett had also turned in false reports of plots to kill Presidents Johnson and Nixon, "unsupported by independent evidence." The panel also falsely claimed that Somersett did not divulge his advance knowledge of JFK's death "until after the President's assassination," thus fraudulently suppressing his report from November 9, 1963.[47]

Roy Frankhouser closed out the decade by attaching himself to Lyndon LaRouche's second presidential campaign as a "security consultant" in 1979. Fresh from peddling suspect "revelations" on the JFK assassination to the HSCA, Frankhouser had prior connections to LaRouche via the former's National Caucus of Labor Committees, formed at Columbia University in 1968 with an eye toward subverting the Students for a Democratic Society. In 1979 Frankhouser touted his links to U.S. intelligence agencies—suitably redacted for right-wing consumption—and snagged a lucrative post on LaRouche's campaign staff. At the time, neither knew that connection would land them both in court, and subsequently in federal prison.[48]

CHAPTER 15

Under Fire

Insider Rick Cooper described the years from 1979 to 1984 as "a state of relative stagnancy" for "the mainstream White Nationalist Movement." During that period, he wrote, none of the movement's leaders—Stoner, Fields, Matt Koehl, James Warner, David Duke—were "gainfully employed," but "lived off their mailing lists," banishing subordinates who demonstrated superior skills. Those named, Cooper alleged, each "had something to hide in his personal life and/or background," typically rumors of "Jewish blood" or homosexuality. At the same time, those years marked "a period of transition from the old Movement to the new Movement," slowly replacing profiteers with "Viking-type youth who have no leaders and are their own kings and queens."[1]

As usual, the truth is more complex.

Party supporter David Duke prepared to leave the Klan in December 1979, quietly establishing America's fourth National Association for the Advancement of White People. In January 1980 Duke offered his mailing list to rival Bill Wilkinson, but Wilkinson arrived for the handoff with reporters instead of cash, sparking a scandal that crippled Duke's Knights. Duke ceded his Klan to Don Black, allegedly stripping headquarters of cash and office machines, and set his sights on politics, while some of his grand dragons cried foul. Jerry Dutton charged Duke with using Klan funds to refurbish his house; Jack Gregory said Duke absconded with funds from a series of Florida rallies.[2]

Black's reign with the Klan was short lived. In 1981 he hatched a plan—perhaps with Duke's assistance—to seize the island nation of Dominica with a small force of American and Canadian fascists, including former Mississippi bomber Joe Daniel Hawkins. ATF agents exposed the plot in April, arresting the conspirators to crush Black's "Operation Red Dog"—dubbed "the Bayou of Pigs" by reporters. One suspect killed himself, while seven defendants pled guilty to federal charges, receiving suspended sentences. In June 1981 jurors convicted Black and Hawkins, resulting in eight-year sentences and $13,000 fines, while acquitting two others. Black was imprisoned until 1985.[3]

Before the Dominica debacle, Ed Fields attended Black's first substantial Klan rally and joined Black—with Duke and Robert Miles—for Glenn Miller's April "Hitler Fest" at Benton, North Carolina, honoring *Der Führer's* birthday and supporting racists charged with murdering five Communists in Greensboro the previous year. That same month, Jesse Stoner teamed with Bill Wilkinson to rouse riotous mobs against civil rights protests in Wrightsville, Georgia. (Sheriff Roland Attaway, in office since 1960, permitted the attacks on marchers and federal mediators, retaining his badge until debilitation from a stroke forced his retirement in June 1985.) Fields moved on to confer with British Nazis in England, then joined Stoner to welcome Belgian fascists to Atlanta, in October. Miller capitalized on his new notoriety to found the Carolina Knights of the KKK, becoming the Tarheel State's dominant Klansman.[4]

***

Jesse Stoner made the party's headlines in 1980. On January 8, the U.S. Supreme Court refused to hear his appeal of his bombing indictment, and he surrendered in Birmingham three days later. Trial began on May 12, with prosecution witnesses including Hugh Morris and two policemen instrumental in the 1958 sting operation, Tom Cook and G. L. Pattie. (First asked to testify in 1977, Morris worried that police had bombed the church, telling Bill Baxley, "I'd make a better witness for the defense if the defense only knew it.") Stoner named Morris as the plot's originator and denied participation in the bombing, or that he had ever advocated violence. Unconvinced, jurors convicted him on May 14, imposing a 10-year sentence, but Stoner remained free on appeal, filing on May 16 as a candidate in Georgia's August Democratic U.S. Senate primary.[5]

Party leaders branded him ineligible, but a federal judge disagreed and Stoner pressed on with the campaign, polling 19,664 votes out of 1,029,300 ballots cast, placing fifth in a field of six contenders. Judge Charles Crowder denied his new trial motion in September, and Georgia's Supreme Court disbarred Stoner on November 7, 1980, but his appeals continued. Alabama's Court of Criminal Appeals upheld his conviction on April 20, 1982, followed by the state's supreme court on August 13. An appeal to the U.S. Supreme Court delayed execution of Stoner's sentence, but that body rejected him on January 10, 1983, while Stoner led a Klan rally in Cleburne, Texas, railing against Cuban and Vietnamese immigrants. Last seen with James Venable on January 23, Stoner failed to surrender the following day, whereupon Alabama issued an arrest warrant. On January 28 the DOJ charged him with unlawful flight to avoid confinement.[6]

Thus began Stoner's odyssey "on the lam," pursued by G-men and bounty hunters employed by Alabama bondsman Sonny Kyle Livingston—a former Klansman, denials notwithstanding, who confessed racist bombings in 1957 but won acquittal from white jurors regardless. On February 1 Livingston claimed Stoner was in Mississippi. Ed Fields placed him in Georgia, echoed by skip tracers who reported a Stone Mountain sighting. By February 7, trackers feared he might be headed for South Africa, but G-men looked closer to home, watching Venable's home and Byron De La Beckwith's. Anonymous callers sent lawmen scuttling to New York and Florida. Questioned in prison, Danny Joe Hawkins "thought" he might know Stoner's location but refused to divulge it. Robert Chambliss, also interviewed, smirked and called G-men "Catholic sons of bitches." April brought reported sightings from Mexico, plus rumors that Stoner was hiding with fugitive Posse Comitatus killer Gordon Kahl. (Fields denied it, saying, "He never associated with tax extremists and never would.") In Alabama, the Southern Poverty Law Center received mocking postcards from Las Vegas and elsewhere, signed by Stoner as "Chief of the High Command of the Aryan Resistance."[7]

In May FBI agents raided an Atlanta apartment (empty) and logged a Georgia reporter's claim of a whispered phone call from Stoner. Sonny Livingston groused that Stoner had skipped on $20,000 bail after paying only $400 down: "I feel he's let me down and I don't understand it. He's hurting himself." Finally, on June 2, Stoner surrendered in Mobile, telling journalists he'd run because "I wanted to live a little longer." Boasting that he had "completely outfoxed" the FBI, he considered writing a handbook for others on the run. James Venable opined, "I think J.B. was broke."[8]

With Stoner caged at last, his lawyer voiced fears that Stoner might "die mysteriously," charging that jailers withheld vital medication prescribed for his client's diabetes and high blood pressure. On November 8, 1983, authorities moves Stoner to a prison north of Birmingham, sharing a hospital ward with Robert Chambliss until Dynamite Bob died on October 29, 1985. By then, Stoner's last appeal, claiming he'd been denied a fair and speedy trial, had also been denied.[9]

***

While Stoner dodged incarceration, Joseph Franklin continued his cross-country rampage. In January 1980 he killed black victims Lawrence Reese and Leo Watkins in separate Indianapolis sniper attacks. In May, he murdered hitchhiker Rebecca Bergstrom in Wisconsin's Mill Bluff State Park and wounded National Urban League president Vernon Jordan in Fort Wayne, Indiana. In June he killed cousins Dante Brown and Darrell Layne in Cincinnati; murdered Kathleen Mikula and Arthur Smothers in Johnstown, Pennsylvania; robbed a bank in Burlington, North Carolina; then killed hitchhikers Vicki Durian and Nancy Santomero in Pocahontas, West Virginia. August saw him murder Ted Fields and David Martin in Salt Lake City. Kentucky police arrested Franklin in September but he escaped from jail, recaptured in Florida on October 28. Utah federal jurors convicted him in March 1981, for violating the civil rights of victims Ted Fields and David Martin, imposing two consecutive life sentences. A separate state trial doubled those terms in June 1981. Dispatched to a federal lockup in Illinois, Franklin suffered 15 stab wounds from a gang of black inmates in February 1982. Six months later, jurors convicted him of violating Vernon Jordan's civil rights. In 1983 Franklin confessed to shooting Larry Flynt and bombing the Amitay home in Maryland. In March 1984 he confessed the Bergstrom, Durian and Santomero slayings, but prosecutors took a wrong turn in the latter cases, convicting innocent suspect Jacob Beard in 1993. (Jurors acquitted Beard at a second trial in 2000.) In July 1984 Franklin received 15 to 20 years for bombing the Chattanooga synagogue, plus six to 10 years for possessing explosives. February 1986 saw him convicted in Wisconsin, for killing Alphonse Manning, Jr., and Toni Schwenn.[10]

Edward Fields addresses his New Order Knights of the KKK in Cedartown, Georgia, scene of multiple terrorist acts in 1981 (National Archives).

When Ed Fields rallied with Don Black's Klan in Birmingham, in 1980, he announced formation of his own faction with Nazi overtones, the New Order Knights. The group's first public appearance occurred in Cedartown, Georgia, in 1981, after the town's Zartic Foods plant imported Mexican workers to replace whites earning higher salaries. Fields created an "American Labor Union" to protest, somehow managing to draw black and white workers together on his picket lines. Two Hispanic "scabs" were murdered, one allegedly for dating a white girl, and jurors acquitted the suspects despite an eyewitness account from one of the slayers. Gunmen fired on other homes, and robed Klansmen beat a black teenager on Main Street. Before turmoil subsided, the prosecution's witness from the murder trial died in a house fire with arson suspected. Fields emerged triumphant from the skirmish, at least in the short term.[11]

In early 1982 the New Order Knights rallied, burned crosses, and scattered leaflets throughout Georgia. Police shut down a May rally in Spaulding, for violating local ordinances, and Fields sued in vain, claiming 500 to 600 members in his courtroom testimony, touting plans to make Georgia "the number one Klan state in the nation." Watchers pegged NSRP membership below 1,000, though *The Thunderbolt* reached 15,000 subscribers. In July 1982 Jesse Stoner traveled to Idaho, joining Don Black, Robert Miles and others for the Second Annual Aryan Nations Congress. With denial of his first appeal by Alabama's Supreme Court in August, R. B. Montgomery stepped in as the party's national chairman, replaced in June 1983 by Willie Wilson of Jacksonville. In early September Emory Burke addressed the Fifth General Convention of the National Alliance in Chicago. Later that month James Venable convened a Klan unity rally at Stone Mountain. David Duke graced the meeting, where the New Order Knights and Don Black's dwindling empire joined four other groups to forge a new Confederation of Klans.[12]

Nineteen eighty-three was a traumatic year for the NSRP. Stoner formally resigned on January 22 and went on the lam. In August the party's executive committee expelled Ed Fields, accusing him of "personal immorality" and diverting money to his Klan. Fields maintained control of *The Thunderbolt,* while Willie Wilson launched a rival newsletter. Rick Cooper claims Fields then emptied the party's bank account, before his May 1984 arrest for allegedly burglarizing party headquarters, stealing files and $5,000 worth of office equipment while holding a gun on R. B. Montgomery. Dueling civil suits were eventually settled out of court, and Fields avoided criminal conviction, but his New Order Knights collapsed by 1985. Through it all, both sides professed support for Jesse Stoner.[13]

Elsewhere, party stalwart Bertrand Comparet died in October 1983, but few noted his passing amidst headlines generated by The Order, a fascist group whose leader—Jay Robert Mathews—declaring war on "ZOG," America's supposed Zionist Occupation Government. A collection of Klansmen and Nazis, spawned at the Aryan Nations compound, The Order assassinated Jewish radio host Alan Berg in Denver; robbed banks and gave the proceeds to various fascist leaders including Glenn Miller; executed "snitches" in their ranks; and dabbled in counterfeiting. When member Robert Martinez turned informer to avoid prison, *The Thunderbolt* published his photo to aid vengeful Nazis. Mathews died in a shootout with FBI agents on December 8, 1984, and most of his disciples wound up in prison, with sentences ranging from three to 250 years.[14]

In 1983 the fading CDL hired John Coleman, who billed himself as "the World's Greatest Intelligence Expert," producing a series of audiotapes on "the secrets of the Kennedy assassination." Eustace Mullins branded Coleman an impostor who plagiarized material from Mullins and Lyndon LaRouche, while the *National Socialist Liberator* attacked "'Dr. John Coleman,' aka John Clarke and likely actually one Joseph Pavlonsky, of Russian Khazarian [Jewish] origin." Still Coleman persevered for a decade, publishing

Sedition trial defendants Louis Beam (left) and Richard Butler (center) join Jesse Stoner and an unidentified companion (in Rebel uniform) for a celebration of the Klan's 1866 creation in Pulaski, Tennessee (National Archives).

The Conspirators' Hierarchy: The Committee of 300 in 1992, while the CDL withered to a shadow of its former self.[15]

Georgia's Supreme Court permanently disbarred Jesse Stoner on April 6, 1984, but he continued his appeals. The Eleventh Circuit Court of Appeals rejected his last bid, a habeas corpus petition, on January 16, 1985. While he sat in prison, Ed Fields remained active outside the party, joining Richard Butler and other fascist leaders at Robert Miles's Michigan farm and "church" in October 1985. The *New York Times* took note but got it wrong, calling Fields the NSRP's director and dubbing it "a racist group in Birmingham." Rally spokesmen called for an alliance with Stoner's old enemies, the Black Muslims, for a joint campaign against Jews.[16]

Nineteen eighty-four was another national election year. Glenn Miller entered North Carolina's Democratic gubernatorial campaign in May but polled only 5,790 votes out of 955,799 cast, running eighth in a 10-man race, emerging to rename his Carolina Knights the White Patriot Party, swapping robes for camouflage fatigues and claiming 5,000 recruits. After founding a branch of Robert Miles's Mountain Church in Pennsylvania, during 1983, Roy Frankhouser attached himself to Lyndon LaRouche's presidential campaign as "an expert in security matters" and began manipulations that would produce federal conspiracy charges three years later. Before that axe fell, in 1985, Frankhouser launched his *Race and Reason* cable TV program in Berks County, remaining on-air for over a decade.[17]

The big news for Nazis in 1984 was the Populist Party, founded by Willis Carto and Robert Weems, a Mississippi Klan leader and NSRP member named as the new party's

Left: Perennial far-right presidential candidate Lyndon LaRouche hired NSRP member Roy Frankhouser as his "security expert" in 1983, ultimately landing both of them in federal prison (Library of Congress). *Right:* Following parole, Jesse Stoner launched a new, homophobic "Crusade Against Corruption" with familiar taints of racism (National Archives).

first chairman. Ronald Reagan proved unstoppable that year, but the Populists fielded Robert Eugene Richards for president—a 1950s Olympian-turned-minister, dubbed "the Vaulting Vicar"—with Liberty Lobby activist Maureen Salaman as his running mate. The team polled 66,236 votes nationwide, running sixth in a field of seven contenders and trailing Lyndon LaRouche by 12,471 ballots.[18]

Encouraged by the growth of his WPP, Glenn Miller entered North Carolina's Republican senate primary in May 1986, claiming a paltry 6,662 votes out of 209,825 cast. Ed Fields received an invitation to speak at July's Sixth Annual Aryan Nations Congress but failed to appear. Jesse Stoner, paroled in November, celebrated Bill Baxley's gubernatorial defeat as "divine." Back in Marietta, he founded a "Crusade Against Corruption," printing posters that read "Praise God for AIDS," hailing the newly epidemic disease as heavenly vengeance against gays, "jews and negroids" [*sic*].[19]

Members of the NSRP and Klan assaulted a staff member of the Center for Democratic Renewal in Marietta, in February 1986. ADL observers found the NSRP "in disarray" by December and "moribund ... essentially out of business" three months later. Stoner and Ed Fields surfaced in Georgia's Forsyth County during January 1987, whipping David Holland's Southern White Knights into frenzied attacks on civil rights marchers that landed the attackers in court, compelled by an SPLC lawsuit to pay their victims $800,000 in damages. Marietta police jailed David Duke and Don Black for reckless conduct and blocking a highway. Stoner continued addressing Klan rallies in March 1987 and Ed Fields billed issue #321 of *The Thunderbolt,* near year's end, as his "most important ever." In 1988 he changed the paper's title to *The Truth at Last* and released a new booklet of musings titled *The Jewish Origins of Communism.*[20]

Racist demonstrators prepare to attack civil rights marchers in Forsyth County, Georgia, in January 1987 (Library of Congress).

Eloise Witte, once Cincinnati party chairman and "Grand Empress" of the National Knights, resurfaced in her native North Carolina in 1986, decrying the arrival of Laotian refugees in Marion, shopping on Main Street beside local whites. Most of the women, she complained, were "pregnant out to here," and were "carrying six or seven more babies in their hands, in carts, in slings, in just about everything but strollers." Witte fumed at the increase in sales of rice and "got riled up" against clergymen who invited the new settlers. "Now that these churches have decided to play stork for the county," Witte railed, "I hope they will not only pay for the keep of these Laotians, but do something about their birth rate. They have just about bred themselves out of a place at the world's table. If we fall heir to another 100 to 400 families, 15 years from now we will probably be called Laos, North Carolina."[21]

Accounts of the NSRP's dissolution in March 1987 differ widely. Fields still blames the FBI's illegal COINTELPRO operation, officially discontinued 16 years earlier, but others disagree. Rick Cooper wrote: "This internal dissension was not as a result of any Anti-Defamation League plot or government COINTELPRO operation, but was something that was destined to happen sooner or later. Fields is a money-grubber and there were those on the NSRP staff who did not like Fields personally because he had at least two wives, patronized prostitutes, frequented discos and misused NSRP funds." Much of that was libelous, if false—but no lawsuit resulted.[22]

Glenn Miller's legal problems continued while the NSRP disintegrated. In January 1985 he signed an agreement with the SPLC to cease paramilitary training in exchange for dismissal of a pending lawsuit against him. July 1986 saw him caught running another armed camp and convicted of contempt, sentenced to 12 months in prison with six months suspended, also ordered to sever all contact with fellow Nazis. In April 1987 Miller mailed 5,000 copies of a "Declaration of War," proclaiming: "I ask for no quarter. I will give none. I declare war against Niggers, Jews, Queers, assorted Mongrels, White Race traitors, and despicable informants." Miller specifically threatened SPLC chief Morris Dees and established a "point system" for murder of federal officials. Rather than launch a war, however, Miller hid in a trailer at Ozark, Missouri, where authorities arrested him—with three cohorts and a substantial arsenal—on April 30. Following his May indictment on multiple charges, Edward Fields supported Miller and helped bankroll his defense. Despite his willingness to testify against fellow recipients of The Order's bank loot, Miller was convicted and served three years in prison, emerging as a protected witness in 1990.[23]

December 1987 saw Roy Frankhouser convicted of obstructing a federal investigation into credit card fraud by Lyndon LaRouche's 1984 campaign. Standing mute on the Fifth Amendment, Frankhouser drew a sentence of three years with a $50,000 fine in February, then was compelled to testify against LaRouche at his separate trial, convicting LaRouche in December 1988 with a 15-year sentence imposed. Frankhouser appealed his own conviction in April 1989, rejected in July.[24]

In February 1988 the DOJ indicted 14 fascists for sedition, including members of The Order and recipients of their bank loot. Charges did not touch the NSRP, though Edward Fields raised money for defendant Robert Miles, while Glenn Miller appeared as a prosecution witness, hoping to reduce his 1987 sentence. Judge Morris Arnold freed one suspect for lack of evidence and jurors acquitted the rest on April 8. William Gale died on April 28, while Fields addressed the National Democratic Front's White Unity Day in North Carolina, taped an interview for Tom Metzger's *Race and Reason* series, but found no Klansmen willing to picket the July Democratic National Convention in Atlanta. Don Black capped the year by marrying David Duke's ex-wife Chloe.[25]

On November 11, 1988, Jesse Stoner rallied 84 members of seven rival Klans outside Powder Springs, Georgia, burning a cross and blaring racist messages via loudspeaker toward the all-black Macedonia Baptist Church, opened in October. Officials denied prior requests for a rally in Smyrna, but a farmer donated his land for the hate fest, he said, to "send a message to the church members."[26]

The Populist Party mounted its most determined presidential campaign in 1988, nominating David Duke. Ralph Forbes, head of the ANP's Western Division, served as Duke's campaign manager, while party chairman Robert Weems retained a seat on the national executive committee. A month before his March nomination, Duke surfaced in New Hampshire's obscure vice presidential primary, running as a Democrat and claiming a surprise victory with 10,531 votes, as ballots cast for his two rivals totaled 33. Duke staged an energetic campaign, zigzagging across the country, securing a place on ballots in 12 states. Oddly, his running mate in some was Trenton Stokes from Arkansas, in others Dr. Floyd Parker from New Mexico. On election day the curious triumvirate claimed 47,043 votes nationwide—.05 percent of all ballots cast. The ADL, despite its claim of NSRP dissolution in 1987, reported the "defunct" party supporting Duke's campaign throughout.[27]

Undaunted by defeat, Duke switched his party affiliation to Republican in December

Jesse Stoner with unidentified companion, on the fringe of a Klan rally at Stone Mountain, Georgia, in 1988 (Stuart Rome).

1988, entering and winning an open primary to succeed retiring State Representative Charles Cusimano of Metairie in January 1989. In February's special election runoff he beat rival John Treen by a margin of 227 votes. His defection notwithstanding, the Populists still welcomed Duke as a speaker for their March convention in Chicago, and he went on to serve a single term in Louisiana's House of Representatives before David Vitter ousted him in 1991.[28]

As the decade closed, Ed Fields continued publishing *The Truth At Last* and saw David Craig's True Knights of the KKK distribute copies in Woodstock, Georgia, on May 27, 1989. On September 2 he joined Richard Butler for a march through Gainesville, sponsored by the Invisible Empire and Southern White Knights. The parade drew 300 racists, including 70 skinheads, while speakers attacked Gainesville's Hispanic residents. Afterward, some 700 celebrants flocked to James Venable's property at Stone Mountain for the largest local rally in decades.[29]

CHAPTER 16

Last Gasp?

The NSRP's dissolution left some party stalwarts at loose ends, while others soldiered on as if nothing had changed. Ed Fields announced formation of a new Emergency Committee to Suspend Immigration on May 30, 1990, targeting Hispanics. Two days later Jesse Stoner declared his candidacy for lieutenant governor of Georgia, hyping the race at a Klan rally on June 30, but balloting on July 17 brought another defeat. He garnered 30,804 votes out of 947,108 cast, placing seventh in a field of nine contenders—consoled by defeating black state legislator Bobby Hill. Party ally David Duke sought a Senate seat from Louisiana, aided by James Warner and Don Black, running second in a two-man race on October 6, with 607,391 votes out of 1,396,113 cast.[1]

In legal news, Louisiana prosecutors reopened Oneal Moore's murder case in 1990—the first of three renewed investigations—but no charges resulted before prime suspect Ernest McElveen died in February 2003. Glenn Miller finished his three-year prison term in 1990, renamed "Frazier Glenn Cross" upon entering the federal Witness Security Program as a long-haul trucker, preaching anti–Semitism on the highway while he found "the freedom of the open road is gloriously exhilarating." Late in 1999 he privately published 1,000 copies of a memoir, *A White Man Speaks Out*, relating his journey from NSRP recruit to militant fascist ex-convict.[2]

In Canada, while the NSRP no longer existed, Nazi skinheads still peddled copies of *The Thunderbolt* around Edmonton, Alberta, as late as February 1990. Two months later, on April 14, one of them—Daniel Joshua Sims—joined others to assault sexagenarian radio commentator Keith Rutherford at his home, leaving him permanently blind. Sims received a wrist-slap sentence of 60 days in June.[3]

Party alumnus Joseph Paul Franklin faced more serious penalties in the century's final decade. In August 1990 he confessed to killing Ted Fields and David Martin in Utah. In 1994 he admitted slaying Gerald Gordon, followed by a 1995 confession to wounding Vernon Jordan. A November 1996 radio interview captured his admission of killing Vicki Durian and Nancy Santomero because "they dated black people." Convicted of Gordon's murder in February 1997, Franklin drew a death sentence. Over the next two months he confessed to the murders of Dante Brown, Darrell Layne, Kathleen Mikula, Arthur Smothers, and Raymond Taylor. Conviction in the Brown and Lane murders brought Franklin a 40-year sentence in October 1997. In 1998 he admitted killing Mercedes Masters, Harold McIver, and William Tatum, slapped with two consecutive life sentences in the latter case. November 1999 brought his confession to killing Johnny Brookshire 21 years earlier.[4]

Party stalwart Byron De La Beckwith lived quietly in Tennessee, supporting Jesse

A check written by Byron De La Beckwith to Jesse Stoner for unspecified "expenses" in February 1996, two years after Beckwith's Mississippi murder conviction and life sentence (National Archives).

Stoner's Crusade Against Corruption and similar causes, until Mississippi prosecutors ordered his third arrest in December 1990 for slaying Medgar Evers. Stoner, described by relatives as a "constant presence" in Beckwith's life for "30-odd years," rallied to his defense. Initially confident of acquittal, Beckwith faced an integrated jury at trial and was convicted of murder on February 5, 1994, receiving a life sentence. Mississippi's Supreme Court denied his appeal, and Beckwith died in prison on January 21, 2001. Edward Fields attended his Chattanooga funeral.[5]

When not mourning old friends, Fields kept busy with his true work, publishing *The Truth at Last* and overseeing its distribution from Dalraida, Georgia, where copies were strewn about lawns on March 5, 1991, to Montgomery, Alabama, where Fields joined a Klan protest at SPLC headquarters four days later. May 18 saw the launch of a national speaking tour with old friend John Tyndal, lately leader of the British National Party. Fields also continued his alliance with the Populist Party, appearing at rallies in June and September 1991. July found Robert Weems and Eustace Mullins tapped to address the First National Identity-Christian Conference in Reidsville, North Carolina, where Weems lectured on "Internationalism and How it Relates to Race, Nation, and Faith." Brochures for the rally featured advertisements for books including *God's Call to Race, Our Nordic Race,* and *White Race—True People of Israel.*[6]

Observers found "no active members other than Stoner" in his Crusade Against Corruption during 1992, but members of the Christian Party rallied to hear him speak at Lyerly, Georgia, on May 3, joined by spokesmen from the SS of America and two rival Klans. Ed Fields pressed on with his anti-immigration efforts, claiming 65,000 signatures on one petition, and joined the Klan for its annual pilgrimage to Pulaski, Tennessee. He also launched a National Campaign to Expose the Holocaust and joined the Atlanta Committee for Historical Review, led by attorney and Holocaust denier Sam Dickson, self-proclaimed on Stormfront as "a responsible right-wing extremist," attending a speech by British Holocaust denier David Irving in October. When Governor Zell Miller declared plans to remove a depiction of the Confederate battle flag from Georgia's state banner,

Fields joined Populist Party chief C. Ray Harrelson's Committee to Save Our State Flag, gaining 7,000 members for the party, though they lost the fight in 2001.[7]

James Warner's then-wife, Debra (née Coleman), resurfaced in 1992, mailing local teacher Sharon Zeller a demand that Debra's son Scott be excluded from any classes dealing with "certain politically sensitive issues ... that would expose him to teachings contrary to her own opinions." Those issues clarified in 1993, when Debra listed herself as secretary of the New Christian Crusade Church. When she sought a seat on the St. Bernard Parish Council in 1995, Zeller released Debra's letter to a daily newspaper, which published excerpts from it and her letters to the editor, condemning U.S. aid to Israel. Reportedly separated from James by then, though still sharing a home, Coleman-Warner fanned the flames by appearing with David Duke at a District 1 State Senate campaign forum, saying of her former husband, "I am not a racist. I do not share his views in any way." She won the first round of voting, then lost a runoff to incumbent Councilman Clay Cosse, despite—or because of—Duke's public support. Debra then sued Zeller and the parish school board, claiming publication of her letter violated her First Amendment right to free speech without fear of retaliation (in this case, her loss of both the election and a private job). The district court upheld a portion of her claim in 1999, a judgment affirmed at the federal level in 2000.[8]

Consciously or otherwise, Patrick Buchanan bore the white supremacist banner in 1992's presidential election. A thinly veiled anti–Semite and Holocaust denier, who orchestrated Ronald Reagan's visit to a German SS cemetery in 1985, he was branded by the ADL as an "unrepentant bigot" who "repeatedly demonizes Jews and minorities and openly affiliates with white supremacists." Ed Fields agreed, devoting front-page coverage to Buchanan's campaign in *The Truth At Last,* and when Buchanan's fliers blanketed Georgia, they bore the newsletter's return address. Another choice for racists that year was Bo Gritz, running for the Populist Party on the slogan "God, Guns and Gritz." Come November, Gritz received 106,152 votes nationwide, with his strongest showings in Idaho and Utah.[9]

Presidential candidate Pat Buchanan in 1992. NSRP headquarters distributed his campaign literature, bearing the party's return address (Library of Congress).

Disappointed at the polls, Ed Fields pressed on to create the America First Party in June 1993. His move capitalized on dissension within the failing Populist Party, as Fields heralded the new movement at a "National Unity Convention" in Clemmons, South Carolina, with Fields named as secretary and Ray Harrelson tapped as treasurer. Emory Burke addressed the first meeting, with French Nazis Guillaume Fabien and Michel Faci of the Euronationalist Party. America First's national council also welcomed Richard Butler from Aryan Nations as a guest speaker, and David Duke graced its meetings. In what spare time remained, Fields worked with Klan leaders Dave Holland, Thom Robb, Frank Shirley, and Bill Hoff; shared a mailing address with British skinhead leader Cliff Warby; picketed a "Queer Family Picnic" in Marietta with skinheads; led local Nazis cheering Holocaust denier David Irving in DeKalb County; and joined racist lawyer Kirk Lyons to protest construction of the U.S. Holocaust Memorial Museum in Washington.[10]

In 1993, rapper Ice Cube surprised Jesse Stoner with a mention in his song "My Skin Is My Sin," on the *Lethal Injection* album.[11]

Roy Frankhouser made more unwelcome headlines in 1993, indicted on assault charges related to a stabbing at a 1992 Klan rally in Cumberland County, Pennsylvania, but jurors acquitted him on April 28, accepting Frankhouser's story that a Klan security guard and several skinheads attacked him as he entered the rally convened by Imperial Wizard James Farrands.[12]

Nineteen ninety-four was a quieter year. Jesse Stoner addressed a Rebel Knights rally in Cumming, Georgia, but he was absent when marchers brandished his Crusade Against Corruption signs during an August march in Cobb County. Ed Fields addressed the Populist Party's national convention, complaining about the number of Jews on President Clinton's cabinet, and visited England as a guest of John Tyndall's British National Party. Early NSRP member Wallace Allen died in January 1995, after repeating his plea of innocence to the Atlanta temple bombing. In February, Boston jurors convicted Roy Frankhouser of conspiring to obstruct justice when he advised the New Dawn Hammerskins to destroy evidence of their cemetery desecrations and assaults on black residents. Judge Patti Saris sentenced him to 25 months in prison. Three months later, on May 2, Oren Potito died in Florida.[13]

John Crommelin died at home on November 2, 1996. Critics including the *Columbia Journalism Review* blasted the *Montgomery Advertiser* for "repressing its institutional memory," printing a laudatory obituary that ignored decades of public bigotry to praise Crommelin as a "hero" and "true American" deserving of "high praise," revered for his "daring exploits, "superb skills," and "outspokenness ... as the savior of naval aviation."[14]

By 1996 Ed Fields was broadcasting short-wave "America First Radio" via World Wide Christian Radio from Nashville, Tennessee, and addressing the Second Annual White Rights Rally of David Duke's NAAWP in Winter Haven, Florida. Columbians veteran Holt Gewinner died on October 23, at age 81. The year's big news was Pat Buchanan's bid for the Republican presidential nomination, his most successful race to date, but adding more stains to his reputation. February saw campaign co-chairman Larry Pratt—spokesman for Gun Owners of America, who shared stages with Aryan Nations leaders—resign, while denying any taint of bigotry and blaming "orchestrated smears" before New Hampshire's primary. One day later, Susan Lamb, Buchanan's campaign manager in Duval County, Florida, quit when she was exposed as Jacksonville's NAAWP leader. Shaken, Florida campaign manager Randy Lakel told reporters, "There's no room for bigotry, racism or anti–Semitism. None. No room at all."[15]

Twenty years after convicting Bob Chambliss, Alabama prosecutors reopened the BAPBOMB case once more. Herman Cash escaped indictment, having died in 1994, while 90-year-old brother Jack repulsed investigators with a terse "no comment." A grand jury indicted Bobby Cherry and Tom Blanton, Jr. (already jailed in Texas for raping his stepdaughter) for murder on May 17, 2000, Cherry's lawyer claiming Bobby rejected an offer of probation for a guilty plea to transporting explosives across state lines. Jurors convicted Blanton on May 1, 2001, imposing four life sentences with parole possible. Cherry stalled trial for another year, claiming dementia and poor health, but jurors finally

Deputies escort former NSRP member Tom Blanton, Jr., from court following his May 2001 murder conviction in the Birmingham "BAPBOMB" case (National Archives).

convicted him on May 22, 2002. He died in prison on November 18, 2004. Blanton remains incarcerated at this writing, eligible for release since April 2016 but with no parole hearing scheduled.[16]

In December 1997 President Clinton chose Madeleine Albright to succeed Warren Christopher as Secretary of State. Newspapers bared her background as a Czech Jew turned Episcopalian in 1959, who only learned of her grandparents' murder by Third Reich Nazis in adulthood. A year after Albright's confirmation, David Duke castigated "Jews who supposedly don't know they are Jewish until after they are appointed to office. Dr. Edward Fields of *The Truth At Last* and I publicly talked about her Jewish pedigree for two years before she supposedly knew of it."[17]

While Fields and Duke gloated, Roy Frankhouser faced trial for harassing Bonnie Jouhari and her daughter in Reading, Pennsylvania. Jouhari worked at the Reading-Berks Human Relations Council, aiding victims of discrimination, which put her in Frankhouser's crosshairs. The SPLC took Jouhari's case and won, resulting in an order that Frankhouser apologize on his *White Forum* TV show and in local newspapers, undergo sensitivity training, perform 1,000 hours of community service, and pay Jouhari 10 percent of his income for a decade.[18]

Spring 1998 brought news of John Kasper's death on April 7, a forgotten man outside Nazi circles. In June, Fields associate and America First Party chairman Jeff Wilkerson organized a new speaking tour for David Irving. Three months later Ed Fields and Jesse Stoner visited Zinc, Arkansas, to address a Klan meeting, before Fields cosponsored a National Patriot's Conference in Auburndale, Florida, with ex-militia leader Dan Daniels. In December Roy Frankhouser became a "pastor" of the Mountain Church of Jesus Christ, led from Michigan by Robert Miles, conducting services at home, before an altar draped with Klan flags and featuring pictures of Adolf Hitler, but Berks County officials rejected his bid for tax-exemption, citing lack of proof that he had been ordained.[19]

Few noticed the passing of Alton Wayne Roberts—ex–Klansman, party member, convicted slayer of three civil rights activists, and betrayer of fellow terrorists to a lethal police ambush—at age 61, on September 11, 1999. He died where he had earned his reputation, in Meridian, while those who mourned him carefully avoided making news.[20]

The 21st century began with new legal conflicts. On May 17, 2000, officers in Ozark County, Missouri, arrested ex-party chaplain Gordon Winrod for kidnapping eight of his 60 grandchildren from their parents in 1994 and '95, to indoctrinate them. Two were later returned to their families in North Dakota, but the remainder engaged in a four-day standoff with police before surrendering. Conviction at trial, in January 2001, brought Winrod a 30-year sentence. Two victims also filed a civil lawsuit, recovering $26 million in damages for their abductions. Paroled in May 2012, Winrod returned to his farm, still railing against the "Jewdiciary" that imprisoned him.[21]

While Winrod sat in jail, Ed Fields spent 2001 promoting William Pierce's National Alliance—belatedly joining in 2003—and imprisoned *Führer* Matthew Hale's Creativity Movement, formerly the World Church of the Creator. In Pennsylvania, Roy Frankhouser wrangled with city officials who denied permission for his American Knights of the KKK to stage demonstrations. Emory Burke, lately a speaker for the National Alliance, died on November 20, 2002, ten years after publishing a novel, *The Unlifted Curse*, that warned readers: "We Caucasians must breed only with Caucasians, and obey the natural law that thunders through the whole world of living beings: Thou shalt breed only with thine own kind!"[22]

Early NSRP member Neuman Britton joined Aryan Nations when the party dissolved, rising to stand as Richard Butler's hand-picked heir in 1998, married by then to Posse Comitatus "martyr" Gordon Kahl's widow. Plans for expansion at Hayden Lake went awry with Britton's death from melanoma on August 18, 2001. Butler failed to choose a new successor before heart failure killed him in September 2004, leaving his movement split into four rival factions.[23]

A stroke left Jesse Stoner paralyzed on his left side in 2001, confined to bed at a rest home in Lafayette, Georgia. His legal guardian, the Rev. Ronald Ragon, lobbied for a move to Chattanooga, but found that when administrators learned the patient's name, "then suddenly they're full." Granting a final interview in July 2004, Stoner apparently regretted nothing but his present immobility. "If I was still active, I'd still be the same," he said. "I'd like to go out and make a speech. Some thought coming into this institution would change me, but a person isn't supposed to apologize for being right." He conceded "defeat of the white people against race-mixing," but had no qualms about his fate in the hereafter. Describing himself as a "soldier of Christ," he declared, "I guess God will put his hand on my head and bless me." Withered to 110 pounds from his old fighting weight, Stoner died on April 23, 2005, from complications of pneumonia. He was buried three days later at Chattanooga's Forest Hills Cemetery, near the foot of Lookout Mountain.[24]

Stoner missed the NSRP's revival in June 2005, concurrent with aged Klansman Edgar Ray Killen's trial and conviction for the 1964 slayings of three civil rights workers in the "Mississippi Burning" case. Based in Philadelphia, Mississippi, the group's anonymous leader pledged dedication to "vigorously defending the Rights, Traditions, Heritages and Culture of the White

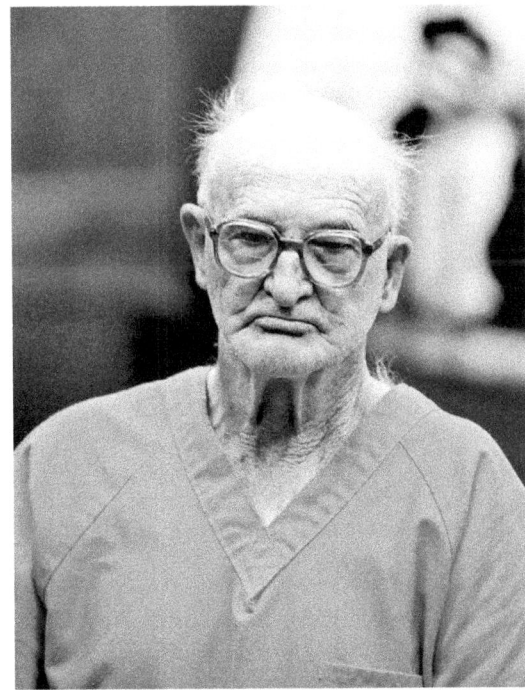

Ex-Klansman Edgar Ray Killen's trial for the "Mississippi Burning" murders revived the NSRP in Philadelphia, Mississippi, during 2005 (National Archives).

people of America." The party vanished from national listings of hate groups in 2006, but that was not the story's end.[25]

Settled in Aurora, Missouri, by 2002, Glenn Miller found himself banned from Stormfront's website as a "snitch," but soon switched to Alex Linder's Vanguard News Network, posting more than 12,000 comments under the screen name "Rounder." In 2006 Miller tried his hand at politics once more, seeking to represent the 7th Congressional District. His campaign ads evoked memories of Stoner's, but Miller failed more dramatically, winning 23 votes out of 241,072 cast and running last in a four-person field.[26]

Joseph Franklin's legal problems multiplied in the new century. In 2006, after he'd spent nine years on death row for killing Gerald Gordon, a federal judge stayed Franklin's death sentence pending inquiries into Missouri's lethal injection system. An appellate court reversed that decision in July 2007, and the U.S. Supreme Court found Missouri's methods constitutional the following year. More appeals stalled Franklin's death until November 20, 2013, when he was executed at the state prison in Bonne Terre.[27]

"Wild Bill" Hoff went next, long since departed from New York and the NSRP, serving as East Coast director of Jeffrey Schoep's National Socialist Movement. On December 8, 2006, he swerved in front of a semi trailer on Highway 148 near Enoree, South Carolina, killed instantly in the collision.[28]

After two years of quiescence, Mississippi's NSRP resurfaced on Stormfront in June 2007, with a post from Philadelphia Klansman "Knightrider1961." As he explained (uncorrected):

> The National States Rights Party, established in 1958 and revived in 2005, is once again stepping forward as a viable political party for White Americans!
>
> While there are many "Third Political Parties" out there, few, if any, are oriented towards the exclusive interests of White Christian Americans. In fact, many are Jewish co-opted and boast about having negro members.
>
> On the other hand, the National States Rights Party is an exclusively WHITE, CHRISTIAN political party devoted to the preservation, protection, and advancement of AMERICA'S WHITE CHRISTIAN MAJORITY!
>
> The goals of the NSRP include:
>
> * Repeal of the Civil Rights Act of 1964 and Voting Rights Act of 1965 along with all other anti–White "Civil Rights" laws.
>
> * Full protection of the Right To Keep And Bear Arms as provided for under the Second Amendmend of the U.S. Constitution.
>
> * Withdrawl of diplomatic relations with and full sunctions against all nations that are anti–American, anti–Christian, and anti–White. Especially Red China, Cuba, and Israel.
>
> * Protection of America's natural resorces and environment without penalizing legitimate sportsmen and util;izing energy resources.
>
> * Reinstituting segregation in public facilities, the Armed Forces and public schools as originally provided by the U.S. Supreme Court in Plessy v. Ferguson.
>
> * Safeguarding America's borders with stringent safeguards including, electrified fences; patrols by the U.S. Army; prosecution of those aiding illegal aliens.
>
> * Repeal of NAFTA, GATT, and other legislation that harms America's workforce.
>
> At this time the NSRP does not have a website due to circumstances beyond our control. But make no mistake about it, the National States Rights Party is here and here to stay!
>
> Anyone interested in joining the NSRP can write:
> National States Rights Party
> National Headquarters
> P.O. Box 886
> Philadelphia, Miss. 39350-0886[29]

On November 7, for the benefit of any persons left confused, "Knightrider" wrote:

Qualifications for membership in the NATIONAL STATES RIGHTS PARTY

* Must be a White; Christian U.S. citizen; 18 years of age or older; registered to vote; regularly practices their right to vote; is in agreement with the party's basic platform and is of good moral character.
NOTE Persons ineligible to join are basically: non–Whites (Any admission of non–White ancestry, no matter how remote) this includes but not limited to: negroes, orientals, Mexicans, Puerto Ricans, jews, American Indians, East Indians and Arabs; homosexuals/bisexuals; drug addicts; alcoholics; non–Christians (atheists, agnostics, pagans, etc.); convicted sex offenders.[30]

"Knightrider1961" returned to the Web in September 2008, declaring:

While there are a number of candidates contending for President of the United States; both the "mainstream" nominees of the Democrat and Republican parties, and those representing certain other political parties as well. While the NSRP does not have a nominee for this high office during the 2008 election, and has chosen not to endorse any of the current candidates at this time, the NSRP feels compelled to issue the following statement.

During the past several presidential elections White Americans have had very little to choose from among the available candidates running. Usually finding themselves having to cast their vote for the "lesser of two evils," or for who they wanted NOT to win. But even when the winner was the candidate we didn't want to win, there was limit on what the new president could do or cause.

This year it's different, VERY different. Right now we are faced with something that was far too frightening for even our fathers fighting for our cause during the sixties, to contemplate or mention as a possibility to rally our people during those desperate times. The prospect of a negro being elected President of the United States!

And it's not just that this is a mixed blooded mongrel spawn of a African savage straight from the dark continent and a wretched White skank who defiled her race. No, it's much more that even THAT. It is a fact that the current Democrat nominee for president is one of the most radical Marxists ever to enter American politics. With an agenda that includes complete gun control; sex education for the youngest children; abortion on demand even at the latest terms; and obliging the most anti–American dictators, such as Hugo Chavez; just to name a few.

On Tuesday, Nov 4th, every White American should go to the polls with just one thing in mind...........STOP BARACK HUSSEIN OBAMA!!!!![31]

As a footnote, two days later, he cautioned: "There is a segment of White activists who view the moslems as allies. The National States Rights Party is NOT among them!"[32] At press time for this volume, no more had been heard of "Knightrider1961" or his renascent NSRP.

Roy Frankhouser died on May 15, 2009, at Reading's Spruce Manor Nursing home, where he had been confined for three years. Lacking known survivors, Berks County's coroner searched in vain for someone to claim his body.[33]

Glenn Miller set his sights on Congress once again in 2010, this time pursuing a Missouri Senate seat as an independent write-in candidate. Critics argued that he only used the podium to grab airtime, having alerted Vanguard News that "stations are required to run advertising for candidates." Over objections from Missouri Attorney General Chris Koster and the Missouri Broadcasters Association, Miller landed interviews with Alan Colmes and Howard Stern, supported by a verdict from the FCC in proclaiming, "It's Not Against the Law to Be White, Yet." The message ultimately failed, as Miller polled only seven votes among 1.9 million cast, running dead last in a field of seven rivals.[34]

Humiliation at the polls lit Miller's fuse. On April 13, 2014, he drove through the

Glenn Miller, aka "Frazier Glenn Cross," salutes jurors after they recommended his execution for multiple murders in August 2015 (National Archives).

streets of Overland Park, Kansas, a suburb of Kansas City, fatally shooting three persons outside the Jewish Community Center of Greater Kansas City and Village Shalom, a Jewish nursing home. While Miller believed his three victims—ranging in age from 14 to 69—were Jews, in fact all three were Gentile Protestants. Arrested the same day, he faced murder charges at arraignment, where Judge Thomas Ryan rejected his claim that the slayings were "necessary" and authorized by the Declaration of Independence. Jurors convicted Miller at trial on August 24, 2015, and recommended execution, a sentence formally imposed on November 10. Miller's answer to the court was a stiff-armed salute and a shouted, "Sieg Heil!" Don Black, on Stormfront, called Miller a "homicidal whack job," then admitted he had known of Miller's "character flaws" since the 1980s but kept silent for the sake of "Movement unity."[35]

Six months after Miller's murder spree, on October 10, 2014, founding party member Matt Koehl died peacefully in his sleep at the New Order's "Nordland" property in Wisconsin. Age 79, he had escaped the curse of violence that claimed his predecessor's life 47 years earlier.[36]

Octogenarian Edward Fields kept mum on Miller's rampage and Koehl's passing, preoccupied with turning out *The Truth At Last* and hyping it on Stormfront. Articles available online—though Fields himself shuns email—include such titles as "Did Six Million Really Die?"; "Clinton's Fanaticism for Race Mixing"; "Do Americans Want a Colored Nation?"; "The Martyrdom of Julius Streicher" [executed for Nazi war crimes in 1946]; "Judaism, a racist, exclusivist religion"; and "The Name Changers"—an exposé of Jews in Hollywood, alerting readers that "Every single one of the original Jewish developers of the movie indus-

An estimated 120 groups espouse variations of Nazi doctrines in the United States, as of 2016 (National Archives).

try divorced their Jewish wives and married beautiful Christian starlets." All that and more is available to subscribers for $18 per year.[37]

The NSRP may be gone, at least for now, but Fields enjoys an audience and Jesse Stoner is revered today among the members of at least 99 Fascist groups in the United States. They include 23 overt Nazi organizations with 119 chapters in 46 states, 58 "white nationalist" cliques active in 29 states, and 18 Nazi skinhead gangs with loyalists in 35 states. Sympathetic ears are also found among 21 Christian Identity "ministries" and in the 97 chapters of eight competing neo-Confederate groups clamoring for secession.[38] If bigots have learned anything from history it is endurance and the will to persevere.

Appendix A:
NSRP Constitution (1958)

(typos uncorrected)

PREAMBLE

We of the National States Rights Party believe in our Lord Jesus Christ and the Christian heritage of our people. We believe in the great White race and the necessity for the preservation of our race and the Nation which the Whiteman created out of the wilderness on this continent. We believe in the principles laid down by our forefathers in the United States Constitution and in the Bill of Rights contained therein. We believe in preserving the Race of our forefathers which built civilizations out of jungles and which gave art, culture, inventions, freedom and justice to the entire world. We will not allow the blood of our people to be polluted with that of black, yellow, jewish or mongrel people. We know that only the pure White Race can preserve this Nation and the freedom handed down to us by our ancestors. All that is patriotic, good, clean and decent springs forth from the foundations of our White folk. These high standards of living do not, and cannot, exist in the non–White backward areas of the world, except where the Whiteman maintains a foothold of control. Therefore, we dedicate our lives and fortunes to the expansion and goals of the National States Rights Party. We feel that only through a political movement can we unit our people and bring the government back into the hands of the White Christian majority.

We dedicate ourselves to the task of saving America and the White race and the preservation of the pure blood of our forefathers, so that all future generations which come after us will be born as White children with a creative intelligence that will strengthen our civilized influence over the world for the good of all mankind. Therefore, we join together for these honorable purposes as outlined in this Constitution and By-laws of the National States Rights Party.

We struggle for—Christ, Race, Nation!

ARTICLE I—NAME

Sec. 1: The name of this political organization shall be the National States Rights Party, This is a political party.

ARTICLE II—OBJECTS

Sec. 1: The objects of this Party are as stated in this Constitution and By-Laws and in the official platform of the National States Rights Party.

ARTICLE III—MEMBERSHIP

Sec. 1: Any White person, who subscribes to the Christian aims, principles, objectives, platform and Constitution of the National States Rights Party, and is of good moral character, may become a member of this Party after his or her application has been approved by the Secretary of the National Executive Committee, unless the National Chairman objects or refused to ratify the granting of membership to said applicant. Any person of Asiatic, African or Jewish blood or ancestry can never be a member of this Party and the same prohibition applies to every White person who is married to such a person.

Sec. 2: The first year's dues and initiation fee must accompany the application for membership. All initiation fees and dues are given by an applicant and by members as contributions to this Party's general fund and treasure and are accepted on that basis by this Party and its various committees and chapters and officers.

Sec. 3: Every applicant for membership must agree to abide by the discipline and Constitution of this Party and agree to work for the fulfillment of its program, aims and purposes. Protestants and Catholics, native-born and foreign-born are all welcome in this Party, so long as they are loyal white racists who give their political loyalty to this Party and its National Chairman.

Sec. 4: A member must give his full political loyalty to the National States Rights Party, and may not belong to any other political party, except in those states where this Party functions as a party within a party in the primaries and conventions of the Democratic or Republican parties. As a general rule, such will only be done when a state's election laws are unconstitutional and rigged to bar this Party from the general election ballot. Our National Chairman shall make the final decisions on such matters. Membership in this Party cannot be purchased or transferred to another person.

ARTICLE IV— NATIONAL EXECUTIVE COMMITTEE

Sec. 1: The National Executive Committee of the National States Rights Party shall consist of a Chairman, Vice Chairman, and at least four other members, and not more than thirteen other members. The Chairman and Vice Chairman of said committee shall be known as the National Chairman and National Vice Chairman.

Sec. 2: The term of office for members of the National Executive Committee shall be for four years, unless, in the interval, a National Convention holds a new election for membership on said committee at a convention called for that purpose. Except as provided above, a National Convention for the purpose of transacting general Party business and electing members of said committee shall be held in the fourth calendar year after the prior election of said committee. Members of said committee shall serve until their successors have been elected or appointed; new members have the right to immediately assume their offices.

Sec. 3: The National Executive Committee shall meet at the call of its Chairman; except, that by written request of a majority of the members of said committee, and notification of the other members, a meeting may be held without a call from the National Chairman. The National Chairman shall designate the place of all meetings of said committee.

Sec. 4: The National Executive Committee shall conduct any and all affairs, business, policy, strategy and activities of the National States Rights Party between conventions of said Party, and have full power to perform those duties which are expected of such committee. Said committee is similar to a borad of directors.

Sec. 5: The National Executive Committee shall have the power to abolish or reorganize any local chapter, or unit, or state organization, or committee, or any other subordinate part of this Party. It may revoke the charter of any chapter, unit, committee, or any other subordinate part of this Party that violates of goes contrary to the platform, program, aims, and purposes of this Party, or violates this Constitution and By-Laws.

Sec. 6: When the National Executive Committee is not in session, its Chairman, the National Chairman, shall have all of the powers, authority, rights and duties that given to the National Executive Committee in sections 4 and 5 of this Article, and exercise them to the best of his ability. His decisions, instructions and orders are immediately effective and binding, but may be appealed to the next meeting of the National Executive Committee.

Sec. 7: The National Executive Committee may remove from office any officer of this Party at the national, state, local or chapter level for disorderly conduct within the Party, using obstructionist acts or words, disruptionist activity within or against the Party, rumor-mongering, disloyalty to this Party or its National Chairman, violation of this Constitution and By-Laws, or other cause, and appoint a successor for such office. Any such officer who is so removed by the National Chairman shall immediately cease holding his office and surrender all books, funds, and monies to the National Chairman or to his (the appellant officer's) successor in office. Any officer who is so removed by the National Chairman, after being removed from office, may appeal to the next meeting of the National Executive Committee. Said committee may grant a hearing if it considers the appeal to have merit and its decision shall be final.

Sec. 8: All property of local chapters, units, committees and other parts of this Party shall be held in their own names, or by trustees in their names as parts of this Party. In case of the revocation of any charter, or authorization, to said chapters, units, committees and other parts of this Party, all of their property and funds, including title to it, shall go into the treasury of the National Executive Committee; the same procedure shall take place in case of voluntary dissolution of any of the above mentioned subordinate parts of this Party. The National Chairman, as a Trustee of this Party and a Trustee of this Party's National Executive Committee may go into any court to enforce this, or any other section of this Constitution and By-Laws, or he may appoint another Trustee to perform said function.

Sec. 9: When vacancies occur on the National Executive Committee, the National Chairman shall appoint successors who shall hold office until the next election of members to said committee by a National Convention of this Party.

Sec. 10: When there are less than fifteen members on the National Executive Committee, the National Chairman may increase the membership of the National Executive Committee to fifteen, but, except for filling vacancies, should not appoint more than two new members in a twelve month period. The National Chairman shall increase the membership of said committee by making appointments in writing. The National Chairman should never let vacancies reduce the membership of said Committee to less than six and neither he nor the National Convention are required to ever have the full fifteen members on said committee so that there will usually be a place on said committee for a new person with ability.

ARTICLE V—
DUTIES OF NATIONAL OFFICERS

Sec. 1: The National Chairman shall preside over every National Convention of this Party, and at all meetings of the National Committee and the National Executive Committee. He may delegate the duty of presiding. He may call a meeting of any committee, at any level, chapter or unit or any other subordinate part of this Party, whenever he deems it advisable by giving reasonable notice to members of any such committee, unit, chapter, or other subordinate part. He shall have full authority to call special National Conventions of this Party for the purpose of transacting any business that is mention in the call or notice—any other matters will be out of order. He shall have full authority in hiring and discharging salaried employees and other employees and determining the salaries or compensation to be paid.

Sec. 2: The National Chairman shall enforce this Constitution and By-Laws, appoint all committees and trustees not otherwise provided for, and perform such other duties as are usual to the office of National Chairman or that may be rendered by this Party. Any and all other matters and authority not specifically covered in this Constitution and By-Laws shall come under the jurisdiction, authority, and duties of the National Chairman.

Sec. 3: Being the Chief Executive of this Party, the National Chairman shall have and hold supreme power and authority within this Constitution and By-Laws in all administrative matters, and to act in any and all matters not prescribed herein, when in his judgment, the best interests of this Party so warrant.

Sec. 4: The National Chairman may delegate authority to his subordinate executives of administrative officers as he may deem necessary, and revoke such delegated authority at his own discretion, but the national authority of this Party shall ever center and be vested in him and shall not be divided.

Sec. 5: The National Chairman shall specify the duties of all officers regardless of rank or station of whatever committee, chapter, unit, or subordinate part of this Party and shall require such duties to be properly performed on penalty of removal from office.

Sec. 6: Regardless of duties, responsibilities and authority delegated and granted to other National Officers in this Constitution and By-Laws and in this Article, the National Chairman may take duties, responsibilities and authority away from any of them and assign the same to another National Officer. This is required of the National Chairman any time that any National Officer fails to properly perform his duties or becomes untrustworthy, in the discretion and judgment of the National Chairman.

Sec. 7: The National Chairman shall designate which National Officer, or Officers, shall handle the funds, monies, real property and personal property of the National Executive Committee and take whatever measures are necessary to safeguard such assets of said committee. He shall have supreme supervision over all departments of this Party.

Sec. 8: The National Chairman shall have authority to issue instructions and orders covering any matter not specifically set forth in this Constitution and By-Laws, or emphasizing any matter in said Constitution, and all such instructions and orders must be respected and obeyed promptly. and faithfully by all members of this Party on penalty of expulsion. In case of such expulsion, notification by mail is sufficient notice.

Sec. 9: The National Chairman shall issue charters to chapters, specify conditions on which charters shall be issued, and shall have poser to open and close chapters or chapters in his discretion or upon request of a chapter. He shall have full and unchallengable authority to suspend or revoke charters of chapters for cause.

Sec. 10: Whenever a question, problem or issue of paramount importance to the interest, well-being, success or prosperity of this Party arises, not provided for in this Constitution and By-Laws, the National Chairman shall have full power to determine such matter, question, problem or issue, and his decision shall be final.

Sec. 11: The National Chairman shall transact all business of this Party between sessions of the National Executive Committee and between National Conventions; adopt measures in the interest of the Party, etc. He shall receive and make decisions in regard to the reports of the officers, committees and chapter of the Party. He may delegate authority as he deems necessary.

Sec. 12: The National Chairman shall call nominating conventions of this party before each election in which the Party participates. Unless otherwise stated in calling such conventions, nominations will be the only order of business.

Sec. 13: The National Chairman shall have full administrative authority in giving effect to the policies of the National States Rights Party, and in supervising its activities.

Sec. 14: The National Chairman shall retain legal talent and attorneys for the National Executive Committee and this Party and make such available to Party members and friends of this Party, at his discretion, when he thinks that a case deserves such legal assistance. This applies to both criminal and civil cases since our enemies persecute us in every way possible. Also, when he thinks that a case deserves such, he may also pay court costs and fines out of the treasury of the National Executive Committee or a legal or special fund.

Sec. 15: The National Chairman is empowered to establish special funds for the work of the Party, such as a Press Fund, Defense Fund, Legal Fund, building fund, organizing fund, campaign funds, etc.. Records of income and outgo of all such funds shall be kept.

Sec. 15: The National Vice Chairman shall act as National Chairman in the absence of the National Chairman. In case of the death, resignation or removal of the National Chairman from office, the National Vice Chairman shall become the National Chairman until the next National Convention, at which time the National Convention shall elect a National Chairman. The National Vice Chairman shall aid the National Chairman in the fulfillment and performance of his duties in whatever way possible. He is the second highest ranking officer of this Party.

Sec. 16: The Secretary of the National Executive Committee shall be appointed by the National Chairman, subject to ratification by a majority vote of those committee members present and voting at a meeting of said committee. Said Secretary is not required to be a member of said committee. He shall follow the instructions of the National Chairman and keep and maintain whatever records are necessary and shall also receive and keep safely all important papers and documents of said committee and this Party and issue membership cards. He shall notify all members in arrears of the amount of their indebtedness. When called upon to do so by the National Chairman, he shall submit his books and records to be checked and audited. He shall never reveal, divulge or otherwise allow any records, reports, membership lists, etc., to fall into other hands or in any way divulge the names or addresses of any Party members without the consent of the National Chairman or National Director. He may issue charters and authorizations to chapters and units and subordinate local and state committees of this Party when approved and signed by the National Chairman. The National Chairman may delegate any of the duties of the Secretary of said Committee to any other National Officer.

Sec. 17: The Treasurer of the National Executive Committee shall be appointed by the National Chairman, subject to ratification by said committee by a majority vote of those committee members present and voting at a meeting of said Committee. Said Treasurer is not required to be a member of said committee. He shall keep a financial record of the business of the National Executive Committee, and make reports to the National Chairman or National Committee when called upon to do so. When called upon by the National Chairman to do so, he shall submit his books and records to be audited by an auditing committee or an accountant chosen by the National Chairman. He shall make reports that are required by law. The National Chairman or National Director may hire a bookkeeper or accountant to help the Treasurer perform his duties, in fact, hire as much assistance for him as he needs. The Treasurer of said committee shall not handle or control or deposit any funds or monies of said committee unless so directed by the National Chairman. The National Chairman, at his own discretion, may delegate the duties of the Treasurer to any other National Officer.

Sec. 18: The Director of the National Executive Committee shall be appointed by the National Chairman, subject to ratification of said committee by a majority of those committee members present and voting at a meeting of said committee. He shall be the National Chairman's Chief of staff in directing the work of the Party and chief of staff at the National Headquarters of the National States Rights Party. He is in charge of all publicity and printed matter published by the National Executive Committee of this Party and is solely responsible for what is edited or published. He is empowered to establish and operate an official organ of the National Executive Committee, other newspapers and magazines, as well as to publish and distribute pamphlets and books. He shall aid Party members seeking information on given subjects. He shall be in charge of all publicity, press releases and dissemination of all official information of said committee, except when the National Chairman orders otherwise. He shall be custodian of the Party library and shall keep files on all subjects concerning the Party, including information on the enemies of this Party and their activities. The Party press should attempt to finance itself; however, with the consent of the National Chairman, the National Director, for the furtherance of his work, may use money and funds from the treasury of the National Executive Committee of this Party, may appeal to Party members and friends of the Party for funds, and control and expend those funds, subject to the authority of the National Chairman.. He may, with consent of the National Chairman, incorporate any of his activities. He shall make reports to the National Chairman whenever called upon to do so. He shall hire and pay salaries or wages to employees at National Headquarters and have authority to discharge any such employees. When so directed by the National Chairman, the Director, otherwise known as the National Director, shall have possession of the monies, funds and assets of the National Executive Committee of this Party and take whatever precautions are required by the National Chairman to protect said monies, funds, assets, securities, bonds, stocks, real property or other things of value. The same applies to special funds. He, as well as any other member so designated by the National Chairman, may hold real or personal property as a Trustee for the National Executive Committee and special funds. The National Chairman, anytime, at his own discretion, may delegate the duties of the National Director to any other National Officer.

Sec. 19: At the expiration of his term of office, by resignation, death, removal, or otherwise, each officer shall turn over to his successor, or the National Chairman, however the National Chairman directs, all monies, funds, property, title to property, papers, records, books and any other assets belonging to this Party that he may have in his possession or under his control. This rule applies to all National Officers and to all other officers and trustees throughout the Party, at all levels.

Sec. 20: All National Officers shall hold office until their successors are installed in office, unless their is an objection by either the National Chairman or the National Executive Committee.

Sec. 21: In addition to the National Chairman and the National Director being Trustees, the National Chairman may appoint other trustees for the National Executive Committee and special funds, and may authorize other Party committees, chapters and units to appoint or elect trustees for themselves, and he may prescribe their functions, conditions and terms of office, and revoke their authorizations and commissions when, in his discretion, he thinks such necessary.

Sec. 22: The National Chairman shall appoint a Sergeant-at-Arms, and Assistants, to have charge of the doors of any and all meetings over which he presides. The Sergeant-at-Arms shall bar enemies of the Party from entering Party meetings, assist the Chairman in preserving order and perform such other duties as may from time to time be assigned to him by the National Chairman. The National Organizer, subject to the National Chairman, shall have charge of the organizing work of the Party. He shall make regular reports to the National Executive Committee. The National Organizer's task shall be the establishment of local chapters and units. He shall call upon the Party and all of its members for assistance.

ARTICLE VI—NATIONAL COMMITTEE

Sec. 1: The National Committee shall consist of all members of the National Executive Committee; all National Officers; all state and local directors, co-ordinators and organizers; the chairman, vice chairman and secretary of every Party committee where this Party has a county committee on condition that said officers of county committees are listed on the records at National Headquarters; every Chairman of a state central or executive committee of this Party; and every Chapter Leader and Chapter Secretary.

Sec. 2: All members of the National Committee must be approved by the National Executive Committee. A member of the National Committee may be suspended or expelled from said Committee by the National Chairman. In that case, the member may appeal to the next meeting of the National Executive Committee.

Sec. 3: The National Committee shall convene the day preceeding the National Convention and at other times and places as decided by the National Chairman.

Sec. 4: The National Secretary shall notify National Committee members of record at least 7 days in advance of special called meetings of the National Committee.

Sec. 5: The purpose of the National Committee is to advise this Party's National Convention.

ARTICLE VII—NATIONAL CONVENTIONS

Sec. 1: The regular National Convention of the National States Rights Party for the purpose of transacting general business of the Party on all subjects and for the purpose of electing this Party's National Executive Committee shall be held on a date to be selected by the National Chairman, and each National Convention to follow, Providence along preventing, shall be held not later than the fourth calendar year after the previous regular National Convention. At his discretion, the National Chairman may call such a regular National Convention at an earlier time, or any other time. Except for the regular National Convention that is required every four years by this section, the National Chairman may call special National Conventions, at any other times, for special Party business.

Sec. 2: The legislative body and the final authority of the National States Rights Party shall be its National Convention. The National Chairman shall determine the place of each National Convention, as well as each meeting of the National Convention and the National Executive Committee. The National Chairman shall determine the details of each such committee meeting and each National Convention and supervise their operations.

Sec. 3: The rules of parliamentary law or Robert's rules of order shall never be applicable to meetings of the National Convention or any other meeting of the National States Rights Party because such rules would permit enemies to disrupt the meetings of our Party.

Sec. 4: The National Convention shall be composed of every member of the National States Rights Party who is in good standing on the membership records at National Headquarters and who also has a membership card to attest same.

Sec. 5: The National Chairman may call nominating conventions at any time, any where in the Nation, to nominate candidates for public office at the national, state or local level. Voting rights will be vested in every member in good standing in the area affected who attends. Unless otherwise stated in the call of nominating conventions, the only business will be nominations for public office, and all other business shall be out of order.

Sec. 6: While Party business is the primary function of our conventions, the National Chairman is empowered to ask outstanding individuals to speak.

ARTICLE VIII—ORGANIZATION

Sec. 1: There shall be four levels of organization of this Party, as follows: national, state, local and chapter.

Sec. 2: The National Secretary may accept applications for membership in any place where there is no chartered chapter. Such members shall be considered members at large. He may also accept applications for membership at large where there are chartered chapters.

Sec. 3: When appropriate, the National Chairman shall establish state, district, county, ward and precinct executive, or central committees. The main purpose of such committees shall be to place this Party's candidates on the ballot and conduct election campaigns, but shall have no authority over chapters, except as provided by the National Chairman. Provisional and initial officers of all such committees shall be appointed by the National Chairman, who, at his discretion, may fill all vacancies as they occur. All decisions by such committees shall be by majority vote with the National Chairman having the right to veto.

Sec. 4: All Party members, chapters and committees should always bear in mind that the purpose of the National States Rights Party is to win our goals in a 100 percent legal and political way by gaining political power through the ballot and general political activity. It is therefore vital that all Party member, officers, chapters and committees make every effort to elect our candidates to political office.

Sec. 5: No member, officer, chapter, unit or committee may give this Party's endoursment to any candidate for public office, except with the approval of the National Chairman. All such candidates must be openly pledged to support this Party's platform, program and policies.

Sec. 6: All chapters, units, committees and officers are required to keep the National Chairman informed as to all of their activities.

Sec. 7: Membership cards in the National States Rights Party shall be issued only by the National Secretary or National Director upon receipt of the yearly membership contribution. Each member of a chapter must be a member in good standing on the records of the National States Rights Party at National Headquarters and have a membership card verifying same.

Sec. 8: The annual contribution for members shall accompany application for membership. Following annual contributions shall be sent to Nationals Headquarters on or before the expiration date on each membership card, but each member shall be allowed a grace period after said expiration of sixty days. If a member has not renewed by then, the National Secretary shall remove his name from the membership list and the local chapter shall do the same.

Sec. 9: The amount of the annual national contribution to National Headquarters for members shall be determined from time to time by this Party's National Executive Committee. Such should be paid before the expiration date on a member's card, so as to save the expense of sending notices to members.

Sec. 10: Every member may receive a copy of this Party's official newspaper each time that it is published.

Sec. 11: Only members in good standing shall hold office or vote in any Party convention, or chapter or committee meeting. This section does not apply to members of the National Executive Committee or National Officers, even though they should make contributions to the Party when able to do so.

Sec. 12: All members shall send their membership contributions directly to National Headquarters. However, to prevent procrastination, chapter officers and other officers should remind and assist members with this matter so that they will remain in good standing.

Sec. 13: Income may be derived as provided in this Constitution or the National Executive Committee may obtain income from sources other than annual membership contributions. Members and friends of this Party are urged to give extra contributions when able.

Sec. 14: Chapters, units and committees of this Party may raise money for their activities and political action by whatever legitimate means they deem fit.

Sect. 15: Before any application can be accepted, it must be sent to National Headquarters. The National Secretary may approve or reject any application. An appeal from his decision may be made to the National Chairman, whose decision shall be final.

Sec. 16: Collections may be take up at meetings of this Party. Voluntary contributions from members and friends should be encouraged in order to strengthen the Party.

Sec. 17: The National Chairman has the authority to examine and inspect the books and records of any and all chapters, committees, members and officers that are in regard to the business of this Party or any part of it, or he may designate some other officer or member to do it. He is also authorized, when funds are available to do so, to hire a bookkeeper or an accountant to install a bookkeeping system for any chapter, unit or committee of this Party, always taking into consideration that any such system must be simple enough to function in said chapters, units or committees when none of their officers are bookkeepers or accountants.

Sec. 18: Insofar as is possible in a political organization with a voluntary membership, and insofar as talented persons and financial means are available, the National Chairman shall cause a suitable budget system to be installed throughout this Party.

Sec. 19: The National States Rights Party's desire is for members who will take an active part in building this Party and electing it to local, state and national political power so that our program and platform can become reality. Members should regularly read and distribute Party literature, attend meetings without fail, assist in placing this Party's candidates on the ballot, support and vote for all or our Party's candidates for public office and otherwise participate in furthering the cause of a free White America.

Sec. 20: When and where appropriate, the National Chairman shall commission directors, organizers, and co-ordinators of Party activities at local, district, and state levels, and each such Party officer shall have whatever authority is delegated to him in the commission from the National Chairman, but shall have no authority to commit a civil wrong or tort or defamation and no authority to subject the National Chairman, the National Executive Committee, other committees and chapters, or anyone else in this Party to any financial obligations or debts.

Sec. 21: At the expiration of his term of office, by death, resignation, removal or otherwise each person who is an officer in any part of this Party at any level, or who holds a position of trust, shall turn over to his successor or the National Chairman all monies, funds, property, papers, records, documents and books belonging to this Party that he may have in his actual or constructive possession, however directed by the National Chairman.

Sec. 22: The National Chairman shall have the authority and right to revoke any appointments, commissions, or delegation of authority that he has, at any time, now or in the future, granted to any officer, member, chapter, unit, committee or anybody else.

Sect. 23: Except where otherwise provided, the decisions of all meetings of this Party's chapters and state, local, district ward and precinct committees shall be decided by a majority vote of those members in good standing in attendance who are entitled to attend. However, any such vote that is contrary to this Constitution or in violation of this Party's platform, principles and program or not in accord with the policies of the National Chairman should be declared out of order by the presiding officer because such a vote is null and void from the beginning. Any member may report any vote or decision that is as described as above to the National Chairman for a ruling. The National Chairman's ruling is immediately effective and binding upon all concerned, but may be appealed to the next meeting of the National Executive Committee. The National Chairman may veto the action, vote or decision of any subordinate part of this Party on his own initiative in which case the veto and decision is immediately effective and binding, but may also be appealed to the next meeting of the National Executive Committee.

Sect. 24: The National Chairman may veto any act of the National Convention, in which case it will take a majority of two thirds of those voting to override his veto. The same applies to any action of the National Committee. However, if two thirds of the votes in a meeting of the National Committee are adverse to the National Chairman, he may refer the entire matter to the National Convention.

Sec. 25: The National Executive Committee will decide its business by a majority vote of those members present and voting. However, the National Chairman has the authority to veto any vote or action of the National Executive Committee, regardless of whether he is present or absent. However, if two thirds of those members of said committee who are present and voting vote to override his veto, it will be considered a vote of no confidence in him; then, the National Chairman must accede to the two thirds vote of said committee or immediately call a regular National Convention for the purpose of electing a new National Executive Committee and the transaction of general Party business.

Sec. 26: Any member of the National Executive Committee, including the National Chairman, may be expelled or removed from said committee by a meeting of said committee where at least two thirds of those committee members present and voting do vote for such removal, suspension, or expulsion. Or, at such a meeting, any member of said committee, including the National Chairman, may be only suspended under conditions as determined by a two thirds vote. In such cases, both the accused and any accuser or accusers who are members of said committee shall have their usual right to vote. However, if the National Chairman is removed, expelled, or suspended by a two thirds vote of the National Executive Committee, said committee, upon demand of the National Chairman, must immediately issue a call for a regular National Convention for the election of a new National Executive Committee and the transaction of general Party business, and set the sate of said convention within sixty days. At said convention, the deposed or suspended National Chairman shall have the right to attend, speak, and be a candidate for re-election to said committee.

Sec. 27: No member of the National Executive Committee may be removed, expelled or suspended, except as provided in section 26 above, or by a National Convention, unless he has filed a legal action in a court against the National Chairman, the National Executive Committee or any of its members, or against any National Officer. In that case, on that ground alone, he must be removed by the National Chairman alone, or by a majority vote of the National Executive Committee; otherwise there would be a conflict of interest.

ARTICLE IX—
OFFENSES, PENALTIES, EXPULSIONS

Sect. 1: Offenses against this Party shall be divided into two classes:–major offenses and minor offenses.

Sec. 2: Major offenses shall consist of the following subsections: (1) Treason against this Nation; (2) violations of this Party's Constitution and By-Laws; (3) conspiring or working against the Party in any way; (4) disloyalty to this Party or its National Chairman, or both; (5) working for the Jew-controlled F.B.I., or giving its agents any information about this Party, or any of its officers or members. This subsection is in recognition of the fact that thee F.B.I. is the action-arm of the Jews against all patriotic White Christian Americans, that it violates the U.S. Constitution, violated the rights of the States, and that the F.B.I. is unnecessary and must be abolished before it completely suppresses American freedom; (6) working for or giving information to any political police or group or entity that is against this Party; (7) spying on this Party for any person or group or entity; (8) any pro–Jewish act or statement; (9) any act of statement that shows a hatred or lack of love toward our White Race; (10) making false charges against any Party officer or member; (11) making any charges against any Party officer or member without specifically citing relevant and material evidence to support the charges; (12) rumor mongering that is harmful to this Party; (13) interference with any Party activity after it has been properly authorized; (14) excessive or habitual drunkenness; (15) polluting the White blood stream through miscegenation; (16) voting against any candidate of this Party who is running for public office; (17) misuse or theft of any Party property; (18) any acts or words that disrupt a Party meeting or that interfere seriously with peace and harmony within the Party;—we cannot afford to tolerate any disruptionist, regardless of whether he is an agent for the enemy, or a natural-born disruptionist; (19) support of any Jewish, communist, or race-mixing organization by word or deed; (20) failure to vote when this Party's candidates are on the ballot; (21) associating socially with negroes; (22) filing a legal action in any court against the National Chairman, or any other Party leader, the National Executive Committee or any of its members, any National Officer, any chapter, unit, or committee, subordinate part or officer of the Party in regard to any of the affairs or business of this Party, instead of resorting to the procedures and provisions of this Constitution for a remedy—except that this does not apply when the National Executive Committee or National Chairman authorizes a suit or it is allowed or ordered by another article or section of this Constitution; (23) and, the repeated commission of a minor offense shall constitute a major offense.

Sec. 3: Minor offenses against his Party shall be as listed in the following subsections: (1) Failing to regularly attend Party meetings; (2) bad conduct in public; (3) failure to have a friendly attitude toward other Party members; (4) vulgarity or profane language prior to or during a Party meeting; (5) coming to a Party meeting while under the influence of alcohol; (6) disorderly conduct at a Party meeting or when associating with other Party members; (7) failure to help authorized Party officers conduct a peaceful and orderly meeting; (8) becoming a victim of Jewish or any other enemy propaganda; (9) failure to perform the citizenship duties of jury service and voting at every opportunity.

Sec. 4: All offenses enumerated above as minor offenses shall be tried by the Chapter Leader or highest ranking Party officer directly concerned with the alleged offense. For conviction of a minor offense, the maximum penalty shall be a reprimand, suspension of membership for ten days or a five dollar fine. Any interested Party member who is dissatisfied with a conviction or an acquittal may appeal to the highest ranking Party officer in his area, then to the highest ranking Party officer in his state, and, after that, to the National Chairman.

Sec. 5: All charges against a Party member involving a major offense under this Constitution shall be in writing and specify the specific act or acts or words charged, which shall be submitted to the Investigating Committee of the chapter, unit, or committee of which the accused is a member, or in whose jurisdiction the alleged offense was committed, or to the highest ranking Party officer in the area for referral to an investigating committee. The Investigating Committee shall then investigate same and determine the sufficiency of the charges. If the charges are sufficient, the Investigating Committee shall order the accused to stand trial.

Sec. 6: Every chapter, unit and committee except the National Executive Committee, should either have a standing regular Investigating Committee or one should be appointed from time to time, as the need arises. Other Party officers such as directors, co-ordinators, et cetera, may appoint such committees when needed and convoke tribunals to try charges.

Sec. 7: In all chapters, except for those members who are biased against the accused, all members shall form a tribunal to hear and decide the case, with the Chapter Leader as presiding officer, unless he is the accused. The case shall be decided by majority vote. The same procedure shall be used by units and committees, and higher ranking officers. If convicted or a major offense, the maximum penalties shall be reprimand, fine of not more than fifty dollars, suspension or expulsion. Ostracism may be added to any of these penalties. The member who is convicted shall have the right to appeal up the Party's chain of command, even to the National Executive Committee which is this Party's highest Tribunal. In case of expulsion, the National Secretary may ratify the expulsion by dropping the expelled member from membership on the records at National Headquarters, unless the National Chairman objects; otherwise, he may allow the member who has been expelled from a chapter, unit, committee, or Party at the local area to continue as a member at large, subject to any ruling by the National Executive Committee or National Chairman. Only relevant evidence shall be admitted to any trial. From the filing of charges, all following steps in regard to trial and appeal must be taken within a reasonable time.

Sec. 8: Anything else in this Article notwithstanding, regardless of how contrary, any chapter by majority vote, may drop any member from membership in the chapter for any offense, or no offense, and said member shall then return to the status of a member at large or apply for membership in another chapter, unless he has also been dropped from membership at National Headquarters.

Sec. 9: The National Executive Committee may take original jurisdiction in any case, may hold a new trial regardless of conviction or acquittal before a lower tribunal and may review any case tried at a lower level, and its decision shall be final.

Sec. 10: Any accused who fails to appear for trial, in person or by representative, shall be deemed as guilty as charged.

Sec. 11: Any member who fails to respect the penalty imposed on another member shall receive the same penalty as if he himself were guilty of that offense.

Sec. 12: Any State Director may expel any member in his state from this Party, without a trial; where there is no State Director, the State Co-ordinator shall have this authority; in any state where there is no State Director or State Co-ordinator, someone else designated by the National Chairman shall have such authority.

Sec. 13: The National Chairman may expel any member or officer anywhere from this Party, members of the National Executive Committee alone excepted, without a trial. This authority should especially be used against undercover agents of all enemy organizations, especially the undercover agents and pimps of the F.B.I. which is trying to disrupt and persecute all patriotic White Christian organizations that are against the Jews, communists and negroes.

Sec. 14: Such orders of expulsion as outlined in sections 12 and 13 of this Article shall be immediately binding and effective, but may be appealed within a reasonable time to the National Executive Committee, this Party's Supreme Tribunal. If said committee thinks that there might be merit in any such appeals, it may grant a trial or otherwise review the expulsions and its decision shall be final.

Sec. 15: The National Chairman has the authority to pardon any member convicted of any offense.

ARTICLE X—EMBLEM, FLAG AND SLOGAN

Sec. 1: The slogan of the National States Rights Party shall be: Honor, Pride, Fight—Save the White!

Sec. 2: The emblem of the National States Rights Party shall be The Thunderbolt.

Sec. 3: We are loyal to and honor the American flag as our Nation's flag. We use the Thunderbolt flag and the Confederate flags as our Party's flags. We use them because they let all of our friends and enemies know where we stand and that we are against the Jews, communists, negroes, negro-lovers and their F.B.I. protectors and all of their puppets and allies because they are our enemies. They are our enemies because they are the enemies of God, the White race and our Nation. The Thunderbolt and Confederate flags also tell the world that we stand for a free White Christian America. In using the Confederate flag, we use it as a symbol of the White race and White supremacy, not as a sectional emblem. We are White racists, not sectionalists, and we strive to preserve the White race throughout this Nation and in every nation where the White race dwells.

ARTICLE XI—LOCAL CHAPTERS AND UNITS

Sec. 1: A local chapter shall consist of three or more members of the National States Rights Party who are in good standing on the records at National Headquarters. Each chapter shall have the following officers: Leader, Assistant Leader, Secretary, and Sergeant at Arms. It may also have an Assistant Secretary, and Assistant Sergeant at Arms. Any of the aforementioned officers, except the Assistant Sergeants at Arms, may also be elected Treasurer.

Sec. 2: Each chapter shall hold an annual election of chapter officers at its first regular meeting in December of each year, unless at an earlier meeting, the chapter voted to hold the election of chapter officers at a later meeting in December. Said December election is for officers for the following calendar year and they shall be installed in their respective offices at the first chapter meeting in January unless their predecessors resign before then, in which case they will be installed then. Present chapter officers shall hold office until new officers are installed. Installation of new officers shall merely consist of a notification to the National Chairman that they are willing to serve and to abide by this Party's Constitution; or, by appearing at the chapter meeting and pledging to do that and joining with the other newly elected officers in reciting the Weekly Lecture as it appears in the Official Meeting Procedure for chapters. Any time that a chapter elects officers, it must immediately notify National Headquarters and the election of said officers must be ratified by National Chairman. All officers-elect and all other chapter members must be in good standing on the records at National Headquarters.

Sec. 3: The Leader shall preside over all meetings of the chapter. He may call special meetings of the chapter as the need arises. He shall be in charge of the affairs of the chapter with the exception of the duties assigned to other officers and see that other chapter officers perform their duties. The Leader should make every effort to hold one meeting every week, preferably at the same time and place. He shall appoint all committees and transact such other duties and business as are usual to the office of Leader or that may be rendered by a Party chapter. In addition to presiding over chapter meetings, he should furnish active leadership to the local chapter or unit in its meetings and all other activities and loyally support the National Chairman and his administration of Party affairs. He should not allow the chapter to become a mere debating society and a breeder of disunity because out Party's platform, Constitution, program and aims are already agreed upon, thereby leaving little room for argument.

Sec. 4: The Secretary shall keep a true record of all resolutions and decisions of a chapter and of all unusually important proceedings of the local chapter or unit, including financial reports, but should not waste time on keeping detailed minutes, and shall never take down the words, or subject matter, of anyone speaking in a chapter meeting. He shall keep a file of the membership of the chapter or unit and record their annual dues payments to National Headquarters, and when said dues expire and make certain that they are paid on time, preferably before they expire. He shall also collect any local dues that may be levied by the chapter and turn them over to the Treasurer or Trustee of the chapter. If the chapter finances itself by voluntary collections instead of by levying local dues, the Secretary shall collect and record the amount of the collections and then turn the sums collected over to the Treasurer or Trustee. He shall make certain that all chapter members maintain themselves in good standing at National Headquarters and, if any member lets his annual payment of dues to National Headquarters become in arears for more than sixty days, the Secretary shall drop him from membership in the chapter and so notify the next chapter meeting.

Sec. 5: The Treasurer of a chapter shall keep a financial record of all of the chapters income and disbursements and give a receipt for all monies and funds received and obtain receipts for all disbursements and keep them available for inspection by the chapter officers, the National Chairman and other properly authorized persons. He shall notify all members in arrears of annual dues to National Headquarters and of dues to the local chapter. He shall make any financial reports that are required by law. He shall keep financial records and shall turn his books over to an auditing committee or an accountant for checking when ordered to do so by the unit or chapter leader or by the National Chairman. He shall make a financial report to the Leader each month; however, if he happens to also be the leader, he shall make the monthly report to a meeting of the chapter or unit. He shall make all payments authorized or ordered by a majority vote of the chapter or unit, by the Constitution and By-Laws, or by the National Chairman. If the chapter so votes, the Treasurer may perform all of these duties, except for letting a Trustee hold and disburse all chapter funds and monies as provided above, in accordance with Section 21 of Article V of this Constitution.

Sec. 6: The Sergeant at Arms, subject to the orders of the Leader, shall have charge of the doors and only admit qualified members and invited friends to meetings. As a general rule, only chapter members in good standing should be allowed to attend regular chapter meetings and friends should only be invited to special meetings or regular meetings when prior permission is obtained from the chapter Leader or one of his superior officers. The National Chairman, and any Party officers designated by him, always have the right to attend any chapter meeting. The Sergeant at Arms shall check the membership cards of all chapter members and other members who attend each meeting and report any that have expired, or are about to expire, to the Leader and the Secretary. He shall open and close the meeting hall and quickly assist the Leader in preserving order and shall perform such other duties as may from time to time be assigned to him.

The Sergeant at Arms may have a First Assistant and other Assistants. He and his assistants may be known as the Security Guard of the chapter, and the Sergeant at Arms may also be known as the chapter's Security Chief. They shall function as a bodyguard for the National Chairman and other Party officers when called upon to do so. If any Security Guard of any chapter wishes to wear uniforms, said uniforms shall consist of a White shirt, this Party's arm-band or Thunderbolt patch, and a Thunderbolt lapel pin. It must be a dress uniform. No outlandish uniforms are allowed; no boots, no Sam Brown belts, et cetera. If any headgear is used, prior permission must be obtained from National Headquarters. All members of the Security Guard must be polite, courteous, clean and well-behaved at all times and must not wear their uniforms except when performing Party business. At all times, they must obey all laws of their State and this Nation which are in accord with the United States Constitution, and they must rigidly abide by this Party's Constitution and By-Laws and obey all orders from and by loyal to this Party's National Chairman. The powers and duties of each Chapter's Security Guard are as defined in this article and section and limited thereto. In most respects it will stand on the same footing as any other chapter committee and give due respect and obedience to the chapter Leader and his superiors. It shall in no way function as a private police.

All Security Guards are a part of chapters and all co-ordination and direction of said Guards about the chapter level shall be as ordered by Directors of Party activity at the local, county or area levels who have been commissioned by the National Chairman. Where there are no such Party Directors, Party Co-ordinators shall have that authority. There shall by no Security Guard officers, except at the chapter level and at National Headquarters where the National Sergeant at Arms, subject to the National Chairman, is responsible for security. In regard to the chain of command from National Headquarters to Security Guards of chapters, it shall be through the regular chain of Party officers. There shall be no Security Guard officers at the state or any other level of Party organization, except for National Headquarters and each local chapter, as specified above.

Sec. 7: For the purpose of owning real property or other assets of a chapter, a chapter may elect one or more Trustees to legally hold such property in their own names, AS Trustees for the chapter as is the practice with other unincorporated organizations. Also, a Trustee may be elected to hold and disburse chapter monies and funds so that the Treasurer of the Chapter may have more time to concentrate upon bookkeeping and other Party duties. A Trustee must at all times be in good standing on the records at National Headquarters and only be elected or appointed in accordance with this Article and Section 21 of Article V of this Constitution and other applicable articles and sections of this Constitution and must, while serving, always abide by this Party's Constitution and By-Laws and the orders of the National Chairman. He must keep the same kind of records as are required of the Treasurer and under the same conditions.

Sec. 8: A chapter may have an initiation for new members, but it shall be dignified and involve no physical pain or suffering whatsoever. Any hazing is hereby forbidden. As a general rule, an initiation of new members should only consist of having them agree to and read aloud the pledge that is contained in the Weekly Lecture as it appears in the Official Meeting Procedure of this Article. Swearing and oaths are not permitted. This is not an oath bound organization.

Sec. 9: All chapter members should be present at every meeting unless they have a valid excuse. Only chapter members in good standing have the right to vote in chapter meetings and all chapter business shall be decided by a majority vote of those present and voting, but any voting or resolution that is contrary to or violates this Constitution or fails to accord with the aims, principles and platform of this Party or the policies of the National Chairman shall be void ab initio and a nullity, and shall so be declared out of order and null and void by the chapter Leader. If the chapter Leader fails to so declare, any member may bring the matter to the attention of his superior Party officers and the National Chairman for appropriate action.

Sec. 10: The rules of parliamentary law or Robert's rules of order shall never apply at any meeting of any chapter or any meetings of any committee of any chapter. The Leader shall determine the rules of order in accordance with the provisions of this Article, subject to the approval of the National Chairman. At all levels, our Party's officers and leaders are expected to have initiative in leading our Party toward being elected to national political power and not to preside over debating societies which, as a matter of nature, only breed disunity.

Sec. 11: When the Leader is absent, the Assistant Leader shall preside at chapter meetings. If both of the aforementioned officers are absent, the Secretary shall preside, then the Assistant Secretary, the Sergeant at Arms. Any officer who is absent for two consecutive meetings without giving a valid excuse shall have his office filled for the remainder of his term by a majority vote of those present and voting.

Sec. 12: The chapter Leader may place a time limit on any report of committees or the discussion of any subject, provided the time limit applies equally to all concerned. He shall limit speeches to 30 minutes, and not allow any member to speak over 5 minutes unless consent is obtained before the meeting begins. He shall keep all chapter business and discussions relevant to our Party's goals and shall declare anyone out of order who says anything that is irrelevant and not in accord with this Constitution and the policies of our National Chairman.

Sec. 13: When a new chapter is formed, provisional officers may be appointed by the Organizer of the chapter, subject to the approval of the National Chairman. A chapter must then obtain a Charter from National Headquarters by filing a written application for it and said chapter shall have no authority until the National Chairman grants it a Charter.

Sec. 14: All chapters are encouraged to hold regular meetings, preferably every week, and actively participate in public affairs. Every county should have at least three local chapters, regardless of how small the county. The Party's desire is to have many small chapters in each areas instead of one or two large chapters. Members attend meetings wit more regularity when they only have to go a short distance to a meeting. Having many small chapters also makes it possible to avoid personality conflicts by only placing members who are affable and friendly toward each other in each chapter, thereby promoting peace and harmony throughout our Party.

Sec. 15: Chapter meetings shall begin at a predetermined time and end promptly at a pre-set time and not be allowed to drag on indefinitely. General discussion, social activities, refreshments and entertainment must not begin until the chapter meeting has officially closed and ended. No alcoholic beverages must be allowed prior to or during a meeting.

Sec. 16: The chapter Leader shall be the only official spokesman for his chapter, shall only speak for his chapter and no other part or officer of the Party, and only say or write what he is authorized to say or write by his chapter that is in accordance with the policies of his superior officers and the National Chairman. He shall not say or write anything defamatory or libellous about anybody while speaking or writing in his official capacity. He is solely responsible for his own statements.

Sec. 17: Any member of a chapter or a member at Large may be expelled from his chapter and this Party by the National Chairman.

Sec. 18: Each chapter shall make a regular brief report of its activities to the National Chairman.

Sec. 19: Candidates for membership in a chapter shall make written application on one of this Party's regular application forms and supply other reasonable information that is required by a chapter. The chapter shall have an Investigating Committee which shall investigate all applications for membership and make every effort to investigate prospective applicants before they apply for membership so as to prevent an unsuitable person from ever making a formal application, thereby preventing hard feelings. It is a much better policy for a chapter to decide upon the acceptability of a person before he is given an application form.

Members may request the Investigating Committee to make a recommendation, one way or the other, before an application is made and the chapter may then vote on whether to extend an invitation to apply, or not, to a prospective applicant. The voting requirements will be the same as if the person had filed a written application and will determine the matter.

When a candidate for membership files an application for membership, the Investigating Committee shall look into the matter and make a report to the chapter. For the applicant to be accepted as a member of the chapter, he must meet all of the membership requirements specified in this Constitution and three fourths of those chapter members must vote for his acceptance. That is true, regardless of whether the applicant is already a member at large of this Party, or a member of another chapter. Further, before any application can be accepted by a chapter, except on a tentative basis, it must be sent to National Headquarters for approval or rejection by the proper National Officer.

Sec. 20: Chapters and units are not required to accept members at large or members from other chapters, but the members of each and every chapter must be in good standing on the records at National Headquarters, as evidenced by an up-to-date membership card from the National Secretary or National Director. A member who is dropped or expelled from membership in a local chapter or unit may continue as a member at large, unless his membership is then revoked by National Headquarters, without objection by the National Chairman.

Sec. 21: A member of a chapter may make charges against any other Party member, inside of outside of his chapter, but the charges, procedure and trial must be in accordance with Article IX of this Constitution.

Sec. 22: Each chapter may have a Youth Movement which shall stand on the same footing as any other chapter committee. They may only wear uniforms, if any, as prescribed in Section 5 of this Article. All members of each Youth Movement must be under the age of nineteen. Each chapter's Youth Movement must be supervised by either the chapter Leader or some responsible adult member designated by him. For student youths under the age of nineteen who are not gainfully employed, the National executive Committee may require an annual contribution to National Headquarters that is less than for other members; chapters may decide what, if any, dues such Youth Movement members must pay to the chapter in which they hold membership.

The Youth Movement shall used the same Official Meeting Procedure that is prescribed in this Article for chapters, except, that the words: "The Youth Movement of" shall be placed before the words "Chapter No. ____." Further, each Youth Movement shall refrain from having committees within it, except when the chapter leader says that such are necessary for it to function and authorizes same. Each member of a chapter's Youth Movement must be in good standing on the records at National Headquarters, the same as all other members.

Any dues or assessments for a Youth Movement shall be determined by its sponsoring chapter, and discipline will be maintained by the chapter in accordance with the usual procedures, as outlined in Article IX of this Constitution. Every member of a Youth Movement must be a law-abiding citizen who is polite, courteous, clean and well-behaved.

Where possible, each chapter should provide gyms and weight lifting equipment for its Youth Movement.

Each Youth Movement must obey the orders of its chapter leader. All co-ordination and direction of Youth Movements above the chapter level shall be as ordered by Directors of Party activities at the local, county or area level who have been commissioned by the National Chairman. Where there are no such Party Directors, Party Co-ordinators shall have that authority. There shall be no Youth Movement officers, except at the chapter level. In regard to the chain of command from National Headquarters to Youth Movements of chapters, it shall be through the regular chain of Party officers. There shall be no Youth Movement officers at the state or any other level of Party organization, except for each local chapter. The National Chairman may appoint a National Youth Director at National Headquarters to formulate programs for chapter youth movements.

Sec. 23: Upon exceeding 25 members, a chapter may be divided into two chapters by the National Chairman, or be chartered by the National Chairman as a local unit. However, this is in the discretion of the National Chairman and is not a requirement.

Sec. 24: It is recommended that each chapter, in addition to having an Investigating Committee, have the following committees as it needs the services of such committees: Membership Committee to maintain contact wit all chapter members and to phone members and remind them of date and place of next meeting and of special meetings; Organizing Committee to solicit desirable persons for membership in the chapter; Educational Committee to distribute this Party's literature; Election Day Committee to transport members and friends to the polls to vote for our candidates for public office and to phone others and urge them to vote, both before and on election day; Voter Registration Committee; Welfare Committee to help needy Party members, and others, to visit the sick and attend funerals of Party members and friends, etc.; Campaign Committee to campaign for our Party's candidates for public office; Fund Raising Committee; and Recreation and Picnic Committee for those purposes and to also be in charge of the chapter's celebration of various holidays. Any of the above committees may be combined into once committee. The Chapter Leader shall appoint other committees as recommended by the National Chairman, and as needed.

Sec. 25: OFFICIAL MEETING PROCEDURE

The order of business for local chapters and units shall be as follows:

(1) Military-style march music (on tape or record or by a live band) until the Chapter Leader is ready to open the meeting.

(2) Chapter Leader: "I now officially proclaim that this meeting of Chapter No. ___ of the State of _____ is duly open for the dispatch of business. Sergeant at Arms,, you may now admit all qualified members of this chapter (and invited guests, if an open meeting), but guard well the doors to this place and allow no enemies in this meeting.

(3) The Leader, or any member designated by him, shall lead the members, and any others present, in saying the following Christian prayer: "Our Father, Who are in Heaven, the Author of all good; Thou who dids't create our White race and so proposed that the White race should fill a distinct place and perform a specific work for Your Glory, we thank You for creating the White nations on this earth and making the White race more intelligent and superior to all other races, and we pray for You to bless us with the strength and the victories to preserve the White race and the power to prevent the other races from mixing with our White race. We pray to be blessed with a White Christian America for Whites only. Please use us, Your children, the White race, as your instruments in this world so that Your will shall be done.

Please bless us White people with unity and peace and harmony among ourselves. Please guide all officers and members of this Party toward friendship for each other and please prohibit rumor-mongering and defaming among out own ranks. Please bless us all with the strength to not believe false charges against our White co-workers in this struggle and please encourage us to speak ill of all loyal White Christians who are working with us in the National States Rights Party. Please bless the National States Rights Party, all of its chapters, units, committees, members, leaders, and especially our National Chairman, and please inspire all of us to become more active in the service of this great Party. Please bestow greater blessings and victories than ever before upon our White race so that it will live as long as the world stands. We glorify You and give thanks to You in the Name of our Lord Jesus Christ. Amen."

(4) The Leader, or a member designated by him, shall lead the assembled members in the pledge of allegiance to the Flag.

(5) The members may now sing a patriotic song.

(6) <u>Weekly Lecture on Party Principles</u>

The chapter Leader, or a member designated by him, shall re-affirm this Party's position by saying: "This is our pledge. This Party, our National States Rights Party, is a patriotic political party which is working to free our Nation from the Jews. Our freedom will be won in a completely legal and political way. When our Party is elected to national political power, new judges will be appointed and laws and Constitutional amendments will be enacted that will free our Nation from the Jews forever.

"Our Party believes in Anti-Jewism because it is a leading Christian virtue and an essential patriotic virtue. Anti-Jewism says that America belongs rightful to us Americans, not to the Jews; Jew-devils have no place in a White Christian nation. When our Party is elected to national political power, the Government will expel the Jews and confiscate their ill-gotten wealth for the benefit of the American people. When the Jews are gone, we Americans will own rich America.

"The National States Rights Party is against communism in any and every form. Communism is Jewish! Communism is one of the Jew plans, along with the Untied Nations organization and other world government schemes, to destroy us and conquer the world. Revolutions, no-win wars, internationalism, economic chaos, inflations, starvations, unemployment and depressions are deliberately designed by the Jews to promote their communistic plans. In every communist country, the Jews are the ruling race.

Almost all communist spies are Jews. Our party proposes for the Government to expel all communists from this Nation. Without the Jews, there would be NO communism!

"Our Party stands for Jesus Christ, restoration of the U.S. Constitution, America First, Trial by Twelve Jurors, Freedom of speech, press and assembly, American Independence, and the other great principles stated in our Party's Constitution and official platform.

"We are against the Jews, communists, negroes and their allies because they are our enemies. Also, we are against the United Nations, world government, foreign give-aways, political police, secret police, race-mixing and Jewish monopoly because they all endanger our White way of life.

"The National States Rights Party believes in White Supremacy, the White race and its preservation throughout the world, a free White America, and only White Christian immigration. We know that all civilizations worthy of the name have been created by the White race. No White nation has ever maintained its civilization after allowing the blood of non–Whites to mongrelize its people.

"When elected to power, our Party will completely separate the races and give all Africans in America a rich country of their own in Africa.

"All laws that are contrary to our Party's platform and program must either be declared unconstitutional by the courts or repealed. The Supreme Court and other courts must have new judges who will interpret the United States Constitution and all state constitutions in accordance with the original intent of the founders of this Nation, such behind embodies in our Party's platform and program.

"We call upon all members to do their duty for this Party, attend all of your chapter and other meetings, maintain peace and harmony with other members, vote for our Party's candidates in every election, make certain that your friends vote and help our National Chairman and other members elect our candidates to public office. We plan to win.

"This is our pledge as we also pledge our loyalty to the National States Rights Party, its Constitution, and to the National Chairman. We further pledge to our National Chairman that we shall never believe or give credence to any lies that the enemy directs against him or this Party or any of its members.

"Our pledge is given upon our honor as members of the great White race. Honor, Pride, Fight—Save the White!"

(7) Unfinished business.

(8) Submission of names of prospective applicants so that a vote can be take on whether or not to invite them to join before they submit applications for membership. Said names may be voted on immediately if enough is known about them or they may be referred to the Investigating Committee for a report on them. If three fourths of the vote is for acceptance, that is final without another vote after the application is filed.

(9) Applications for membership in the Party and the chapter will be read, discussed and referred to the Investigating Committee if more information and recommendations are needed. To be accepted into chapter membership, three fourths of those members present and voting must vote for the applicant. If rejected, the application should be immediately forwarded to National Headquarters for consideration as an applicant for membership at large. If accepted, the application and initiation fee should be immediately rushed to National Headquarters with a recommendation that it be accepted by the National Secretary and that a membership card be issued to the applicant.

(10) Reports of committees.

(11) Reading of communications from National Headquarters and from State and local Party directors and Party co-ordinators.

(12) Reports of chapter officers.

(13) Announcements.

(14) Statement by Chapter Leader about Party activities and general political developments in accordance with his duty to furnish active leadership.

(15) General business.

(16) Speeches in accordance with this Constitution and By=Laws and the aims, principles, platform and program of the National States Rights Party.

(17) Chapter Leader: "I now proclaim this meeting of Chapter No. ____ of the National States Rights Party in the State of _____ duly ended and closed. This chapter will meet again next _____ (day of week), on the ___ day of _____, 19__. Fellow White people, one and all, good night." The members shall then respond with a victory cheer of their own choosing.

(18) Military-style band music shall then be played as the members depart, or until a social gathering starts.

ARTICLE XII—AMENDMENTS

Sec. 1: This Constitution (and By-Laws) of the National States Rights Party may be amended by a two-thirds vote of the National Convention at any National Convention which is a regular national convention for the purpose of transacting general business of this Party, or at any National Convention which is called for the purpose of changing or amending this Constitution, but not at any other kind of national convention. Said Constitution may be amended or changed by a majority vote of the National Convention where specifically permitted by the National Chairman. Such permission is the only authority that our National Chairman cannot delegate to another.

ARTICLE XIII—
MISCELLANEOUS PROVISIONS

Sec. 1: Every chapter, unit, committee, officer, organizer, director, co-ordinator and member of this Party is to refrain from committing any civil wrongs or torts or libels of defamations against any person or entity; and if any such acts are committed, only the person or persons committing such acts are responsible for such acts and not this Party or any officer, member, chapter, unit or committee of this Party.

Sec. 2: No officer or member of this Party may incur any debts or financial obligations that would be binding upon any other officer or member of this Party, unless the other officer or member personally signs the instrument of indebtedness.

Sec. 3: Every chapter, officer, member, committee, or other part of this Party must identify itself (or himself) with anything that it (or he or she) publishes in print, on picket signs and otherwise, such as listing chapter number and address and name of officer responsible, and is hereby forbidden to commit defamation, libel or slander. Further, no person may speak for this Party or its chapters or any other parts of it without proper authorization. Every one in this Party is solely responsible for what he writes or says and the National Chairman, the National Executive Committee, each chapter, each unit, each committee, each officer, each director, each co-ordinator and each member is in no way responsible for the defamations and torts that might possible be committed by others in this Party—the same as one Democrat or Republican is nor responsible for what other Republicans or Democrats say or do.

Sec. 4: There are cases where unauthorized persons, even non-members, have purported to speak for this Party. This must stop.

Sec. 5: No member or officer of this Party may incur any debts or financial obligations for the National Chairman, the National Executive Committee, or any chapter, unit or committee or any other part of this Party or any member or officer, except as provided in sections 6 and 7 below.

Sec. 6: The National Chairman may allow any chapter, unit or committee to incur debts or financial obligations of a contractual nature only, which bind only that chapter, unit or committee, as such, and none of its members of officers or any other persons or committees.

Sec. 7: The National Chairman or the National Director may incur debts and financial obligations of a contractual nature to help the National Executive Committee function, but such debts and financial obligations shall only be binding upon the Treasury and income of the National Executive Committee, but shall not be binding upon anyone else unless some other person personally signs as a surety.

Sec. 8: All officers, trustees, members and any other persons who handle funds or other things of value that belong to this Party or any of its subordinate parts shall keep a written record of all transactions including income and outgo, and receipts where possible.

Sec. 9: Any bylaws or rules and regulations adopted by any chapter or committee or other part of this Party must be in accordance with this Constitution and be approved by the National Chairman.

Sec. 10: Only an authorized officer can speak, act, picket or demonstrate for the various chapters, committees and units of this Party, and he must have advance authorization. He must also have prior authorization to have Party members and others in said picket lines and demonstrations.

Sec. 11: No chapter, unit, committee or subordinate part of this Party may become incorporated in any state or otherwise, except by specific written permission from the National Executive Committee. Such permission may only be granted in unusual cases because political parties should not be incorporated. The National Executive Committee may permit publications to be incorporated.

THE THUNDERBOLT

Why We Choose To Struggle under the Sign of The Thunderbolt

The Thunderbolt is an ancient symbol of the White race. It is the thunder from the heavens which first awed out forefathers as they looked into the storm clouds and listened to the thunderous roar. The White race has always used different forms of the flash of light to symbolize strength and power. The Thunderbolt has always been a warning to the Whiteman's enemies. The flash was a rune in the first alphabet of our White folk. Today, there are some U.S. armored divisions and bomber wings which proudly wear the Thunderbolt patch on their shoulders. The Tennessee State police wear it on their uniforms. It is the symbol of the United Cerebral Palsy Fund and many other organizations and businesses. The flag of the National States Rights Party is the patriotic red, white and blue. The red stands for the pure red blood of our White people which we seek to preserve for our posterity as long as the world exists. The blue represents the vast future of our White people stretching into time and eternity: as long as God's blue sky is above us, the great White race shall live. The cross in the background of booth our Thunderbolt and Confederate flags is the Cross of St. Andrew which was part of the battleflag of the Confederacy. It represents the persecutions that our forefathers, and we, have endured so that we would be free White Christian Americans and reminds us that we too must generously give, sacrifice and suffer, if necessary, so that the White race will continue to live. The white circle stands for the purity of our White womanhood and our beloved little White children who are the basic reason for our united stand; we struggle for them. We are ordained by God to save the White race so that civilization will exist as long as the world stands. With this Thunderbolt banner and the White racist Confederate flag, we march forward knowing that WE WILL WIN!

Appendix B:
"Why Vote States Rights" (1960)

Why Vote States Rights?

The Jews, Communists and Negroes have their own political parties, including the corrupt Republican and Democratic parties. We White Americans have our political party—the National States Rights Party. Our Party represents the great White [race] that produced civilization, the Bill of Rights, Magna charta [sic], and the other great documents which recognize our God-give rights as free men.

Both the Democratic and Republican Parties are controlled by the Jew-Communists and cater to the Jewish and Negro bloc votes. Their degenerate platforms demand Communist "civil rights" laws that would destroy both American Freedom and the White Race. That is why patriots throughout the country are organizing better for the purpose of placing the National States Rights Party on the ballot in 1960. We are tired of choosing the lesser of two evils as offered to us by the two old parties because the lesser evil is still evil. In 1960 loyal White Americans are voting for [the] Presidential candidate of the National States Rights Party.

Don't Vote Against Yourself

The old trick of the unprincipled politicians is to tell you that you are throwing away your vote unless you vote for either the Democratic or Republican candidates. Their candidates, in effect, are running on platforms that call for the destruction of States Rights and our Race. If you vote for them, you are doing worse than wasting your vote. You are voting against the White Race, against American liberty, and even against yourself. Remember, there is no real difference between the two old parties; they are both against you.

They are the same. Under the Democratic Party they called it the Internal Revenue *Bureau*. Under deceitful Ike, the Republicans call it the Internal Revenue Service. It is the same old robbery bureau under either name.

TWO-PARTY TREASON

Under the Democrats, we were taxed to give money to foreign nations, including the evil Communists, and the same policy is followed under the Republicans. The internationalist traitors in the Democratic party surrendered American sovereignty and independence to the race-mixing, Jew-Communist United Nations Organization and N.A.T.O. The internationalist traitors of the Republican Party have consumated [*sic*] & strengthened that same betrayal of America. We charge that The Democratic and Republican parties, with their Jewish bi-partisan foreign policy, gave half the world to Communism, even refusing aid to the White Christian Hungarians when they temporarily had their Country free of the Jew-Communist yoke in 1956. The leaders of the Democratic party had close fraternal and political relations with the Communist dictator of Russia, Stalin: Truman referred to bloody Stalin as "good old Joe." Ike, the Republican, after giving central Europe to the Communists, has chummy drinking parties with the red monster Khruschev [*sic*]. During World War II, Ike had drunken meetings with Zhukov and the other evil Communist generals where debauchery reigned supreme.

BETRAYAL

Democrat Truman was President at the time that Russia blocked the American land routed to Berlin resulting in the Berlin airlift. At that time the United States possessed the atomic bomb and Russian didn't. Instead of backing down and resorting to airlift, why didn't Truman tell the Communists to pull out of German and all of Eastern Europe or be atom bombed? Why did Truman let the Communists stay in German and Eastern Europe when he could easily have forced them out under threat of atomic bombardment which they could not have survived? Even better, why didn't he force them to surrender and proceed to also free the Russian people from their Jew-Communist tyrants? So much for the Democratic party. Now for the treason of the Republican party. Ike was in England at the time Germany invented the guided missiles and rained them down on England during World War II. Even though the guided missiles were not accurate then, any layman could see that they would be perfected and become a more important weapon of war than the airplane. Ike saw the missiles in their infancy. Yet, when stupid Ike became President, he refused to spend more than a few tax dollars for American development of the missiles, thereby allowing his Communist buddies, such as Khruschev [*sic*] and Zhukov to get dangerously ahead of the United States. Ike should be impeached and prosecuted for treason. Even before he became president, while commanding American troops in Europe, Ike turned the German guided missiles factory and its scientists over to the reds. He also gave the German submarine factories and their scientists to the Communists resulting is [*sic*] the present Communist submarine threat to America. Eisenhower, the Republican, like his Democratic predecessors, has never shown any dislike for Communists and Communism. Vote for those two old parties and you will be voting for the death penalty for your country.

DEMO-REPUB FARM CHAOS

Both the Republican and Democratic parties are responsible for the farm depression. They have spent our tax money to develop agriculture in foreign countries, thereby shrinking the market for America's agricultural products and allowing an invasion or our farm markets at home. That is the basic cause of the depressions on our farms. They have taxed our farmers and other citizens to build up farm competition where labor is cheap. Both old parties are guilty of sabotaging the American farmer.

Both the Democratic and Republican parties are cutting the throats of the American business man and the American working man by building up foreign industry which uses cheap sweat-shop labor. Those foreign products are then sold in America to undermine our industries. The old parties don't represent America; they represent International Jewish finance. The Democratic and Republican parties represent the Communist-Jewish Conspiracy which is rapidly conquering our America and smothering our liberties.

OLD PARTIES FOR COMMUNISM

The evil Communist party was the first party to announce a platform for a so-called civil rights program that would kill liberty and our White race. That criminal party was the first party to demand that the White Race be wiped out with race-mixing which they call integration. Now, the Republican and Democratic parties have adopted that part of the Communist party's platform in full. They are using the subversive F.B.I. to enforce the Communist "civil rights" plot against White America. There is no real difference between the two old parties. If *you* vote for either the Democratic, or Republican, candidate for President, you will be voting for the death of the White Race. Nixon, the Republican candidate, was admittedly a secret member of the NAACP for ten years before openly bragging about it only a few years ago and he continues as one of the NAACP's leading members. Apparently Senator Lyndon Johnson will be the Democratic candidate for President. Johnson is responsible for the evil civil rights bill of 1957. He hopes to become President by selling the White people of America down the river or racial pollution. Johnson has betrayed the White Race to promote his own selfish political ambition. At this very moment, Johnson is conspiring to pass an un–Constitutional anti–White civil rights bill through the Senate; he is willing to destroy the Bill of Rights, States Rights, and the White Race merely to get a vain chance at the Presidency. Some cheap Southern politicians are supporting Johnson; they are not real segregationists and should be retired from public office at the next elections. If a Southern senator or governor says that he is for both Lyndon Johnson and Segregation, he is lying because it is impossible to be for both. If the Democrats don't nominate Johnson, they will nominate some other enemy of the White Race. Any Southern politician who supports Johnson for President is a traitor to the White Race.

VOTE STATES RIGHTS

Appendix C: NSRP Platform (1980)

RACIAL POLICY

1. We believe in the creation of a wholesome White Folk Community, with a deep spiritual consciousness of a common past and a determination to share a common future.

2. We favor complete separation of all non–Whites and dissatisfied minorities from our White Folk Community.

3. We demand that intermarriage between Whites and non–Whites be outlaws in all states not already having such legislation.

4. We demand that total segregation be maintained in the nation's schools, and that only members of the White Folk Community be allowed to engage in the educational and cultural activities of our White society.

5. We believe that segregation should be restored to the nation's armed forces, to rebuild morale and fighting efficiency.

6. We believe it better that only members of our White Folk Community be allowed to take part in the affairs of government or serve in the courts.

7. We demand a policy of non-interference in the cultural affairs of other races.

8. We favor creation of a National Repatriation Commission, to encourage the voluntary resettlement of Negroes in their African homeland, with fullest financial and economic assistance toward that end.

9. We approve the removal of all alien minorities, dissatisfied with our American way of life and the republic for which we stand.

10. We favor the preservation of Indian national life in America, and the unlimited development of reservation facilities.

11. We believe that immigration should be restricted to select White individuals.

12. We demand the impeachment or removal from office otherwise of any public official who advocates race-mixing or mongrelization.

ECONOMIC POLICY

1. We believe that the workers, farmers, businessmen and professional people of our nation should work together as a team, placing the greater good of our White Folk Community above any individual or group interest.

2. We approve of labor unions, run by honest White men and free of subversive influence.

3. We believe that the farmer should get a fair price for his product in a free market.

4. We believe that the government should refrain from competing with private enterprise, and from interfering in the hiring policies of private business.

5. We demand that Congress alone exercise its constitutional right to issue debt and interest-free currency, based on the production of goods and rendition of services in America.

6. We favor protection of the White American producer by limiting foreign trade to the direct exchange of surplus products.

7. We believe that the purchasing power of the consumer should be raised proportionately as science increases the power to produce.

8. We demand that the confiscatory taxation policies of the federal government be ended immediately.

SOCIAL POLICY

1. We favor combined civic effort in every individual state to eliminate slum, flood and dust-bowl conditions.

2. We favor creation of proper outlets for the White youth of our nation to encourage the development of mind and muscle, and provide for instruction in the highest racial ideals.

3. We demand the complete reorganization of our educational system, so that every White citizen is afforded full opportunity to realize his vocational ambitions.

4. We demand the elimination of all ideology and influences from the movies, television, radio, newspaper and all other phases of our national life, which tend to cause the degeneration and disintegration of our White Folk Community.

5. We demand the creation of a clean and honest White government,, which will provide the basis for a sound economy, with full employment and improved living conditions for White citizens of every age.

STATES' RIGHTS POLICY

1. We demand that the federal government cease interfering with the sovereign rights of the states, as guaranteed by the Constitution.

2. We demand that the federal government stop issuing judicial decrees which violate state sovereignty.

3. We demand that the federal government stop fostering thought-control, and refrain from violating the traditional social customs of the individual states.

4. We demand the removal of all federal control over the national guard units and law enforcement agencies of the states.

5. We demand that all states exercise their authority to stop the secret-police tactics employed against them by the federal government.

6. We demand that the states uphold their right to investigate, prosecute and obtain conviction of subversives within their borders.

FOREIGN POLICY

1. We approve the strengthening of cultural and moral ties among the White nations, in view of the world-wide survival crisis which the White Man faces.

2. We demand that White Christian boys never be sent to fight on foreign soil to appease the interests of an alien minority.

3. We demand that all financial and moral support for the State of Israel cease, for the rebuilding of Arab-American friendship.

4. We demand and end to the policy of foreign give-aways.

5. We oppose any international entanglement whereby this Republic would tend to lose its sovereignty and freedom.

WHITE MEN UNITE!

Chapter Notes

Citations from sources listed in the bibliography are presented in abbreviated form. One-time citations from sources not included in the bibliography include all relevant details.

Introduction

1. Myer, pp. 277–313.
2. Joel Krieger, ed. *The Oxford Companion to Comparative Politics.* New York: Oxford University Press, 2012; p. 120.
3. Alec Campbell, "Where Do All the Soldiers Go? Veterans and the Politics of Demobilization," in Diane E. Davis, Anthony W. Pereira, eds., *Irregular Armed Forces and their Role in Politics and State Formation.* New York: Cambridge University Press, 2003; pp. 110–111.
4. Otis Mitchell, *Hitler's Stormtroopers and the Attack on the German Republic, 1919–1933.* Jefferson, NC: McFarland, 2008.
5. Jules Archer, *The Plot to Seize the White House.* New York: Skyhorse, 1973; Sally Denton, *The Plots Against the President: FDR, A Nation in Crisis, and the Rise of the American Right.* New York: Bloomsbury, 2012.
6. Myers, pp. 314–375.
7. Chalmers, *Hooded,* pp. 322–3.
8. Barkun, pp. 53–4, 129, 142–3, 183–5.
9. "Wesley Swift," http://en.metapedia.org/wiki/Wesley_Swift; *Para-Military Organizations,* pp. CR-1 and CR-2.
10. Richard Steele, *Free Speech in the Good War* (New York: St. Martin's, 1999), pp. 43–45; "NYC Trial of Christian Front Members Begins," http://skepticism.org/timeline/june-history/6697-nyc-trial-christian-front-members-begins.html.
11. "Great Sedition Trial of 1944," http://en.metapedia.org/wiki/Great_Sedition_Trial_of_1944.
12. *Ibid.*
13. *Ibid.*
14. *Ibid.*
15. *Ibid.*

Chapter 1

1. Dudley, pp. 263–4; Weisenburger, pp. 832–4; "Atlanta Police Department," http://www.atlantapd.org/apdhistory.aspx; Patterson, pp. 203–4; "American Gentile Army," http://en.metapedia.org/wiki/American_Gentile_Army.
2. Harold Henderson, "Eugene Talmadge (1884–1946)," http://www.georgiaencyclopedia.org/articles/government-politics/eugene-talmadge-1884-1946; "Vigilantes Inc.," http://en.metapedia.org/wiki/Vigilantes_Inc.; Patterson, pp. 204–6; "Samuel W. Roper," http://en.metapedia.org/wiki/Samuel_W._Roper.
3. Patterson, pp. 205–7.
4. "Emory Burke," http://en.metapedia.org/wiki/Emory_Burke; Edward Hatfield, "Columbians," http://www.georgiaencyclopedia.org/articles/history-archaeology/columbians; Greene, p. 235; Weisenburger, pp. 826–32.
5. "Homer Loomis," http://en.metapedia.org/wiki/Homer_Loomis; Edward Hatfield, "Columbians," http://www.georgiaencyclopedia.org/articles/history-archaeology/columbians; Greene, p. 235; Kennedy, pp. 141–2; Weisenburger, pp. 836–9.
6. "Homer Loomis," http://en.metapedia.org/wiki/Homer_Loomis; Weisenburger, pp. 821–2, 836, 839; "The Columbians," http://en.metapedia.org/wiki/The_Columbians; Charles Garcia, "Was Columbus Secretly a Jew?" CNN, May 24, 2012; "John H. Zimmerlee," http://en.metapedia.org/wiki/John_H._Zimmerlee; Greene, p. 235.
7. Dudley, pp. 264–5; Patterson, pp. 207–8; Weisenburger, pp. 821–2, 839–40; "The Columbians," http://en.metapedia.org/wiki/The_Columbians; Kennedy, pp. 132–3; Greene, pp. 33–4.
8. Edward Hatfield, "Columbians," http://www.georgiaencyclopedia.org/articles/history-archaeology/columbians; Dudley, p. 264.
9. "The Columbians," http://en.metapedia.org/wiki/The_Columbians.
10. *Ibid.*; Weisenburger, pp. 826, 840; Greene, p. 34; "Homer Loomis," http://en.metapedia.org/wiki/Homer_Loomis; Patterson, p. 208.
11. "*The Thunderbolt* (American)," http://en.metapedia.org/wiki/The_Thunderbolt_%28American%29; FBI Files, William Allen; Edward Fields, personal communication with the author.
12. Weisenburger, pp. 840–2.
13. Martin; "Jesse Benjamin 'J. B.' Stoner," http://www.ourcampaigns.com/CandidateDetail.html?CandidateID=76937; Webb, "Freedom for All?"; Webb, *Rabble,* p. 155; McWhorter, p. 133; "The McCallie School," https://en.wikipedia.org/wiki/The_McCallie_School.
14. "J. B. Stoner," http://en.metapedia.org/wiki/J._B.

_Stoner; Group Research Report, p. 1; "St. Augustine Ku Klux Klan Rally," http://www.drbronsontours.com/bronsonstaugustinekkk2.html; Webb, "Freedom for All?"; Massengill, p. 276; Greene, p. 158.

15. Webb, "Freedom for All?"; Kennedy, pp. 70–1; Group Research Report, p. 1; HUAC *Hearings Part 5*, p. 3810.

16. Greene, pp. 41–2; "George Michael Bright," http://en.metapedia.org/wiki/George_Michael_Bright; FBI Files, Wallace Allen; "Ira Jett," http://en.metapedia.org/wiki/Ira_Jett; Weisenburger, p. 824; "Ralph Childers," http://en.metapedia.org/wiki/Ralph_Childers; Kennedy, p. 127; "The March (1945)" https://en.wikipedia.org/wiki/The_March_%281945%29; "Dwight D. Eisenhower," https://en.wikipedia.org/wiki/Dwight_D._Eisenhower.

17. Weisenburger, p. 825.

18. "Holt J. Gewinner," http://sortedbyname.com/pages/g104091.html; "Holt J. Gewinner," http://en.metapedia.org/wiki/Holt_J._Gewinner; "The Order of Black Shirts," http://en.metapedia.org/wiki/American_Fascisti; Patterson, p. 208; Kennedy, pp. 129–30, 157–8.

19. "Edward Fields," http://en.metapedia.org/wiki/Edward_Fields; "Marist School (Georgia)," https://en.wikipedia.org/wiki/Marist_School_%28Georgia%29; Group Research Report, p. 1.

20. Hatfield, "Columbians," http://www.georgiaencyclopedia.org/articles/history-archaeology/columbians; Weisenburger, pp. 825–6; "The Columbians," http://en.metapedia.org/wiki/The_Columbians; Weisenburger, p. 846; Kennedy, p. 139.

21. Kennedy, p. 133; "Earnest Sevier Cox (1880–1966)," http://www.encyclopediavirginia.org/Cox_Earnest_Sevier_1880-1966; "Earnest Sevier Cox," https://en.wikipedia.org/wiki/Earnest_Sevier_Cox.

22. Kennedy, pp. 138–142; "Max Nelsen," http://en.metapedia.org/wiki/Max_Nelsen; *The Jewish Floridian*, April 21, 1950; "Allen C. Shuler," http://en.metapedia.org/wiki/Allen_C._Shuler.

23. "The Columbians," http://en.metapedia.org/wiki/The_Columbians; Kennedy, p. 139; "George E. Deatherage," http://en.metapedia.org/wiki/George_E._Deatherage; "George Van Horn Moseley," http://en.metapedia.org/wiki/George_Van_Horn_Moseley; McWhorter, p. 54.

24. Kennedy, pp. 17–19, 120–8, 138–42, 157–8; "Non-Sectarian Anti-Nazi League," http://en.metapedia.org/wiki/Non-Sectarian_Anti-Nazi_League; Dudley, pp. 266–7, 271; Weisenburger, pp. 823, 832–5; "Girl Secret Agent Helps Expose the Columbians," *St. Petersburg Times*, December 11, 1946; "Blond Who Helped Spy on Columbians Had Danger Signal," *Milwaukee Journal*, December 14, 1946.

25. Greene, *The Temple Bombing*, p. 156.

26. Kenney, pp. 134–6; "Blond Who Helped Spy on Columbians Had Danger Signal," *Milwaukee Journal*, December 14, 1946; Weisenburger, p. 830.

27. Weisenburger, p. 826; Hatfield, "Columbians," http://www.georgiaencyclopedia.org/articles/history-archaeology/columbians; Kennedy, p. 131; John H. Zimmerlee, http://en.metapedia.org/wiki/John_H._Zimmerlee.

28. Weisenburger, pp. 843–4; "1946 Georgia lynching," https://en.wikipedia.org/wiki/1946_Georgia_lynching.

29. Weisenburger, p. 844.

30. Weisenburger, pp. 844–5; Dudley, p. 269; Hatfield, "Columbians," http://www.georgiaencyclopedia.org/articles/history-archaeology/columbians.

31. Greene, pp. 143–4, 156; Dudley, p. 269; Weisenburger, p. 821; Kennedy, p. 128.

32. Weisenburger, pp. 845–6; Kennedy, pp. 123–30.

33. Hatfield, "Columbians," http://www.georgiaencyclopedia.org/articles/history-archaeology/columbians; Dudley, pp. 265, 269–72; Kennedy, pp. 148–50; "Toy Hitlers," *Newsweek* 28 (November 11, 1946): 31.

34. Weisenburger, pp. 846–7; "The Columbians," http://www.ourgeorgiahistory.com/ogh/The_Colombians; Kennedy, pp. 128, 154–6, 158–9; Wolfgang Saxon, "Lawrence D. Duke Sr., 86; Fought the Klan in Georgia," *New York Times*, April 1, 1999; Dudley, pp. 270–1; Weisenburger, p. 824; "Ira Jett," http://en.metapedia.org/wiki/Ira_Jett; "Columbian Seeking Bond," *Pittsburgh Post-Gazette*, December 16, 1946.

35. Scott Buchanan, "Three Governors Controversy," http://www.georgiaencyclopedia.org/articles/government-politics/three-governors-controversy; Kennedy, pp. 163–8; Patterson, pp. 208–9.

36. Kennedy, pp. 143–7.

37. "Atlanta Police Department," http://www.atlantapd.org/apdhistory.aspx; Dudley, p. 267, 274; Group Research Report, p. 1; Kennedy, p. 139; Weisenburger, pp. 252–3.

38. "James Venable," http://en.metapedia.org/wiki/James_Venable; Weisenburger, p. 852; Greene, p. 145; Weisenberger, pp. 853–4,

39. Weisenburger, pp. 855–6; Homer Loomis, http://en.metapedia.org/wiki/Homer_Loomis; Greene, p. 145; Attorney General's List of Totalitarian, Fascist, Communist, Subversive, and Other Organizations http://everything2.com/title/Attorney+General%2527s+List+of+Totalitarian%252C+Fascist%252C+Communist%252C+Subversive%252C+and+Other+Organizations

40. Peter Kuznick, "We Can Learn a Lot from Truman the Bigot," *Los Angeles Times*, July 18, 2003; "The Rise and Fall of Jim Crow," http://www.pbs.org/wnet/jimcrow/stories_events_truman.html; "1948 Democratic National Convention," https://en.wikipedia.org/wiki/1948_Democratic_National_Convention.

41. McWhorter, pp. 37, 67–8; Nunnelley, pp. 12, 14–16, 34–5.

42. "Dixiecrat," https://en.wikipedia.org/wiki/Dixiecrat; McWhorter, pp. 69–71; Velie, pp. 14–15; Executive Order 9981: Desegregation of the Armed Forces (1948), http://www.ourdocuments.gov/doc.php?flash=true&doc=84.

43. "Progressive Party (United States, 1948)," https://en.wikipedia.org/wiki/Progressive_Party_%28United_States,_1948%29; McWhorter, pp. 63–5; "Dixiecrat," https://en.wikipedia.org/wiki/Dixiecrat.

44. "Gerald L. K. Smith," http://en.metapedia.org/wiki/Gerald_L._K._Smith; "Harry A. Romer," http://en.metapedia.org/wiki/Harry_Romer; "Jesse Benjamin 'J. B.' Stoner," http://www.ourcampaigns.com/CandidateDetail.html?CandidateID=76937; "Tennessee's 3rd congressional district," https://en.wikipedia.org/wiki/Tennessee's_3rd_congressional_district.

45. "Kurt Mertig," http://en.metapedia.org/wiki/Kurt_Mertig; "Citizens Protective League," http://en.metapedia.org/wiki/Citizens_Protective_League; "National Renaissance Party," http://en.metapedia.org/wiki/National_Renaissance_Party; "James H. Madole," http://en.metapedia.org/wiki/James_Madole; "Frederick Charles Weiss," http://en.metapedia.org/wiki/Fred_Weiss.

46. "National Renaissance Party," http://en.metapedia.org/wiki/National_Renaissance_Party; "James H. Madole," http://en.metapedia.org/wiki/James_Madole; "Nationalist Action League," http://en.metapedia.org/

wiki/Nationalist_Action_League; Cooper, "Brief History"; "Eustace Mullins," http://en.metapedia.org/wiki/Eustace_Mullins; "Matt Koehl," http://en.metapedia.org/wiki/Matt_Koehl.
47. "Chicago and Its Suburbs," http://areachicago.org/chicago-and-its-suburbs; White Circle League of America, http://en.metapedia.org/wiki/White_Circle_League_of_America; Joseph Beauharnais, http://en.metapedia.org/wiki/Joseph_Beauharnais.
48. FBI Files, White Circle League of America.
49. Weisenburger, p. 856; "Homer Loomis," http://en.metapedia.org/wiki/Homer_Loomis.
50. "Emory Burke," http://en.metapedia.org/wiki/Emory_Burke; Weisenburger, pp. 856–7.
51. Weisenberger, p. 855; Dudley, p. 268; "Ira Jett," http://en.metapedia.org/wiki/Ira_Jett,
52. John H. Zimmerlee, http://en.metapedia.org/wiki/John_H._Zimmerlee.
53. Max Nelsen: http://en.metapedia.org/wiki/Max_Nelsen.
54. "Edward James Smythe," http://en.metapedia.org/wiki/Edward_James_Smythe.
55. *Ibid.*
56. Velie, p. 15; Greene, p. 158; "St. Augustine Ku Klux Klan Rally," http://www.drbronsontours.com/bronsonstaugustinekkk2.html; "Associated Klans of America," http://en.metapedia.org/wiki/Associated_Klans_of_America.
57. "Edward Fields," http://en.metapedia.org/wiki/Edward_R._Fields; Group Research Report, p. 1; Greene, p. 157.
58. Greene, p. 157.
59. *Ibid.*, p. 158.
60. *Ibid.*; Group Research Report, p. 1; "Emmett Morris," http://en.metapedia.org/wiki/Emmett_Morris; "Edward Fields," http://en.metapedia.org/wiki/Edward_Fields; Greene, pp. 159–61.
61. "Edward Fields," http://en.metapedia.org/wiki/Edward_Fields; Webb, "Freedom for All?"; Chalmers, *Hooded*, p. 344.

Chapter 2

1. *Brown v. Board of Education of Topeka*, 347 U.S. 483 (1954) and Brown v. Board of Education of Topeka, 349 U.S. 294 (1955).
2. "Edward Fields," http://archive.adl.org/learn/ext_us/fields.html?xpicked=2&item=Fields.
3. Webb, "Freedom for All?"; J. B. Stoner, "The Philosophy of 'White Racism'" (Atlanta: n.d.); "List of nationalist meetings and demonstrations in America," http://en.metapedia.org/wiki/List_of_nationalist_meetings_and_demonstrations_in_America; Group Research Report.
4. "Massive Resistance," https://en.wikipedia.org/wiki/Massive_resistance; "Southern Manifesto on Integration (March 12, 1956)," http://www.pbs.org/wnet/supremecourt/rights/sources_document2.html.
5. McMillen, *Citizens' Councils*; "White Citizens' Councils," http://en.metapedia.org/wiki/Citizens_Council; "Original Ku Klux Klan of the Confederacy," http://en.metapedia.org/wiki/Original_Ku_Klux_Klan_of_the_Confederacy; "Seaboard White Citizens' Council," http://en.metapedia.org/wiki/Seaboard_White_Citizens_Council.
6. James Kaetz, "Autherine Lucy," http://www.encyclopediaofalabama.org/article/h-2489; McWhorter, pp. 97–9, 103.
7. McWhorter, pp. 37, 99–101, 114, 123–8, 180–1; "Asa Carter," http://www.encyclopediaofalabama.org/article/h-2427, Weisenburger, p. 857.
8. "John Kasper," http://en.metapedia.org/wiki/John_Kasper.
9. *Ibid.*; "Ezra Pound," https://en.wikipedia.org/wiki/Ezra_Pound; Webb, *Rabble*, pp. 49–50; "Eustace Mullins," http://en.metapedia.org/wiki/Eustace_Mullins.
10. Webb, *Rabble*, pp. 53–4, 72–3; McMillen, p. 106; Gordon, pp. 28, 30; "Desegregation of Sturgis High School," http://history.ky.gov/desegregation-of-sturgis-high-school; "Millard Grubbs," http://en.metapedia.org/wiki/Millard_Grubbs.
11. Griffin; Gordon, p. 28; "Clinton High School," http://www.tn4me.org/article.cfm/a_id/111/minor_id/26/major_id/11/era_id/8; Carroll Van West, "Clinton Desegregation Crisis," http://tennesseeencyclopedia.net/entry.php?rec=279; Webb, *Rabble*, p. 52.
12. Griffin; "Clinton High School," http://www.tn4me.org/article.cfm/a_id/111/minor_id/26/major_id/11/era_id/8.
13. "John Kasper," http://en.metapedia.org/wiki/John_Kasper; Gordon, p. 29; Egerton; Webb, *Rabble*, pp. 88–95; *Kasper v. Tennessee* 326 S.W.2d 664 (1959).
14. Webb, "Freedom for All?"; Alfred Friendly Jr., "The Bigot They Are," *The Harvard Crimson*, March 26, 1957.
15. "John G. Crommelin," http://en.wikipedia.org/wiki/John_G._Crommelin; "John G. Crommelin," http://www.ourcampaigns.com/CandidateDetail.html?CandidateID=19159; Group Research Report; Webb, *Rabble*, p. 124.
16. Edward Fields, http://archive.adl.org/learn/ext_us/fields.html?xpicked=2&item=Fields; Group Research Report.
17. ADL, *Extremism*, 98; "Edward Fields," http://en.metapedia.org/wiki/Edward_Fields.
18. Elijah Muhammad, *Message to the Blackman in America* (Chicago: Muhammad Mosque of Islam, 1965), pp. 330–335.

Chapter 3

1. FBI Files, NSRP.
2. *Ibid.*
3. *Ibid.*; Group Research Report; "United White Party," http://en.metapedia.org/wiki/United_White_Party; "Christian Anti-Jewish Party," http://en.metapedia.org/wiki/Christian_Anti-Jewish_Party; "Wallace Allen," http://en.metapedia.org/wiki/Wallace_Allen; "Ned Dupes," http://en.metapedia.org/wiki/Ned_Dupes; "Daniel Kurtz," http://en.metapedia.org/wiki/Dan_Kurtz; "Matt Koehl," http://en.metapedia.org/wiki/Matt_Koehl.
4. "Wallace H. Allen," http://en.metapedia.org/wiki/Wallace_Allen; "DeWest Hooker," http://en.metapedia.org/wiki/DeWest_Hooker; FBI Files, DeWest Hooker; Schmaltz, pp. 28–9.
5. *Greenville* (SC) *Piedmont,* November 26, 1957; "Edward Fields," http://en.metapedia.org/wiki/Edward_Fields.
6. FBI Files, John Kasper; "John G. Crommelin," http://en.metapedia.org/wiki/John_G._Crommelin.
7. "List of nationalist meetings and demonstrations in America" http://en.metapedia.org/wiki/List_of_nationalist_meetings_and_demonstrations_in_America#1955–1959; "Political Broadsides, 1957 and 1960," http://louisville.libguides.com/c.php?g=158720&p=1040061.
8. "James W. Cole," http://en.metapedia.org/wiki/

James_W._Cole; "James W. 'Catfish' Cole," https://en.wikipedia.org/wiki/James_W._%22Catfish%22_Cole; "North Carolina Knights of the Ku Klux Klan," http://en.metapedia.org/wiki/North_Carolina_Knights_of_the_Ku_Klux_Klan; William Shires, "Defendants are Lawyers," *High Point* (NC) *Enterprise*, September 18, 1965; "Bad Medicine for the Klan," Life, January 27, 1958, pp. 27–8; Jefferson Currie II, "The Ku Klux Klan in North Carolina and the Battle of Maxton Field," *Tar Heel Junior Historian* 44:1 (Fall 2004); Nicholas Graham, "January 1958: The Lumbees face the Klan," *This Month in North Carolina History*, January 2005; Chick Jacobs and Venita Jenkins, "The Night the Klan Met Its Match," *Fayetteville* (NC) *Observer*, January 18, 2008; "Cole Says His Rights Violated," *Greensboro* (NC) *Daily News*, January 20, 1958; "Kluxer Jailed for Posing as a Private Eye," *Gastonia* (NC) *Gazette*, February 3, 1959; Dew James, "'Sergeant' Cole, Partner Await Grand Jury Action," *Florence* (SC) *Morning News*, March 7, 1959; "Court Convicts 'Gumshoe' Cole and Sleuth Pal," *The Robesonian* (Lumberton, NC), March 31, 1959.

9. "AL Governor—D Primary," http://www.ourcampaigns.com/RaceDetail.html?RaceID=80045; Weisenburger, p. 858; George Kellman, "Anti-Jewish Agitation," *The American Jewish Year Book* 61 (1960): 41–48; "AL Governor—Runoff," http://www.ourcampaigns.com/RaceDetail.html?RaceID=80046; McWhorter, pp. 107–8, 131.

10. "Matt Koehl," http://en.metapedia.org/wiki/Matt_Koehl.

11. FBI Files, NSRP; Duffee, p. 6; "List of nationalist meetings and demonstrations in America," http://en.metapedia.org/wiki/List_of_nationalist_meetings_and_demonstrations_in_America#1955-1959.

12. "List of nationalist meetings and demonstrations in America," http://en.metapedia.org/wiki/List_of_nationalist_meetings_and_demonstrations_in_America#1955-1959; Simonelli, pp. 28–9, 117; Group Research Report, pp. 1, 2, 6; "Oren F. Potito," http://en.metapedia.org/wiki/Oren_F._Potito; "James K. Warner," http://en.metapedia.org/wiki/James_K._Warner; "National Citizens Protective Association Inc.," http://en.metapedia.org/wiki/National_Citizens_Protective_Association; "John W. Hamilton," http://en.metapedia.org/wiki/John_W._Hamilton; "Joseph Beauharnais," http://en.metapedia.org/wiki/Joseph_Beauharnais; "Arthur B. Cole," http://en.metapedia.org/wiki/Arthur_B._Cole; "White Circle League of America," http://en.metapedia.org/wiki/White_Circle_League_of_America; *Beauharnais v. Illinois*, 343 U.S. 250 (1952); "F. Allen Mann," http://en.metapedia.org/wiki/F._Allen_Mann; FBI Files, NSRP; "Peter L. Xavier," http://en.metapedia.org/wiki/Peter_Xavier.

13. Group Research Report, pp. 2, 6; "John Kasper," http://en.metapedia.org/wiki/John_Kasper; Greene, p. 207.

14. Group Research Report, pp. 1, 3, 7; FBI Files, NSRP; "List of nationalist meetings and demonstrations in America," http://en.metapedia.org/wiki/List_of_nationalist_meetings_and_demonstrations_in_America#1955-1959; "National States Rights Party," http://en.metapedia.org/wiki/National_States_Rights_Party; "John G. Crommelin," http://www.ourcampaigns.com/CandidateDetail.html?CandidateID=19159; "KY Governor—D Primary," http://www.ourcampaigns.com/RaceDetail.html?RaceID=382582; "KY Governor," http://www.ourcampaigns.com/RaceDetail.html?RaceID=174295.

15. Group Research Report, p. 2; "The Thunderbolt (American)," http://en.metapedia.org/wiki/The_Thunderbolt_%28American%29; *Thunderbolt*, October 1958.

16. Chalmers, *Hooded*, p. 344.

17. FBI Files, NSRP; "James Bagwell," http://en.metapedia.org/wiki/James_Bagwell.

18. *Thunderbolt*, October 1958.

19. *Thunderbolt*, July 1958; "States' Rights Party," https://en.wikipedia.org/wiki/States'_Rights_Party; "National States Rights Party," http://en.metapedia.org/wiki/National_States_Rights_Party; "Realpolitical Institute," http://en.metapedia.org/wiki/Realpolitical_Institute; "Max Nelson," http://en.metapedia.org/wiki/Max_Nelsen.

20. "Realpolitical Institute," http://en.metapedia.org/wiki/Realpolitical_Institute; "Max Nelson," http://en.metapedia.org/wiki/Max_Nelsen; FBI Files, Realpolitical Institute; "Edward Fleckenstein," http://en.metapedia.org/wiki/Edward_Fleckenstein; Cooper, "Brief History."

21. Greene, p. 214; Webb, *Rabble*, p. 132.

22. "National States Rights Party," http://en.metapedia.org/wiki/National_States_Rights_Party.

23. Webb, "Counterblast."

24. "John Kasper, the National States Rights Party, and the Demise of the Old South," http://mauryk2.com/2010/11/06/john-kasper-the-national-states-rights-party-and-the-demise-of-the-old-south; Webb, "Counterblast"; Cooper, "Brief History."

25. *Report of the Legislative Investigation Committee*, p. 69.

26. "John Kasper," http://www.ourcampaigns.com/CandidateDetail.html?CandidateID=4498.

27. "William Potter Gale," http://en.metapedia.org/wiki/William_Potter_Gale; Levitas, pp. 61–2, 66–7.

28. "Wesley Swift," http://en.metapedia.org/wiki/Wesley_Swift; "Betrand Comparet," http://en.metapedia.org/wiki/Bertrand_Comparet; "San Jacinto Capt," http://en.metapedia.org/wiki/San_Jacinto_Capt; "Richard Butler," http://en.metapedia.org/wiki/Richard_Butler; Simonelli, p. 116; "Christian Knights of the Invisible Empire," http://en.metapedia.org/wiki/Christian_Knights_of_the_Invisible_Empire; Group Research Report, pp. 9–10.

29. ADL, *Extremism*, p. 86; "James Oviatt," http://en.metapedia.org/wiki/James_Oviatt; Boylan.

Chapter 4

1. McWhorter, pp. 58, 73–4.

2. Michael and Judy Newton, *Racial and Religious Violence in America* (New York: Garland, 1991), pp. 434–5.

3. Drabble, "FBI, COINTELPRO … Tennessee"; Greene, pp. 5, 227; Webb, "Freedom for All?"; Murphy, p. 17; Parker, p. 9.

4. Murphy, pp. 13–14, 17; Parker, pp. 9–10; Newton, *Invisible Empire*, pp. 134–5; McWhorter, p. 132.

5. Murphy, p. 13; Newton, *Invisible Empire*, pp. 134–5.

6. Murphy, p. 17; Newton, *Invisible Empire*, pp. 134–5.

7. Nunnelley, pp. 36, 75, 77, 79; McWhorter, p. 130.

8. "J. B. Stoner, 81, Fervent Racist and Benchmark for Extremism, Dies," *New York Times*, April 29, 2005; Murphy, p. 14; McWhorter, p. 133.

9. "William Hugh Morris," http://en.metapedia.org/wiki/William_Hugh_Morris; McWhorter, pp. 130, 132–3; "Bethel Baptist Church (Birmingham, Alabama)," https://en.wikipedia.org/wiki/Bethel_Baptist_Church_%28Birmingham,_Alabama%29; Newton, *Ku Klux Terror*, p. 80.

10. McWhorter, pp. 132–3.

11. McWhorter, p. 133; Newton, *Ku Klux Terror,* p. 82.
12. McWhorter, p. 133; Newton, *Ku Klux Terror,* p. 83.
13. Greene, pp. 228–230; McWhorter, p. 133.
14. Greene, pp. 230; McWhorter, p. 134.
15. Greene, pp. 230–1.
16. McWhorter, p. 134–5; Nunnelley, p. 79.
17. Nunnelley, p. 180.
18. "Clinton Desegregation Crisis," http://tennesseeencyclopedia.net/entry.php?rec=279; "1958 School Blast United a Divided Tennessee Town," *Los Angeles Times,* October 16, 1988.
19. Greene, pp. 1–2, 254–7.
20. Webb, "Counterblast."
21. *Ibid.*; Green, pp. 270–87; Kirkham, Levy and Crotty, p. 345
22. Group Research Report, p. 3; "William Scott Stephenson," http://en.metapedia.org/wiki/William_Scott_Stephenson; "*The Virginian,*" http://en.metapedia.org/wiki/The_Virginian; Greene, pp. 297–300.
23. Greene, pp. 223, 282–6, 288, 300–3, 309–22, 403–6; Kellman, pp. 42–3.
24. Webb, "Counterblast"; Greened, pp. 305–9, 333–73; Kellman, pp. 42–3.
25. Greene, pp. 403–4, 407–8, 411–13.
26. McWhorter, p. 200.
27. FBI Files, Millard Grubbs; "List of nationalist meetings and demonstrations in America," http://en.metapedia.org/wiki/List_of_nationalist_meetings_and_demonstrations_in_America#1955–1959; Kellman, p. 44; HUAC, *Hearing Part 2,* pp. 2039, 2049; *Kasper v. State of Tennessee* 326 S.W.2d 664 (1959).
28. Rodnell Collins and A. Peter Bailey, *Seventh Child: A Family Memoir of Malcolm X* (New York: Citadel, 2000), pp. 213–18.
29. Martinelli, pp. 35–6.
30. Keller, "J. B. Stoner"; HUAC, *Hearings Part 5,* p. 3810; Kellman, p. 44; Alfred Friendly Jr., "The Bigot They Are," *The Harvard Crimson,* March 26, 1957; Chalmers, *Hooded,* p. 344; Mandy Baca, "Miami Black History: 1940s to 1960s," https://thenewtropic.com/miami-black-history-1940s-1960s.
31. "George Lincoln Rockwell," http://en.metapedia.org/wiki/George_Lincoln_Rockwell; Cooper, "Brief History"; Simonelli, p. 77; Weisenberger, p. 858.
32. Cooper, "Brief History"

Chapter 5

1. Cook, pp. 3–4.
2. Civil Rights Act of 1960 (Public Law 86–449, 74 Stat. 89); Webb, "Counterblast."
3. "National States Rights Party," http://en.metapedia.org/wiki/National_States_Rights_Party; "Edward Fields," http://archive.adl.org/learn/ext_us/fields.html?xpicked=2&item=Fields; Cobbs and Smith, p. 72; McWhorter, p. 201; FBI Files, NSRP; Group Research Report, p. 6; "List of nationalist meetings and demonstrations in America," http://en.metapedia.org/wiki/List_of_nationalist_meetings_and_demonstrations_in_America#1955–1959; Dr. Fields communication with the author; "Ann Bishop," http://en.metapedia.org/wiki/Ann_Bishop; Roy Reed, *Faubus: The Life and Times of an American Prodigal* (Fayetteville: University of Arkansas Press, 1997), 9. 265.
4. Jack Schnedler, "Little Rock: A Look Back," http://showtime.arkansasonline.com/e/media/central/timeline.html1959; Roy Reed, *Faubus,* p. 257; McMillen, *Citizens' Council,* pp. 283–4.
5. National States' Rights Party, http://en.wikipedia.org/wiki/National_States%27_Rights_Party; "Wolfsangel," https://en.wikipedia.org/wiki/Wolfsangel; "Edward Fields," http://archive.adl.org/learn/ext_us/fields.html?xpicked=2&item=Fields.
6. FBI Files, Roy Frankhouser; "Roy Frankhouser," http://en.metapedia.org/wiki/Roy_Frankhouser#Biography; HUAC, *Hearings Part 4,* p. 3348.
7. "John G. Crommelin," http://www.ourcampaigns.com/CandidateDetail.html?CandidateID=19159; Cooper, "Brief History"; Eric Pace, "John Crommelin, 94, Dies," *New York Times,* November 12, 1996; "John G. Crommelin," http://en.wikipedia.org/wiki/John_G._Crommelin.
8. Tully, pp. 231–2; Parker, p. 17; Group Research Report, p. 9.
9. "John Kasper," http://www.ourcampaigns.com/RaceDetail.html?RaceID=385079.
10. "U.S. Klans, Knights of the Ku Klux Klan," http://en.metapedia.org/wiki/U.S._Klans,_Knights_of_the_Ku_Klux_Klan; Cook, p. 126; "Robert Davidson," http://en.metapedia.org/wiki/Robert_%E2%80%9CWild_Bill%E2%80%9D_Davidson.
11. Webb, "Freedom for All?"
12. "Adolf Eichmann," http://en.metapedia.org/wiki/Adolf_Eichmann; Group Research Report, pp. 3, 4; Cook, p. 172.
13. Cook, pp. 171–2.
14. Cooper, "Brief History."
15. "National States' Rights Party," http://en.wikipedia.org/wiki/National_States%27_Rights_Party; Rice, p. 128.
16. Greene, p. 163.
17. Rice, p. 127; David Pietrusza, "1960: LBJ vs. JFK vs. Nixon," http://www.davidpietrusza.com/1960-third-parties.html; Edward Fields personal communication with the author, December 28, 2015.
18. "National States Rights," http://www.ourcampaigns.com/PartyDetail.html?PartyID=1871; *Report of the Florida Legislative Investigating Committee,* p. 68; "Orval E. Faubus," http://www.ourcampaigns.com/CandidateDetail.html?CandidateID=4200; "List of nationalist meetings and demonstrations in America," http://en.metapedia.org/wiki/List_of_nationalist_meetings_and_demonstrations_in_America#1955-1959.
19. "New Orleans school desegregation crisis," https://en.wikipedia.org/wiki/New_Orleans_school_desegregation_crisis; Cook, pp. 202, 204.
20. "Leander Perez," https://en.wikipedia.org/wiki/Leander_Perez; Alan Wieder, "The New Orleans School Crisis of 1960: Causes and Consequences," *Phylon* 48 (2nd Quarter 1987): 122–131; Drabble, "The FBI, COINTELPRO … Louisiana"; Cook, p. 203;
21. "New Orleans school desegregation crisis," https://en.wikipedia.org/wiki/New_Orleans_school_desegregation_crisis; Cook, p. 203.
22. FBI Files, NSRP.
23. "List of nationalist meetings and demonstrations in America," http://en.metapedia.org/wiki/List_of_nationalist_meetings_and_demonstrations_in_America#1960s; "Fighting American Nationalists," http://en.metapedia.org/wiki/Fighting_American_Nationalists; Group Research Report, p. 2; "Nordiska Rikspartiet," http://en.metapedia.org/wiki/Nordic_Reich_Party; "British National Party (1960-1967)," http://en.metapedia.org/wiki/British_National_Party_%281960-1967%29; "John Bean," http://en.metapedia.org/wiki/John_Bean.
24. Mississippi State Sovereignty Commission Files, https://inspireactionproject.com/2014/04/28/letter-

from-j-b-stoner-grand-wizard-kkk-to-elijah-muhammad-photo-from-mississippi-state-sovereignty-commission-files.

25. *Morgan v. Virginia* 328 U.S. 373 (1946); *Boynton v. Virginia*, 364 U.S. 454 (1960); *Keys v. Carolina Coach Company*, 64 MCC 769 (1955); Arsenault, pp. 11–55.

26. Parker, pp. 19–20; Arsenault, pp. 147–76; Fleming, "Death of Willie Brewster"; Group Research Report, p. 9; McWhorter, p. 203; Trymane Lee, "Ku Klux Klan Violence: Town Near Appalachian Mountains Tries To Shake Memories," *Huffington Post*, July 18, 2011.

27. McWhorter, pp. 167, 178, 197–8, 201; May, pp. 26–30, 34.

28. McWhorter, pp. 199–203, 205, 208; May, p. 35.

29. McWhorter, pp. 212–13, 217.

30. May, pp. 41–4, 45; Parker, pp. 20–22.

31. May, pp. 46–7; McWhorter, pp. 240–1, 247; Parker, p. 20; FBI Files, NSRP; Michael Ollove, "FBI's mole in Klan was as horrifyingly brutal as the rest," *Baltimore Sun*, June 5, 2005; Michael Kaufman, "Gary T. Rowe Jr., 64, Who Informed on Klan In Civil Rights Killing, Is Dead," *New York Times*, October 4, 1998.

32. May, p. 364.

33. Donald Grant, *The Way It Was in the South: The Black Experience in Georgia* (New York: Birch Lane Press, 1993), pp. 381–2; "Jerry Dutton," http://en.metapedia.org/wiki/Jerry_Dutton; HUAC, *Hearings Part 4*, p. 3345.

34. "List of nationalist meetings and demonstrations in America," http://en.metapedia.org/wiki/List_of_nationalist_meetings_and_demonstrations_in_America #1960s; Webb, *Rabble*, p. 191.

35. Lee Formwalt, "Albany Movement," http://www.georgiaencyclopedia.org/articles/history-archaeology/albany-movement; Parker, pp. 27–8.

36. Armbrister, pp. 81–2; Boylan; *Report of the Florida Legislative Investigation Committee*, p. 74; Edward Fields, personal communication with the author; *Para-Military Organizations in California*, pp. NSRP-9 and NSRP-10.

37. *Para-Military Organizations in California*, pp. NSRP-9 through NSRP-11.

38. Cooper, "Brief History"; Drabble, "The FBI, COINTELPRO ... Nazification"; Duffee, pp. 202–6; Schmaltz, pp. 152–3.

39. Group Research Report, p. 8; "The Winrod Legacy of Hate," http://www.adl.org/combating-hate/domestic-extremism-terrorism/c/the-winrod-legacy-of-hate.html; "John Kasper," http://en.metapedia.org/wiki/John_Kasper; "The Intruder," http://www.imdb.com/title/tt0055019; "Emory Burke," http://en.metapedia.org/wiki/Emory_Burke; "Robert A. Bowling," http://en.metapedia.org/wiki/Robert_A._Bowling; "Jerry Dutton," http://en.metapedia.org/wiki/Jerry_Dutton; "James K. Warner," http://en.metapedia.org/wiki/James_K._Warner; *DeGuello Report*; "Oren Fr. Potito," http://en.metapedia.org/wiki/Oren_F._Potito; "Robert Lee Lewton," http://en.metapedia.org/wiki/Robert_Lee_Lewton.

40. "John G. Crommelin," http://www.ourcampaigns.com/CandidateDetail.html?CandidateID=19159; Boylan; "William P. Gale," http://www.ourcampaigns.com/RaceDetail.html?RaceID=386045; "John Kasper, the National States Rights Party, and the Demise of the South," http://mauryk2.com/2010/11/06/john-kasper-the-national-states-rights-party-and-the-demise-of-the-old-south.

41. FBI Files, NSRP; Group Research Report, p. 9; "National States' Rights," http://www.ourcampaigns.com/PartyDetail.html?PartyID=1871.

42. Sherrill, *Gothic*, p. 268; Flowers, p. 44; Newton, *White Robes*, p. 133; "George C. Wallace," http://www.ourcampaigns.com/CandidateDetail.html?CandidateID=4038.

43. "List of nationalist meetings and demonstrations in America," http://en.metapedia.org/wiki/List_of_nationalist_meetings_and_demonstrations_in_America #1960s; FBI Files, NSRP; Group Research Report, p. 2.

44. "Clyde Kennard," https://en.wikipedia.org/wiki/Clyde_Kennard; "James Meredith," https://en.wikipedia.org/wiki/James_Meredith.

45. FBI Files, NSRP; Doyle, pp. 29, 81, 98–9, 128; Lord, p. 184; John Doar report to the DOJ, https://www.justice.gov/crt/foia/file/661946/download; "List of American military officers opposed to Jewish supremacism," http://en.metapedia.org/wiki/List_of_American_military_officers_opposed_to_Jewish_supremacism.

46. *Para-Military Organizations in California*, p. CR-2.

47. Doyle, pp. 96–7; Webb, *Rabble*, p. 145; "Edwin A. Walker," http://www.ourcampaigns.com/CandidateDetail.html?CandidateID=120949.

48. John Doar report to the DOJ; Doyle, pp. 92, 97, 134; Boylan; Dorman, pp. 50, 68; Sherrill, *Gothic*, p. 281.

49. Webb, *Rabble*, pp. 145–6; Doyle, pp. 163–6, 187, 213–16. 269. 280; Dorman, pp. 81, 114; John Doar report to DOJ; "Edwin Walker," https://en.wikipedia.org/wiki/Edwin_Walker; FBI Files, NSRP.

50. Armbrister; John Doar report to DOJ; Dorman, pp. 115, 188–9, 264–66; Doyle, p. 311; Webb, *Rabble*, p. 163; James H. Meredith SMMSS (MUM00594), http://www.olemiss.edu/depts/general_library/archives/finding_aids/MUM00594.html; Massengill, p. 163; "Ole Miss riot of 1962," https://en.wikipedia.org/wiki/Ole_Miss_riot_of_1962; HUAC, *Present-Day*, p. 89.

51. Webb, *Rabble*, pp. 148–9; Doyle, 309–10; "Did Lee Harvey Oswald Shoot at General Edwin Walker?" http://22november1963.org.uk/did-lee-oswald-shoot-general-edwin-walker; Benjamin Epstein and Arnold Forster, *Report on the John Birch Society 1966* (New York: Random House, 1966), p. 15; "Edwin Walker," https://en.wikipedia.org/wiki/Edwin_Walker; *DeGuello Report*; "Liberty Lobby," http://en.metapedia.org/wiki/Liberty_Lobby#Liberty_Lobby_Board_of_Policy_members.

52. McWhorter, p. 303; Group Research Report, p. 2; "Evall G. Johnson," http://en.metapedia.org/wiki/Evall_G._Johnston; "*The Georgia Tribune*," http://en.metapedia.org/wiki/The_Georgia_Tribune; "American National Party," http://en.metapedia.org/wiki/American_National_Party; McWhorter, p. 173–4.

53. "Daniel Burros," http://en.metapedia.org/wiki/Daniel_Burros; *DeGuello Report*; "Marshall Field," https://en.wikipedia.org/wiki/Marshall_Field; Orison Marden, "How Marshall Field succeeded," https://mises.org/library/how-marshall-field-succeeded; "John H. Morrell," http://uipress.lib.uiowa.edu/bdi/DetailsPage.aspx?id=277; "Edward Fields," http://en.metapedia.org/wiki/Edward_Fields; "Armour and Company," https://en.wikipedia.org/wiki/Armour_and_Company.

Chapter 6

1. Carter, pp. 165–6; "The Inaugural Address of Governor George C. Wallace, January 14, 1963," http://digital.archives.alabama.gov/cdm/singleitem/collection/voices/id/2952/rec/5; McWhorter, p. 311; FBI Files, NSRP; Group Research Report, pp. 2, 4, 7, 12; Schmaltz, p. 173; "Selma Figure Known Here," *Dallas Morning News*, January 25, 1965.

2. HUAC, *Present-Day*, p. 89; *Report of the Florida Legislative Investigation Committee*, pp. 74–5; *Para-Military Organizations in California*, p. NSRP-10.

3. Sherrill, "A Look Inside," pp. 27–8.
4. Armbrister, p. 82; Group Research Report, p. 7; "Dewey Taft," en.metapedia.org/wiki/Dewey_Taft; "List of American military officers opposed to Jewish supremacism," http://en.metapedia.org/wiki/List_of_American_military_officers_opposed_to_Jewish_supremacism.
5. McWhorter, pp. 311–13, 317–18, 320, 322, 352, 357; Cobbs and Smith, pp. 73, 79–80.
6. McWhorter, pp. 341, 361–2; Group Research Report, p. 4.
7. Stanton, pp. 6, 74, 88; McWhorter, p. 425; Group Research Report, p. 9.
8. Group Research Report, p. 4; McWhorter, pp. 129, 425, 428.
9. Forster and Epstein, *Report on the Ku Klux Klan*, p. 31.
10. Group Research Report, pp. 4–5; McWhorter, p. 473; Carter, pp. 139–40.
11. McWhorter, pp. 456–9, 479–80.
12. Massengill, pp. 10, 163, 201; Webb, "Freedom for All?"
13. Group Research Report, p. 5, 6; Sherrill, "A Look Inside," p. 29.
14. Carter, pp. 166–7.
15. McWhorter, pp. 473–4.
16. The Martin Luther King, Jr. Papers Project, http://kingencyclopedia.stanford.edu/primarydocuments/630800-009.pdf; Group Research Report, pp. 5, 11.
17. Carter, p. 167; McWhorter, p. 491.
18. McWhorter, pp. 479–80, 482, 485.
19. McWhorter, pp. 479–85; Group Research report, p. 9; Drabble, "From White Supremacy to White Power"; Armbrister, p. 82; HUAC, *Present-Day Ku Klux Klan*, p. 14; HUAC, *Hearings Part 2*, p. 2114; "Edward Fields," http://en.metapedia.org/wiki/Edward_Fields.
20. Group Research Report, p. 2; Carter, pp. 168–9.
21. McWhorter, p. 493.
22. Group Research Report, p. 5; Clark, pp. 171–2; May, p. 83; McWhorter, pp. 495, 498.
23. McWhorter, pp. 501–2.
24. McWhorter, pp. 499–503, 507–8.
25. May, pp. 85–6; McWhorter, pp. 507–8; Cobbs and Smith, p. 83; Carter, pp. 173–4; "Robert C. Gafford," http://obits.al.com/obituaries/birmingham/obituary.aspx?pid=161086902; Edward Fields personal communication with the author.
26. "Thomas Tarrants," http://en.metapedia.org/wiki/Thomas_Tarrants; Nelson, pp. 24, 206–7.
27. McWhorter, pp. 504, 507, 536; Group Research Report, p. 5; Cobbs and Smith, p. 186; FBI Files, NSRP.
28. F. Erik Brooks, "Sixteenth Street Baptist Church," http://www.encyclopediaofalabama.org/article/h-1744; McWhorter, pp. 492–3, 506, 508, 516; Cobbs and Smith, pp. 89, 98–99, 186–7; HSCA, *Final Report*, p. 377.
29. Mendelsohn, p. 96; McWhorter, p. 531.
30. McWhorter, pp. 536, 557.
31. Cobbs and Smith, p. 199; McMillan, "The Birmingham Church Bomber."
32. McWhorter, pp. 539, 540–3; McMillan, "The Birmingham Church Bomber."
33. McWhorter, pp. 547–9, 552, 556, 561, 565.
34. McWhorter, pp. 552–3.
35. McWhorter, pp. 554–5.
36. HUAC, *Hearings Part 4*, p. 3232; May, p. 98; John Archibald and Jeff Hansen, "Death spares scrutiny of Cash in bomb probe," *Birmingham News*, September 7, 1997; Stanton, p. 80; Cobbs and Smith, p. 187.
37. Boylan; HUAC, *Hearings Part 5*, p. 3669.
38. McMillan, "New Bombing Terrorists"; HUAC *Hearings*, Vol. 2, pp. 2215–16, 2222–24, 2227–30.
39. McWhorter, p. 562; FBI Files, Jesse Benjamin Stoner.

Chapter 7

1. Turner, pp. 106–7.
2. *Ibid.*, p. 107; Report filed by FBI Agent Charles Paul Rose, December 4, 1963; "Dr Stanley L Drennan," http://www.findagrave.com/cgi-bin/fg.cgi?page=gr&GRid=40986831; *Stanley L. Drennan, M.D., Appellant, v. Patricia Harris, Secretary of Health, Education and Welfare and Blue Shield of California, Appellees*, 606 F.2d 846 (9th Cir. 1979).
3. Boylan.
4. "Constitution Party (United States, 1952), http://en.metapedia.org/wiki/Constitution_Party_%28United_States,_1952%29; "List of nationalist meetings and demonstrations in America," http://en.metapedia.org/wiki/List_of_nationalist_meetings_and_demonstrations_in_America; "Kenneth Goff," http://en.metapedia.org/wiki/Kenneth_Goff; "Curtis B. Dall," http://en.metapedia.org/wiki/Curtis_Dall.
5. Boylan; "List of nationalist meetings and demonstrations in America," http://en.metapedia.org/wiki/List_of_nationalist_meetings_and_demonstrations_in_America; "Archibald Roberts," https://en.wikipedia.org/wiki/Archibald_Roberts; FBI Files, Joseph Milteer.
6. Boylan.
7. McWhorter, p. 562.
8. Boylan.
9. Turner, pp. 58–9.
10. *Ibid.*, p. 59.
11. *Ibid.*
12. Christensen, "King Assassination"; "Joseph Milteer: Miami Prophet, or Quitman Crackpot?" http://mcadams.posc.mu.edu/milteer.htm.
13. FBI Files, Joseph Milteer; Christensen, "JFK, King."
14. "Transcript, Milteer-Somersett, November 9, 1963," http://cuban-exile.com/doc_051-075/doc0062c.html.
15. "Jack William Brown," http://en.metapedia.org/wiki/Jack_William_Brown; HUAC, *Present-Day*, p. 57; FBI Files, NSRP; Drabble, "The FBI, COINTELPRO ... Tennessee"; Newton, *Unsolved*, pp. 41–2; FBI Files, Joseph Milteer.
16. "Marietta, Georgia," https://en.wikipedia.org/wiki/Marietta,_Georgia; "Gas Believed Tragedy Cause in Georgia," *Anderson* (Indiana) *Herald*, November 1, 1963; "At Least 12 Are Killed in Georgia Gas Blast," *Progress-Index* (Petersburg VA), December 6, 1957.
17. "Joseph Milteer: Miami Prophet, or Quitman Crackpot?" http://mcadams.posc.mu.edu/milteer.htm; "Odd Happenings On The Day of The Assassination, Pt. 2," http://alt.conspiracy.jfk.narkive.com/VnPgJpFX/odd-happenings-on-the-day-of-the-assassination-pt-2.
18. Christensen, "JFK, King."
19. *Ibid.*
20. FBI Files, Joseph Milteer.
21. *Ibid.*; Boylan.
22. FBI Files, Joseph Milteer.
23. Christensen, "JFK, King."
24. *Ibid.*
25. *Ibid.*
26. *Ibid.*
27. *Ibid.*
28. Boylan.
29. *Ibid.*

30. Gerald McKnight, *Breach of Trust: How the Warren Commission Failed the Nation and Why* (Lexington: University Press of Kentucky, 2004), p. 11.
31. Group Research Report, p. 12; "Selma Figure Known Here," *Dallas Morning News*, January 28, 1965; "James Robinson," http://en.metapedia.org/wiki/James_Robinson.
32. "George E. Butler," http://spartacus-educational.com/JFKbutler.htm; Richard Lindberg and John Tuohy, "Jack Ruby, Organized Crime and the Kennedy Assassination," http://richardlindberg.net/articles/chicago_mob.html; Ray Zauber, "George Butler: His Word Was Law," *Oak Cliff* (TX) *Tribune*, January 10, 1980; William Turner, *The Police Establishment* (New York: G. P. Putnam's Sons, 1968), pp. 188–195.
33. Bryan Woolley, "At its peak, Ku Klux Klan gripped Dallas," *Dallas Morning News*, May 15, 2010; HUAC, *Present-Day Ku Klux Klan*, p. 161; Newton, *White Robes*, pp. 167, 175.
34. Newton, *White Robes*, pp. 140–141; Scott Parks, "Extremists in Dallas created volatile atmosphere before JFK's 1963 visit," *Dallas Morning News*, October 12, 2013; Ray Zauber, "George Butler: His Word Was Law," *Oak Cliff* (TX) *Tribune*, January 10, 1980.
35. Newton, *White Robes*, p. 141.
36. Christensen, "A Miami police informant."
37. *Ibid.*
38. *Fields v. City of Fairfield*, 375 U.S. 248 (1963); Webb, "Freedom for All?"

Chapter 8

1. "Florida Timeline," http://fcit.usf.edu/florida/docs/f/fltime.htm; "The Massacre of the French," https://www.nps.gov/foma/learn/historyculture/the_massacre.htm.
2. "Florida's Quadricentennial in St. Augustine: Crosses to Bear," http://studiohourglass.blogspot.com/2014/06/floridas-quadricentennial-in-st.html; "Florida's Quadricentennial in St. Augustine: Crosses to Bear," http://studiohourglass.blogspot.com/2014/06/floridas-quadricentennial-in-st.html.
3. *Racial and Civil Disorders in St. Augustine*, pp. 2–3, 29; Larry Goodwin, "Anarchy in St. Augustine," *Harper's*, January 1965; "Dr. Robert B. Hayling," http://www.drbronsontours.com/bronsonstaugustinekkk2.html; HUAC, *Present-Day*, p. 87; HUAC, *Hearings Part 5*, p. 3661–2.
4. Larry Goodwin, "Anarchy in St. Augustine," *Harper's*, January 1965; "Dr. Robert B. Hayling," http://www.drbronsontours.com/bronsonstaugustinekkk2.html.
5. HUAC, *Present Day Ku Klux Klan*, pp. 28, 54–5; "Dr. Robert B. Hayling," http://www.drbronsontours.com/bronsonstaugustinekkk2.html; Armbrister, pp. 81–2.
6. *Racial and Civil Disorders in St. Augustine*, pp. 3–4, 31; HUAC, *Present-Day*, p. 87; HUAC, *Hearings Part 5*, pp. 3661–2; Gillette and Tillinger, pp. 115–19.
7. Gillette and Tillinger, p. 117.
8. "St. Augustine Ku Klux Klan Rally," http://www.drbronsontours.com/bronsonstaugustinekkk2.html; Gillette and Tillinger, p. 115; Larry Goodwin, "Anarchy in St. Augustine," *Harper's*, January 1965; *Racial and Civil Disorders in St. Augustine*, p. 4.
9. *Racial and Civil Disorders in St. Augustine*, p. 31; "Dr. Robert B. Hayling," http://www.drbronsontours.com/bronsonstaugustinekkk2.html; Armbrister, p. 82; "St. Augustine Ku Klux Klan Rally," http://www.drbronsontours.com/bronsonstaugustinekkk2.html.
10. Newton, *Invisible Empire*, pp. 163–4.
11. "Dr. Robert B. Hayling," http://www.drbronsontours.com/bronsonstaugustinekkk2.html; *Racial and Civil Disorders in St. Augustine*, pp. 4, 32; Larry Goodwin, "Anarchy in St. Augustine," *Harper's*, January 1965.
12. *Racial and Civil Disorders in St. Augustine*, pp. 5, 33; "Dr. Robert B. Hayling," http://www.drbronsontours.com/bronsonstaugustinekkk2.html.
13. HUAC, *Present-Day*, pp. 117–18; HUAC, *Hearings Part 4*, pp. 3234–5; HUAC, *Hearings Part 5*, pp. 3669, 3678, 3690; "Dr. Robert B. Hayling," http://www.drbronsontours.com/bronsonstaugustinekkk2.html; "St. Augustine Ku Klux Klan Rally," http://www.drbronsontours.com/bronsonstaugustinekkk2.html.
14. HUAC, *Present-Day*, pp. 117–18; HUAC, *Hearings Part 4*, pp. 3234–5; "Dr. Robert B. Hayling," http://www.drbronsontours.com/bronsonstaugustinekkk2.html; Drabble, "The FBI, COINTELPRO-WHITE HATE ... Florida."
15. HUAC, *Hearings Part 5*, p. 3686.
16. "Dr. Robert B. Hayling," http://www.drbronsontours.com/bronsonstaugustinekkk2.html; *Racial and Civil Disorders in St. Augustine*, pp. 6–7, 9, 34, 36–7; Drabble, "The FBI, COINTELPRO-WHITE HATE ... Florida"; Larry Goodwin, "Anarchy in St. Augustine," *Harper's*, January 1965.
17. *Racial and Civil Disorders in St. Augustine*, pp. 39–40; "Dr. Robert B. Hayling," http://www.drbronsontours.com/bronsonstaugustinekkk2.html.
18. *Racial and Civil Disorders in St. Augustine*, pp. 13–17, 40–2; "Dr. Robert B. Hayling," http://www.drbronsontours.com/bronsonstaugustinekkk2.html; Larry Goodwin, "Anarchy in St. Augustine," *Harper's*, January 1965.
19. *Report of the Florida Legislative Investigation Committee*, pp. 67–8.
20. *Racial and Civil Disorders in St. Augustine*, pp. 20–1, 42–4; "Changing of the Guard," https://www.splcenter.org/fighting-hate/intelligence-report/2001/changing-guard-0; "Dr. Robert B. Hayling," http://www.drbronsontours.com/bronsonstaugustinekkk2.html; Garrow, p. 68; Larry Goodwin, "Anarchy in St. Augustine," *Harper's*, January 1965.
21. *Racial and Civil Disorders in St. Augustine*, pp. 22–3, 45; "Dr. Robert B. Hayling," http://www.drbronsontours.com/bronsonstaugustinekkk2.html; FBI Files, Jesse Benjamin Stoner.
22. *Racial and Civil Disorders in St. Augustine*, pp. 47, 49; "Dr. Robert B. Hayling," http://www.drbronsontours.com/bronsonstaugustinekkk2.html; HUAC, *Hearings Part 5*, p. 3687.
23. HUAC, *Present-Day*, pp. 117–18; Drabble, "The FBI, COINTELPRO-WHITE HATE ... Florida.
24. "Party Is Linked to Florida Strife," *New York Times*, August 1, 1964.
25. "Dr. Robert B. Hayling," http://www.drbronsontours.com/bronsonstaugustinekkk2.html; *Racial and Civil Disorders in St. Augustine*, p. 59.
26. "Sheriffs of the 20th Century," http://www.sjso.org/wp-content/uploads/2012/10/20th-cen-sheriffs.pdf; "Dr. Robert B. Hayling," http://www.drbronsontours.com/bronsonstaugustinekkk2.html.

Chapter 9

1. FBI Files, NSRP.
2. *Ibid.*
3. *Ibid.*; "List of nationalist meetings and demonstrations in America," http://en.metapedia.org/wiki/List_of_nationalist_meetings_and_demonstrations_in_America#1955–1959; *DeGuello Report*.

4. "James P. Thornton," http://en.metapedia.org/wiki/James_P._Thornton; *DeGuello Report*; Cooper, "Brief History."
5. "Thomas Tarrants," http://en.metapedia.org/wiki/Thomas_Tarrants; Nelson, p. 24–5, 206–7.
6. "National States Rights Party," http://en.metapedia.org/wiki/National_States_Rights_Party; "Marietta, Georgia," https://en.wikipedia.org/wiki/Marietta,_Georgia; "A century after Jewish Man's Lynching, Georgia town unsettled," CBS News, August 26, 2015.
7. FBI Files, NSRP; "Jerry Dutton," http://en.metapedia.org/wiki/Jerry_Dutton; "National White Americans Party," http://en.metapedia.org/wiki/American_States_Rights_Party; Schmaltz, p. 319–20; Sherrill, "A Look Inside," p. 29; Cooper, "Brief History"; McWhorter, p. 557; Daniel Johnson, "National White Americans Party," http://blogs.brown.edu/hallhoag/2013/11/14/national-white-americans-party; FBI Files, NSRP.
8. Jones, pp. 32, 41; William Turner, "The Minutemen," *Ramparts* (January 1967): 69–76.
9. Jones, pp. 27–8.
10. FBI Files, NSRP; "List of nationalist meetings and demonstrations in America," http://en.metapedia.org/wiki/List_of_nationalist_meetings_and_demonstrations_in_America#1960s.
11. Jones, pp. 111, 299–301, 378, 383; Turner, "The Minutemen," pp. 69–70, 72; "Jail Term for Minuteman Postponed," *Los Angeles Times*, November 25, 1964; FBI Files, NSRP.
12. Sherrill, "A Look Inside," p. 27.
13. "John G. Crommelin," http://www.ourcampaigns.com/CandidateDetail.html?CandidateID=19159.
14. "William P. Gale," http://www.ourcampaigns.com/CandidateDetail.html?CandidateID=58365&ShowAllEvent=Y; Boylan; "Christian Defense League," http://en.metapedia.org/wiki/Christian_Defense_League.
15. Carter, pp. 198–225.
16. William Jones, *The Wallace Story* (Marion, AL: American Southern Publishing Co., 1966), pp. 324, 327, 340; Clifton White, *Suite 3505: The Story of the Draft Goldwater Movement* (New Rochelle, NY: Arlington House, 1967), p. 15; Chalmers, *Hooded*, pp. 383–4; "1964 Presidential Election Results," http://uselectionatlas.org/RESULTS/national.php?year=1964.
17. "U.S. President National Vote," http://www.ourcampaigns.com/RaceDetail.html?RaceID=1941; HUAC, *Present-Day*, p. 13; "MT District 1," http://www.ourcampaigns.com/RaceDetail.html?RaceID=142687; FBI Files, NSRP; "John Kasper," http://en.metapedia.org/wiki/John_Kasper.
18. "List of nationalist meetings and demonstrations in America," http://en.metapedia.org/wiki/List_of_nationalist_meetings_and_demonstrations_in_America#1960s; FBI Files, NSRP; Cooper, "Brief History."
19. FBI Files, COINTELPRO—WHITE HATE GROUPS.
20. Michael Newton, *The FBI Encyclopedia* (Jefferson, NC: McFarland Publishing, 2003), pp. 69–72.
21. FBI Files, COINTELPRO—WHITE HATE GROUPS.
22. Newton, *The FBI Encyclopedia*, pp. 69–72.
23. Drabble, "From White Supremacy to White Power"; George Lincoln Rockwell, *This Time the World!* (Liverpool, WV: J. V. Morgan, 1961), p. 166; Drabble, "The FBI, COINTELPRO—WHITE HATE ... Florida."
24. Kenneth O'Reilly, *Racial Matters: The FBI's Secret File in Black America, 1960-1972* (New York: The Free Press, 1989), pp. 180, 200, 224.

Chapter 10

1. *Para-Military Organizations in California*, pp. NSRP-11, NSRP-16, and CR-3.
2. FBI Files, NSRP; "Watts riots," https://en.wikipedia.org/wiki/Watts_riots.
3. "Selma to Montgomery March (1965)," http://kingencyclopedia.stanford.edu/encyclopedia/encyclopedia/enc_selma_to_montgomery_march; "1965: Selma & the March to Montgomery," http://www.crmvet.org/tim/timhis65.htm#1965selmacourthouse; "Sheriff Jim Clark, segregationist icon, dies at 84," Associated Press, June 6, 2007.
4. "Selma & the March to Montgomery," http://www.crmvet.org/tim/timhis65.htm#1965selmacourthouse; Schmaltz, pp. 235–6; "James Robinson," http://en.metapedia.org/wiki/James_Robinson.
5. "Selma to Montgomery March (1965)"; Robbie Brown, "45 Years Later, an Apology and 6 Months," *New York Times*, November 15, 2010; Alston Fitts, "Bloody Sunday," http://www.encyclopediaofalabama.org/article/h-1876.
6. Tully, pp. 221–2; "Selma to Montgomery March (1965)"; Nancy Klann-Moren, "March 7, 1965, Selma, Alabama, Bloody Sunday, 48 years ago, today," http://www.nancyklann-moren.com/march-7-1965-selma-alabama-bloody-sunday-48-years-ago-today; "Kendrick, Thomas Randall, 1943–," http://crdl.usg.edu/people/k/kendrick_thomas_randall_1943/?Welcome.
7. "Selma to Montgomery March (1965)"; "1965: Selma & the March to Montgomery"; Sherrill, "A Look Inside," p. 30.
8. May, pp. 150–183, 298–315.
9. *Ibid.*, pp. 184–210; Edward Fields personal communication with the author.
10. *Ibid.*, pp. 234–5, 243–50, 263–5, 301, 303.
11. FBI Files, Millard Dee Grubbs.
12. *Ibid.*
13. Boylan; Cheri Seymour, *Committee of the States: Inside the Radical Right* (Sandy, OR: CPA Book Publishers, 1991), p. 86; "Posse Comitatus Act," https://en.wikipedia.org/wiki/Posse_Comitatus_Act.
14. HUAC, *Hearings Part 5*, p. 3811; Parker, p. 101; "List of racially-motivated bombings," http://www.bhamwiki.com/w/List_of_racially-motivated_bombings#1965.
15. "Confronting the Klan in Bogalusa With Nonviolence & Self-Defense," http://www.crmvet.org/tim/tim65b.htm#1965bogalusa.
16. *Ibid.*
17. *Ibid.*
18. *Ibid.*; Drabble, "The FBI, COINTELPRO—WHITE HATE ... Louisiana"; Kritstone Denholm, "Chasing Ghosts in a Civil Rights Era Cop Killing," http://www.policemag.com/channel/patrol/articles/print/story/2010/10/chasing-ghosts.aspx; Richard Serrano, "Answers Elusive in 1965 Slaying," *Los Angeles Times*, July 26, 2002.
19. Drabble, "The FBI, COINTELPRO—WHITE HATE ... Louisiana"; Lance Hill, *The Deacons for Defense: Armed Self-Defense and the Civil Rights Movement* (Chapel Hill: of North Carolina Press, 2004), pp. 311–2; University "Ernest Raphael 'Ray' McElveen," *Bogalusa Daily News*, February 18, 2003; Denholm, "Chasing Ghosts"; HUAC, *Present-Day*, p. 124.
20. "Confronting the Klan in Bogalusa With Nonviolence & Self-Defense"; Drabble, "The FBI, COINTELPRO—WHITE HATE ... Louisiana; Hill, *The Deacons for Defense*, pp. 131–2.
21. Hill, *The Deacons for Defense*, pp. 131–2; Seth

Hague, "Niggers Ain't Gonna Run This Town," http://www.loyno.edu/~history/journal/1997-8/Hague.html.
22. "Confronting the Klan in Bogalusa With Nonviolence & Self-Defense"; Parker, pp. 116; HUAC, *Hearings Part 5*, p. 3821.
23. Parker, p. 116; Michael Newton, *Unsolved Civil Rights Murder Cases, 1934–1970* (Jefferson, NC: McFarland Publishing, 2016), pp. 227, 229.
24. Parker, p. 101; HUAC, *Present-Day*, p. 14; Webb, *Rabble*, p. 177.
25. Parker, p. 101; "Ten Years for Alabama Slayer," *New York Herald Tribune*, European Edition, December 3, 1965.
26. Fleming, "Guns, Bombs and Kenneth Adams"; Michael Newton, *Unsolved Civil Rights Murder Cases, 1934–1970* (Jefferson, NC: McFarland, 2016), pp. 76–7.
27. Fleming, "Memories of a Dark Time"; Fleming, "The Agent, the Judge, and the Trial"; "Ten Years for Alabama Slayer," *New York Herald Tribune*, European Edition, December 3, 1965.
28. "Ten Years for Alabama Slayer," *New York Herald Tribune*, European Edition, December 3, 1965; Fleming, "The Agent, the Judge, and the Trial"; Parker, p. 101; "Convicted Slayer of Negro Shot to Death in Alabama," *New York Times*, November 6, 1966; *Hubert Damon Strange v. State*, 197 So. 2d 447 (1967).
29. "Voting Rights Act of 1965," http://kingencyclopedia.stanford.edu/encyclopedia/encyclopedia/enc_voting_rights_act_1965; "Sheriff Jim Clark, segregationist icon, dies at 84," Associated Press, June 6, 2007; Sherrill, *Gothic Politics*, p. 313; "Col. Al Lingo Resigns," *Montgomery Advertiser*, September 17, 1965; "Lingo Bids For Negro Vote," *Alabama Journal*, April 13, 1966; "Ex-Trooper Chief, Lingo, Dies at 59," *Birmingham Post-Herald*, August 18, 1969.
30. Sherrill, "A Look Inside," pp. 26–7.
31. FBI Files, NSRP; *Brandenburg v. Ohio*, 395 U.S. 444 (1969).
32. HUAC, *Hearings Part 4*, pp. 3373, 3400–02, 3407, 3433–4, 3476.
33. Drabble, "The FBI, COINTELPRO—WHITE HATE … Florida."

Chapter 11

1. May, pp. 171–2; HUAC, *Present-Day*, pp. 1–2.
2. Frank Donner, *The Un-Americans* (New York: Ballantine, 1967); Walter Goodman, *The Committee: The Extraordinary Career of the House Committee on Un-American Activities* (New York: Farrar Straus & Giroux, 1968); Kenneth O'Reilly, *Hoover and the Unamericans: The FBI, HUAC, and the Red Menace* (Philadelphia: Temple University Press, 1983).
3. HUAC, *Testimony Part 5*, p. 3827.
4. HUAC, *Present-Day*, pp. 14, 25, 34, 36, 107; HUAC, *Testimony, Part 5*, pp. 3656, 3665, 3667, 3674, 3679, 3682, 3681, 3688, 3694, 3700, 3705, 3710, 3714, 3717, 3728, 3743, 3748, 3752, 3768, 3804–24.
5. HUAC, *Testimony Part 3*, pp. 2698–2701; HUAC, *Testimony Part 5*, pp. 3497, 3525–46, 3700–04.
6. HUAC, *Testimony Part 4*, pp. 3342–63; HUAC, *Testimony Part 5*, pp. 3804–24.
7. Ibid.
8. Drabble, The FBI, COINTELPRO-WHITE HATE … Florida."
9. William Bryk, "Old Smoke: The Death of Daniel Burros: A Jewish Klansman who did more than just hate himself," http://www.nypress.com/old-smoke-the-death-of-daniel-burros-a-jewish-klansman-who-did-more-than-just-hate-himself.
10. HUAC, *Present-Day*, p. 36; HUAC, *Hearings Part 2*, p. 3354; HUAC, *Hearings Part 4*, pp. 3321–2, 3338–9, 3368.
11. "Nazi Icon Part African American?" http://niksnest.blogspot.com/2007_04_01_archive.html.
12. "Brother of Neo-Nazi Leader William Hoff Jr. Speaks Out," https://www.splcenter.org/fighting-hate/intelligence-report/2007/brother-neo-nazi-leader-william-hoff-jr-speaks-out.
13. "Nazi Icon Part African American?" http://niksnest.blogspot.com/2007_04_01_archive.html.
14. HUAC, *Hearings Part 5*, p. 3697.
15. "John G. Crommelin," http://www.ourcampaigns.com/CandidateDetail.html?CandidateID=19159; Sherrill, "A Look Inside," pp. 7, 25, 26, 29; "James D. Johnson," https://en.wikipedia.org/wiki/James_D._Johnson.
16. "Lester Maddox," *The Guardian*, June 25, 2003; "Bo Callaway," https://en.wikipedia.org/wiki/Bo_Callaway; "Lester Maddox," http://www.ourcampaigns.com/CandidateDetail.html?CandidateID=4197.
17. Sherrill, "A Look Inside," p. 29; Martin; Edward Fields, personal communication with the author.
18. Sherrill, "A Look Inside," pp. 29–30; "National White Americans Party," http://en.metapedia.org/wiki/National_White_Americans_Party_%281966%29; "National White Americans Party," http://blogs.brown.edu/hallhoag/2013/11/14/national-white-americans-party; "Samuel Irving Newhouse Sr.," https://en.wikipedia.org/wiki/Samuel_Irving_Newhouse,_Sr.
19. Sherrill, "A Look Inside," p. 29; Cooper, "Brief History"; *Birmingham News*, November 9, 1966.
20. HUAC, *Present-Day*, p. 89; Parker, pp. 143–4; "Timeline: Seattle CORE 1961–1968," http://depts.washington.edu/civilr/CORE_timeline.htm; "Capturing the Movement: Before and After the Civil Rights Act of 1964 in Photographs," http://www.mdhs.org/underbelly/2014/06/30/capturing-the-movement-before-and-after-the-civil-rights-act-of-1964-in-photographs.
21. Princess Anne *Marylander and Herald*, August 11, 1966; *Carroll, et al. v. The President and Commissioners of Princess Anne County*, 247 Md. 126 (1967), 230 A.2d 452; "States Righters Charged with Riots in Baltimore," *St. Petersburg Times*, July 30, 1966; *Lynch et al. v. State of Maryland*, 2 Md. App. 546 (1967), 236 A.2d 45.
22. *Lynch et al. v. State of Maryland*; FBI Files, NSRP.
23. *Lynch et al. v. State of Maryland*; Parker, p. 143.
24. *Lynch et al. v. State of Maryland*; Parker, pp. 143–4; "States Righters Charged with Riots in Baltimore," *St. Petersburg Times*, July 30, 1966.
25. "States Righters Charged with Riots in Baltimore," *St. Petersburg Times*, July 30, 1966; *Carroll, et al. v. The President and Commissioners of Princess Anne County*; "Johnny Rebel (singer)," https://en.wikipedia.org/wiki/Johnny_Rebel_%28singer%29.
26. *Carroll, et al. v. The President and Commissioners of Princess Anne County*.
27. Ibid.
28. Ibid.
29. Ibid.
30. Ibid.
31. Ibid.; HUAC, *Present-Day*, p. 89; Parker, p. 144; *Lynch et al. v. State of Maryland*; FBI Files, NSRP.
32. Drabble, "FBI Covert Operations"; Sherrill, "A Look Inside," p. 27.
33. "Chicago Campaign (1966)," http://kingencyclopedia.stanford.edu/encyclopedia/encyclopedia/enc_chicago_campaign.
34. Frank James, "Martin Luther King Jr. in Chicago," http://www.chicagotribune.com/news/nationworld/

politics/chi-chicagodays-martinlutherking-story-story.html.
35. Schmaltz, pp. 290–1; FBI Files, NSRP.
36. Sherrill, "A Look Inside," p. 27; "Chicago Campaign (1966)"; "Civil Rights Act of 1968," https://en.wikipedia.org/wiki/Civil_Rights_Act_of_1968; Peter Babcox, Noam Chomsky, Judy Collins, Harvey Cox, and Edgar Z. Friedenberg, et al., "The Committee to Defend the Conspiracy," *The New York Review of Books*, June 19, 1969.
37. Drabble, "The FBI, COINTELPRO—WHITE HATE ... Florida."
38. "Lurleen Burns Wallace," http://www.ourcampaigns.com/CandidateDetail.html?CandidateID=42070; Carter, pp. 278, 295, 320.
39. Bill Jones, The Wallace Story (Northport, AL: American Southern Publishing Co., 1966), pp. 329–332.
40. Carter, p. 295.

Chapter 12

1. FBI Files, NSRP.
2. *Ibid.*
3. Sherrill, "A Look Inside," p. 27, 30; Parker, pp. 156–7; Desegregation and Civil Rights, http://www.wisconsinhistory.org/turningpoints/tp-049/?action=more_essay.
4. Sherrill, "A Look Inside," p. 27.
5. HUAC, *Present-Day*, pp. 18, 62; Chalmers, *Hooded*, p. 387.
6. Nelson, pp. 115, 119, 150, 159.
7. Parker, pp. 169–71, 199–200; Nelson, p. 46.
8. Nelson, pp. 80; Matthew Schaefer, "Joseph Hawkins," Channel 9, WAFB (Baton Rouge, LA), June 30, 2012.
9. Newton, *Ku Klux Klan in Mississippi*, p. 174.
10. "MS Lt. Governor—D Primary," http://www.ourcampaigns.com/RaceDetail.html?RaceID=662649.
11. Newton, *Ku Klux Klan in Mississippi*, pp. 177–8; Nelson, p. 23.
12. Nelson, pp. 142–6.
13. *Ibid.*, pp. 25–6, 30–2; "Encyclopedia of Southern Jewish Communities—Beth Israel—Jackson, Mississippi," http://www.isjl.org/mississippi-jackson-beth-israel-encyclopedia.html; Gary Zola, "What Price Amos? Perry Nussbaum's Career in Jackson, Mississippi," in *The Quiet Voices: Southern Rabbis and Black Civil Rights, 1880s to 1990s* (Tuscaloosa: University of Alabama Press, 1997), p. 239; Randy Sparks, *Religion in Mississippi* (Oxford: University Press of Mississippi, 2001), p. 239.
14. Drabble, "The FBI, COINTELPRO-WHITE HATE ... Florida."
15. *Ibid.*
16. *Tampa Tribune*, September 9, 1967.
17. Drabble, "The FBI, COINTELPRO-WHITE HATE ... North Carolina."
18. Cooper, "Brief History"; "George Lincoln Rockwell," http://en.metapedia.org/wiki/George_Lincoln_Rockwell; "John Patler," http://en.metapedia.org/wiki/John_Patler.
19. Sherrill, "A Look Inside," p. 29.
20. "George Lincoln Rockwell," http://en.metapedia.org/wiki/George_Lincoln_Rockwell; "Matt Koehl," http://en.metapedia.org/wiki/Matt_Koehl; Cooper, "Brief History"; "American Nazi Party," http://en.metapedia.org/wiki/American_Nazi_Party#New_Order.
21. Nelson, pp. 61–2.
22. "Judge William Harold Cox," http://law2.umkc.edu/faculty/projects/ftrials/price&bowers/Cox.htm;

"Mississippi Burning Trial: A Chronology," http://law2.umkc.edu/faculty/projects/ftrials/price&bowers/miss_chrono.html; Parker, pp. 65–8.
23. Drabble, "The FBI, COINTELPRO-WHITE HATE ... Mississippi"; Nelson, pp. 66, 69, 79; "Jurors Clear a Klan Leader of Submachine Gun Charge," *New York Times*, January 19, 1968; "Thomas Tarrants," http://en.metapedia.org/wiki/Thomas_Tarrants.
24. Nelson, pp. 139–41.
25. *Ibid.*, pp. 140–1.
26. *Ibid.*, pp. 106–7; Michelle Simmsparris, "Significance of Black Church Burnings," http://academic.udayton.edu/race/06hrights/waronterrorism/churchburn01a.htm.
27. Nelson, p. 134–5, 160, 162; Jack Nelson, "Klansmen Recruited by States Rights Party: FBI Agents Investigating Racist Group in Connection with Mississippi Violence," *Los Angeles Times*, May 30, 1968.

Chapter 13

1. "Martin Luther King, Jr. Chronology," http://kingencyclopedia.stanford.edu/encyclopedia/chronologyentry/1956_01_30; Wexler and Hancock, pp. 21–31; Boylan; Christensen, "King Assassination."
2. Newton, *Hate Crime*, p. 1; Peter Levy, "The Dream Deferred: The Assassination of Martin Luther King, Jr., and the Holy Week Uprisings of 1968," in Jessica Elfenbein, Thomas Hollowak, and Elizabeth Nix (eds.), *Baltimore '68: Riots and Rebirth in an American City* (Philadelphia: Temple University Press), pp. 3–25; Lyndon Baines Johnson, "Letter to the Speaker of the House Urging Enactment of the Fair Housing Bill," April 5, 1968.
3. Newton, *A Case*, pp. 113–128; HSCA *Final Report*, p. 381.
4. Christensen, "King Assassination"; HSCA *Final Report*, pp. 402–404.
5. Newton, *A Case*, pp. 99–101, 110–12; HSCA *Final Report*, p. 381.
6. Newton, *A Case*, pp. 173–183.
7. *Ibid.*, pp. 183–194.
8. Huie, "The Story of James Earl Ray."
9. Huie, "Why James Earl Ray murdered Dr. King."
10. *Ibid.*
11. Huie, "The One and Only," p. 26.
12. Maloney.
13. *Ibid.*
14. Drabble, "The FBI, COINTELPRO-WHITE HATE ... Mississippi"; Congregation Beth Israel (Meridian, Mississippi), https://en.wikipedia.org/wiki/Congregation_Beth_Israel_%28Meridian,_Mississippi%29; Nelson, pp. 113, 120–1, 137–41, 147–72.
15. Nelson, pp. 173–87; "Mississippi Spy Exposes Three Frame-Up Case," *Thunderbolt*, November 1968; "Thomas Tarrants," http://en.metapedia.org/wiki/Thomas_Tarrants.
16. Drabble, "The FBI, COINTELPRO-WHITE HATE ... Mississippi"; Jack Nelson, "Klansmen Recruited by States Rights Party: FBI Agents Investigating Racist Group in Connection with Mississippi Violence," *Los Angeles Times*, 30 May 1968.
17. "Kathy Ainsworth," http://en.metapedia.org/wiki/Kathy_Ainsworth; "Who Was the Girl in the Polka Dot Dress?" http://web.archive.org/web/20040611213431/members.fortunecity.com/wernerhoff/rfk5.html.
18. "Racial Shooting in Berea."
19. *Ibid.*; CBS Evening News, September 4, 1968; FBI Files, NSRP.
20. Marc Perrusquia, "Records give up-close look at

James Earl Ray's every move in jail," *Commercial Appeal* (Memphis), April 10, 2011; HSCA *Final Report,* p. 382.
 21. Why Did James Earl Ray Plead Guilty? http://mlkmurder.blogspot.com/2013/08/why-did-james-earl-ray-plead-guilty.html.
 22. Anthony Lewis, "Beyond a Shadow of a Doubt," *New York Times,* April 26, 1968.
 23. "John G. Crommelin," http://www.ourcampaigns.com/CandidateDetail.html?CandidateID=19159; "William P. Gale," http://www.ourcampaigns.com/CandidateDetail.html?CandidateID=58365&ShowAllEvent=Y.
 24. Newton, *White Hoods,* p. 164; Maloney; Carter, pp. 300, 365–6, 367–9.
 25. Sherrill, "A Look Inside," pp. 27–8.
 26. "Youth for Wallace," http://en.metapedia.org/wiki/Youth_for_Wallace; "National Youth Alliance," http://en.metapedia.org/wiki/National_Youth_Alliance; "Revilo P. Oliver," http://en.metapedia.org/wiki/Revilo_P._Oliver; "Richard Cotton," http://en.metapedia.org/wiki/Richard_Cotton; "Austin J. App," http://en.metapedia.org/wiki/Austin_App.
 27. "American Independent Party," http://en.metapedia.org/wiki/American_Independent_Party.
 28. Waldron and Hartmann, pp. 388, 495–498.
 29. *Ibid.,* pp. 510–11; HSCA *Final Report,* p. 394.
 30. Waldron and Hartmann, pp. 517–22.
 31. *Ibid.,* pp. 498, 604–6; Christensen, "King Assassination"; Department of Justice, "V. Wilson's Allegations," http://www.justice.gov/crt/v-wilsons-allegations; Newton, *A Case,* pp. 90–1.
 32. Christensen, "King Assassination."
 33. Waldron and Hartmann, pp. 729, 770.
 34. FBI Files, NSRP;
 35. *Ibid.*; "List of nationalist meetings and demonstrations in America," http://en.metapedia.org/wiki/List_of_nationalist_meetings_and_demonstrations_in_America#1955–1959.
 36. FBI Files, NSRP.
 37. *Ibid.*
 38. "William Potter Gale," http://en.metapedia.org/wiki/William_Potter_Gale; "Posse Comitatus," http://en.metapedia.org/wiki/Posse_Comitatus.
 39. Drabble, " The FBI, COINTELPRO ... North Carolina"; Group Research Report; Newton, *White Robes,* p. 165.
 40. "Brother of Neo-Nazi Leader William Hoff Jr. Speaks Out," https://www.splcenter.org/fighting-hate/intelligence-report/2007/brother-neo-nazi-leader-william-hoff-jr-speaks-out; "Nazi Icon Part African American?" http://niksnest.blogspot.com/2007_04_01_archive.html.

Chapter 14

 1. FBI Files, NSRP.
 2. *Ibid.*
 3. *Ibid.*; Chet Huntley, "Reverend Carl McIntire leads Washington, DC march for victory tomorrow," NBC News, April 3, 1970; "Carl McIntire's Victory March," KGDN 630 Radio (Seattle, WA), April 7, 1970; *Thunderbolt,* August 1970.
 4. FBI Files, NSRP; *Thunderbolt,* August 1970.
 5. *Thunderbolt,* August 1970; FBI Files, NSRP.
 6. FBI Files, NSRP; Webb, *Rabble,* pp. 195–6. 205; Martin; "Jesse Benjamin Stoner," http://www.ourcampaigns.com/CandidateDetail.html?CandidateID=76937; Judith Smith, *Political Brokers: People, Organizations, Money, and Power* (New York: Liveright, 1972), p. 307.
 7. FBI Files, NSRP; H. Michael Barrett, "The 1970 Split In The NSWPP: A First Hand Account," http://home.alphalink.com.au/~radnat/usanazis/barrett.html; ADL, *Extremism,* p. 56; Don Black, https://www.stormfront.org/forum/t22074; "Man Acquitted of Shooting Nazi," *The Dispatch* (Lexington, NC), November 25, 1970; Bridges, p. 40; Duke, p. 294.
 8. FBI Files, NSRP; *The Thunderbolt,* August 1970; "John G. Crommelin," http://www.ourcampaigns.com/CandidateDetail.html?CandidateID=19159.
 9. "Wesley Swift," http://en.metapedia.org/wiki/Wesley_Swift; Rick Cooper, "Brief History"; "William Luther Pierce," http://en.metapedia.org/wiki/William_Luther_Pierce; "National Youth Alliance," http://en.metapedia.org/wiki/National_Youth_Alliance.
 10. "Black September and the Frankhouser File," http://larocheplanet.info/pmwiki/pmwiki.php?n=Library.UnityNow2; *DeGuello Report*; *Jouhari/Horton v. United Klans of America/Frankhouser,* Case Number 03-98-0692-8 & 03-98-0797-8 (1998).
 11. FBI Files, NSRP; Noam Chomsky, "Domestic Terrorism: Notes on the State System of Oppression," *New Political Science* 21 (September 1999): 303–324.
 12. Turner, p. 113; ADL, *Extremism,* p. 145; Edward Fields, "Personal News Letter," February 1971; "James K. Warner," http://en.metapedia.org/wiki/James_K._Warner; "Sons of Liberty," http://en.metapedia.org/wiki/Sons_of_Liberty_%28publishers%29; "New Christian Crusade Church," http://en.metapedia.org/wiki/New_Christian_Crusade_Church; "Christian Vanguard," http://en.metapedia.org/wiki/Christian_Vanguard; *Ray v. Foreman, Huie and Hanes.*
 13. "Leroy Gibson Persecuted in North Carolina: Federal Government and Communists Trying to Frame White Patriot" *Thunderbolt* November 1973; "How FBI 'Cointelpro' Disrupted Right Wing" *Thunderbolt* July 1975; "List of nationalist meetings and demonstrations in America," http://en.metapedia.org/wiki/List_of_nationalist_meetings_and_demonstrations_in_America; Bridges, p. 43; Newton, *White Hoods,* p. 174.
 14. Steve Flowers, "Steve Flowers Inside the Statehouse," October 12, 2005; "George C. Wallace," http://www.ourcampaigns.com/CandidateDetail.html?CandidateID=4038; "1972 Presidential General Election Results," http://uselectionatlas.org/RESULTS/national.php?year=1972&minper=0&f=1&off=0&elect=0U.S.
 15. *Thunderbolt,* September 1972; ADL, *Extremism,* pp. 80–1, 136; Webb, "Freedom for All?"; Webb, *Rabble,* pp. 184–7, 199–201.
 16. ADL, *Extremism,* pp. 80–1.
 17. Michael Fraase, "Mississippi as an inequality microcosm," http://www.farces.com/mississippi-as-an-inequality-microcosm.
 18. "Rev. Lynch, 'Fireball Segregationist,' Dies," *Florida Times-Union* (Jacksonville), October 7, 1972; Don Black, https://www.stormfront.org/forum/t22074; Sims, p. 155; Edward Fields personal communication with the author.
 19. "Roy Frankhouser," http://en.metapedia.org/wiki/Roy_Frankhouser; Joyce Gemperlein, "LaRouche Probe Snares Man with a Past of Hate," *Philadelphia Inquirer,* November 10, 1956; "Black September and the Frankhouser File," http://larocheplanet.info/pmwiki/pmwiki.php?n=Library.UnityNow2; ADL, *Extremism,* p. 84.
 20. FBI Files, NSRP.
 21. *Ibid.*
 22. Flynn and Gerheart, pp. 65–79.
 23. "James Clayton Vaughn Jr., AKA Joseph Paul Franklin," http://maamodt.asp.radford.edu/Psyc%20405/serial%20killers/Franklin,%20Joseph%20Paul.pdf.

24. Drabble, "FBI COINTELPRO ... Mississippi"; Massengill, pp. 1, 3–4, 266–291, 299–300.
25. Sher, pp. 50–1; FBI Files, NSRP.
26. FBI Files, NSRP; *Macon Telegraph*, May 23, June 28, July 18, and August 14, 1974; "Jesse Benjamin Stoner," http://www.ourcampaigns.com/CandidateDetail.html?CandidateID=76937; Jack Bass and Walter DeVries, *The Transformation of Southern Politics: Social Change and Political Consequence Since 1945* (Athens: University of Georgia Press, 1976), p. 156.
27. *Cason v. City of Jacksonville*.
28. ADL, *Extremism*, pp. 84–5; "Black September and the Frankhouser File," http://laroucheplanet.info/pmwiki/pmwiki.php?n=Library.UnityNow2.
29. ADL, *Extremism*, pp. 19, 59, 145; Bridges, pp. 35–6, 40–3, 53–4; *DeGuello Report*.
30. Miller, *White Man Speaks*.
31. Illinois Legislative Investigating Committee, p. 49.
32. Church Committee Vol. 6, *Federal Bureau of Investigation*, http://www.aarclibrary.org/publib/church/reports/vol6/contents.htm; "National States Rights Party," http://en.metapedia.org/wiki/National_States_Rights_Party; FBI Files, Jesse Benjamin Stoner.
33. "Knights of the Ku Klux Klan," http://en.metapedia.org/wiki/Knights_of_the_Ku_Klux_Klan_%281975%29; "Jerry Dutton," http://en.metapedia.org/wiki/Jerry_Dutton; Bridges, pp. 75, 77–9, 105; Webb, *Rabble*, p. 132.
34. "List of nationalist meetings and demonstrations in America," http://en.metapedia.org/wiki/List_of_nationalist_meetings_and_demonstrations_in_America; "International Anti-Semitic Congress," *Patterns of Prejudice* 10 (1976): 11; Bridges, pp. 58–65.
35. "Lester Maddox," http://www.ourcampaigns.com/CandidateDetail.html?CandidateID=4197.
36. "James K. Warner," http://en.metapedia.org/wiki/James_K._Warner; ADL, *Extremism*, pp. 3–4, 146–7; S. R. Shearer, "Anti-Semitism & the Economic Crisis: The Two Go Hand-in-Hand," http://www.antipasministries.com/html/file0000315.htm.
37. *DeGuello Report*; "Affairs of the Association," *The Southwestern Historical Quarterly* 25 (July 1921–April 1922): 79.
38. Bridges, p. 72; Neighbors Network, *Shadow*, p. 4; "Order of Flemish Militants," https://en.wikipedia.org/wiki/Order_of_Flemish_Militants; FBI Files, Jesse Benjamin Stoner; "League of St. George," https://en.wikipedia.org/wiki/League_of_Saint_George; Ray Hill and Andrew Bell, The Other Face of Terror—Inside Europe's Neo-Nazi Network (London: Collins, 1988), pp. 165–6, 185–9, 255–6; Martin Lee, *The Beast Awakens* (New York: Warner Books, 1997), p. 192.
39. "James Clayton Vaughn Jr., aka Joseph Paul Franklin," http://maamodt.asp.radford.edu/Psyc%20405/serial%20killers/Franklin,%20Joseph%20Paul.pdf.
40. Murray Schumach, "Cowan Was 'Nice Man' to Some in New Rochelle, but to Others 'Real Prejudiced Backer of Nazis.'" *New York Times*, February 15, 1977; Robert McFadden, "Nazi Sympathizer Also Wounds 5 in Wild Attack Followed by Siege at Moving Company." *New York Times*, February 15, 1977; Ira Leibowitz, "Probe of 'Son of Sam' terror cult documents satanic underground," *Executive Intelligence Review* 14 (August 14, 1987): 65.
41. Boylan; ADL, *Extremism*, p. 56; "James Earl Ray's Brother Stays at Stoner Headquarters," *Florence* (AL) *Times—Tri Cities Daily*, February 20, 1978.
42. Cobbs and Smith, pp. 155, 182; McWhorter, pp. 573–4; FBI Files, Jesse Stoner.
43. Baxley to Fields, February 28, 1976.
44. FBI Files, Jesse Stoner; Donald Grant, *The Way It Was in the South: The Black Experience in Georgia* (New York: Birch Lane Press, 1993), p. 441; J. B. Stoner flier, "Opposed to Civil Rights Laws"; Webb, "Freedom for All?"; "Jesse Benjamin Stoner," http://www.ourcampaigns.com/RaceDetail.html?RaceID=382406.
45. *Final Report of the Select Committee on Assassinations*, pp. 3–6, 360–370.
46. *Ibid.*, pp. 377–383; FBI Files, Jesse Stoner.
47. *Final Report of the Select Committee on Assassinations*, pp. 402–404; "Joseph Adams Milteer," http://www.findagrave.com/cgi-bin/fg.cgi?page=gr&GRid=6337479&ref=wvr.
48. "The Complete File on Roy Frankhouser," http://jfkcountercoup2.blogspot.com/2012/08/the-complete-file-on-roy-frankhouser.html; Gregory Rose, "The Swarmy Life and Times of the NCLC," *National Review*, March 30, 1979; John Mintz, "Defense Calls LaRouche, Followers 'Most Annoying'; Trial Begins for Leesburg Group Accused of Obstructing Probe Into Its Fund-Raising," *Washington Post*, December 18, 1987.

Chapter 15

1. Rick Cooper, "Brief History."
2. Bridges, pp. 75–78, 85–88, 106; Rick Cooper, "Brief History."
3. Stewart Bell, *Bayou of Pigs: The True Story of an Audacious Plot to Turn a Tropical Island into a Criminal Paradise* (Mississauga, Ontario: John Wiley & Sons, 2008); "2 Guilty in New Orleans for Plot on Dominica Invasion," *New York Times*, June 21, 1981.
4. "Edward Fields," http://archive.adl.org/learn/ext_us/fields.html?xpicked=2&item=Fields; ADL, *Extremism*, p. 136; "List of nationalist meetings and demonstrations in America," http://en.metapedia.org/wiki/List_of_nationalist_meetings_and_demonstrations_in_America; "Wrightsville, Georgia, Racial Demonstrations," CBS News, April 12, 1980; Donald Grant, *The Way It Was in the South: The Black Experience in Georgia* (New York: Birch Lane Press, 1993), pp. 449–51; Drabble, "The FBI, COINTELPRO ... North Carolina."
5. FBI Files, Jesse Stoner; Greene, p. 408; Webb, "Freedom"; McWhorter, p. 134; *Atlanta Constitution*, July 31, 1980; "Jesse Benjamin Stoner," http://www.ourcampaigns.com/CandidateDetail.html?CandidateID=76937.
6. FBI Files, Jesse Stoner;
7. *Ibid.*
8. *Ibid.*; *Stoner v. Graddick*; *Washington Post*, February 12 and June 3, 1983; Holley; Nunnelley, p. 137.
9. FBI Files, Jesse Stoner; McWhorter, p. 575.
10. "James Clayton Vaughn Jr., AKA Joseph Paul Franklin," http://maamodt.asp.radford.edu/Psyc%20405/serial%20killers/Franklin,%20Joseph%20Paul.pdf.
11. ADL, *Extremism*, 80; ADL, *Hate Groups*, p. 9; Neighbors Network, *Shadow*, p. 3; Wells.
12. Neighbors Network, *Shadow*, p. 3; ADL, *Extremism*, pp. 39–40, 57, 74, 144; "List of nationalist meetings and demonstrations in America," http://en.metapedia.org/wiki/List_of_nationalist_meetings_and_demonstrations_in_America; Sher, p. 184.
13. ADL, *Extremism*, p. 137; ADL, *Hate*, p. ADL, *KKK*, pp. 11–12; "Edward Fields," http://archive.adl.org/learn/ext_us/fields.html?xpicked=2&item=Fields; Webb, *Rabble*, p. 208; Cooper, "Brief History"; Neighbors Network, *Shadow*, p. 4.
14. "Bertrand Comparet," http://en.metapedia.org/wiki/Bertrand_Comparet; Massengill, p. 301; Brent

Smith, *Terrorism in America: Pipe Bombs and Pipe Dreams* (Albany: State University of New York Press, 199), pp. 66–76.

15. Boylan; "Eustace Mullins," http://www.whale.to/c/check.html; "Elizabeth, Queen of the Jews," http://www.lyndonlarouche.org/fascism29.htm; John Coleman, *The Conspirators' Hierarchy: The Committee of 300* (Carson City, NV: America West Publishers & Distributors, 1992).

16. Webb, *Rabble*, p. 208; *Stoner v. Graddick*; Wayne King, "White Supremacists Voice Support of Farrakhan," *New York Times*, October 12, 1985.

17. "Frazier Glenn Miller Jr.," http://www.ourcampaigns.com/CandidateDetail.html?CandidateID=38408; ADL. *Extremism*, p. 85; "Roy Frankhouser," http://laroucheplanet.info/pmwiki/pmwiki.php?n=Cult.RoyFrankhouser; Kelly.

18. Ridgeway, pp. 147–9; Bridges, p. 136; "U.S. President National Vote," http://www.ourcampaigns.com/RaceDetail.html?RaceID=1936.

19. "Frazier Glenn Miller Jr.," http://www.ourcampaigns.com/CandidateDetail.html?CandidateID=38408; "Edward Fields," http://archive.adl.org/learn/ext_us/fields.html?xpicked=2&item=Fields; Webb, *Rabble*, p. 208; Webb, "Freedom for All?"; *Atlanta Constitution*, November 13, 1986.

20. Center for Democratic Renewal, pp. 34–5; ADL, *Hate*, pp. 37–8; "Edward Reed Fields," http://en.metapedia.org/wiki/Edward_R._Fields; Bridges, pp. 128–30; Neighbors Network, *Shadow*, p. 5; "Forsyth County Civil Rights March, January 1987, http://www.aboutnorthgeorgia.com/ang/Civil_Rights_March,_January,_1987; Drabble, "COINTELPRO—WHITE HATE ... Georgia"; *McKinney v. Southern White Knights*, 934 F.2d 1265, No. 90-8512, 1991; Donald Grant, *The Way It Was in the South*, pp. 554–5.

21. Spencer Sherman, "The Hmong's Blue Ridge Refuge," http://aliciapatterson.org/stories/hmongs-blue-ridge-refuge.

22. Edward Fields, personal letter to the author, December 6, 2015; Rick Cooper, "Brief History."

23. "Fugitive Racist Leader Is Captured in Missouri," *New York Times*, May 1, 1987; Suall and Lowe; "Glenn Miller," http://en.metapedia.org/wiki/Glenn_Miller.

24. Ronald Ostrow and Kevin Roderick, "Extremist's Ex-Aide Disclosed Alleged Statement FBI Tells of Threat by LaRouche," *Los Angeles Times*, October 10, 1986; Joyce Gemperlein, "LaRouche Probe Snares Man with a Past of Hate," *Philadelphia Inquirer*, November 10, 1986; John Mintz, "Judge Delays Trials of LaRouche, Six Associates; Case of Former Ku Klux Klan Leader Frankhouser Is Severed and Will Be Tried First," *Washington Post*, October 21, 1987; Matthew Wald, "LaRouche Taken in by Aide, Trial Told," *New York Times*, December 10, 1987; "Roy Frankhouser," http://laroucheplanet.info/pmwiki/pmwiki.php?n=Cult.RoyFrankhouser; Kelly.

25. "Charges Announced," CBS News, February 18, 1988; "Edward Fields," http://archive.adl.org/learn/ext_us/fields.html?xpicked=2&item=Fields; "Fort Smith Sedition Trial," http://en.metapedia.org/wiki/Fort_Smith_Sedition_Trial; Neighbors Network, *Shadow*, p. 5; "Woman with Ties to White Supremacists Represents School for Blacks and Hispanics," Fox News, July 30, 2008.

26. FBI Files, Jesse Stoner.

27. Schmaltz, p. 339; "Willis Carto and the IHR," http://www.nizkor.org/faqs/ihr/ihr-faq-04.html; "NH U.S. Vice President—D Primary," http://www.ourcampaigns.com/RaceDetail.html?RaceID=393638 ; Bridges, pp. 136–8; "us President National Vote," http://www.ourcampaigns.com/RaceDetail.html?RaceID=1935; ADL, *Hate Groups*, p. 3.

28. "David Duke," http://www.ourcampaigns.com/CandidateDetail.html?CandidateID=4279; Jason Berry, "A Master Racist Jumps Parties to Land in the Louisiana Legislature," *Los Angeles Times*, February 26, 1989.

29. Neighbors Network, *Hatred in Georgia*, 1993, pp. 20, 30; Neighbors Network, *Shadow*, p. 5.

Chapter 16

1. Neighbors Network, *Hatred 1990*, pp. 17, 27–8, 30; Neighbors Network, *Shadow*, p. 5; Jesse Stoner, http://www.ourcampaigns.com/CandidateDetail.html?CandidateID=76937; Bridges, p. 175; "LA U.S. SENATE," http://www.ourcampaigns.com/RaceDetail.html?RaceID=3516.

2. "On This Day," https://lcrm.lib.unc.edu/blog/index.php/tag/ernest-ray-mcelveen; "Ernest Raphael 'Ray' McElveen," http://files.usgwarchives.net/la/washington/obits/2003/bogalusad/february.txt; James Hill, "Ex-KKK Leader Was Given a New Identity Years Before Shooting," ABC News, April 24, 2014.; ADL, "Frazier Glenn Miller's Violent Comeback," http://www.adl.org/combating-hate/domestic-extremism-terrorism/c/frazier-glenn-millers-violent-comeback.html.

3. Kinsella, pp. 176–184.

4. "James Clayton Vaughn Jr., AKA Joseph Paul Franklin," http://maamodt.asp.radford.edu/Psyc%20405/serial%20killers/Franklin,%20Joseph%20Paul.pdf.

5. Massengill, pp. 2, 6, 9, 10; *De La Beckwith v. State*; "Edward Fields," http://archive.adl.org/learn/ext_us/fields.html?xpicked=2&item=Fields.

6. Neighbors Network, *Hatred 1991*, pp. 19, 20, 27, 29, 40; Neighbors Network, *Shadow*, p. 5; "Edward Fields," http://archive.adl.org/learn/ext_us/fields.html?xpicked=2&item=Fields; "Willis Carto and the IGR," http://www.nizkor.org/faqs/ihr/ihr-faq-04.html.

7. Neighbors Network, *Hatred 1992*, pp. viii, ix, 11, 14; Neighbors Network, *Shadow*, pp. 5–6; Edward Fields," http://archive.adl.org/learn/ext_us/fields.html?xpicked=2&item=Fields; John Sugg, "A Kinder, Gentler Racism," http://clatl.com/atlanta/a-kinder-gentler-racism/Content?oid=1266094; "Flag of Georgia (U.S. State)," https://en.wikipedia.org/wiki/Flag_of_Georgia_%28U.S._state%29.

8. Joanna Weiss and Karen Turni, "Candidate Linked to White Supremacist Group," *Times-Picayune* (New Orleans), November 14, 1995; "Election Results by Precinct," http://staticresults.sos.la.gov/10211995/10211995_44_8720_Precinct.html; *Warner v. St. Bernard Parish School Board*.

9. Ben Shapiro, "Pat Buchanan, Anti-Semite," *Front Page Magazine*, March 1, 2012; ADL, "Patrick Buchanan: Unrepentant Bigot" May 21, 2009; Neighbors Network, *Hatred 1992*, pp. viii, ix, 2, 5, 14, 26; Neighbors Network, *Shadow*, p. 5; "James 'Bo' Gritz," http://www.ourcampaigns.com/CandidateDetail.html?CandidateID=4270.

10. Neighbors Network, *Hatred 1993*, pp. 3, 13, 17, 62; Neighbors Network, *Shadow*, p. 5; Edward Fields," http://archive.adl.org/learn/ext_us/fields.html?xpicked=2&item=Fields.

11. "My Skin Is My Sin" lyrics, http://www.lyricsmode.com/lyrics/i/ice_cube/my_skin_is_my_sin.html.

12. Kelly.

13. Neighbors Network, *Hatred 1993*, p. vi; "Edward Fields," http://archive.adl.org/learn/ext_us/fields.html?xpicked=2&item=Fields; Greene, pp. 403–4, 411; Frank

Murray, "Vague federal obstruction laws create legal headaches," *Washington Times*, August 21, 1998; "Oren F. Potito," http://en.metapedia.org/wiki/Oren_F._Potito.

14. Eric Pace, "John G. Crommelin, 94, Dies," *New York Times*, November 12, 1996; "John G. Crommelin," http://www.ourcampaigns.com/CandidateDetail.html?CandidateID=19159.

15. "Edward Fields," http://archive.adl.org/learn/ext_us/fields.html?xpicked=2&item=Fields; "Holt J. Gewinner," http://sortedbyname.com/pages/g104091.html; "Buchanan Aide Leaves Campaign Amid Charges," *The Union Leader* (Manchester, NH), February 16, 1996; "Another Buchanan Aide Tied to Supremacists," *Spokesman Review* (Spokane, WA), February 17, 1996.

16. John Archibald and Jeff Hansen, "Death spares scrutiny of Cash in bomb probe," *Birmingham News*, September 7, 1997; "1963 Birmingham church bombing timeline," http://www.cnn.com/2013/09/13/us/birmingham-bombing-timeline/index.html; Yvonne Lamb, "Birmingham Bomber Bobby Frank Cherry Dies in Prison at 74," *Washington Post*, November 19, 2004; "Thomas Edwin Blanton Jr.," http://www.doc.state.al.us/InmateHistory.aspx.

17. Michael Dobbs, "Albright's Family Tragedy Comes to Light," *Washington Post*, February 4, 1997; David Duke, *My Awakening* (Covington, LA: Free Speech Press, 1998), p. 321.

18. "Klansman must pay 10% of his income and apologize to housing worker in bias lawsuit settlement," *Jet*, May 29, 2000, p. 9.

19. " Frederick John Kasper Jr.," http://en.metapedia.org/wiki/John_Kasper; INSERT OTHER "Edward Fields," http://archive.adl.org/learn/ext_us/fields.html?xpicked=2&item=Fields; "White supremacist plans appeal for church," York (PA) *Daily Record*, December 4, 1998.

20. "Alton Wayne Roberts," https://en.wikipedia.org/wiki/Alton_Wayne_Roberts.

21. "The Winrod Legacy of Hate"; Associated Press, "White Supremacist Pastor Convicted," January 15, 2001; "Supremacist sentenced to 30 years in prison for abductions," *Lawrence* (KS) *Journal-World*, March 20, 2001; Associated Press, "Minister to Pay $26M for Abduction." Associated Press. May 4, 2002; "Winrod to Be Released from Prison May 11," *Ozark County Times* (MO), April 19, 2012.

22. Edward Fields," http://archive.adl.org/learn/ext_us/fields.html?xpicked=2&item=Fields; Charles Lardner, "City, Uncertain What to Expect, Braces for KKK rally," *Intelligencer Journal* (Lancaster, PA), September 8, 2001; "Emory Burke," http://en.metapedia.org/wiki/Emory_Burke.

23. "Neuman Britton," http://archive.adl.org/presrele/extremism_72/3203_72.html; "Lawsuit may force Aryan move to San Diego area," *Idaho Statesman*, September 5, 2000; Erin Massey, "Escondido white supremacist dies," *San Diego Union-Tribune*, August 21, 2001; Cooper, "Brief History."

24. Ben Torpy, "No Remorse: An Old Bigot Wastes Away," *Atlanta Journal-Constitution*, July 22, 2004; "J. B. Stoner; bombed black church in 1958," *Boston Globe*, April 28, 2005.

25. ADL, "White People's Party Attempts Political Activity," July 21, 2005; "The Year in Hate," SPLC *Intelligence Report* no. 157 (Spring 2015): 45.

26. "Glenn Miller," http://en.metapedia.org/wiki/Glenn_Miller; "Frazier Glenn Miller Jr.," http://www.ourcampaigns.com/CandidateDetail.html?CandidateID=38408.

27. "James Clayton Vaughn Jr., AKA Joseph Paul Franklin," http://maamodt.asp.radford.edu/Psyc%20405/serial%20killers/Franklin,%20Joseph%20Paul.pdf; "Joseph Paul Franklin, white supremacist serial killer, executed in Missouri," CBS News, November 20, 2016.

28. "Brother of Neo-Nazi Leader William Hoff Jr. Speaks Out," https://www.splcenter.org/fighting-hate/intelligence-report/2007/brother-neo-nazi-leader-william-hoff-jr-speaks-out; "Nazi Icon Part African American?" http://niksnest.blogspot.com/2007_04_01_archive.html.

29. "National States Rights Party," https://www.stormfront.org/forum/t395206.

30. Ibid.

31. Ibid.

32. Ibid.

33. Kelly.

34. "Glenn Miller," http://en.metapedia.org/wiki/Glenn_Miller; Thomas Wellborn, "Glenn Miller, Proud KKK Leader, Runs for Senate from Missouri," http://www.alan.com/2010/04/03/glenn-miller-proud-kkk-leader-runs-for-senate-from-missouri/#; "Frazier Glenn Miller Jr.," http://www.ourcampaigns.com/CandidateDetail.html?CandidateID=38408.

35. "Glenn Miller," http://en.metapedia.org/wiki/Glenn_Miller; Gene Hartley, White supremacist Glenn Miller from Aurora faces 2 murder charges," Channel KY3 (Springfield, MO), April 15, 2014; "Frazier Glenn Miller argues in court that the murders he committed in Kansas were 'necessary,'" *Times of Israel*, July 18, 2015; "White supremacist convicted of Jewish site killings," CBS News, August 31, 2015; "White supremacist Frazier Glenn Miller sentenced to die" (September 8, 2015), https://www.newshub.org/white-supremacist-frazier-glenn-miller-sentenced-die-18412530.html#; Catherine Shoichet, "Judge sentences Frazier Glenn Cross to death," CNN, November 11, 2015.

36. "Matt Koehl Passes into History," http://www.theneworder.org/news/2014/11/matt-koehl-passes-into-history.

37. "The Truth at Last," https://www.stormfront.org/truth_at_last/index2.htm; "The Truth at Last Archives," http://israelect.com/reference/WillieMartin/NameChangers.htm.

38. "The Year in Hate," SPLC *Intelligence Review* mo. 157 (Spring 2015): 45–48.

Bibliography

Books

Adams, Don. *From an Office Building with a High-Powered Rifle: One FBI Agent's View of the JFK Assassination*. Walterville, OR: Trine Day, 2012.

Anti-Defamation League. *Extremism on the Right*. New York: ADL, 1983.

———. *Hate Groups in America*. New York: ADL, 1988.

———. *The KKK and the Neo-Nazis*. New York: ADL, 1984.

Arsenault, Raymond. *Freedom Riders: 1961 and the Struggle for Racial Justice*. New York: Oxford University Press, 2006.

Ayton, Mel. *Dark Soul of the South: The Life and Crimes of Racist Killer Joseph Paul Franklin*. Dulles, VA: Potomac, 2011.

Bailey, Elaine. *Explosion in Villa Rica*. Douglasville, GA: Lillium, 2011.

Barkun, Michael. *Religion and the Racist Right: The Origins of the Christian Identity Movement*. Chapel Hill: University of North Carolina Press, 1996.

Bartley, Numan. *The Rise of Massive Resistance: Race and Politics in the South During the 1950s*. Baton Rouge: Louisiana State University Press, 1969.

Branch, Taylor. *Pillar of Fire: America in the King Years, 1963–65*. New York: Simon & Schuster, 1999.

Bridges, Tyler. *The Rise of David Duke*. Oxford: University Press of Mississippi, 1995.

Carlson, John [pseud.]. *Under Cover*. New York: E. P. Dutton, 1943.

Carter, Dan. *The Politics of Rage: George Wallace, the Origins of the New Conservatism, and the Transformation of American Politics*. Baton Rouge: Louisiana State University Press, 2000.

Center for Democratic Renewal. *They Don't All Wear Sheets: A Chronology of Racist and Far Right Violence, 1980–1986*. Atlanta: CDR, 1987.

Chalmers, David. *Hooded Americanism: The History of the Ku Klux Klan*. Durham, NC: Duke University Press, 1987.

Clark, E. Culpepper. *The Schoolhouse Door: Segregation's Last Stand at the University of Alabama*. New York: Oxford University Press, 1993.

Cobbs, Elizabeth, and Petric Smith. *Long Time Coming*. Birmingham, AL: Crane Hill, 1994.

Collins, Rodnell. *Seventh Child: A Family Memoir of Malcolm X*. New York: Citadel, 2000.

Cook, James. *The Segregationists*. New York: Appleton-Century-Crofts, 1962.

Dorman, Michael. *We Shall Overcome*. New York: Delacorte, 1964.

Doyle, William. *An American Insurrection: James Meredith and the Battle of Oxford, Mississippi, 1962*. New York: Anchor, 2003.

Epstein, Benjamin, and Arnold Forster. *The Radical Right: Report on the John Birch Society and Its Allies*. New York: Random House Trade Paperbacks, 1967.

———. *Report on the John Birch Society*. New York: Random House, 1966.

Flynn, Kevin, and Gary Gerheart. *The Silent Brotherhood*. New York: Signet, 1990.

Forster, Arnold, and Benjamin Epstein. *Danger on the Right*. New York: Random House, 1964.

———. *Report on the Ku Klux Klan*. New York: Anti-Defamation League, 1966.

Garrow, David. *St. Augustine, Florida, 1963–1964: Mass Protest and Racial Violence*. New York: Carlson, 1989.

Gillette, Paul, and Eugene Tillinger. *Inside Ku Klux Klan*. New York: Pyramid, 1965.

Greene, Melissa. *The Temple Bombing*. Reading, MA: Addison-Wesley, 1996.

Higham, Charles. *American Swastika: The Shocking Story of Nazi Collaborators in Our Midst from 1933 to the Present Day*. New York: Doubleday, 1985.

Hill, Lance. *The Deacons for Defense: Armed Resistance and the Civil Rights Movement*. Chapel Hill: University of North Carolina Press, 2004.

Jones, J. Harry. *The Minutemen*. Garden City, NY: Doubleday, 1968.

Kaplan, Jeffrey. *Encyclopedia of White Power: A Sourcebook on the Radical Racist Right*. Lanham, MD: AltaMira, 2000.

Kellman, George. "Anti-Jewish Agitation." In *The American Jewish Year Book 61* (New York: American Jewish Committee, 1960), pp. 41–49.

Kennedy, Stetson. *The Klan Unmasked*. Gainesville: University Press of Florida, 1990.

Kinsella, Warren. *Web of Hate: Inside Canada's Far Right Network*. New York: HarperCollins, 2001.

Kruse, Kevin. *White Flight: Atlanta and the Making of Modern Conservatism*. Princeton, NJ: Princeton University Press, 2005.

Levitas, Daniel. *The Terrorist Next Door: The Militia Movement and the Radical Right*. New York: Thomas Dunne, 2004.

Lord, Walter. *The Past That Would Not Die*. New York: Harper & Row, 1965.

MacDonald, Andrew [pseud.]. *Hunter*. Hillsboro, WV: National Alliance, 1989.

Marsh, Alec. *John Kasper and Ezra Pound: Saving the Republic*. New York: Bloomsbury Academic, 2015.

Massengill, Reed. *Portrait of a Racist: The Real Life of Byron De La Beckwith*. New York: St. Martin's, 1997.

May, Gary. *The Informant: The FBI, the Ku Klux Klan, and the Murder of Viola Liuzzo*. New Haven, CT: Yale University Press, 2005.

McMillan, George. *The Making of an Assassin*. New York: Little, Brown, 1976.

McMillen, Neil. *The Citizens' Council: Organized Resistance to the Second Reconstruction, 1954–64*. Champaign: University of Illinois Press, 1971.

McWhorter, Diane. *Carry Me Home: Birmingham, Alabama: The Climactic Battle of the Civil Rights Revolution*. New York: Simon & Schuster, 2001.

Mendelsohn, Jack. *The Martyrs: Sixteen Who Gave Their Lives for Racial Justice*. New York: Harper & Row, 1966.

Muhammad, Elijah. *Message to the Blackman in America*. Phoenix, AZ: Secretarius Memps, 1997.

Myers, Gustavus, edited and revised by Henry Christman. *History of Bigotry in the United States*. Oakville, ON: Capricorn, 1960.

Nelson, Jack. *Terror in the Night: The Klan's Campaign Against the Jews*. Oxford: University Press of Mississippi, 1996.

Newton, Michael. *A Case of Conspiracy*. Los Angeles: Holloway House, 1980.

_____. *The Invisible Empire: The Ku Klux Klan in Florida*. Gainesville: University Press of Florida, 2001.

_____. *Ku Klux Terror: Birmingham, Alabama, from 1966–Present*. Atglen, PA: Schiffer, 2013.

_____. *The Ku Klux Klan in Mississippi: A History*. Jefferson, NC: McFarland, 2010.

_____. *Unsolved Civil Rights Murders, 1934–1970*. Jefferson, NC: McFarland, 2016.

_____. *White Robes and Burning Crosses: A History of the Ku Klux Klan from 1966*. Jefferson, NC: McFarland, 2014.

Nunnelley, William. *Bull Connor*. Tuscaloosa: University of Alabama Press, 1991.

Parker, Thomas (ed.). *Violence in the U.S.*, vol. 1, 1956–67. New York: Facts on File, 1974.

Patterson, William (ed.). *We Charge Genocide: The Historic Petition to the United Nations for Relief From a Crime of The United States Government Against the Negro People*. New York: Civil Rights Congress, 1951.

Reed, Roy. *Faubus: The Life and Times of an American Prodigal*. Fayetteville: University of Arkansas Press, 1999.

Rice, Arnold. *The Ku Klux Klan in American Politics*. Washington, D.C.: Public Affairs, 1962.

Ridgeway, James. *Blood in the Face: The Ku Klux Klan, Aryan Nations, Nazi Skinheads, and the Rise of a New White Culture*. New York: Thunder's Mouth, 1995

Rosenthal, A. M., and Arthur Gelb. *One More Victim: The Life and Death of a Jewish Nazi*. New York: New American Library, 1967.

Rowe, Gary. *My Undercover Years with the Ku Klux Klan*. New York: Bantam, 1976.

Schmaltz, William. *Hate: George Lincoln Rockwell and the American Nazi Party*. Lincoln, NE: Brassey's, 1999.

Sher, Julian. *White Hoods: Canada's Ku Klux Klan*. Vancouver, BC: New Star, 1980.

Sherrill, Robert. *Gothic Politics in the Old South*. New York: Grossman, 1968.

Simonelli, Frederick. *American Fuehrer: George Lincoln Rockwell and the American Nazi Party*. Champaign: University of Illinois Press, 1999.

Sims, Patsy. *The Klan*. New York: Stein and Day, 1978.

Stanton, Mary. *Freedom Walk: Mississippi or Bust*. Oxford: University Press of Mississippi, 2003.

Tarrants, Thomas, III. *The Conversion of a Klansman: The Story of a Former Ku Klux Klan Terrorist*. New York: Doubleday, 1979.

Terry, Maury. *The Ultimate Evil*. Lyndhurst, NJ: Barnes & Noble, 2000.

Tully, Andrew. *The FBI's Most Famous Cases*. New York: Dell, 1965.

Turner, William. *Power on the Right*. Berkley, CA: Ramparts, 1971.

Waldron, Lamar, and Thom Hartmann. *Legacy of Secrecy: The Long Shadow of the JFK Assassination*. Berkeley, CA: Counterpoint, 2009.

Wallace, Max. *The American Axis: Henry Ford, Charles Lindbergh, and the Rise of the Third Reich*. New York: St. Martin's, 2004.

Webb, Clive. *Rabble Rousers: The American Far Right in the Civil Rights Era*. Athens: University of Georgia Press, 2010.

Wexler, Stuart, and Larry Hancock. *The Awful Grace of God: Religious Terrorism, White Supremacy, and the Unsolved Murder of Martin Luther King, Jr*. Berkeley, CA: Counterpoint, 2012.

Zatarain, Michael. *David Duke: Evolution of a Klansman*. Gretna, LA: Pelican, 1990.

Articles

Armbrister, Trevor. "Portrait of an Extremist." *Saturday Evening Post* (August 22, 1964): 80–83.

"At Least 12 Are Killed in Georgia Gas Blast." *Progress-Index* (Petersburg VA), December 6, 1957.

Blumberg, Janice. "The Bomb That Healed: A Personal Memoir of the Bombing of the Temple in Atlanta, 1958." *American Jewish History* 73 (1983).

Christensen, Dan. "JFK, King: Miami Links." *Miami Magazine*, September 1976.

———. "King Assassination: FBI Ignored Its Miami Informer." *Miami Magazine*, October 1976.

———. "A Miami Police Informant, a Prophetic Racist and Fresh Questions about JFK's Death." *Florida Bulldog*, November 12, 2013.

"Columbians Seeking Bond." *Pittsburgh Post-Gazette*, December 16, 1946.

Cooper, Lisa. "Our History: The Villa Rica Explosion." *Douglasville* (GA) *Patch*, March 11, 2013.

"Cowan Had 4 Pistols but Not One Permit." *New York Times*, February 16, 1977.

Denholm, Kristine. "Chasing Ghosts in a Civil Rights Era Cop Killing." *Police*, October 2010.

Drabble, John. "The FBI, COINTELPRO-WHITE HATE and the Decline Ku Klux Klan Organizations in Alabama, 1964–1971." *Alabama Review* 61 (February 2008): 3–47.

———. "The FBI, COINTELPRO-WHITE HATE and the Decline of Ku Klux Klan Organizations in Mississippi, 1964–1971." *Journal of Mississippi History* 66 (Winter 2004): 353–401.

———. "From White Supremacy to White Power: The FBI's COINTELPRO-WHITE HATE Operation and the 'Nazification' of the Ku Klux Klan in the 1970s." *American Studies* 48 (Fall 2007): 49–74.

Dudley, J. Wayne. "'Hate' Organizations of the 1940s: The Columbians, Inc." *Phylon* 42 (1981): 262–274.

Egerton, John. "Walking into History: The Beginning of School Desegregation in Nashville." *Southern Spaces*, May 4, 2009.

Fleming, John. "The Death of Willie Brewster: The Agent, the Judge and the Trial." *Anniston Star*, March 23, 2009.

———. "The Death of Willie Brewster: Finding Strength in the Pain." *Anniston Star*, March 25, 2009.

———. "The Death of Willie Brewster: Guns, Bombs, and Kenneth Adams." *Anniston Star*, March 24, 2009.

———. "The Death of Willie Brewster: Memories of a Dark Time." *Anniston Star*, March 22, 2009.

"Four Arrested in Murders." *Southern Courier*, September 4–5, 1965.

Gordon, Arthur. "Intruder in the South." *Look* 21 (February 19, 1957): 27–31.

Group Research Inc. "National States Rights Party." April 8, 1964.

Holley, Joe. "Virulent Segregationist J. B. Stoner Dies." *Washington Post*, April 28, 2005.

Huie, William. "The One and Only." *Skeptic* 18 (March/April 1977): 25–27.

———. "The Story of James Earl Ray and the Plot to Kill Martin Luther King, Part 2." *Look* 32 (November 26, 1968): 86–89.

———. "Why James Earl Ray Murdered Dr. King." *Look* 33 (April 15, 1969): 102–112.

"J. B. Stoner; Bombed Black Church in 1958." *Boston Globe*, April 28, 2005.

Keller, Larry. "Deputy Sheriff's Murder Still Unsolved." *SPLC Intelligence Report* 134 (Spring 2009).

———. "J. B. Stoner, Junkyard Dog." *SPLC Intelligence Report* 137 (Spring 2010).

Kelly, Dan. "Longtime KKK Leader Roy E. Frankhouser Jr. of Reading Dies." *Reading* (PA) *Eagle*, May 16, 2009.

Martin, Douglas. "J. B. Stoner, 81, Fervent Racist and Benchmark for Extremism, Dies." *New York Times*, April 29, 2005.

McFadden, Robert. "Nazi Admirer Also Wounds 5 in Wild Attack Followed by Siege at Moving Company." *New York Times*, February 15, 1977.

McMillan, George. "The Birmingham Church Bomber." *Saturday Evening Post* (June 6, 1964): 15–19.

———. "The Klan Scourges Old St. Augustine." *Life* (June 26, 1964).

———. "New Bombing Terrorists of the South Call Themselves NACIREMA—America Spelled Backward." *Life* 11 (October 1963).

Murphy, Robert. "The South Fights Bombing." *Look* 23 (January 6, 1959): 13–17.

"Nacirema: Violent Group Revealed." *Spartanburg* (SC) *Herald*, November 2, 1965.

"New Rochelle Gunman Kills 5 and Then Himself." *New York Times*, February 15, 1977.

Schumach, Murray. "Cowan Was 'Nice Man' to Some in New Rochelle, but to Others 'Real Prejudiced' Backer of Nazis." *New York Times*, February 15, 1977.

Sherrill, Robert. "A Look Inside the Invisible Empire." *New South* (Spring 1968): 4–30.

Suall, Irwin, and David Lowe. "The Hate Movement Today: A Chronicle of Violence and Disarray." *Terrorism* 10 (1987): 345–364.

"The Religious Roots of Domestic Terrorism." *Daily Beast*, August 7, 2015.

Velie, Lester. "The Klan Rides the South Again." *Collier's* 122 (October 9, 1948): 13–15, 74–75.

Weisenburger, Steven. "The Columbians, Inc.: A Chapter of Racial Hatred from the Post-World War II South." *Journal of Southern History* 69 (November 2003): 821–860.

Wieder, Alan. "The New Orleans School Crisis of 1960: Causes and Consequences." *Phylon* 48 (1987): 122–131.

Dissertations and Theses

Blaisdell, Mary Ellen. "The National States Rights Party." University of Florida, 1964.

Duffee, E. B. Jr. "The National States Rights Party." University of Maryland, 1968.

Martinelli, Amy. "A Moderate Calm? Florida's Struggle Over School Desegregation After *Brown*, 1955-1961." University of Florida, 2007.

Webb, Clive. "Freedom for All? Blacks, Jews, and the Political Censorship of White Racists in the Civil Rights Era." *American Jewish History* 94 (December 2008): 267–297.

Wells, Lynn. "The Cedartown Story: The Ku Klux Klan & Labor in 'The New South.'" *Labor Research Review* 1 (1986): 71–79.

Official Documents

Cason v. City of Jacksonville. No. 73–3102, 497 F.2d 949 (1974).

De La Beckwith v. State. 707 So. 2d 547 (Miss. 1997), cert. denied, 525 U.S. 880 (1998).

Federal Bureau of Investigation Files: Bombing of Sixteenth Street Baptist Church; COINTELPRO—White Hate Groups; Democratic Nationalist Party; Robert B. DePugh; F. Allen Mann; Jesse Benjamin Stoner; Frederick John Kasper; Gerald Lyman Kenneth Smith; Kenneth Goff; Millard Grubbs; Minutemen; National Association for the Advancement of White People; National Knights of the Ku Klux Klan; National Renaissance Party; National States Rights Party; National Youth Alliance; Realpolitical Institute; Roy E. Frankhouser Jr.; Sam Adams Committee; Wallace Allen; William Pierce.

Final Report of the House Select Committee on Assassinations, U.S. House of Representatives, Ninety-Fifth Congress. Washington, D.C.: U.S. Government Printing Office, 1979.

Illinois Legislative Investigating Committee. *Ku Klux Klan: A Report to the Illinois General Assembly*. Chicago: ILIC, 1976.

James Earl Ray, Plaintiff-Appellant, v. Percy Foreman, William Bradford Huie, and Arthur J. Hanes, Sr., Defendants-appellees. 441 F.2d 1266 (6th Cir. 1971).

J. B. Stoner, Petitioner-Appellant, v. Charles Graddick, Attorney General of Alabama; and Freddie Smith, Commissioner of the Alabama Department of Corrections, Respondents-Appellees. 17 Fed. R. Evid. Serv. 366, No. 83-7535, 1985.

John Kasper v. State of Tennessee. 326 S.W.2d 664 (1959).

Joseph Carroll, et al., Petitioners, v. President and Commissioners of Princess Anne, et al. 393 U.S. 175 (89 S.Ct. 347, 21 L.Ed.2d 325), 1968.

Kirkham, James, Sheldon Levy, and William Crotty. *Assassination and Political Violence: A Staff Report to the National Commission on the Causes and Prevention of Violence.* New York: Bantam, 1970.

Loomis v. State. Court of Appeals of Georgia, Division No. 2, December 3, 1948.

Para-Military Organizations in California. Sacramento: California Attorney General's Office, 1965.

The Present-Day Ku Klux Klan Movement, Report by the Committee on Un-American Activities, House of Representatives, Ninetieth Congress. Washington, D.C.: U.S. Government Printing Office, 1967.

The Present-Day Ku Klux Klan Movement, Hearings Before the Committee on Un-American Activities, House of Representatives, Ninetieth Congress, Vols. 1–5. Washington, D.C.: U.S. Government Printing Office, 1967.

Racial and Civil Disorders in St. Augustine. Tallahassee: Florida Legislative Investigating Committee, 1965.

Report of the Florida Legislative Investigating Committee. Tallahassee: Florida Legislative Investigating Committee, 1965.

U.S. Department of Justice. Oxford Riot Files, September 16, 1963.

Warner v. St. Bernard Parish School Board. No. 96–1839, 99 F.Supp.2d 748 (2000).

Internet Sources

"Assassinations: Miami link, Part I." http://cuban-exile.com/doc_101-125/doc0122.html.

Boylan, D. "A League of Their Own: A Look Inside the Christian Defense League," http://cuban-exile.com/doc_026-050/doc0046.html.

"Confronting the Klan in Bogalusa with Nonviolence & Self-Defense (Jan–July 1965)." http://www.crmvet.org/tim/tim65b.htm#1965bogalusa.

Cooper, Lisa. "The Villa Rica Explosion." http://www.drbronsontours.com/bronsonhistorypageamericancivilrights.html.

Cooper, Rick. "A Brief History of White Nationalism." http://www.hugequestions.com/Eric/TFC/History-of-White-Nationalism.html.

Cuban Information Archives. http://cuban-exile.com.

Drabble, John. "The FBI, COINTELPRO-WHITE HATE, and the Ku Klux Klan in Florida, 1964–

1971." http://www.geocities.ws/drabbs/workingpapers.html.

———. "The FBI, COINTELPRO-WHITE HATE, and the Ku Klux Klan in Georgia, 1964–1971." http://www.geocities.ws/drabbs/workingpapers.html.

———. "The FBI, COINTELPRO-WHITE HATE, and the Ku Klux Klan in Louisiana, 1964–1971." http://www.geocities.ws/drabbs/workingpapers.html.

———. "The FBI, COINTELPRO-WHITE HATE, and the Ku Klux Klan in North Carolina, 1964–1971." http://www.geocities.ws/drabbs/workingpapers.html.

———. "The FBI, COINTELPRO-WHITE HATE, and the Ku Klux Klan in South Carolina, 1964–1971," http://www.geocities.ws/drabbs/workingpapers.html.

———. "The FBI, COINTELPRO-WHITE HATE, and the Ku Klux Klan in Tennessee, 1964–1971." http://www.geocities.ws/drabbs/workingpapers.html.

———. "The FBI, COINTELPRO-WHITE HATE, and the Ku Klux Klan in Virginia, 1964–1971." http://www.geocities.ws/drabbs/workingpapers.html.

———. "FBI Covert Operations and Suppression of Ku Klux Klan Violence, 1964–1971." http://www.geocities.ws/drabbs/workingpapers.html.

"Edward Fields." http://archive.adl.org/learn/ext_us/fields.html?xpicked=2&item=Fields.

Encyclopedia of Alabama. http://www.encyclopediaofalabama.org.

Encyclopedia of Arkansas History & Culture. http://www.encyclopediaofarkansas.net.

Ernie Lazar FOIA Collection. https://archive.org/details/lazarfoia.

"The 54th Anniversary of the Dynamite Bombing of Hattie Cotton Elementary." http://enclave-nashville.blogspot.com/2011/09/54th-anniversary-of-dynamite-bombing-of.html.

Griffin, Robert. "The Tale of John Kasper." http://www.robertsgriffin.com/TaleKasper.pdf.

Hague, Seth. "'Niggers Ain't Gonna Run This Town': Militancy, Conflict and the Sustenance of the Hegemony in Bogalusa, Louisiana." http://www.loyno.edu/~history/journal/1997-8/Hague.html.

Maloney, J. J. "James Earl Ray." http://hrsbstaff.ednet.ns.ca/waymac/African%20Canadian%20Studies/MLK%20Assassination%20Investigation/james_earl_ray%20by%20Maloney.htm.

Metapedia: The Alternative Encyclopedia. http://en.metapedia.org/wiki/Main_Page.

Miller, F. Glenn. *A White Man Speaks Out.* http://www.whty.org/book.

"National States Rights Party." https://www.stormfront.org/forum/t395206.

Neighbors Network. *Hatred in Georgia, 1989.* https://radicalarchives.files.wordpress.com/2013/03/1989-hatred-in-georgia.pdf.

———. *Hatred in Georgia, 1990.* https://radicalarchives.files.wordpress.com/2013/01/1990-hatred-in-georgia.pdf.

———. *Hatred in Georgia, 1991.* https://radicalarchives.files.wordpress.com/2013/01/1991-hatred-in-georgia.pdf.

———. *Hatred in Georgia, 1992.* https://radicalarchives.files.wordpress.com/2013/01/1992-hatred-in-georgia.pdf.

———. *Hatred in Georgia, 1993.* https://radicalarchives.files.wordpress.com/2013/01/1993-hatred-in-georgia.pdf.

———. *The Shadow of Hatred: Hate Group Activity in Cobb County,* https://radicalarchives.files.wordpress.com/2013/03/shadow-of-hatred.pdf.

Neely, Jack. "The Poet and the Terrorist: The Strange Story of John Kasper." http://www.metropulse.com/stories/features/poet-terrorist-strange-story-john-kasper.

New Georgia Encyclopedia. http://www.georgiaencyclopedia.org.

"1960: JFK vs. LBJ vs. Nixon." http://www.davidpietrusza.com/1960-third-parties.html.

"1965: Selma & the March to Montgomery." http://www.crmvet.org/tim/timhis65.htm#1965selmacourthouse.

Pietrsusza, David. "1960: LBJ vs. JFK vs. Nixon," http://www.davidpietrusza.com/1960-third-parties.html.

Presidential Election Results, 1964, John Kasper. http://www.statemaster.com/graph/pre_1964_pop_vot_for_joh_kas-1964-popular-votes-john-kasper.

"Racial Shooting in Berea on 1 Sep. 1968." Berea Encyclopedia, http://bereaencyclopedia.blogspot.com/2005/05/racial-shooting-in-berea-on-1-sep-1968.html.

"The Religious Roots of Domestic Terror." http://www.thedailybeast.com/articles/2015/08/07/the-religious-roots-of-domestic-terror.html.

St. Augustine Civil Rights, 1960–1965. http://www.drbronsontours.com/bronsonhistorypageamericancivilrights.html.

"St. Augustine Ku Klux Klan Rally, September 18, 1963." http://www.drbronsontours.com/bronsonstaugustinekkk2.html.

Tennessee Encyclopedia of History and Culture. http://tennesseeencyclopedia.net/index.php.

The Truth at Last. https://www.stormfront.org/truth_at_last/index2.htm.

Wikipedia: The Free Encyclopedia. https://www.wikipedia.org.

"The Winrod Legacy of Hate." http://www.adl.org/assets/pdf/combating-hate/The-Winrod-Legacy-of-Hate.pdf.

Index

Aaron, Edward 33
ABC News 132, 176
Action (newsletter) 85
Adams, Donald 109, 113
Adams, Hugh 67
Adams, Kenneth 74, 75, 76, 80, 82, 88, 103, 104, 138, 174
Adams, P.M. 22
Admiral Semmes Hotel 128
Adolf Eichmann Trial Facts Committee 68
Ainsworth, Kathryn 157, 158, 160, 167, 180, 182
Ainsworth, Ralph 157
Akin, James 13, 20, 23
Alabama 12, 24, 25, 32, 33, 37, 38, 43, 45, 47, 50, 52, 56, 67, 68, 70, 74
Alabama Christian Movement for Human Rights 55
Alabama Knights of the Ku Klux Klan 67, 74, 75, 76, 77, 80, 84, 87–88, 90, 95, 99, 101, 111, 114, 122, 125, 126, 127, 130, 137, 138, 139, 141, 145, 146, 151, 152, 154, 160, 161, 163, 165, 169, 171, 176, 180, 185, 186, 187, 190, 192, 199, 201
Alabama State Fair 146
Alabama States Rights Party 128
Albright, Madeleine 202
Alderman, Garland, Sr. 8
Alexander, Dennis 148
Alien Registration Act 8
Allen, Karl 68
Allen, Wallace 43, 45, 56, 58, 59, 201
America, Awake! (book) 8
America First Committee 5, 9, 15
America First, Inc. 8
America First Party 25, 200, 202
America First Radio 201
America in Danger! (newsletter) 8
America Salutes the Heroes of Nashville (pamphlet) 42
American Anti-Communist Society 28
American Bilbo Club 27
American Bulletin (newsletter) 12
American Civil Liberties Union 86, 113

American Committee to Free Cuba 126
American Council of Christian Churches 152
American Destiny Party 5
The American Eagle (pamphlet) 43
American Fascisti Association 4
American Gentile Army 11
American Gentile Protective Association 8, 10
American Independent Party 169
American Independent Youth Alliance 180
American Jewish Committee 36, 67
American Labor Union 192
American League for the Defense of Jewish Rights 18
American Legion 3, 4, 5, 51
American National Party 85
American National-Socialist Party 10
American Nationalist (newsletter) 58, 130
American Nationalist Confederation 4
American National Socialists 9
American Nazi Party 43, 45, 63, 64, 67, 68, 72, 78, 79, 85, 91, 100, 124, 125, 128, 144, 150–151, 158, 159, 176, 180, 182, 196
American Party 170, 174
American States Rights Association 33
American States Rights Party 125, 132, 146
American Vigilant Intelligence Federation 4
American Vigilante Patriots 8
American White Guard 5
Americanism Defense League 5
Americans for Democratic Action 100
Americans for Preservation of the White Race 84, 155, 157
Ancient City Gun Club 116, 117
Anderson, William 99
Andrews, E.E. 22
Andrews, T. Coleman 38, 47, 101

Anglo-Saxon Christian Congregation 7
Anglo-Saxon Clubs of America 17
Anspach, Norman 145, 171
Anti-Communist Christian Association 134
Anti-Defamation League (ADL) 3, 50, 53, 63, 67, 78, 116, 146, 158, 159, 167, 176, 179, 180, 184, 194, 195, 196, 200
App, Austin 169
Arizona 100, 127, 178
Arkansas 65, 67, 69, 70, 102, 126, 127, 134, 145, 152, 157, 169, 172, 175, 185, 196, 202
Armbrister, Trevor 77, 78, 84
Armontrout, Bill 167
Armstrong, Louis 52
Arnall, Ellis 21, 22, 145, 146
Arnold, Morris 196
Aryan Nations 7, 126, 180, 192, 194, 200, 201, 203
Ash, William 185
Asher, Courtland 8
Asone, Gaetano 5
Aspinwall, Leon 142
Associated Klans of America 28
Associated Press 85
Association of Georgia Klans 11, 14, 16, 18, 21, 22, 27
Atlanta Committee for Historical Review 199
Atlanta Constitution (newspaper) 14, 56, 58, 175
Atlanta Journal (newspaper) 20
ATTACK! (newsletter) 169
The Attack (newsletter) 78
Austin, Henry 136
Avery, Harry 165
AWAKE Movement 102

Bagwell, James 47
Bagwell, Robert 126
Bailey, Christopher 68
Baker, Wilson 130
Ballentine, Donald 142
"BAPBOMB" (FBI case) 97, 186, 201, 202
Bardin, Thomas 126
Barker, Bob 174, 179
Barnes, Sidney 157, 163

Index

Barnett, Ross 80, 81, 82, 83, 84, 89, 152, 157
Baton Rouge Morning Advocate (newspaper) 184
Battle, W. Preston 165
Baxley, Bill 186, 190, 194
Baxter, C.M. 47
Baxter, David 8. 10
Bay of Pigs invasion 100
Beach, Henry 172
Bean, John 72-73
Beard, Jacob 191
Beauharnais, Joseph 27, 46, 47, 58, 72, 101
Belgium 185
Bell, Arthur 5
Benjamin, Dale 47
Bennett, Thomas 137
Bergman, Walter 76
Berkowitz, David 186
Bethel Baptist Church 54, 55, 56, 85, 186
Bilbo, Theodore 13, 15, 27, 62
Bing, Norman 186
"Birmingham Daily Bulletins" 89
Birmingham News (newspaper) 146
"Birmingham Plan" 24
Bishop, Ann 65, 70, 72, 125
Bishop, William 19
Black, Chloe 178, 196
Black, Don 176, 179, 182, 186, 189, 191, 192, 194, 196, 198, 206
Black, Jerrold 139
Black Armed Guard 44, 134
Black Front 16
Black Legion 9, 10, 17
Black Muslims *see* Nation of Islam
Black September 179
"Black Tuesday" (1929) 3
Blackwell, Charles 142
Blackwell Real Estate 155
Blanton, Thomas, Jr. 85, 91, 95, 97, 98, 201-202
Blanton, Thomas, Sr. 91, 97
Blevins, Clarence 138
"Bloody Sunday" (Selma, AL) 132
Blue Shirts of Canada 5
B'nai B'rith 3
Bogalusa Voters & Civic League 134
Bogan Junior College 171
bombings: Alabama 33, 52-56, 74, 76, 85, 87, 88, 89, 91, 94, 95-99, 102, 104, 109, 110, 116, 134, 152, 163, 186, 188, 190-191, 201-202; Arkansas 65-66, 67; Florida 52-53, 117-118, 119, 122, 142; Georgia 19, 20, 52, 56-59, 65, 107-108, 201; Louisiana 71, 137, 180; Maryland 185, 191; Mississippi 83, 155, 156, 157, 158, 159, 160, 161, 167, 189; North Carolina 52, 178; Ohio 140, 142; Tennessee 36, 37, 52, 56, 185, 191; Wisconsin 153
Bond, Julian 187
Botnick, Adolph 167, 180

Boutwell, Albert 87, 93, 134
Bowers, Samuel 154, 155, 157, 159, 160, 161, 167
Bowling, Richard 50, 56, 59, 77, 82, 87, 125
Bowling, Robert 31, 50, 55, 56, 58, 59, 77, 79, 82
Brackett, George 110
Brailsford, William 147-148, 176
Branch, H.V. 53
Brandenburg, Clarence 139
Bremer, Arthur 178
Brennemann, Otto 8
Brewer, Albert 178
Brewster, Willie Sr. 138-139
Bright, George 15, 45, 46, 50, 56, 58-59, 77
British Israelism 5
British National Party 199, 201
British Union of Fascists 73
Britton, Frank 130
Britton, Neuman 51, 78, 86, 120, 130, 158, 174, 175, 203
Britton, Patricia 175
Britton, Rufus 78, 86
Brock, James 118, 119, 122
Broenstrupp, Howard 8
Brookshire, Johnny 185, 198
The Broom (newspaper) 8, 28
Brown, Dante 191, 198
Brown, Harry 107
Brown, Jack 98, 101, 103, 104, 105, 106, 107, 109, 110, 163
Brown, Robert 100
Brown v. Board of Education of Topeka 31, 33, 43, 52, 65, 74, 80, 163
Bruce, Melvin 82, 84
Brumback, Oscar 8
Brunson, Charles 117
Bryant, Farris 118, 120, 121
Bryant, Joseph 47, 172
Buchanan, John, Jr. 141
Buchanan, Patrick 200, 201
Buckley, Travis 142, 180
Bundy, Edgar 152
Burbank, Thomas 136
Bureau of Alcohol, Tobacco, and Firearms (ATF) 177, 179, 180, 181, 182, 189
Burke, Emory 12, 13, 14, 15, 16, 17, 19, 20, 21, , 22, 23, 27, 33, 43, 45, 46, 64, 78-79, 82, 86, 107, 125, 192, 200, 203
Burke, James 108
Burns, Haydon 53
Burros, Daniel 85, 143-144, 184
Busbee, George 186-187
Bush, William 159
Butler, George 111-113
Butler, Richard 51, 126, 180, 193, 197, 200, 203
Butler, Smedley 4
Byrd, Garland 145
Byrd, Harry, Sr. 31, 152

Cagle, Charles 76, 87, 88, 89, 91, 94, 97, 98
Cagle, Helen 88

Cahaba River Group 91, 95, 98
Calabria, Marie 78
California 8, 10, 51, 58, 78, 79, 86, 100, 101, 117, 120, 122, 124, 126, 130, 133, 161, 163, 169, 172, 174, 176, 178, 179, 180, 182
California League Against Communism 7
California Rangers 7, 51, 126
Callaway, A.W. 19
Callaway, Howard, Sr. 145-146
Cameron, William 3
Camp Nordland (NJ) 5, 7
Canada 5, 80, 163, 164, 174, 179, 198
Capt, San Jacinto 51
"Captain X" 86
Cardel, Paul 148
Carden, Noah 163
Carlton, Gerald 182
Carmack, Barney 95
Carolina Knights of the Ku Klux Klan 190, 193
Carroll, Joseph 147, 148, 149, 150, 158
Carter, Asa 32, 33, 34, 35, 36, 38, 50, 53, 65, 80, 86, 87, 88, 93, 95, 152, 169, 188
Carter, Jimmy 145, 176, 180, 183
Carto, Willis 124, 152, 169, 170, 176, 182, 193
Cassara, Jack 186
Cash, Herman 89, 91, 95, 98, 186, 201
Cash, William "Jack" 88, 89, 91, 95
Castorina, Paul 4
Castro, Fidel 100, 101, 109
Catholic Church 13, 16, 28, 60, 67, 69, 71, 72, 85, 117, 127, 134, 138, 143, 153, 158, 185, 190, 210
Caulfield, Jack 181
Caulk, Jack 103, 107
CBS News 75, 168, 176
CDL Report (newsletter) 124
Center for Democratic Renewal 194
Central Intelligence Agency (CIA) 33, 171, 183
Chain-Ganged by the Jewish Gestapo (booklet) 27
Chambliss, Robert 33, 52, 53, 65, 75, 87, 89, 91, 93, 94, 95, 97, 98, 102, 186, 190, 191, 201
Cheney, Irwin 116
Cherry, Bobby 95, 98, 201-202
Chicago Freedom Movement
Childers, James 16, 19, 20, 21, 22
Christ of the Ozarks 157
Christenberry, Herbert 136, 137
Christensen, Dan 110-111
Christian Anti-Communism Crusade 152
Christian Anti-Jewish Party 28, 29, 31, 43, 47, 50, 56
Christian Crusade 152
Christian Crusaders League 23
Christian Defense League 7, 51, 78, 100, 102, 117, 124, 126, 130, 184, 186, 192, 193

Christian Front 7, 19, 25, 43
Christian Guard 181
Christian Identity religion 5, 7, 82, 86, 133, 178, 180, 183, 199, 207
Christian Knights of the Invisible Empire 51, 102
Christian Knights of the Ku Klux Klan 38, 60, 62, 63, 73, 74
Christian Military Defense League 125
Christian Nationalist Crusade 7, 17, 23
Christian Nationalist Party 25, 46
Christian Party 9, 38, 39, 40–41, 60, 199
Christian Patriots Crusade 46
Christian Vanguard (newsletter) 124, 178, 183
Christians, George 5
Christopher, Warren 202
Church, Frank 183
Church League of America 152
Church of Jesus Christ—Christian 7, 45, 51, 78, 100, 102, 180
Citizens' Commission to Investigate the FBI 177
Citizens' Councils 32, 33, 34, 36, 36, 37, 38, 43, 54, 56, 63, 64, 66, 67, 71, 82, 88, 101, 110, 130, 134, 136, 141, 152, 169, 170
Citizens for Brailsford Committee 148
Citizen's National Law Enforcement Commission 58
Citizens Protective League 10, 25
Civil Rights Act of 1960 65
Civil Rights Act of 1964 121, 204
Clark, Frank 8, 9
Clark, Jim 82, 130, 131, 132, 139, 152
Clark, Ramsey 164
Clement, Frank 36, 42
Clinton, Bill 201, 202, 206
Cochran, Paul 122
COINTELPRO (FBI operation) 128–129, 155, 158, 177, 180, 181, 195
Cole, Arthur 46
Cole, Carolyn 43
Cole, James 43–45, 46, 47, 59, 60, 61, 142
Cole, Nat 33, 74
Coleman, Bill 122
Coleman, John 184, 186, 192–193
Coleman, Tom 138
Coleman-Warner, Debra 184, 200
Colescott, James 5, 15
Colfield, Mrs. C.C. 103, 110
Collins, Leroy 53
Colorado 33, 101
Columbia Press Service 8
Columbia University 33, 188, 201
Columbian Workers Movement 13
Columbians Inc. 13–23, 27–28, 45, 47, 91, 107, 201
Columbus, Christopher 13
The Coming Red Dictatorship (book) 82

Commercial Appeal (newspaper) 159
Committee of Concern 160
Committee of Conscience 155
Committee of One Million 5
Committee to Free Ezra Pound 49
Committee to Save Our State Flag 200
Common Sense (newsletter) 105, 107
Commoner Party 11
Communist Party USA 128
Comparet, Bertrand 51, 126, 184, 192
Confederate Underground 52, 56, 58
Confederation of Klans 192
Congress of Freedom 109, 110
Congress of Racial Equality (CORE) 74, 134, 146, 148, 149
Connor, Eugene "Bull" 24, 25, 33, 52, 53–56, 74–75, 76, 80, 87, 88, 93, 130
Conrad, Earl 15
Conservative Party of America 93
The Conservative Viewpoint (newsletter) 101
The Conspirators' Hierarchy (book) 193
Constitution Party 38, 47, 101, 107, 109, 110, 157, 171
Cook, James 65
Cook, Tom 55, 74, 76, 88, 190
Cooper, Noel 132
Cooper, Rick 25, 49, 50, 64, 68, 159, 189, 192, 195
Coordinating Council of Community Organizations 150
Copling, John, Jr.
Coral Gables High School 157
Corley, Luther 56, 58
Cotten, Richard 101, 169, 183
Cottonmouth Moccasin Gang 163
Couch, William, Jr. 16
Coughlin, Charles 7, 10, 19
Council of Statehood 128
Courtney, Kent 71
Covington, Harold 182
Cowan, Edna 46, 47
Cowan, Frederick 186
Cox, Earnest 17
Cox, William 159
Craig, Calvin 82, 99, 145
Craig, David 197
Craig, Marilyn 59
Creativity Movement 203
Creel, Robert 88
Crommelin, John, Jr. 37–38, 43, 45, 46, 56, 67, 68, 69, 79, 82, 87, 95, 124, 126, 133, 145, 163, 169, 176, 183, 201
Cross, Frazier *see* Miller, Glenn
The Cross and the Flag (newsletter) 170
Crowder, Charles 190
Crowder, Lee 65
Crowe, Alton 136
Crowe, Dorman 135, 136
Crowe, Robert 136

Crowe, William 99
Crown-Zellerbach Corporation 134
Crusade Against Corruption 194, 199, 201
Crusader (newsletter) 182, 183
Crusader White Shirts 5
Cuba 82, 100, 101, 106, 126, 171, 190, 204
The Cult of Equality (book) 62
Cunningham, Hugh 84, 89
Curtis, Merritt 101
Cusimano, Charles 197

Dade County Board of Instruction 63
Daley, Richard 150, 151
Dall, Curtis 101, 109
Dallas County Voters League 130
Dallas Police Association 112
Daniels, Dan 202
Daniels, Jonathan 138
Davidson, Meyer 167
Davidson, Robert 67
Davis, Lawrence 115, 117, 118, 120, 123, 130
Day, Edward 89
Deacons for Defense and Justice 134–135
Dearborn Independent (newspaper) 3
de Aryan, Constantine 8
Deatherage, George 4, 8, 17
Dees, Morris 196
The Defender (newsletter) 8
DeFries, Ira 138
DeFries, Johnny 138, 139
DeGuello Report 182, 184
De La Beckwith, Byron 84, 89, 142, 155, 180, 182, 183, 190, 198–199
Delenne, Hugh 95
del Valle, Pedro 101, 133, 169
Democratic Nationalist Party 27, 42, 47
Democratic Party 11, 24, 38, 45, 46, 47, 50, 67, 70, 79, 126, 127, 144, 145, 146, 169, 176, 178, 179, 181, 190, 193, 196, 205, 210
Dennett, Prescott 8
Dennis, Delmar 155
Dennis, Lonnie 9
de Priest, Hudson 8
DePugh, Robert 69, 80, 125–126, 153, 161, 179
DeShazo, Albert 91, 125
de Shishmareff, Paquita 8
Devil's Advocates Motorcycle Club 183
DeVore, Jimmy 58–59
Dewey, Thomas 25
Dickinson, William 126
Dickson, Sam 199
Diebel, Hans 8, 10
Dilling, Elizabeth 5, 8, 101
Dilys, Joseph 183
Dixie Klans 72, 107
Dixiecrats 24–25, 47
Dixon, Frank 24, 25

Dixon, Thomas, Jr. 12, 24
Doar, John 81, 82, 136
Documented Proof: Jews Behind Race Mixing (pamphlet) 43
Dominica 189
Dorsey, George 20
Dorsey, Mae 20
Douglas, Alan 153
Douglas, Paul 24
Doyle, Thomas 83
Doyle, William 132
Drennan, Stanley 100
Droege, Wolfgang 183
Duffee, Eldridge, Jr. 45
Duke, Daniel 12, 18, 19, 20, 21, 22–23
Duke, David 176, 178, 180, 182, 183, 184, 185, 186, 189, 192, 194, 196, 197, 198, 200, 201, 202
Dupes, Ned 43, 45, 46, 72, 124, 125, 174
Durian, Vicki 191, 198
Dutton, Jerald 76, 79, 82, 86, 87, 89, 91, 97, 125, 132, 146, 183, 189

Eastland, James 159
Eastview Klavern (Birmingham) 74, 76, 80, 87, 88, 89, 91
Eaton, William 132, 133
Edmondson, Robert 8
Edwards, Eldon 59, 63, 67, 107
Eicher, Edward 10
Eichmann, Adolf 68
Eisenhower, Dwight 16, 42, 65, 234
Eldridge, Charles 168
Eldridge, R.D. 139, 142, 168, 171, 174–175
Elmhurst, Ernest 9, 10, 12
Emergency Committee to Suspend Immigration 198
England 165, 171, 174, 189, 201, 234
Episcopal Church 12, 138, 155, 202
Eubanks, Goldie, Sr. 117
Eugenical News (magazine) 17
Euronationalist Party 200
Evers, Medgar 89, 90, 115, 142, 155, 180, 199

Fabien, Guillaume 200
Faci, Michel 200
Fair Employment Practices Commission 25
Fair Housing Act of 1968 151
Fallaw, Eunice 116
Farley, Michael 95, 97
Farley, Richard 158
Farmer, Saxon 136, 137
Farris, Chuck 153
Fascist League of North America 4
Faubus, Orval 65–66, 69–70, 72
Federal Bureau of Investigation (FBI) 7, 10, 20, 28, 33, 34, 42, 43, 45, 46, 47, 53, 55, 56, 60, 65, 67, 75, 76, 77, 78, 82, 86, 87, 89, 97, 98, 99, 100, 102, 103, 109, 111, 113, 117, 118, 122, 124, 125, 128, 129, 131, 132, 133, 138, 140, 143, 150, 151, 153, 155, 158, 159, 161, 162, 163, 167, 169, 170, 171, 172, 174, 175, 177, 179, 181, 183, 188, 190, 192, 195
Federal Communications Commission 179, 187, 205
Federal Community Relations Service 134
Federal Witness Protection Program 76, 198
Federated Ku Klux Klan 54
Felmet, John 59
Fernenx, Frank 8
Field, Marshall 85
Fields, Dolores 47
Fields, Edward 16, 20, 23, 28, 30, 31, 38, 42, 43, 45, 47, 50, 59, 61, 65, 68, 69, 72, 74, 75, 76, 77, 78, 79, 82, 85, 87, 88, 89, 90, 91, 93, 94, 95, 97, 98, 113, 124, 125, 128, 129, 130, 132, 133, 138, 146, 151, 153, 154, 171, 172, 174, 175, 176, 178, 179, 181, 184, 185, 186, 189, 190, 191–192, 192, 193, 194, 195, 196, 197, 198, 199–200, 201, 202, 203, 206, 207
Fields, Ted 191
The Fiery Cross (newsletter) 91
Fighting American Nationalists 72, 128
Finch, James 133
First National Identity-Christian Conference 199
First Union Baptist Church 161
Fish, Hamilton III 141
Fleckenstein, Edward 49
Florida 16, 17, 18, 45, 53, 55, 63, 69, 72, 79, 82, 87, 98, 109, 110, 111, 115–123, 130, 140, 142, 143, 145, 151, 153, 157, 158, 163, 164, 165, 171, 174, 179, 180, 181, 181, 188, 189, 190, 191, 201, 202
Florida Advisory Committee to the U.S. Commission on Civil Rights 115
Florida Council on Human Relations 116
Florida East Coast Railway 117
Florida Legislative Investigating Committee 122
Florida States' Rights Party 82
Florida Memorial College 123
Flynt, Larry 185, 191
Folsom, James 25, 130
Foote, Steven 126
Forbes, Ralph 196
Ford, Henry 3, 4
Foreman, Percy 165, 178
Forster, Arnold 50
Fort Benning (GA) 100
Fort McClellan (AL) 138
Fraase, Michael 179
France 39
Frank, Leo 79, 125
Frankhouser, Roy 66–67, 72, 77, 87, 91, 113, 126, 141, 142, 143, 144, 159, 177, 179, 181, 182, 184, 188, 193, 196, 201, 202, 203, 205
Franklin, Benjamin 180
Franklin, Joseph 180, 185–186, 191, 198, 204
Free Emory Burke Committee 23
Free Will Hour (radio program) 44
Freedman, Benjamin 184
Freedom of Information Act 1, 177
"freedom rides" 74–76, 100, 153
Friends of the New Germany 4
Friends of Progress 8
From an Office Building with a High-Powered Rifle (book) 113
Frontier (journal) 47
Fruchtbaum, Renee 19
Fry, Leslie *see* de Shishmareff, Paquita
Fuisher, Granville 158

Gafford, Robert 95, 98
Gale, William 51, 78, 79–80, 82, 98, 100, 101, 102, 111, 117, 126, 133, 163, 169, 172, 180, 196
Garland, Reuben, Sr. 59
Garland, William 51
Garner, Elmer 8, 10
Garner, James 8
Garrett, Floyd 75–76
Garrison, Jim 101
Garvey, Marcus 17
Gaston, A.G. 95
Gaston Motel 88, 89, 163
Gayman, Dan 183
Gelber, Seymour 98, 109, 164, 171
Gelston, George 149
Gentry, Robert 98, 117, 143
Georgia 11–23, 30, 43, 47, 52, 53, 56, 58, 66, 72, 77, 82, 91, 100, 101, 403, 105, 107–108, 109, 110, 113, 125, 127, 140, 145–146, 151, 152, 154, 169, 175, 179, 181, 183–184, 185, 186–187, 190, 191–192, 193, 194, 197, 198, 199, 200, 201, 203
Georgia Bureau of Investigation 11
Georgia School of Technology 13, 19
The Georgia Tribune (newspaper) 85
German-American Bund 5, 7, 8, 9, 10, 25, 66, 68, 158, 183, 200
German-American Republican League 25
Germany 3–4, 8, 13, 16, 25
Gewinner, Holt 4, 16, 201
Gibson, Leroy 178
Gilbert, Keith 163
"God Bless America" (song) 28
Godfrey, Donald 117, 118, 122, 142
God's Call to Race (book) 199
Goebbels, Paul Joseph 8, 180
Goff, Kenneth 86, 87, 101, 111
Goldwater, Barry 89, 100, 127
Goodwin, John 11
Gordon, Gerald 185, 198, 204
Gover, John 133
Grabifker, Charles 51
Graham, Billy 56
Grant, George 126
Grant, Madison 12, 17

Index

Grantham, Jack, Sr. 142
Gray, James, Sr. 145
Graymont Elementary School (Birmingham) 93
Great Britain 185
Greater Jackson Clergy Alliance 157
Green, Mattie 107
Green, Samuel 11, 14, 22, 28
Greene, Melissa 59
Gremillion, Jack 136
Griffin, Barton 117, 118, 122, 143
Griffin, Kenneth 47, 56, 57, 58
Griffin, William 8, 69
Gritz, Bo 200
Grubbs, Millard 34, 43, 45, 46, 58, 133
Guihard, Paul 83
Gun Owners of America 201
Gunderson, Jack 127
Gunn, Roy 161–162, 167

Haegele, Anton 5
Hale, Dallas 168
Hale, Matthew 203
Hall, John 94, 97, 98
Hamilton, John 45–46, 101
Hanes, Arthur, Jr. 165
Hanes, Arthur, Sr. 33, 87, 133, 165, 166, 178
Harding, George 111
Hargis, Billy 85, 87, 152
Harmony Boys Quartet 80
Harrelson, C. Ray 200
Harris, Roy 56
Hart, Merwin 101
Hartmann, Thom 170, 171
Hartsfield, William 19, 57
Hattie Cotton Elementary School (Nashville) 36, 37
Hauser, James 116
Hawkins, Joe Daniel 155, 155, 157, 158, 167, 190
Hawkins, Joe Denver 155
Hayling, Robert 115, 116, 118, 122
Hays, Brooks 134
Head Start program 155, 161
Headley, Walter 164
Healey, Raymond 17
Heinemann, Jerome 172, 174
Hendel, Edwin 148
Hendrix, William 45, 46, 53, 56–57, 69
Hennes, Lou 176
Hensley, Don 47
Hicks, Robert 134, 135
High Command of the Aryan Resistance 190
Hill, Bobby 198
Hill, Hattie 136
Hill, Lister 38
Hilton, Nancy 185
Hines, Clifford 20
Hitler, Adolf 3–4, 10, 13, 15, 16, 17, 20, 25, 33, 37, 64, 68, 86, 100, 126, 158, 174, 175, 185, 186, 189, 202
The Hoax of the Twentieth Century (book) 184

Hockett, Fred 36, 63, 82
Hoff, Sheldon 144–145
Hoff, William, Jr. 91, 141, 144, 173, 200, 204
Hoff, William, Sr. 144–145
Hoffa, Jimmy 170
Holland, Dave 194, 200
Hollywood Palladium 163
The Holocaust (TV mini-series) 184
Holocaust deniers 169, 184, 199, 200, 201
"Holy Week Uprisings" 163
Hooker, DeWest 43
Hoover, J. Edgar 20, 53, 77, 98, 102, 111, 113, 128, 129, 135, 151, 177, 183
Hornsby, Marion 11, 21, 22, 23
Houghton, Troy 126
Howard, Lawrence 101
Hudgins, Robert 141
Hudson, Charles 8, 25
Hughes, Dudley, Jr. 168
Hughes, Richard 144
Huie, William 165–166, 178
Humphrey, Hubert 24, 139, 142
Hunt, H.L. 113
Hunt, Nelson 113
Huntsville Times (newspaper) 146
Hurst, Kennedy 126
Hustler (magazine) 185

Ice Cube 201
Idaho 25, 100, 126, 180, 183, 192, 200
Illinois 24, 46, 47, 124, 174, 176, 177, 178, 180, 182–183, 191
Indiana 10, 16, 46, 47, 65, 101, 107, 109, 110, 126, 174, 180, 181, 191
Industrial Workers of the World 3
Ingram, Troy 91
The International Jew (book series) 3
International Patriotic Congress *see* World Nationalist Congress
Interstate Commerce Commission 74
The Intruder (film) 78
Invisible Empire Knights of the Ku Klux Klan 183
Iowa 30, 38, 47, 85
Irving, David 199, 201, 202
Israel 68, 69, 172, 185, 200, 204, 238
Italy 3, 34

Jackson, James 116
Jackson, Jesse 150
Jackson, Jimmy 133
Jackson, Wharlest 155, 156
Jackson Daily News 167
Jenkins, Clyde 116
Jett, Ira 15–16, 21, 27
The Jewish Origins of Communism (book) 194
Jewish War Veterans 20
John Birch Society 51, 86, 91, 102, 124, 125, 152, 169, 184

Johnson, Frank, Jr. 132
Johnson, James 145
Johnson, Jess 21
Johnson, Lyndon 121, 126, 127, 129, 139, 188, 235
Johnson, Milton 136
Johnston, Evall 23, 85
Joliet Army Ammunition Plant 177
Jones, Ellis 8, 10
Jones, Frank 20
Jones, H.G. 86
Jones, James 91, 158, 172
Jones, Marcus 93, 102
Jones, Penn, Jr. 112
Jordan, Vernon 191, 198
Jouhari, Bonnie 202
Jung, Harry 4
Junior Citizens' Council 35

Kahl, Gordon 190, 203
Kallenberg, Bernard 143
Kappl, Thea 27
Kasper, John 32, 33–37, 38, 43, 46, 51, 52, 56, 60, 63, 67, 69, 78, 124, 127, 170, 202
Kay, Everett 103
Kefauver, Estes 67
Kelley, Clarence 55
Kemp, Barry 76
Kendrick, Thomas 132
Kennard, Clyde 80
Kennedy, John 69–70, 72, 98; assassination 100–114, 115, 126, 187, 188, 192
Kennedy, Robert 76, 77, 83, 87, 93, 153, 154, 159, 167, 179
Kennedy, Stephen 60, 63
Kennedy, Stetson 15, 17, 18, 20, 22
Kentucky 34, 38, 43, 45, 46, 47, 127, 133, 168, 174, 185, 191
Kern, Allen 139
Kernbach, Wilfried 176
Kerns, Woody 171
Key, Al 167
Khaki Shirts of America 4
Kiefer, Fred 158
Killen, Edgar 203
Kinard, William 117
King, Alfred 88, 134
King, George, Jr. 51, 111
King, Martin, Jr. 59, 77, 88, 90, 91, 99, 102, 106, 110, 111, 118, 120, 122, 130, 131, 132, 139, 142, 149, 150, 151, 161; assassination 163–171, 187–188
Kirchman, Harry 47
Kirk, Claude 123
Kirkpatrick, F.D. 134
Kite, Clarence 20, 23
Klapprott, August 5, 7, 9
Klavaliers 27
Klavern No. 1 (Atlanta, GA) 11, 14, 15
Klavern No. 297 (Atlanta, GA) 11
Knight, Claxton 134, 136, 137
Knight, James 110
Knight, Jimmie Glenn 138
Knights of the Confederacy 76

Knights of the White Camellia: 1930s 4; 1950s 53
Knowles, Douglas 65
Koehl, Matthias, Jr. 25, 43, 45, 46, 47, 49–50, 59, 67, 68, 72, 78, 79159, 176, 189, 206
Korean War 27
Kornegay, Robert 161
Koster, Chris 205
Kochtitzky, Robert 160
Ku Klux Klan *see* individual factions by name
Kuhn, Fritz 5, 6, 9
Kullgren, William 8
Kunze, Gerhard 9, 10
Kurtz, C. Daniel 43, 45, 58

LaCoste, Rene 183
Lake, Clancy 75
Lakel, Randy 201
Lamb, Susan 201
Lambert, J.G. 5
Landry, Stuart 62
LaRouche, Lyndon 188, 192, 193, 194, 196
Lauderdale, E.A., Sr. 65–66
Laughlin, Harry 17
Laws, Bolitha 10
Layne, Darrell 191, 198
League of Empire Loyalists 72–73
League of St. George 185
Levi, Edward 183
Lewallen, Buford 36
Lewandowski, Ralph 95
Lewis, Evan 151
Lewis, H.A. 133
Lewis, John 74
Lewton, Robert 78, 86
Liberty Lobby 67, 85, 101, 152, 179, 194
Liberty National Bank and Trust 153
Life (magazine) 98, 132–133
"Lincoln Plan" 43
Lindbergh, Charles 5
Linder, Alex 204
Linder, Earl 86
Lindsay, James
Lingo, Albert 80, 83, 87, 88, 89, 90, 91, 93, 94, 97, 98, 132, 138, 139
Little, R.E. 77
Liuzzo, Viola 132, 138, 141, 146
Livingston, Sonny 190
Lloyd, Robert 176
Longshoremen's Union 164
Look (magazine) 165
Loomis, Homer, Jr. 12–14, 15, 16, 18, 19, 20, 21, 22–23
Loomis, Homer, Sr. 23, 27
Lorena Duling Elementary School 157
Lott, Trent 83
Louisiana 25, 71–72, 82, 127, 134–137, 143, 152, 169, 178, 180, 181, 182, 183, 184, 197, 198
Louisiana States' Rights Party 71
Love, Frank 164
Lucy, Autherine 32–33

Ludecke, Kurt 4
Lumbee Indians 44–45
Luna, Don 98
Luthardt, Charles, Sr. 146–147
Luther, Martin 3
Lyman, William, Jr. 8
Lynch, Connie 45, 51, 77–78, 84, 86, 91, 111, 116–118, 120–121, 122, 123, 126, 129, 130, 136, 137, 138, 146–151, 153, 158, 163, 168, 172, 179
Lyons, Kirk 201
Lyons, Robert 77, 113, 147

MacArthur, Douglas 51, 101
Maddox, Allen 146
Maddox, Lester, Sr. 145–146, 179, 181, 183–184
Madole, James
Maerz, Herman 10
Mafia 128, 170, 174
Malcolm X 121
Malcom, Dorothy 20
Malcom, Roger 20
Malone, Wallace 97
Mann, Forrest, Jr. 46, 47
Manning, Alphonse, Jr. 185, 191
Manson, Charles 180
Manucy, Alonzo 121–122
Manucy, Holsted 117, 120, 121, 122
Marcello, Carlos 170–171
Marist School (Atlanta, GA) 16
Marshall, Thurgood 159
Martin, David 191, 198
Martinez, Robert 192
Marx, Karl 184
Maryland 127, 143, 146–150, 168, 169, 172, 176, 178, 180, 185, 191
Maryland State Penitentiary 146
Massachusetts 69, 85, 153
Massenburg Bill (VA) 17
Massey, Albert 151
"Massive Resistance" movement 31
Masters, Mercedes 185, 198
Mathews, Jay 192
Matthews, Laude 155, 180
McCaskey, W.M. 157
McCloud, Lee 103, 104, 107, 109
McDaniel, Donald 8
McDaniel, James, Jr. 125
McElveen, Ernest 135, 136, 137, 198
McFarland, William, Jr. 25
McGill, Ralph 14, 19, 20
McGinley, Conde 101, 107, 184
McIntyre, Carl 152, 174, 175
McIver, Harold 185, 198
McKeithen, John 134, 136
McKeldin, Theodore 148
McKelroy, Paul 155
McMahon, James 113
McMillan, George 97, 98–99, 166–167
McQuirter, James 183
McShane, James 81, 84
McWhorter, Diane 55
McWilliams, Joseph 5, 9–10, 18, 38
Medical Committee for Human Rights 136

Mehdidi, Mohammed 179
Mein Kampf (book) 2, 14, 23, 34, 125, 180, 182
Melvin, E.J. 172
Meredith, James 80, 81, 82, 84
Meridian Star (newspaper)
Mertig, Kurt 10, 25
Metcalf, Lee 89
Metzger, Tom 182, 196
Michigan 9, 10, 179, 181, 193, 202
Midlothian Mirror (newspaper) 112
Mikula, Kathleen 191, 198
Miles, Robert 181, 182, 189, 192, 193, 196, 202
Militant Knights of the Ku Klux Klan 142
Milledgeville State Hospital (GA) 59
Miller, Emmett 67
Miller, Glenn 182, 189–190, 192, 193, 194, 196, 198, 204, 205–206
Miller, John 174
Miller, Steve 134
Miller, Wallace 161
Miller, William 127
Miller, Zell 199
Milteer, Joseph 98, 101, 103–111, 113, 163, 170–171, 188
Minneapolis Business College 27
Minnesota 17, 47
Minutemen 67, 69, 78, 80, 82, 91, 100, 101, 125, 126, 153, 161, 169, 174, 177, 179, 180, 187
Mississippi 13, 24, 25, 32, 62, 80, 81, 82, 84, 88, 89, 127, 129, 134, 135, 136, 145, 152, 154–155, 156, 157–158, 159–161, 163, 167, 169, 171, 180, 182, 189, 190, 193, 199, 203, 204
"Mississippi Burning" case 155, 156, 159, 203
Mississippi College 157
Mississippi Southern College 80
Missouri 23, 84, 125, 166, 196, 202, 204, 205
Mitchell, Porter, Jr. 17
Mobile College 161
Mohr, Gordon "Jack" 181
Monson Motor Lodge 118, 119, 121–122
Montgomery, R.B. 192
Moore, J.R. 161
Moore, Maevella 136
Moore, Oneal 135, 136, 198
Moore, William 87–88
Moore's Ford lynching (GA) 20–21
Morgan, Bill 98
Morgan, Earl 91
Morgan, Wesley 59
Morrell, George 85, 184
Morrell, John 85, 184
Morris, Bill 165
Morris, Emmett 28
Morris, William 53–54, 55, 56, 59, 140, 142, 187–188, 190
Morrisroe, Richard 138
Moseley, George 17, 23, 27

Index

Moseley, Oswald 73
Mountain Church of Jesus Christ 193, 202
"Move Them Niggers North" (song) 149
Muhammad, Elijah 38, 39, 60, 62, 63, 73
Mullikin, Walter 133
Mullins, Eustace, Jr. 25, 34, 47, 49, 67, 68, 192, 199
Murphy, Matthew, Jr. 95, 98, 118, 122, 124, 128, 132–133, 138, 143
Mussolini, Benito 3
"My Skin Is My Sin" (song) 201

Nacirema Inc. 98–99
Nation of Islam 38–41, 60–63, 73–74, 121, 144, 193
National Alliance 170, 176, 192, 203
National Association for the Advancement of Colored People 24, 33, 36, 44, 45, 55, 62, 63, 67, 86, 89, 113, 115, 117, 140, 142, 153, 155, 179, 187, 235
National Association for the Advancement of White People 43, 189
National Campaign to Expose the Holocaust 199
National Caucus of Labor Committees 188
National Citizens Protective Association 46
National Christian Democratic Union 182
National Christian News 79
National Committee to Free America from Jewish Domination 46
National Committee to Secure Justice for the Atlanta Five 58
National Copperheads 8
National Council of Churches 122
National Democratic Front 196
National Emancipation of the White Seed 180
National Fascist Party (Italy) 3
National Front 185
National Gentile League 8, 10
National Knights of the Ku Klux Klan 47, 139–140, 142, 151, 195
National Labor Relations Board
National Labour Party (Britain) 72
National Law Enforcement Committee 133
National Liberty Party 8, 10
National Party 178
National Party (Britain, 1960s) 72, 199, 201
National Patriot's Conference 202
National Renaissance Party 25–27, 43, 67, 72, 128, 176. 179, 184
National Repatriation Committee 50
National Security League 46
National Socialist German Workers' Party (Germany)

National Socialist Liberator (newsletter) 192
National Socialist Movement 204
National Socialist Party of America 182
National Socialist Vanguard 68
National Socialist White People's Party 158–159, 169, 176, 182
National States Rights Conference 38
National States Rights Party: hapter meeting procedure 222–230; constitution and bylaws 209–232; dissolution 195; flag 232; foundation 42–51; internal discipline 219–222; membership 210; officers 47, 212–215; platform 50, 236–238; revival 203–205; uniform 66; youth section 79, 80, 86, 95
National Urban League 191
National White Americans Party 47, 79, 91, 125, 146, 147, 183
National Workers' League 9, 10
National Youth Alliance 169, 176
Nationalist Action League 25
NBC-TV 184
Negron, Leon 93, 98
Nelsen, Maynard "Max" 17, 27, 47, 67, 72, 77, 124
New Christian Crusade Church 178, 180, 182, 183, 200
New Dawn Hammerskins 201
New Deal 4
New Hampshire 12, 169, 196, 201
New Hope Baptist Church 161
New Jersey 5, 7, 33, 49, 91, 141, 144, 172, 174
New Mexico 178, 196
New Order 159, 206
New Order Knights of the Ku Klux Klan 191, 192
The New Patriot (newsletter) 124
New York 7, 10, 12, 15, 16, 19, 23, 25, 34, 43, 47, 49, 60–63, 65, 69, 73, 85, 91, 126, 127, 141, 143, 144, 149, 153, 170, 173, 186, 190, 204
New York Evening Enquirer (newspaper) 8
New York Times (newspaper) 4, 143, 193
Newell Chapel Methodist Church 161
Newhouse, Samuel Sr. 146
Newsweek (magazine) 20
Night Riders: The Inside Story of the Liuzzo Killing (booklet) 146
Nixon, Richard 69, 163, 178, 188, 235
Noble, Robert 8, 10
Non-Sectarian Anti-Nazi League 18, 22
Norden, Eric 177
Nordiska Riksparteit (political party) 72
North Carolina 44, 47, 52, 61, 74, 110, 134, 142, 145, 158, 161, 167, 170, 172, 173, 178, 179, 182, 189, 191, 193, 194, 195, 196, 199

North Carolina Knights of the Ku Klux Klan (1950s) 44, 47, 142
North Carolina Knights of the Ku Klux Klan (1980s) 173
North Dakota 51, 202
Northern Alabama Citizens' Council 32
Northern European Ring 72
Northern Friends of the South 38
Northern Ireland 185
Norton, Richard 147, 148, 149, 150
Nussbaum, Perry 157, 160

Obama, Barrack 205
Odinist Religion & Nordic Faith Movement 178
O'Donnell, William 148
Ohio 17, 46, 47, 65, 139, 140, 142, 163, 168, 171, 174, 185
O'Kelley, Hoke 145
On Target (newsletter) 126
Operation Breadbasket 150
"Operation Hoodwink" 128
"Operation Midnight Ride" 87
"Operation Red Dog" 189
Orchard Villa Elementary School 63, 64
The Order 192, 196
Order of Black Shirts 4, 16
Order of Flemish Militants 185
Oregon 47, 101, 172
Original Ku Klux Klan of the Confederacy 33
Orme, Mrs. J. Henry 5
Orr, John 63
Osgood, Clarence 97
Oswald, Lee 85, 101, 109, 111–113
Our American Destiny (pamphlet) 47
Our Common Cause (newspaper) 8
Our Nordic Race (book) 199
Oviatt, James 51
Ownby, Vester 11, 13, 16, 19
Owsley, Alvin 3, 5
"Oxford Victim Tells Story" (article) 84

Page, Hubert 74, 75, 82
Paine, Michael 113
Paine, Ruth 113
Palmer School of Chiropractic 30, 31, 38
Pan-Aryan Alliance 9
Parker, Floyd 196
Parker, Robert 138
Parks, Robert 67
Parti National Social Chrétien (political party) 5
The Passing of the Great Race (book) 12
Patler, John 85, 159
Patriotic Legal Fund 164
Patriotic National Center and School for Racial Studies and Leadership 80
Patriotic Research Bureau 5
Patterson, John 45, 76

Patterson, Robert 32
Pattie, G.L. 55, 190
Pavlonsky, Joseph *see* Coleman, John
Pearson, Drew 50, 56, 78
Pearson, Roger 124
Peck, James 76
Pelley, William 4, 5, 8, 9, 10
Penland, Betty 18, 19, 20, 23, 27
Pennsylvania 45, 67, 91, 113, 141, 143, 177, 191, 193, 201, 202, 203
People's Progressive Political Party 23
Perez, Leander 71–72
Perrow, Robert 82, 83
Philander Smith College 67
Phillips, Hunter 83
Phillips, John 143
"The Philosophy of 'White Racism'" (essay) 31
The Pickwick Papers (book) 12
Pierce, Frederick 85
Pierce, William 169–170, 176, 178, 184, 203
Pittsburgh Courier (newspaper) 22, 73
Playboy (magazine) 177
Plessy v. Ferguson 31, 204
Plumbers and Steamfitters Local 272 (Atlanta, GA) 14
Poole, Ken 182
Poorbaugh, Earl 149
Pope, Jerrold 168
Populist Party 193–194, 196, 199, 200, 201
Pospisil, Stanley 110
Posse Comitatus 133
Posse Comitatus Act 133, 172, 190, 203
Potito, Oren 45, 79, 80, 82, 83, 86, 125, 184, 201
Pott, Frances 145
Pound, Ezra 33–34, 36, 49
Powell, Claude 170
Powell, John 17
Powell, John (newsman) 158
Powell, Leon 170
Prairie Fire (newsletter) 172, 175
Pratt, Larry 201
Prendergast, J. Gilbert 150
President's Committee on Equality of Treatment and Opportunity in the Armed Services 25
Price, Jack 20
Princeton University 12
Pritchett, Laurie 77, 130
Progressive Party 25
Protestant Statesman and Nation (newsletter) 27
Protestant War Veterans Association 8, 11
The Protocols of the Learned Elders of Zion (book) 3, 34, 124
Pryor, Ralph 144
Publicity (magazine) 8
Pulitzer Prize 56
Pye, Durwood 58

Quarterman, Robert 158

Rabb, Lawrence 155
Raby, Albert 150
Race and Reason (TV show) 193, 196
Racial and National Identity (booklet) 133
Racial Integrity Act (VA) 17
Ragon, Ronald 203
Ramage, Edward 94
Ramsey High School (Birmingham) 93
Randall, Paul 149
Rankin, John 143
Ravan, Howell 187
Ray, James 163, 164–167, 168, 171, 178
Ray, Jerry 165, 176, 186
Ray, John 169
Reading Anthracite Company 181
Reading-Berks Human Relations Council 202
Reagan, Ronald 194, 200
The Real Hate Mongers (booklet) 124
Realpolitical Institute 47, 48
The Rebel (newspaper) 86
Rebel Knights of the Ku Klux Klan 201
Reedy, W.V. 82
Reese, Lawrence 191
Reeves, Gene 185
Reineke, Edwin 126
Remember Mary Phagan Committee 79
Republican Party 25, 46, 50, 80, 100, 126, 127, 145, 158, 169, 181, 194, 196, 201, 205
The Revere (newsletter) 46
Rexair Rainbow Vacuum Cleaner Corporation 27
Richards, Robert 194
Riddlehoover, Charles 140, 142
Ridout, Carl 95
Rights of White People 178
The Rising Tide of Color (book) 12
Robb, Thom 200
Robert E. Lee Klavern No. 508 118, 142
Roberts, Alton 155, 159, 160, 167, 202
Roberts, Archibald 85, 101
Roberts, Raymond 154, 156. 162, 167
Robinson, James 80, 86, 111, 131, 132, 133
Robinson, Johnnie 95
Rockefeller, Winthrop 145
Rockwell, George 43, 45, 46, 58, 63–64, 65, 67. 68, 72, 76, 78–79, 82, 86, 91, 124, 125, 128, 129, 131, 145, 150–151, 158–159
Rodriguez, Emanuel 144–145
Roeder, Manfred 183
Rogers, Creed 135, 136
Rogers, Leslie 56, 58, 59
Rogers, William 60
Romer, Harry 25
Roosevelt, Franklin 4, 24
Roper, Samuel 11, 28

Ropke, Frank 133
Rosecrans, William 117–118, 122
Rotella, Frank, Jr. 91, 126, 141, 144
Rothschild, Jacob 56, 57
Rowe, Gary, Jr. 75, 76, 89, 95, 122, 132, 133, 183, 186
Rozier, Bill 138
Ruby, Jack 111–112
Rucker, Elza 168, 175
Rummel, Joseph 71
Rutherford, Keith 198
Ryan, Richard 178
Ryan, Thomas 206
Sage, Eugene 10

St. Augustine Record (newspaper) 116, 117, 122
Saint James Methodist Church 91
St. Louis Post-Dispatch (newspaper)
Salaman, Maureen 194
Sanctuary, Eugene 8, 101
Sanitation Workers' Union 164
Santomero, Nancy 191, 198
Sapiro, Aaron 3
Sapp, Charles 102, 164
Saris, Patti 201
Saturday Evening Post (magazine) 97
Schepff, Robert 181
Schoep, Jeffrey 204
Schwartz, Fred 152
Schwenn, Toni 185, 191
Schwinn, Herman 8, 10
Scott, Nannie 85
Seaboard White Citizens' Council 32, 34
Seale, Homer 137
"Second Reconstruction" 72
sedition trials 1944 10; 1988 193, 196
Segregation or Death (pamphlet) 36
Self, W.W. "Red" 74, 75
Self-Preservation and Loyalty League 134
Sentinel (magazine) 10
Separation or Amalgamation (pamphlet) 13
Settles, Bernice 72, 125
Shatner, William 78
Shearer, Eileen 169
Shearer, William 169
Shelley, Joseph 115, 117
Shelton, Robert 45, 67, 75, 80, 82, 83, 84, 87, 89, 91, 93, 95, 98, 99, 109, 116, 127, 138, 141, 157, 159, 172, 186
Sherrill, Robert 145, 146, 150, 153, 154, 159, 169
Shipp, James 11, 27
Shirley, Frank 200
Shores, Arthur 91, 94
Shoup, James 111
Shuler, Allen 17
Shuttlesworth, Fred 33, 54–55, 88, 99, 102
Sibley, Goldsmith 20

Index

Sibley, Minnie 20
Sigma Nu fraternity 83
Silver Shirt Legion of America 4, 6, 8, 9, 51, 126, 172
Simmons, William 83
Simpson, Bryan 118, 120, 122, 123
Sims, Charles 181
Sims, Daniel 198
Sims, Donald 137
Sims, J.D. 66
Sims, Larry 95, 97
Sims, Patsy 179
Sirhan, Sirhan 167
The Six Million Swindle (book) 184
Sixteenth Street Baptist Church 52, 76, 95–99, 102, 110, 117, 186, 201–202
Skeptic (magazine) 166
skinheads 197, 198, 201
Slamon, Edward 177, 181
Smith, Al 25
Smith, Arthur 4
Smith, Gerald 5, 7, 10, 15, 17, 18, 23, 25, 27, 46, 157
Smith, Howard 8
Smith, Howard K. 75
Smith, Robert 125
Smith Act 8
Smithson, Claude 77
Smoot, Dan 109
Smyer, Sidney 24
Smythe, Edward 8, 10, 11, 17, 23, 27–28
Sobieski, John 39
Social Credit Party (Canada) 80
Social Republic Society of America 8
Socialist Workers Party 128
Somersett, William 82, 98, 101, 102, 103–110, 111, 163, 164, 171, 188
Sons of Liberty 124, 178
South Africa 190
South Carolina 25, 44, 47, 74, 89, 91, 93, 108, 116, 127, 144, 152, 171, 200, 204
South Carolina Knights of the Ku Klux Klan 47
South Dakota 33
Southern Bible College 43–44
Southern Conference on Bombing 53
"Southern Manifesto" 31
Southern Negro Youth Congress 25
Southern Poverty Law Center 190, 194, 196, 199, 202
Southern White Knights of the Ku Klux Klan 194, 197
Spake, Hugh 170, 171
Spanknoebel, Heinz 4
Sparkman, John 38, 67, 145
Spegal, Donald 117
Spencer, Delia 85
Spiers, Arnold 137
The Spotlight (newsletter) 184
SS of America 199
Stand Up for America: The Story of George C. Wallace (pamphlet) 152
Standring, John 181
State Farm Insurance 53, 54, 59
States' Rights Party 47
The Statesman (newspaper) 11
Stephens, Charles 171
Stephenson, William 58, 85
Stevenson, Adlai 85
Stoddard, Lothrop 12
Stokes, Trenton 196
Stoner, Jesse, Jr. 15, 25, 27, 28, 29, 30, 31, 38–41, 43, 45, 47, 50, 52, 53, 54–56, 59, 60–63, 64, 65, 73–74, 75, 76, 77, 78, 79, 82, 84, 87, 88, 93, 95, 97, 98, 99, 102, 103, 117, 118, 120, 121, 122, 123, 124, 125, 126, 127, 129, 130, 134, 136, 137, 138–139, 142–143, 146, 149, 150, 153, 154, 158, 159, 163, 164, 165, 167, 168, 169, 172, 174, 175–176, 178, 179, 180, 181, 183, 184–185, 186–187, 188, 189, 190–191, 192, 193, 194, 196, 197, 198, 199, 201, 202, 203, 204, 207
Stoner, Jesse Sr. 15
Stoner Anti-Jewish Party 15
The Storm (newsletter) 12
Stormfront 199, 204, 206
Strange, Hubert 138, 139
Streicher, Julius 66, 206
Strickland, C.J. 59
Stuart, Virgil 115, 117, 122, 123
Student Nonviolent Coordinating Committee 77, 130, 132
Students for a Democratic Society 171, 188
Suall, Irwin 67
Sullivan, Charles 155, 157
Swastika League of America 4
Sweden 72
Swift, Wesley 5, 7, 45, 51, 78, 79, 82, 86, 102, 111, 124, 126, 130, 133, 157, 161, 176, 182
Synon, John 152

Taft, Dewey 87, 120, 122
Take Your Choice: Separation or Mongrelization (book) 13
Talmadge, Eugene 11, 12, 16, 22, 66
Talmadge, Herman 22, 23
Tampa Tribune (newspaper) 158
Tarrants, Thomas III 95, 124–125, 157–158, 159. 160–161, 167, 171, 180
Tatum, Bryant 185
Taylor, Glen 25
Taylor, John 181, 183
Taylor, Raymond 185
Teamsters Union 6, 170
Tebault, A.H., Jr. 122
Temple Beth-El (Birmingham, AL) 52, 54, 55
Temple Beth-El (Charlotte, NC) 52
Temple Beth-El (Miami, FL) 52
Temple Beth Israel (Jackson, MS) 157, 158, 159
Temple Beth Israel (Meridian, MS) 167
Tennessee 15, 25, 35, 36, 38, 46, 47, 51, 52, 56, 60, 67, 70, 98, 107, 165, 167, 168, 171, 179, 180, 193, 198, 199, 201, 231
Tennessee Federation for Constitutional Government 36
Texas 16, 78, 82, 98, 101, 102, 110, 111, 113, 143, 165, 169, 178, 180, 201
Thagard, Thomas 131
Thomas, Ernest 134–135
Thomas, Eugene 132
Thomas, George 23
Thompson, Melvin 22
Thompson, Ronald 181
Thornton, James 78, 124, 125
"Three Governors Controversy" (GA) 22
Thunder in the South (book) 23
The Thunderbolt (newspaper) 1, 14, 47, 51, 59, 66, 67, 71, 76, 77, 78, 79, 80, 85, 86, 87, 89, 91, 120, 124, 125, 128, 130, 132, 143, 145, 146, 169, 174, 175, 178, 180, 181, 182, 185, 192, 198
Thunderbolt on the Right (TV documentary) 158
Thurmond, Strom 24, 25, 89, 152
Till, Emmett 165
Tiller, Thomas 158
Time (magazine) 62
Time Inc. 168
Touart, Richard 82
Tougaloo College 159
Townsend, Ralph 8
Trahan, Clifford 149
Treen, David 71, 197
Triggs, Clarence 137
True, James, Jr. 8, 10
True Knights of the Ku Klux Klan 197
Truman, Harry 23–24, 25, 27, 234
The Truth About David Duke (pamphlet) 183
The Truth at Last (newsletter) 1, 194, 197, 199, 200, 202, 206
Tucker, Buddy 180, 183
"Turnaround Tuesday" (Selma, AL) 132
Tyndal, John 199, 201

Ulster Defense Association 185
Ultimatum Conference of Loyal Americans 43, 44, 45
United Americans for Conservative Government 91
United Auto Workers 139, 170
United Christian Posse Association 172
United Florida Ku Klux Klan 98, 116, 117, 122, 142, 151
United Freedom 128
United Klans of America 67, 82, 84, 88, 89, 91, 95, 98, 99, 109, 113, 116, 120, 122, 133, 135, 138, 141, 142, 143–144, 154, 158, 172, 174, 177, 180, 182

United Nations 59, 85, 87, 132, 229, 234
United Press International 56
U.S. Attorney General's list of subversive organizations 23
U.S. Fascists 4
U.S. 5th District Court of Appeals 137
U.S. Holocaust Memorial Museum 201
U.S. House Committee on Un-American Activities 21, 139, 141
U.S. House Select Committee on Assassinations 108, 113, 164, 187
U.S. Klans 45, 56, 59, 63, 67, 76, 107
U.S. Naval Air Force 28
U.S. Secret Service 100, 102, 106, 108, 111, 188
U.S. Senate Select Committee to Study Governmental Operations 183
U.S. Supreme Court 31, 43, 46, 77, 139, 146, 187, 190, 204
United States of America Union of Fascists 5
United White Party 43, 47, 56
University of Alabama 32–33, 88–89
University of Miami 158
University of Minnesota 17
University of Mississippi 81–84
University of Virginia 17
U.S. News & World Report (magazine) 62, 86
Utah 110, 191, 198, 200

Vanguard News Network 204, 205
Venable, James 23, 27, 30, 58, 59, 77, 95, 101, 139, 140, 142, 151, 163, 190, 192, 197
Vick, Raymond 16
Viereck, George 8
Vigilantes Inc. 11
Viking Youth of America 128
Vincent Chapel African Methodist Episcopal Church 155
Virginia 8, 13, 17, 31, 34, 43, 45, 64, 74, 86, 101, 145, 152, 159, 180, 185
Virginia Council on Human Relations 34
The Virginian (magazine) 58, 85
Virginians Awake! (pamphlet) 36
Vitter, David 197
Von Stahl, Ben 133
von Stahrenberg, Peter 10
Voting Rights Act of 1965 139

WAGA-TV (Atlanta, GA) 176
Wagner, Daniel 139–140. 142
Wake, Roy 172, 174, 175
Waldron, Lamar 170, 171
Walker, Edwin 82, 83, 84–85, 86, 87, 89, 101, 113, 184
Wallace, George 45, 80, 83, 86, 87, 88, 89, 90, 91, 93, 94, 95, 97, 98, 126–127, 132, 145, 151, 152, 169, 170, 178–179, 186
Wallace, Henry 25
Wallace, Joseph 14
Wallace, Lurleen 145, 151–152
Waller, Lanier 16, 19, 21, 22
Walter Reed Hospital 110
Ware, James 97
Ware, Virgil 97
Warner, Carol 200
Warner, James 46, 79, 84, 85, 87, 93, 95, 124, 126, 178, 180, 181, 182, 183, 184, 186, 189, 198, 200
Warren Commission 111, 113
Washburn, Lois 8, 10
Washington, George 17, 42
Washington, DC 10, 28, 33, 34, 87, 91, 110, 164, 169, 174, 175, 201
Washington Observer (newsletter) 124
Washington State 9, 47
Watergate scandal 178, 181
Watkins, Leo 191
Watts, Frank 162
Watts riot 130
Wayside Baptist Church 44
We the People 11
Webb, George 75, 76
Webb, Paul 23
Weems, Robert 193–194, 196, 199
Weiss, Frederick 25
West End High School (Birmingham) 93, 95
West Germany 183
West Virginia 171, 191
Western Destiny (newspaper) 181
What World Famous Men Said About the Jews (booklet) 124
Wheat, G. Clinton 100–101
White, Ben 163
White America (book) 17
The White American (newspaper) 125, 146, 147
White Circle League of America 27
The White Circle News (newsletter) 27
White Defence League (Britain) 72
White Democratic Nationalist Party 42

White Forum (TV show) 202
White Knights of the Ku Klux Klan 136, 142, 154, 155, 157, 163, 167
A White Man Speaks Out (memoir) 198
White Marylander (newsletter) 150
White Patriot Party 193, 194
White Race—True People of Israel (book) 199
The White Sentinel (newsletter) 46, 101
White-Slave Traffic Act 102
White Unity Day 196
White Youth Corps 128
Whitman, Ervin 82
Whitman, R.I. 20
Whitman, Robert 87
Whitman, Roy 13
Wilkerson, Jeff 202
Wilkins, Collie 132–133, 138
Wilkinson, Bill 183, 189
Wilkinson, Horace 25
Williams, Joy 185
Williams, Kenneth 109, 113
Willis, Edwin 143
Wilson, Willie 117, 142, 145, 151, 174, 175, 181, 192
Wingrow, Ike 11
Winrod, Gerald 8, 45
Winrod, Gordon 45, 78, 86, 202–203
Wisconsin 126, 185, 191, 206
Witte, Eloise 139–140, 142, 163, 195
World Church of the Creator 203
World Nationalist Congress 180, 183
World Union of Free Enterprise National Socialists 58, 63
World Wide Christian Radio 201
Wright, Fielding 25
Wright, Paul 133
Wulff, Melvin 113

Xavier, Peter 46, 58, 168, 176
The X-Ray (newsletter) 8

Yale University 5
Yates, Bill 134
Young, A.Z. 134
Youth for Wallace 169

Zartic Foods 191–192
Zimmerlee, John 13, 15, 19, 27
"Zionist Occupation Government" 192

www.ingramcontent.com/pod-product-compliance
Ingram Content Group UK Ltd.
Pitfield, Milton Keynes, MK11 3LW, UK
UKHW050538150426
5217IPUK00026B/1991